W9-BBK-784

"Any woman can nurse a baby,"
says Karen Pryor, mother of three.

"And any working woman can
nurse a baby, too,"
adds her daughter, Gale Pryor,
a working mother.

In this essential updated guide, the experienced mother-daughter team offers the latest techniques for successful and satisfying nursing, from your newborn's first weeks through the early months of your child's life and onward.

" . . . a wonderful addition to the resources available to today's breastfeeding mother."
—La Leche League International

Nursing Your Baby

KAREN PRYOR AND GALE PRYOR

POCKET BOOKS

New York   London   Toronto   Sydney   Tokyo   Singapore

The authors of this book are not physicians and the ideas, procedures, and suggestions in this book are not intended as a substitute for the medical advice of a trained health professional. All matters regarding your health require medical supervision. Consult your physician before adopting the suggestions in this book, as well as about any condition that may require diagnosis or medical attention. The authors and publishers disclaim any liability arising directly or indirectly from the use of this book.

POCKET BOOKS, a division of Simon & Schuster Inc.
1230 Avenue of the Americas, New York, NY 10020

Copyright © 1963, 1973, 1991 by Karen Wylie Pryor

Published by arrangement with HarperCollins Publishers

All rights reserved, including the right to reproduce this book or portions thereof in any form whatsoever. For information address HarperCollins Publishers, 10 East 53rd Street, New York, NY 10022

ISBN: 0-671-74548-4

First Pocket Books printing September 1991

10 9 8

POCKET and colophon are registered trademarks of Simon & Schuster Inc.

Cover photo by Karen Pryor

Printed in the U.S.A.

To Jon and Kolya

Acknowledgments

Human lactation and the practical management of breastfeeding are areas in which an extraordinary expansion of knowledge has been taking place since about 1980. We could not have summarized this huge body of new information without the help of many specialists. Foremost among them was our technical editor, Kathleen Auerbach, Ph.D. Dr. Auerbach is editor-in-chief of the *Journal of Human Lactation,* a founder of the International Lactation Consultants Association, until recently assistant professor of Clinical Pediatrics at the University of Chicago School of Medicine, and an adjunct faculty member or consultant to more than a dozen other medical schools. She has an encyclopedic knowledge of the breastfeeding research literature and is much in demand as a medical editor. Her own research is far-ranging: for example, she is the author, with Lawrence Gartner, M.D., of a landmark paper on neonatal jaundice, the senior author of three broad-scale sociological studies of working nursing mothers, and author of a fundamental study on relactation and induced lactation.

Like many of today's researchers, Dr. Auerbach started out as a nursing mother, became a La Leche League group leader, then got an advanced degree, and went into research and teaching. In private practice, and as attending associate at the University of Chicago's teaching hospital, she has helped thousands of women learn to breastfeed. In workshops and seminars in hospitals all over the country she teaches other medical care givers to do the same. Kathy Auerbach has made herself instantly available and kept us on track throughout this project. She has led us to scores of exciting new research reports; she speaks, always, from the viewpoint of the nursing mother; and her competence, energy, and good humor often kept us going when we flagged.

Many other specialists took the time and trouble to review portions of the manuscript related to their own fields. We are grateful to Armond Goldman, M.D., of the University of Houston, preeminent researcher on immunological factors in human milk (as you will see in our reference section), who meticulously corrected chapter 3 and provided us with many references and resources including his own in-press manuscripts. Allan Cunningham, M.D., professor of pediatrics at Columbia University Medical School, reviewed our coverage of his own work on the health of breastfed vs. artificially fed babies and also read and commented on chapter 8. Niles Newton, Ph.D., critiqued chapter 6 and helped us greatly with the endocrinological literature. Lewis Lipsitt, Ph.D., executive director of the American Psychological Association and a specialist on infant learning and behavior, reviewed chapters 4 and 5 and made many cogent suggestions.

Edward Cerutti, M.D., provided us with his bibliographic files on breastfeeding. Marvin Eiger, M.D., toured Karen through Beth-Israel Hospital's lactation clinic. Laura Waxman, M.D., and Kittie Frantz, P.N.P., did the same at the University of Southern California. Kittie Frantz reviewed several chapters and provided us with her series of videotapes on breastfeeding. Via Kittie Frantz, Carl Muchnick, M.D., provided us with an invaluable resource: a continuing file, going back over a decade, of Medline monthly printouts of research abstracts on human milk. Via interlibrary loans the King County Library System in Washington state located all the medical references we asked for (including historical and foreign papers) and delivered photocopies by mail, without charge, usually within a few days of the request, an incredible service that probably knocked a year off the writing time of this book.

Amy Carroll Porter and her daughter Ellen are our beautiful cover photograph subjects.

Jackie Shina and Janet Repucci, both experienced lactation consultants and La Leche League leaders in the Boston area, were of inestimable help to Gale in preparing part 2 of this book. They donated hours of their time to update us on a vast range of subjects, including the role of the lactation consultant and the history of the International Lactation Consultants Association, recent changes in hospital procedures, and current treatment of jaundice. Throughout the research and writing of part 2, Jackie and Janet remained available to answer questions knowledgeably and with insight. Heather Robinson contributed enormously to our information on working mothers who nurse, and to chapter 12. Terry Asquith gave us a crash course on milk banks. We'd also like to thank Miriam Erickson, Boston-area milk bank director; Sandy Erickson of the Denver Milk Bank; and Karen's dear friend Leslie Hawkinson, past board member of La Leche League International, who took care of Gale's son, Max, while we interviewed Sandy. La Leche League staff members provided us with extensive information. Dozens of other professionals sat still for visits or phone interviews; we are grateful to all.

Many nursing mothers read and made valuable comments on portions of the manuscript, including Annette Lindbergh, Kristina Lindbergh, Sharon Lindbergh, Carrie Pryor, Robin Pringle, and our medical illustrator, Amy Carter. Mary Beth Lambe, M.D., another nursing mother, provided Karen with some skilled medical care that was crucial in completing this project. We are grateful to our editors (both of them past working nursing mothers): Beverly Lewis, who conceived of this project, convinced us it needed doing, and edited the manuscript; and Jane Chelius of Pocket Books, who heartened and defended us through three years of writing and research. Finally, we'd like to thank our spouses, Jon Lindbergh and Kolya Leabo, both of whom not only encouraged us but also put up pleasantly with the many drawbacks of being married to a writer.

Karen Pryor
Gale Pryor

Table of Contents

Preface

Karen:

I wrote the first *Nursing Your Baby,* published in 1963, because I was mad: mad at the bad advice and lack of support given to me and to my friends when we chose to breastfeed our babies. Like many mothers in the '50s, I had a hard time nursing my first child, Ted; things were much better the second and third times around, with Michael and then Gale, and I realized I had *learned* what to do. The main obstacle to all mothers' success, I suspected, was *not* physical incapacity, it was our own lack of information. A little library research backed up this hypothesis. I set out to find and share with other mothers the information you need to breastfeed; to write the book I wished I'd had with my own first baby.

The first version of *Nursing Your Baby* was, unavoidably, a book of its times. In 1960, it was generally true that doctors were male, first-time mothers were very young, and no mothers worked, or if they did, they certainly didn't breastfeed. When the paperback edition of the book came out in 1973, the publishers asked for a few minor additions—a section on DDT, a section on marijuana—but we assumed the basic audience hadn't changed much.

Gale:

Well, things had changed a lot by the late 1980s when I started my family. I had a full-time, very demanding job and so did all my friends. If we became mothers we would have no intention of giving up either our work or the satisfactions of breastfeeding. But where was the book for us? *Nursing Your Baby* had helped tens of thousands of new mothers to understand why breastfeeding is so important and how to nurse their babies, but it was a book of another time, when mothers were "girls" and only husbands left home.

In 1986, Karen's publishers asked her if she would do a truly new version of *Nursing Your Baby*. She was dubious: her children were grown and she had moved on to other interests and projects; also, she felt unequipped to write about the full-time working nursing mother, since she had never been one. "How would it be if I wrote that part?" I suggested. We both realized, too, that I could update the language throughout the book, reflecting the changes since the sixties. So our partnership began. We would keep the format of the original book—part 1, a survey of the facts of human lactation, which would be primarily but not entirely Karen Pryor's responsibility, and part 2, a mother-to-mother, month-by-month practical guide to the experience of breastfeeding, which would be primarily my task.

My first child, Max, was born in 1987, and I returned to work full time and also breastfed for almost two years; during that period Karen and I started researching and writing what has become virtually a new book for nursing mothers. We found an enormous amount of new information about breastfeeding, both scientific and practical. We met many women and men who are real "lactophiles," so convinced of the importance of human milk to babies that they are devoting passionate lives of service to this cause, as laboratory scientists, milk bank managers, counselors of mothers, trainers of medical care providers, and in many other roles. We learned a lot, and we hope it will all be useful to you.

Karen:

The scientific discoveries about human milk made in the last decade alone have been astonishing. It seems that the more we investigate, the more we discover how remarkably valuable and specialized this substance is for the benefit of the human organism. I've been excited, too, by all the skilled new management techniques for helping mothers breastfeed and by our increasing understanding of how breastfeeding benefits the mother's body, in long-term ways, as it was meant to do.

One big change that I am especially happy to see is the increasing recognition that breastfeeding involves two people, not just one. When I was writing back in the 1960s, if anything went wrong with lactation, it was inevitably assumed to be the mother's fault; her milk was too thin, she wasn't doing this or that right. Now we know that sometimes the baby also needs to learn and to be encouraged, and many ways have been developed to spot and avoid trouble on the junior side of the partnership.

I saw a poignant example of this in our own family when my older son, Ted, and his wife, Carrie, had a baby girl. Gwen was a great nurser, but sometimes she seemed to have trouble staying on the breast. I was holding her in my arms one evening about a week after her birth when I noticed something I had just been reading about: a heart-shaped dip in the tip of her tongue, a clue to a short frenulum, the tissue under the tongue, which would restrict its movement. Gwen was tongue-tied. Nursing her would take extra care and patience.

Thinking of how hard I had struggled to breastfeed Ted, her father, I turned to him and said, "Stick out your tongue." And he couldn't do it. Ted was tongue-tied himself, and it had very much hampered his own ability to learn to breastfeed. I had attributed all those early struggles to my ignorance. Had Ted been born today, we would have known more about the baby's side of the job and how to spot and overcome problems of that kind. It was a joy to put this kind of information together, knowing that each new discovery or insight we can pass along is going to help some other mother and baby breastfeed.

Karen and Gale:
Much has changed in our culture's attitude toward breastfeeding since the first version of *Nursing Your Baby* was published. Rarely does one hear anymore, even from synthetic-milk manufacturers, that formula is superior to

breast milk. Rarely is a mother treated as if she had taken the "ridiculous notion" into her head to nurse her baby. Breast milk is now acknowledged to be the ideal food for babies and nursing to have many benefits for both mother and child.

Unfortunately, the result of this rather official assent to breastfeeding (sometimes grudgingly given) is a sense of obligation. Breastfeeding today is too frequently considered something a mother does for her baby for three months just to pass on the immunities—then she's "allowed" to stop. While it's true that any amount of breastfeeding benefits a baby, this approach to nursing ignores the joy of breastfeeding. Once learned, breastfeeding can be one of the most fulfilling experiences in a women's life. It is with this awareness, a sense of the satisfaction and joy in nursing, rather than the feeling that it is yet another maternal duty, that we would like our readers to close the pages of the new *Nursing Your Baby*.

PART
I

CHAPTER 1

The Nursing Couple

THE NURSING COUPLE

The oneness of the nursing mother and her baby has always fascinated mankind. Like lovers, they are united both physically and spiritually. Unlike lovers, their union lacks the ambivalence and tensions of sexuality. Christianity is not the only religion that reveres the image of mother and infant as a symbol of pure love. The Egyptians always portrayed their chief goddess, Isis, with the infant Horus nursing at her breast. Mother-goddesses in the Near East preceded Isis; the Madonnas of past and present art follow her. Almost every great artist, from the unknown sculptors of the Hittites to Michelangelo, Mary Cassatt, and Picasso, has used the nursing mother and her child as a subject, and tried to convey in stone or clay or paint the sense of their being two people and yet one.

It is brief, this unity. In many cultures, the baby is weaned in a year or two, and his world expands far beyond his mother's arms. She then becomes a part of her child's life, rather than its center. But this is an intense relationship, for all its brevity. Mother and child share a rapport so complete that it can exert a profound effect on both. Without this mutual understanding, breastfeeding does not proceed successfully; it is as much a part of breastfeeding as is the giving and taking of milk.

Nursing a baby is an art; a domestic art, perhaps, but one that like cooking or gardening brings to a woman the release

3

and satisfaction that only creative work can give. The author Anne Morrow Lindbergh wrote, "When I cannot write a poem, I bake biscuits and feel just as pleased." Nursing gives the same sort of satisfaction and joy. Successful nursing mothers, having enjoyed a long, happy nursing relationship with their babies, often find it hard to understand why others refuse to breastfeed. They may not be able to express in words what they themselves like about nursing. For one mother nursing the baby may be an intense, joyful experience, while for another mother it is as casually routine as pouring a cup of coffee. But all successful nursing mothers tend to feel that breastfeeding is special—and that the bottle-feeding mother just doesn't know what she's missing.

Breastfeeding is special for the baby, too. Drinking from a bottle is a passive experience, but nursing at the breast is a participation sport. Babies can throw themselves into this activity with an endearing, almost comical gusto. Take, for example, this observation, by British novelist Angela Thirkell, of a grandmother watching her daughter nursing her new baby girl: "Edith was sitting in a low chair, her baby in her arms, while the said baby imbibed from nature's fount with quite horrible greed. Her face became bright red, her few dark hairs were dank with perspiration, one starfish hand was clenched on a bit of her nightgown . . . she was victualling herself as far as her adoring grandmother could make out for a six weeks' siege at least." Nobody ever felt that way about a plastic bottle.

THE START OF THE NURSING RELATIONSHIP

The relationship between the nursing mother and her baby begins with physical compatibility. When the mother's milk starts to flow easily, and the baby starts suckling consistently, they can become what psychiatrist M. P. Middlemore named the nursing couple, rather than two strangers. This can happen from the very first feeding, a few minutes after the baby is born. The nursing relationship seems to arise spontaneously, like love at first sight; this is probably the biologically normal situation. In our culture, however, the first nursing is often delayed, and both mother and baby may be under many physical or emotional handicaps. So the nursing relationship begins with a courtship, which may last for days or even weeks. If personalities clash, the courtship may be a stormy one. An occasional baby suffers from birth complications or other problems and does not respond eagerly to the breast. The start of breastfeeding can be difficult, and some mothers are not prepared for that. But with encouragement and the right advice, breastfeeding can be a great success even after a slow start.

For the first day or two after birth, some babies want to lick and play at the breast, rather than nurse. Others, even if prevented from breastfeeding for a week or more, take to nursing on the first try, as if they had been just waiting for the chance. Mothers and babies usually come to an understanding. They enjoy their experiences together more and more. Comfortable, satisfying feedings become the rule. Thus, a happy nursing relationship begins to grow.

THE REWARDS OF NURSING

People who do not breastfeed often assume that the chief reward for the nursing mother is a sense of virtue, the knowledge that in breastfeeding she is doing the right thing for her baby: an intellectual sort of satisfaction. Actually, while the mother is proud that the baby thrives, her reward lies in the peace, even the bliss, of the nursing experience, in the good health she and her baby enjoy, and in being the recipient of the baby's obvious and lavish love. As any nursing mother can tell you, one reward is that breastfeeding, once learned, is a lot less trouble than the chores involved in taking care of an artificially fed baby. And if you are working or in school, and must be away from your baby part of the time, breastfeeding offers enormous satisfaction, because only you can do it.

In addition, breastfeeding is the fastest way to lose weight and get back in shape after pregnancy. Nursing the baby causes your uterus to contract; one mother said that by the time she left the hospital she could see that her stomach was already flatter than those of new mothers who weren't breastfeeding. Also, during pregnancy the body stores special fat reserves in the hips and abdomen that are intended to be used up during milk production. Breastfeeding draws on these supplies. If the mother does not lactate, these special fat deposits can be very hard to get rid of.

BREASTFEEDING: A LEARNED MUTUAL SKILL

In modern industrialized societies a new mother often needs to make tremendous adjustments to the perhaps unfamiliar presence of an infant and to the unfamiliar job of motherhood. On top of that, she is learning a new skill: breastfeeding. Furthermore, she is often learning this skill under biologically bizarre circumstances: alone or among strangers, without experienced mothers to comfort and guide her, without the cultural information and support that nature intended her to have.

People in Western cultures tend to behave as if breastfeeding, like giving a bath, were something you do *to* a baby. In reality, breastfeeding is something you do *with* a baby, something you learn together. Some babies are born experts, others require help. The baby must learn that milk is what she needs, and that her mother's breast is the place to get it. If the breast is hard to grasp, she must learn how to get hold of it. If the milk is slow to start flowing, she may have to acquire more patience and perseverance than she was born with. She must cope with the way she is handled, dressed, or wrapped during nursing, whether that suits her preference or not.

The sweet taste of human milk is a nice payoff for the baby, of course, as is the easing of hunger—but her mother's scent, eyes, voice, touch, and presence, all very important and dear to her, reinforce her nursing behavior, too. And even to a newborn, success breeds success; accomplishing a satisfying feeding is reinforcing in itself.

The mother, meanwhile, must learn how to be comfortable with her baby, and how to read her needs and signals, not just for the breast but for company and other needs. Fortunately, babies are wonderful teachers. And the nursing interaction is full of immediate rewards that make learning easier. The most immediate satisfaction for the mother is that nursing feels good, bringing physical comfort and a flood of hormones that cause feelings of relaxation and peace. The biggest reward, however, is the baby's behavior. Nursing babies, even newborns, love to gaze at and touch their mothers; that's flattering. And watching the baby nurse is fun; it's so gratifyingly clear that you are just what she wants.

The mother tends to feel that her breastfed baby is not a job or a chore, but her partner, her little friend, a member of the team. And this equality is the essence of the nursing relationship. Both partners expend energy; those efforts, on both sides, are reinforced by pleasant consequences. So both partners become even readier to expend that energy again. Breastfeeding is a continuing loop of behavior and reinforcers, an exchange of efforts and satisfactions that is equally rewarding to both mother and baby.

CONTAGIOUS EMOTIONS

As Sibylle Escalona, M.D., has pointed out, emotions are contagious. Even tiny babies can "catch" emotions from their mothers, and as parents of high-strung, colicky babies can testify, upset infants have upset parents, too. Sometimes this creates difficulties, but contagion of emotions can also work in favor of mother and baby. The calmed baby is a soothing armful for the mother. The father's enjoyment of the baby and pride in his wife can soothe mother and baby, too. An experienced, relaxed person can sometimes calm a frantic baby simply by holding him. And so when a baby settles down and begins nursing well, his evident enjoyment and relief convey themselves to the mother, so that she, too, begins to enjoy the feeding.

Some care providers—nurses, midwives, physicians, lactation counselors—convey their own calmness to others, so that everyone around them, mothers and babies alike, begins to feel calm and cheerful. Such a person often has phenomenal success in helping mothers and infants to become happy nursing couples. Sometimes a grandmother or sister or friend provides the confidence-giving wafts of calm enjoyment; sometimes the baby's father is the soothing presence. And once the lactation is well established, the tranquil joy of mother and baby can spread back outward to the rest of the household as well—an extremely valuable contagious emotion.

THE BONDS OF LOVE

An established nursing relationship is not lightly broken. Mother and baby need each other both physically and emotionally. The baby, of course, has a physical need for milk. His emotional need is also great: a need for contact with his mother, and for the love and reassurance he gets through all his senses while nursing, but especially through his highly sensitive mouth. The mother, in turn, has a physical need for the baby to take the milk from her breasts. Moderate fullness is not a discomfort; nevertheless, the letdown reflex that makes the milk flow is relieving, satisfying, like a drink of water when one is thirsty. Also, mothers quickly become fond of nursing, and not just because of the rush of hormones associated with the first flow of milk. In our demanding society, it's lovely to have a legitimate excuse to sit down and do nothing for a while. So a sensation of fullness makes a mother yearn for her baby and for the satisfaction of feeding him. Many mothers learn to look forward to and expect the physical relaxation each time they nurse.

But most of all, perhaps, the mother, like the baby, needs to be shown that she is loved; and the behavior of even a tiny baby at the breast is proof positive of that. His greed is flattering, his blissful enjoyment is contagious, his drunken satiety is a comical compliment. As he grows older, his love of his mother becomes conscious and intense. The baby of

8

three months stares and stares at his mother's face as he nurses, looking into her eyes—loving her with all his soul. At five or six months he plays at the breast, fiddling with a ribbon or button on his mother's dress, patting her lovingly. He smiles out of the corner of his mouth, or puts a hand up to her lips to be kissed, showing her at every feeding how much he loves her. It is quite an experience. Life is not so full of true love that one regards it as commonplace in any circumstances.

We do not wish to imply that the mother and baby who do not breastfeed don't love each other; of course they do. But happy nursing couples feel differently about each other. Mothers who have bottle-fed one or two children and then found that they could breastfeed subsequent babies are poignantly aware of the difference. The physical intimacy of breastfeeding dispels the barriers that always exist between individuals in a way that no amount of conscientious mothering can do. The nursing couple have become a successful team at feedings, and this mutual understanding extends to all the other contacts they make.

Mothers who have reared both bottle-fed and breastfed infants say a nursing baby is "easier." The ease lies not only in being free of the chores of bottle-feeding and the drawbacks of synthetic milks, but in feeling companionable and agreeable with the baby. The nursing baby is often taken along with his mother wherever she goes, not only because he needs his mother's milk, but because he is so little trouble, and she misses him when they are apart. This rapport can continue to be a part of the relationship of mother and child long after weaning.

THE HAPPY NURSING BABY

It is not just in her relationship to her mother that the nursing baby enjoys a casual intimacy that the bottle-fed baby may miss. A happy nursing baby is easier on the whole household. She is always around, but seldom in the way. Siblings can be jealous of any new baby at first (and fathers can be a godsend, amusing an older child while the mother nurses the new one, in the early weeks). But once the family has become accustomed to the newcomer, the nursing couple fit into the family as one individual, the baby simply an extension of the mother, nursing while she reads to other children, nursing while she talks over the day with her husband, or naps, or talks on the phone, or sits down to her own dinner. Perhaps the breastfed baby gets so much bodily attention that she demands less attention in other ways; perhaps, also, her smoothly running insides contribute to her cheerfulness. And almost certainly the learning that goes on at the breast contributes to the baby's attitudes and sociability with others. She may well be the least demanding or troublesome member of the family; so she gets a full share of love and approval from all.

The mother who must go back to work after her baby is born can be extra-appreciative of the happiness breast-feeding brings to her baby. While it may be a bit of trouble to pump or express her milk at work in order to maintain her supply and to avoid using synthetic milk (see chapter 13), the closeness of the nursing relationship becomes even more important to mother and baby if they must be apart during the day. Perhaps someone else gave the baby her milk in a bottle during the day, but breastfeeding illuminates their daily reunions, and gives the baby needed physical and emotional strength. And the mother gains emotional reassurance from the breastfeeding relationship, too. No matter that someone else must care for the baby while she is gone; breastfeeding is one thing no one else can do for the baby but her own mother. In preserving this privilege for herself, a mother also preserves, across the daily separation, the closeness that breastfeeding brings.

INTERFERENCE WITH BREASTFEEDING

Even though today breastfeeding is officially championed throughout the medical industry, it is still not uncommon for a physician to order a baby off the breast for a great variety of trivial and often quite erroneous reasons. Cultural prejudice against breastfeeding is still widespread. One woman firefighter was allowed to bring her baby to work—she had a desk job—but was fired for obscene behavior when she discreetly nursed the baby on the premises; she sued and got her job back. All employers are not sympathetic to the real need for a maternity leave, and such considerations as on-site or nearby day care and flexible hours to accommodate the nursing mother are rare indeed. The mother who stays home to breastfeed is often regarded as unproductive, while the mother who works is often hindered from giving her child the care he needs.

The strength of the bonds that join a nursing couple is most evident, perhaps, when those bonds are broken. It is understandable that some babies object to being weaned to artificial feeding, but people are often aghast at the violent reaction of the nursing mother when some external pressure forces her to stop nursing. The mother does not feel guilty or inadequate, as is often assumed. She is grief-stricken. She may feel as if her nursing baby has been taken away from her. She may bitterly resent the person or circumstance she considers responsible. She may change doctors. She may change jobs. Many a mother has nursed her baby with incredible courage and devotion through illnesses (the baby's or her own) despite hostile critics, unsympathetic doctors, public disapproval, and absence of family support. Many a grandmother who was forced unnecessarily to wean her own babies still gets tears in her eyes as she remembers how she felt. This strength of feeling, this unreasoning determination, does not arise from guilt or neurosis or fear of failure as a mother. It is not stubborn selfishness in the face of "reality." It is good mothering. And it is love, the intense love of the nursing couple.

THE BRIDGE TO INDEPENDENCE

What effect, if any, does this nursing relationship have upon the emotions and personality of the child? Many authorities (anthropologist Ashley Montagu, John Bowlby, Ph.D., and M. Bevan-Brown, M.D., among others) believe that a good nursing relationship is valuable, perhaps essential, for the healthy emotional growth of the infant, and possibly of the mother as well. Dr. Montagu suggests that the human infant is born at nine months because the rapidly growing brain cannot pass through the birth canal much later than that, but that it is not a "mature" product until about nine months later, when it has teeth and a fair amount of mobility. Consequently, the species is adapted to about nine months of additional gestation outside the womb, which ought to provide as fully for the infant's needs as did the complete protection within the womb during the nine months of pregnancy. Perhaps it is relevant that some babies wean themselves rather abruptly and spontaneously at or around the age of nine months, from breast or bottle. While nursing is often continued far beyond the nine-month point, this seems to be the earliest point at which weaning occurs naturally.

The separation of mother and child at birth is a physical and emotional shock to them both. Lactation permits this separation to be accomplished gradually, over a minimum of nine months. Only gradually is the child parted from his old, uterine existence. When the mother feeds him long and often at her breast, this world still consists mainly of her warmth, support, and movements, of her pulse, her voice, her body chemistry. He can acquire understanding of his new world of temperatures, textures, lights, sounds, and people from the familiar home base of her body. And it is gradually, rather than abruptly, that the mother is separated from this extension of herself. Psychologist Sylvia Brodie, in her book *Patterns of Mothering,* describes final weaning from the breast, at nine months or more, as a kind of second birth, in which mother and child are severed spiritually as they were severed physically by the birth.

It seems reasonable to suppose that the gradual transitions provided by breastfeeding are truly beneficial to the infant. Herbert Ratner, M.D., says "the quickest way to make your child independent is to take care of his needs when he is dependent"; and his overriding needs are for the nourishment and the nurturing that breastfeeding provides.

ARE BREASTFED BABIES HAPPIER?

Breastfed babies are indubitably *healthier* than bottle-fed babies, as we shall see in following chapters. But are breastfed babies happier? Do they grow up to be "better adjusted"? No, say the bottle-feeders. Yes, say the breastfeeders. In some schools in Japan, the first question asked when a child enters is, How long was the child breastfed? Practical experience has indicated that the child who was breastfed briefly or not at all has a harder time getting used to school. Surveys in this country designed to discover psychological differences between breastfed and bottle-reared children at school age have had very mixed results, for a rather straightforward reason: most researchers counted a baby that got any breast milk at all as a breastfed baby. Thus, the information about children who were *fully* breastfed—meaning they were fed their mothers' milk exclusively for about six months, with breastfeeding continuing at least through the first year—was jumbled with information about children who were breastfed for a few days or weeks (token breastfeeding) or given synthetic feeds from the start (mixed feeding) and who therefore differed from truly breastfed babies in many ways. Even so, some researchers did find long-term psychological advantages for breastfed children, only to be challenged on the ground that those children were happier because they had mothers with more affectionate natures, who were thus more apt to breastfeed.

As we shall see in later chapters, the critics got it backward: it is not necessarily the mother's affectionate nature that motivates breastfeeding; the breastfeeding experience itself teaches mothers to be affectionate and to be skilled in showing affection. The learning is built into the system, and when it is not interfered with, it works well.

Western medicine tends to think of breastfeeding as

something that involves small infants only. But human babies throughout most of the world remain nursing babies for at least one year, and often two or more. And the older baby derives obvious and perhaps important reassurance from being able to nurse. This is true of other species as well. Cornell University scientists point out that when a person enters a field of goats or sheep, all the babies run in fear to their mothers and immediately begin to nurse. Anthropologists have noted the same thing happening in India and Africa when a stranger enters a remote village: even children of five or six immediately run to their mothers for a reassuring swig of milk. The experienced nursing mother knows that when a toddler is weaning himself he may cease to want the breast for nourishment, but still need it very much when he is frightened or has hurt himself. The older bottle-fed baby gets this kind of comfort from his bottle, a blanket, or his thumb—poor substitutes for a mother's lap and bosom.

Although breastfeeding is generally recommended by medical care givers, it is still customary to tell mothers who don't want to breastfeed that bottle-feeding is just as good, as long as it is combined with plenty of loving care and the baby is held and cuddled as if he were drinking from the breast. The trouble is, cuddling a baby who is taking a bottle is rather like talking to someone who is reading a newspaper. The baby is interested in the bottle, not in the mother. The mother's tendency may be to begin propping the bottle within a few weeks of birth; the baby is more fun to be with at other times.

Perhaps the very affectionate mother, who enjoys giving the bottle, can "fool" the baby by holding him close and smiling and talking to him while he drinks from a bottle, so that feedings are pleasant for them both. Nevertheless, for her at least, the relationship is platonic. It does not involve her body, her hormones, her nervous system. Her response to the baby cannot be the same, and the baby does not have to interact with her in the same way, waiting for the milk to let down, say, or signaling his own satisfaction.

One could speculate that this transfer of the baby's attention from the mother to the bottle and her inevitable abandonment of him at mealtimes, whether it occurs at two months or at five, make the bottle more important than ever as a token of comforting, and that this attachment is at the root of our Western admiration of material things at the expense of the spiritual. Or perhaps this widespread substitution of food for love in the lives of many infants explains why Americans tend to be overweight and overeaters. Perhaps such habits as smoking, drinking, and even talking are but substitutes for the suckling at our mother's breast that was denied us in infancy. In fact, scientists in the field of infant behavior are beginning to agree that the fantastically high level of mental illness in this country is due, at least in part, to our systematic frustration of normal mother-infant relationships, from standardized surgical deliveries to the hospital isolation of infants, rigid child-care systems, and interference with lactation.

WHAT ABOUT THE MOTHER?

The nursing relationship, or lack of it, may well have profound effects upon the personality of the infant. What of the mother? Is she helped in any way by the experience of nursing? Mothers who have experienced a normal nursing relationship, in which mother and baby are a happy nursing couple for many months, are often well aware of the emotional maturity that the experience has brought them. Medical personnel who understand the management of breastfeeding, and who in consequence see many happy nursing mothers, will concur. Successful lactation seems to have a permanent and valuable maturing effect.

Lactation is the final chapter in a woman's biological functioning. It is an oversight to consider, as Kinsey did, that sexual intercourse and its variations are the only significant form of sexual behavior. Men, indeed, have only one biological function related to their sex: intercourse. Women have five: the ovarian cycle, intercourse, pregnancy, childbirth, and lactation. Each of these events has a powerful effect on a woman's life.

We are quite aware of the physical and emotional changes

that take place when a girl reaches puberty and begins the ovarian cycle. The emotional significance and maturing effects of intercourse are reasonably well understood. Pregnancy has become a field of considerable interest to students of human emotions. The emotional repercussions of a poorly managed childbirth vs. the mental and physical rewards of a well-conducted labor and birth are sufficiently recognized for childbirth associations and education programs to have sprung up all over the country. And we are beginning to discover that lactation has long-term health benefits for the mother as well as for the child. But we are still generally unaware of the psychological effects on women of experiencing a normal lactation.

When a woman breastfeeds, she must give herself to the baby. She must let the baby set the pace, make the decisions, do the work. Many mothers cannot do this at first, especially if they have been handed, or have asked for, a fixed set of rules. But most often a woman eventually gets "lazy" and relaxes into a more natural role. She forgets to look at the clock, she doesn't bother to interrupt the baby for her own reasons, she doesn't worry about when or why she wants to eat. She actively gives the baby milk, time, and love, whenever she seems to want it. She lets her move around, start and stop, nurse at her own rate, interrupt her meals or prolong them. She learns to participate in feedings without dominating or deciding anything, to be deeply interested but quite casual about the whole matter.

This is the natural result of successful breastfeeding, no matter what kind of personality the mother has. The woman who doesn't develop this completely casual approach with the first baby often adopts it with her second; that is one reason why many nursing mothers "have more milk" the second time around. This relaxed yet attentive attitude toward ourselves and others is rather foreign to our culture. For many American women, prolonged breastfeeding constitutes their first experience of a truly interactive primary relationship. The richness of the experience depends somewhat, of course, on how long one nurses; those who stop at two months, or four, will necessarily forgo the experiences they would have in nursing their child at eight months or a year. But as long as a woman is nursing, she is putting another's needs first, and at the same time meeting needs of her own. Like the baby, she is learning to give and take.

The experience of breastfeeding can teach a mother how to go about being womanly rather than girlish: a grownup, in short. Her relationship with her husband may change for the better. She may find her work outside the home less stressful. And her relationships with the rest of her family may improve; the sustained two-way relationship with her baby constitutes a useful education.

THE FATHER AND THE NURSING COUPLE

A man usually derives real joy from the sight of his wife nursing his child. Dr. Hugh Smith, the Dr. Spock of eighteenth-century London, wrote, to urge mothers to nurse their babies: "Oh, that I could prevail upon my fair countrywomen to become still more lovely in the sight of men. I speak from the feelings of a man . . . rest assured, when he beholds the object of his soul cherishing and supporting in her arms the propitious reward of wedlock . . . it recalls a thousand delicate sensations to a generous mind." For a mother, then or now, one happy reward of nursing is the glow on her mate's face when he first sees the baby at her breast.

Becoming a father for the first time changes a man's position somewhat. He becomes a major part of a household of three, rather than merely a companion or mate. And in no place is his paternal contribution more valuable than in the nursing relationship. Many a nursing mother is aware that she has nursed her baby successfully, partly because her mate thought she *should* and knew she *could,* whatever the rest of the world said or did.

In the last decades, the custom of enlisting fathers as labor coaches has become more and more widespread. Fathers have avidly plunged into this role. The benefits have been enormous. Primary, of course, is the father's provision of intimate support and care for the mother throughout labor, a human and humane necessity that is conspicuously absent in the standard medical system. The opportunity the father receives to bond with the baby in the emotion-filled hour of birth is also of fundamental importance, for both parent and child.

The father's support for breastfeeding is a continuation of his role as labor coach and may require particularly masculine skills. Recently, in a large metropolitan hospital, one father coached his wife through the safe birth of a baby girl, who was in due course taken to the hospital nursery "for observation." When six hours had passed and the baby had not been returned to their room, the father went to the hospital nursery, walked in, and found a physician he had never met ordering a bottle of sugar water for the baby, a practice deleterious to breastfeeding. The father protested. The physician said he was in charge of the nursery that day and he knew best. "Well, we're breastfeeding," the father said firmly, "and I want this baby to be taken to my wife immediately." The doctor backpedaled. The nurses looked at the father's hospital ID bracelet, which matched the baby's; they put the baby in his arms, he took it back to the room, and in five minutes the beginning of a long and happy nursing relationship had been accomplished; that baby never saw the inside of the nursery again. The father later said, of the showdown in the nursery, "It was fun."

Any little girl in Bali or Beirut grows up with ample experience of observing successful nursing couples, often starting with seeing a sibling at the breast shortly after she herself has been weaned. A new American mother may never have seen a baby nursing, even once, and she may never have held a new baby until her own newborn is put in her arms. Breastfeeding is a learned skill, but brief hospital stays and harried staff mean that a mother may not get the start-up help she needs. In our culture, new fathers have the vital tasks of shielding the mother from interference, and of defending her right to be a natural mother and their baby's inalienable right to its mother's milk.

CHAPTER 2

How the Breasts Function

MAKING MILK: THE MAMMALIAN GIFT

Any woman can nurse a baby. Most women could nurse twins. Medical science has never recorded a case of a woman who gave birth and did not subsequently have milk in her breasts. There is no medical reason, save dangerous infectious disease, mortal illness, or insanity, for preventing a mother from nursing. If you are fit to have a baby you are fit to nurse it.

So we stated in *Nursing Your Baby* in 1963. Today, the medical sleuths have turned up a few rare cases of physical impediments to lactation: a pituitary gland that has ceased to function, for example, and some kinds of breast surgery. And there is one new valid reason, besides major illness or insanity, for preventing a mother from breastfeeding: cocaine addiction. In general, however, the system that has worked since humankind began, and for a considerable time before that, will work for you.

When milk is present, it needs only to be removed for the body to make more milk. The more that is removed, the more will be made. Thus the supply increases as the demand increases. This system is so automatic that it is possible for a woman who has not had a baby in years to produce some milk by putting an infant to her breast. Some mothers in the United States are discovering that they can at least partially nurse an adopted baby long after having weaned their own youngest. It is the custom, in some African tribes, for grandmothers and mothers alike to suckle the babies, thus assuring milk in times of hardship.

It is possible for a mother who did *not* nurse her baby during its first weeks of life to start putting it to the breast at the age of a month, or two months, and by letting the baby suckle, to increase her supply, building up enough secretion to maintain the baby entirely on her own milk. The problem of feeding a baby who is allergic to formula can sometimes be solved in this way. The mother of a premature baby, hospitalized for weeks after birth, can still plan to establish a milk supply and be breastfeeding soon after the baby comes home.

This remarkable function, the ability to produce ample and excellent food for the newborn young, is what separates us mammals from the lower creatures. Lactation probably arose early in the evolution of living creatures. In a sense, it is older than pregnancy. The monotremes, those ancient but still living forms such as the duckbilled platypus, lay eggs like reptiles. But the young, once hatched, drink their mother's milk.

The platypus has no nipples. Milk simply oozes through the pores of the skin on the abdomen, and the baby licks it off. The next step, as shown in marsupials such as the opossum, was the development of the nipple, which serves to collect the milk in one spot, gives the embryo-sized young something to grasp, and prevents accidental separation from the milk supply. Pregnancy—internal gestation—in mammals was the final step in protecting and nourishing the young, long preceded by the giving of milk.

HOW THE BREASTS DEVELOP

The mammary glands, from which the word "mammal" is taken, appear early in the development of the embryo in the form of two thickened bands, the mammary ridges or milk lines, running down the center of the body. In the human species, these milk lines are discernible when the embryo is six weeks old. By the time it is five months along, the nipple, areola or darkened area around the nipple, and the duct system beneath the nipple are all developed. In humans, of course, the mammary glands develop relatively high on the embryonic milk lines, in the chest region. In some other species, the glands may develop low on the milk line, as in hoofed animals, or in serial pairs, as in dogs and cats. The existence of auxiliary pairs of nipples in human beings, either below or above the usual pair, is not uncommon, occurring about twice as often as the birth of triplets. These supernumerary nipples usually, but not always, are nonfunctioning during lactation. Mammary tissue may also exist along the milk lines, without a nipple. Once in a while, such tissue swells during early lactation, but since the milk is not removed, the functioning soon ceases.

When a human baby is born, its breast tissue is usually enlarged, due to the presence of lactation hormones received from the placenta. Regardless of the sex of the child, the glands may actually secrete drops of milk during the first days after birth—what nurses and midwives sometimes call witches' milk. Once this activity ceases, the mammary glands remain inactive, simply growing along with the rest of the body until a year or two before puberty. Then, in girls, the ovaries begin to release increasing quantities of estrogen into the bloodstream, causing the nipples and areolas to enlarge, and the glandular and duct tissue to grow and proliferate.

When menstrual cycles begin, the ovaries give off increased estrogen in amounts that wax and wane cyclically. When estrogen levels are highest, around the midpoint of each menstrual cycle, the major part of breast development takes place. The ducts continue to ramify and branch away from the nipples like tributaries of a river or branches of a tree, and fat is laid down around the duct system, giving the breasts their size and shape. (Buxomness, or the lack of it, is not a good indication of potential ability to lactate; it is mostly a result of the quantity of nonfunctional fatty tissue in the breasts.) The development of the breasts depends not only upon estrogen, but also upon pituitary hormones, which govern general body growth. Once the body is mature and growth has ceased, in the late teens or early twenties, breast growth is not noticeable until and unless the individual becomes pregnant.

BREAST CHANGES IN PREGNANCY

Everyone who becomes pregnant is aware of the changes that pregnancy produces in the breasts, often in the very first weeks. Some women have sensations of fullness and soreness, which normally occur for a day or two before each menstrual period. When these sensations suddenly seem to be going on day after day, the experienced mother goes flying to her calendar to figure out when the new baby might be expected. By the time her next period is overdue, the glands of Montgomery, which lie in the areola in a ring around the nipple, have become prominent. These glands secrete special lubricants that make the areola elastic and flexible, so it can accommodate itself to being drawn into the infant's mouth. (Montgomery described these glands in a famous medical hyperbole as "a constellation of miniature nipples scattered over a milky way.") By the fifth month, the mother may need to buy larger bras; breast tissue is growing. Nipple and areola become larger and darker. By the ninth month, even the new bras may seem tight, partly because the rib cage is also expanding to make room for the baby.

Changes in breast size reflect the preparation of the breasts for lactation and are caused by hormones circulating in the bloodstream. With elegant economy, nature borrows hormones for milk production from the same set that is used to govern the menstrual cycle. The menstrual cycle is maintained by a sort of hormonal round robin, in which the pituitary gland and the ovaries stimulate each other to produce a series of hormones that in the first half of the cycle develop and release an egg, and in the second half of the cycle prepare the uterus for possible pregnancy, should that egg become fertilized.

The ovarian hormone progesterone *(pro-gestation)*, which

22

predominates in the second half of the cycle, causes the uterine lining to thicken. Progesterone also produces premenstrual changes in the breasts: the feeling of tenderness and fullness, and sometimes an actual temporary increase in size. If no pregnancy takes place, progesterone production ceases, and the uterine lining is sloughed away in the menstrual flow. If conception takes place, however, the fertilized egg itself produces a hormone that keeps the ovaries producing progesterone; the uterine lining remains to support the embryo.

About six weeks after conception, the placenta develops and begins to take over the hormone production job. The placenta releases very high levels of estrogen, as well as some progesterone and other hormones, into the body. This combination stimulates tremendous changes in the breasts. Up to now, growth has taken place only in the duct system, which will transport the milk down to the nipples. Once the placenta has developed, a whole new system is added. This is the secretory system that actually makes the milk. The end of every duct branches and rebranches and buds off into little sacs, called the alveoli, which are lined with milk-secreting cells. The alveoli form clusters on their ducts, rather like bunches of grapes on their stems. The increase in breast size during pregnancy is a result mainly of the addition of alveoli to the mammary structure.

In the second half of pregnancy the placenta begins producing prolactin, the *pro-lactation* hormone. This stimulates further growth of the alveoli and also causes them to secrete milk. There is milk in the breasts from the fourth or fifth month of pregnancy; if miscarriage or premature delivery takes place from this time on it is followed by lactation.

If prolactin, which causes milk secretion, is present and the alveoli are capable of producing milk, why don't pregnant women lactate? Prolactin levels in fact are very high everywhere in the body during pregnancy; this hormone does a lot more than just make milk—it is in men's bodies, too. The very high levels of estrogen and progesterone produced by the placenta stimulate breast growth, but another placental product, a prolactin-inhibiting factor, prevents the secretion of milk until the placenta leaves the body.

Milk production is further inhibited by a specific suppressor hormone in the placenta. Once the baby is born and the placenta, with its hormones, is gone, normal milk secretion can start. Lactation researcher Marianne Neifert, M.D., has reported a case of a new mother who could not give milk and also was bleeding a lot; on examination, her uterus proved to have retained a piece of the placenta—enough to stop the breasts from functioning. When that was removed, an ample milk supply developed within twenty-four hours.

PHYSICAL BENEFITS OF LACTATION TO THE MOTHER

The physical benefits that breastfeeding can give to the mother begin in the hour her child is born. As lactation gets under way, the oxytocin released at each feeding causes mild uterine contractions. At first, these contractions can be uncomfortable; however, nursing in the hour of birth contracts the still-active uterus so effectively that it prevents the spasmodic cramping contractions or afterpains that are common when the first nursing is delayed. Throughout the time a mother is nursing, her uterus contracts during and after each feeding. Thus it involutes, or returns to normal size, more rapidly than that of the mother who doesn't nurse.

Breast tissue that has functioned is said to retain its shape over a longer period of years than that which has not. Some doctors think that breasts that have never lactated may be subject to atrophy and are more likely to be prematurely pendulous or shapeless. If lactation is ended abruptly, the breasts may seem soft or flat for a few weeks. By six months after weaning, however, the breasts have usually regained their former shape, whatever that may have been, but may have somewhat less fatty tissue. This makes little difference to the small-breasted woman, since she didn't have much fatty tissue to begin with. The woman with very large breasts may prefer her figure after lactation.

Lactation is actually good for the mother's body. Among other things, it combats the cumulative effects on the figure of several pregnancies. Some of the weight gained in pregnancy represents nutrients such as calcium, which are stored in the mother's body for use during lactation. Special fat depots are laid down during pregnancy, to be drawn on during lactation; this is why a nursing mother need not eat as many calories as she is putting out to stay healthy while breastfeeding. When lactation is suppressed, it is possible that these stored nutrients remain in the body; each pregnancy therefore tends to make the mother a little heavier.

Finally, there is good evidence that lactation protects against some forms of breast cancer and that prolonged lactation (lasting two years or more) offers striking protection against ovarian cancer (see p. 58). There is evidence, also, that lactation offers significant protection, through mechanisms not yet understood, against osteoporosis, the loss of calcium from the mother's skeleton in old age.

HOW LACTATION BEGINS

The instant of birth is a thrilling moment. Usually the mother's urge is to pick up the baby right away and put it to the breast. In modern hospitals, mothers are given the baby and encouraged to nurse in the birth setting immediately after birth, sometimes even before the placenta is delivered and the cord cut. The baby is usually extremely alert and active during the first hour, gazing into its parents' eyes, and ready to "latch on." A vigorous sucking reflex can be elicited in this receptive period. The baby's sucking, through sensory and hormonal responses in the mother's body, causes the uterus to contract, facilitating delivery of the placenta, if that has not already occurred, and reducing postpartum bleeding.

The milk present in the breasts upon giving birth is colostrum, a thick, yellowish fluid crammed with both nourishment and vital antibodies as well as other protective agents. Even one feeding of colostrum provides the baby with important benefits (see chapter 3). Colostrum also has a slightly laxative effect; it serves to clean out the baby's intestines of waste products accumulated during its uterine life (see chapter 4).

Normally, the mother then rests, with the baby in her bed or very close by, so that they can nurse whenever she feels full or the baby peeps. A newborn baby may want to nurse in spurts, sometimes every hour or two; as one researcher has pointed out, a baby's stomach is no bigger than its two fists, breast milk is very digestible, and that newborn is ready to grow. A newborn may take in considerable quantities of high-calorie colostrum, the special milk that is first produced, in the first day or two of life.

Whether the mother nurses sitting up or lying down, she holds the baby flat against her body, facing her, so that he does not have to reach or twist his neck to latch on. In all mothers, whether the areola is large or small, the sinuses lie about the same distance behind the nipple, a distance matching the size of a newborn baby's mouth. While the baby is on the breast, his tongue and jaws apply pressure to the milk sinuses behind the nipple, not to the nipple itself. The nipple is positioned well back in the baby's mouth, where it is virtually untouched during nursing. While a mother's nipples may become tender for a few hours or days, especially with her first baby, proper positioning and frequent, unrestricted nursing enable her breasts to adjust to their new task quickly (see chapter 6).

Outsiders sometimes assume mothers must need sleep that the baby is denying them, but in fact the new mother can doze and nurse at the same time, as she could never do while holding a bottle. The production of milk depends upon the secretion of prolactin, which is stimulated by the baby's suckling. Frequent and unrestricted nursing is important for a good start. Casual, frequent, and unrestricted nursings also benefit the mother physically, and are comforting and reassuring to both her and the baby. Many a mother feels fretful and depressed if her baby is away from her, and actually gets less rest if the baby is taken out of the room.

Within twenty-four to thirty-six hours, the colostrum changes to more mature milk, tailored to the special needs of the newborn. Secretion may be overabundant at first; one pediatrician tells his patients, "Nature doesn't know you didn't have twins." The breasts may often feel full, but the baby is always available to reduce the overload. The supply soon adjusts to the baby's needs.

Babies born in hospitals often lose weight in the first days after birth, owing to separations from the mother, and sometimes to water loss from being too warmly wrapped. They usually turn the corner and begin to gain weight within a few days after birth. Babies that are born at home, or kept with their mothers and allowed to nurse unrestrictedly, may gain weight within a day or two. As the mother gradually resumes her normal activities, she continues to keep the baby near her or with her day and night and to nurse him as long and as often as he wants. During the first month, a baby usually nurses an average of ten or twelve times in a twenty-four-hour period. This implies an average of two hours or more between feedings, but in real life the baby may sometimes want to nurse *every* hour—in the early or late evening, typically—and at other times will go for longer periods—three or four hours, perhaps—without nursing. As the baby grows and becomes more efficient, nursing sessions become shorter and fewer, occurring at longer intervals.

HUMAN PRODUCTION CAPACITY

The power of natural selection, though it has not produced such extreme production capacity as has been bred into the modern dairy cow, has nevertheless made all female mammals relatively good producers of milk. The amount of milk produced is a direct result of the amount removed. Ruth Lawrence, M.D., professor of pediatrics at the University of Rochester Medical School, points out that the mammary gland is not a bladder, and the breast is not a storage tank. The breast is a production device; it is never truly empty, since production is continuous. When the baby is hungrier, perhaps because of a growth spurt, he nurses longer or more frequently. The rate of production then increases until the breasts are again meeting his needs, and also producing a surplus. When he is less hungry for milk and takes a bit less, production is correspondingly diminished.

Peak production capacity is well above normal peak demand. This seems to be just as true for humans as for other species. Hospital milk banks, which collect and store human milk for premature and sick babies, have found that almost any woman who cares to be a donor can produce surplus milk beyond her own baby's needs. Some milk bank donors produce only a few ounces of surplus milk daily; others can donate a pint or more. Such individual variations seem to be entirely within the mammalian safety margin. Some women can produce at least twice as much milk as is needed by the average baby; experienced nursing mothers can usually breastfeed twins. Some mothers have successfully nursed triplets and even quadruplets, though not always without occasional assistance. A woman with a supernormal ability to lactate might be able to nurse more. In previous centuries, such women were often on the staffs of foundling hospitals. (There is a record of a woman in a French orphanage who for a short time maintained seven babies on her own milk.) A woman with an inherited potential at the low end of the normal scale can still produce enough milk for *one* baby.

The existence of the hypogalactic woman, that is, the woman who cannot make enough milk for any baby because she does not have enough alveoli in her breasts, has been postulated but never very clearly demonstrated. What *has* been clearly demonstrated is that, in the presence of prolactin and possibly other lactation hormones, alveoli can be developed by the sucking stimulus alone. This fact, that breastfeeding itself makes the breasts function, means that mothers who start out producing just a few ounces of milk per day may yet be able to produce a quart or more daily after a few months of lactation.

One often hears it suggested that because we in the United States raise so many babies on the bottle, allowing the survival of offspring of mothers who have subnormal lactating ability, we are becoming in truth what the Russians call us in jest: a nation of milkless women. Fortunately, evolution does not work that quickly. The ancient mammalian equipment cannot be rendered nonfunctional in the random breeding of a few generations. Poor lactation in our society is usually due to a multitude of cultural interferences in the lactation process, not to physical incapacity.

THE LETDOWN REFLEX

Certainly, despite normal equipment, a great many civilized women "cannot" nurse a baby. They just don't seem to have enough milk. If prolactin causes milk secretion, why can't we solve the problem of the modern woman who "doesn't have enough milk" by giving her prolactin injections? This has been tried, but it is generally not a success. Almost always, the factor that is limiting the amount of milk a mother has for her baby is not prolactin production; in fact, the hormone does not govern how much milk she is making.

Making milk, so simple and automatic a process when enough sucking stimulation is provided and enough milk is removed, is only half of lactation. *Giving* milk is the other, equally important half. The nursing baby cannot get his mother's milk by himself. Even the powerful mechanical suction of a breast pump can remove no more than about a third of the milk, that milk which lies in the large collecting ducts or milk sinuses directly behind the nipple. The milk in the smaller ducts and alveoli cannot be withdrawn by outside forces; it must be delivered by actions within the breast itself.

This held-back milk is made available to the baby by a reflex within the breast called the letdown reflex. (Dairymen have always spoken of cows "letting down" their milk; hence the term. In England this reflex is sometimes termed "the draught," pronounced *draft*. The name "milk ejection reflex" is also used.) In the milk-secreting lobes of the breast and along the walls of the ducts lie octopus-shaped cells called basket cells, which reach their threadlike arms around the alveoli and along the duct walls. When the letdown reflex operates, all these cells contract. The alveoli are compressed and the duct passages are widened. Fluid rushes from the bloodstream into the sinuses to mix with the milk constituents from the alveoli. The resulting milk is quickly pushed down into the main milk sinuses under the nipple. In early lactation it may even be pushed out of the duct openings to drip or spray from the nipples.

When the baby nurses, he does not actually remove milk by suction. Such suction as he exerts is merely sufficient to keep the nipple in place in the back of his mouth. Then with tongue and jaws he compresses the areola and the large milk sinuses beneath, pressing the milk that is in the sinuses into his mouth. In this way he milks the breast, and this is the way all mammals (except, of course, the platypus) get their milk.

As the baby starts to nurse, the tactile sensations received by the mother trigger the release of the hormone oxytocin, which causes the basket cells to contract. The milk lets down. The letdown reflex functions repeatedly during a single nursing. The baby need hardly make the effort to milk the breast; the milk is pumped into his throat of its own accord. Even a very tiny or weak baby can thus get plenty of milk almost effortlessly.

In fact a newborn baby can be quite overcome by the sudden abundance from a strong letdown reflex. He may choke, gasp, sputter, get milk up his nose, and have to let go to catch his breath while the milk sprays all over the bedclothes and his face. Fortunately, most babies are excited rather than upset by this misadventure, and come back to the breast with avid greed.

A functioning letdown reflex is crucial to the nourishment of the baby, not only because the baby receives just a third of the milk without the letdown action, but because he can receive the fat content of the milk *only* if the milk is let down. It has long been known that the last few swallows of milk are the richest; dairymen distinguish between the thin "fore milk" and the fat-filled "hind milk." F. E. Hytten, M.D., of the University of Aberdeen in Scotland, has shown in an ingenious demonstration with sponges that the fat particles, being sticky, tend to cling to the walls of the alveoli and ducts and to be drawn off last. The fat mixes more evenly in the breast that the baby is not nursing, as letdowns occur; however, some gradation remains. British researcher Michael Woolwich, M.D., identified several babies who were doing poorly because their mothers had been firmly told to nurse only ten minutes on each breast at each feeding; by obediently following that rule, the women were inadvertently feeding their babies only the fore milk from each breast. The babies were suffering from starvation symptoms because they were, in effect, being fed skim milk.

In human milk, 50 percent of the calories come from the fat content. Even if the baby is allowed to nurse unrestrictedly, the fat globules will not reach the baby if the letdown reflex does not occur. An inhibited letdown reflex therefore results in a hungry baby even if a fair amount of fluid is being taken in. The letdown reflex is a simple physical response to a physical stimulus. It is supposed to work like clockwork. Failure of the letdown reflex, however, is the basic cause of most breastfeeding failures. Why?

The letdown reflex needs to be trained, or conditioned, to work reliably; until that happens, this reflex is greatly affected by the mother's circumstances. Any disturbance, particularly in the early days of lactation, can cause inhibition of the letdown reflex. Such stresses as embarrassment, irritation, or anxiety actually prevent the pituitary from secreting oxytocin. Thus, the woman who dislikes breastfeeding or is very much afraid she will fail may actually give less milk than the mother who is interested and hopeful of success. Physical problems such as sore nipples and engorgement (see chapter 2, pp 55–56, and chapter 10, pp. 240–41, 248–49) can cause discomfort that exacerbates the problem by interfering with letdown. And a strong disturbance, such as real anger or fear, sends adrenaline through the system, causing the small blood vessels to contract, so that oxytocin, even if released, does not reach the basket cells that make the milk let down. This is what is happening to the mother whose milk stops flowing—and whose baby starts crying— when a disapproving relative walks into the room.

All too often the hospital setting provides numerous shocks and alarms to new parents, all deleterious to development of a well-conditioned letdown reflex. Fatigue; interruptions; embarrassment; fear and pain; anxiety about money, about work, about children at home, about breast-feeding itself; brusque doctors and disagreeable nurses; these and similar disturbances can be almost unavoidable features of hospitalization for childbirth. Some mothers do not even begin letting down their milk until they leave the hospital, by which time they may have been told they cannot breastfeed because of the baby's excessive weight loss or because the baby is "jaundiced" (a physiologic response to going hungry). Others do all right in the hospital but "lose their milk" on going home, when household responsibilities and family stresses inhibit the letdown reflex. Even the mother who gives her baby a fair amount of milk and who seems to be making a success of breastfeeding may have a still weak or unreliable letdown reflex for the first six weeks or longer.

When the letdown reflex is poorly established, an otherwise minor disturbance—such as guests, a late evening, a cold, a quarrel—is enough to tip the balance, to inhibit the reflex so that milk is left in the breast. Furthermore, the fatty particles in the milk remain in the secretory cells, so that the milk the baby does receive has fewer calories than it would have otherwise. Consequently, the baby gets hungry again sooner than usual. At this point, the mother may be tempted into giving him a bottle. Soon milk secretion is diminished because less milk is being removed. Unfortunately, this is usually regarded by the mother, her family, and all too often her medical care giver, as the beginning of the end of lactation, rather than as a temporary and remediable situation.

At the opposite end of the spectrum is the mother with what has been called an overactive letdown reflex; her letdown is very efficient, the milk supply is abundant, and the baby, while gaining extremely well, chokes and sputters through each feeding, and is gassy and flatulent afterward. The baby, usually a very strong nurser, can never nurse just for comfort, because once at the breast he must gulp or drown; rejection of the breast and early self-weaning can result. This inconvenient overabundance can usually be brought into balance in a week or less by nursing on one breast only, at each feeding, and by changing nursing positions (see chapter 11, pp. 271–72).

The first and most important step in improving an irregular or elusive letdown reflex is to reduce outside stress. New mothers are all too ready to assume that they are simply imperfect people who can't lactate readily, when often their circumstances would make it hard for even the most experienced nurser to let down her milk. In addition to cutting down on her own activities temporarily, a new nursing mother needs to look hard at whatever other stresses she is under—a chaotic household, worries about work, a husband who uses her as a sounding board for his own anxieties, the news on the television, her income taxes due next month, visiting relatives, business entertaining, whatever—and find some way to postpone or mitigate each external stress.

After stress-load reduction, the easiest tool at the mother's disposal for encouraging a good letdown reflex is the nature of the reflex itself. It is very easily conditioned. By exposing the mother to some other constant stimulus, it is possible to "teach" the letdown reflex to operate when needed, even if inhibiting factors are present. Some hospitals have gone so far as to ring a bell when the babies are about to be brought from the nursery. The mothers' milk begins to flow, like the saliva of Pavlov's dog, at the sound of the bell.

Any routine that is customarily followed before nursing, such as drinking a glass of water, bathing the breasts, turning on a favorite music tape, or simply sitting down and unbuttoning, can be a conditioning stimulus for the letdown reflex. The scent of the baby is a powerful conditioning stimulus. Breastfed babies have a sweet fragrance (unlike bottle-fed babies, who smell of sour milk); mothers who have to pump their milk when they are away from the baby sometimes keep the baby's jacket or nightie handy, so the baby's scent will help trigger the letdown.

The letdown reflex can also be conditioned to a time interval. After the first few weeks, some babies settle down to a fairly predictable feeding pattern; the milk may then let down automatically when mealtime rolls around. It's often quite a surprise for a new mother, out at a party for the first time since the baby arrived, to find herself suddenly drenched with milk at 10 P.M.

As the reflex begins to be conditioned, the milk may let down when the mother sees the baby, or hears it cry, or even when she simply thinks of the baby. The letdown reflex can even become conditioned to the mother's emotion as she starts to nurse, letting down whenever she feels a sense of pleasurable anticipation; one mother's milk lets down when she sits down to a good dinner, another's when she steps into a hot tub. One executive mother found that her milk always let down in the "down" elevator of her office building.

Before the letdown reflex becomes well-conditioned, the mother may experience irregular events, such as uncontrolled leaking, milk letting down at the wrong time or not at all, or marked fluctuations in milk production. These are all signs that the letdown reflex is starting to learn what to do; these symptoms decrease as the reflex becomes well-conditioned.

When lactation is well established, the initial letdown in a feeding is very effective; for some mothers this occurs from the first week or even, especially with experienced mothers, from the first feeding. For some women letdown is accompanied by a pins-and-needles or pressured sensation; others never feel a thing. The milk lets down several times in one feeding, even though only the first letdown may be felt. Letdown can be recognized by the gulping sounds the baby makes, swallowing the free-flowing milk. The letdown reflex and the consequent rush of fluid from the bloodstream into the breast occur rapidly; the mother who is producing a lot of milk—for example, while nursing a five- or six-month-old baby—may feel acutely thirsty when her milk lets down.

As the lactation continues, sphincter muscles within the nipples begin to function, putting a stop to leaking and spraying. These sphincter muscles, like a closed drawstring, hold the milk in the breast until the baby relaxes the nipple by suckling. Once these muscles learn their job, the filled milk sinuses may stand out in visible ridges under the areola after the milk lets down, but no dripping or leaking occurs.

The well-conditioned letdown reflex of the experienced nursing mother is the secret of her ample, steady milk production, day in, day out, and of her satisfied baby. She hardly thinks of it; she may not even be aware of it. Her baby wants to nurse, she gives him the breast, and the milk comes; it is infallible. Only when the baby himself begins to lose interest in the breast, which will not occur for at least nine months, does her milk supply diminish and her letdown reflex operate later in the feeding and finally fade away. If the baby were to get sick at this point and want the breast more often, both milk secretion and the letdown reflex would return.

When the letdown reflex is truly secure, even a serious emotional shock may not shake it. And the normal extra efforts that occur in every woman's life—sitting up all night with a sick child, giving a dinner party or a speech, catching the flu—can be withstood.

BREASTFEEDING AND THE MOTHER'S NUTRITION

A nursing mother may produce from 600 to 1,000 milliliters (20–34 ounces) of milk per day, depending on the size and age of the baby; one mother nursing triplets produced 3,000 milliliters of milk a day, or about three quarts. Each 1,000 milliliters of milk requires about 1,000 calories, for the energy in the milk and the energy it takes to manufacture the milk. Not all of this comes from the diet; some of it is drawn from fat reserves laid down in the mother's body during pregnancy.

With anything approaching an adequate diet, most women not only produce plenty of milk but do so without physical detriment. A study of forty-five well-nourished nursing mothers in Texas showed that on a diet of about 2,200 calories a day these mothers gradually lost weight, while their babies were all doing well. The amount or kinds of food they ate had no effect on the amount of milk they produced (the amount of milk, as we have seen, depends on the individual baby's needs).

During lactation, the mother's body adapts to this new demand in several ways. Her gastrointestinal tract actually grows and elaborates, developing more intestinal surface for absorbing food, so that less of what she eats is wasted. She can also more easily absorb foods to which she may be allergic, thus making potential allergens available in the milk, a consideration for families with a history of allergies. Her metabolism lowers somewhat, to save calories; after a full meal, when most people feel hot and show flushed faces, the nursing mother literally heats up less. This metabolic change may also be nature's way of telling the mother to slow down; fortunately, nursing is a good excuse to sit down and rest several times a day.

Unless the mother is actually starving, her body can provide adequate calories and fat even on a substandard diet. But other ingredients, such as vitamins, calcium, and other minerals, normally come from the mother's diet, and nature will see to it that the baby's needs are met first. If these nutritional elements are missing from the mother's diet, her own body stores will inevitably be raided. Inadequate or restrictive diets take their toll; in one study in Nepal, the nursing babies of mothers on very marginal diets were small and growing slowly, but they *were* healthy nursing babies. The mothers, on the other hand, had urinary tract infections, parasites, B-vitamin deficiencies, and many illnesses, including hepatitis.

The diet of prosperous Western women, though it may be ample in calories, may be inadequate in other ways. In 1958, Dr. F. E. Hytten and others found that in civilized England, among women on presumably ample diets, "breast feeding is by no means usually associated with maternal well-being." Hytten found that 44 percent of a group of one hundred lactating women lost weight, felt excessively tired, and suffered from repeated minor infections. Many American mothers try to "diet" by avoiding eating; others subsist on precooked fast food; some are too busy or tired to bother to feed themselves; and some subscribe to vegetarianism and other self-restrictions. All of these customs are likely to result in a diet that is poor in some minerals and vitamins. Adding lactation on top of already poor nutrition drains the mother's reserves, from B-complex vitamins in her liver, to calcium and phosphorus in her bony skeleton. It may be that the complaints of fatigue and barely adequate milk supply that are sometimes made by American nursing mothers are not psychosomatic, as is sometimes assumed, or due to overly demanding lives, but are the result of unsuitable diet.

An old superstition that mothers "lose a tooth for every baby" reflected a time in which most mothers were not receiving enough calcium, and dental care was nonexistent. Modern Western diets, however, are often calcium-poor. Bonnie Worthington-Roberts, Ph.D., professor of nutrition at the University of Washington School of Medicine, points out that if, on a low-calcium diet, you nurse a baby for a year or two, "it doesn't take a genius to figure out where that calcium is going to come from." Calcium intake is particularly important in the adolescent mother, who may still be growing. Research studies suggest that on a junk-food diet a nursing teenager may lose up to 10 percent of her skeletal calcium in four months. Calcium supplementation (1,600 mg daily) can prevent this loss.

Vitamin supplements can help to make up most deficiencies in the nursing mother's diet; supplements show up in the milk right away. Vitamin D, necessary for calcium metabolism, is especially important (see chapter 3, pp. 76–78). You cannot, however, better the norm by taking megadoses; vitamin levels in the milk will stop climbing when the optimum is reached.

The best way to assure an adequate supply of minerals, especially trace elements, to the mammary gland is to eat a varied diet. Many plants, for example, pick up specific trace elements. That whiff of garlic in the salad or onions on the hamburger may seem like a frill, but it brings with it a few sulfur molecules, a crucial element in the oniony flavor and an essential component of some human enzymes. Pioneering breastfeeding-researcher Niles Newton, Ph.D., points out that the action of oxytocin, which governs the letdown reflex, depends on adequate supplies of calcium and also magnesium. A mother having trouble letting down her milk might look into increasing her magnesium intake slightly; leafy greens are one good source.

A nursing mother who complains of fatigue or exhaustion may be suffering from inadequate supplies of B-complex vitamins, which appear to be important in milk production, especially at high levels, as when nursing a totally breastfed baby of fifteen pounds or more. (Researchers have found that a woman is even more likely to be deficient in B-complex vitamins if she was taking oral contraceptives before her pregnancy.) Although most vitamin supplements contain some parts of the B-vitamin group, individual needs vary, and the complete spectrum is more likely to be found in natural sources; mothers have reported dramatic recovery from feelings of exhaustion upon taking brewer's yeast or fenugreek tea, an herbal source of B-complex vitamins (see chapter 10, p. 316).

Perhaps the thyroid gland, which controls the rate of metabolism, is a factor, too. Many women are slightly deficient in thyroid secretion during lactation. Administering thyroid extract to such mothers has been observed not only to relieve such symptoms as excessive fatigue, but also to increase the amount of milk produced in some cases.

Good all-around nutrition is important for the nursing mother's own health; she can't nurse a baby and stay healthy and energetic herself on a diet of soda and potato chips. Pediatrician Eloise Skelton-Forrest, M.D., points out that a mother needn't change all her preferences to eat well. In the first place she needs *enough* food; a nursing mother "is better off eating 2,500 calories of junk [food] than picking at something she hates and getting 800 calories." Second, most people can get the nutrition they need by "reaching into their regular diet"; if for you the basics are tortillas, beans and rice, and chile peppers, fine; these all provide good nutrition.

In general, we all need the same nutritional elements, but some of us need more of one component or can thrive on less of another. An Eskimo, for example, must be able to tolerate a high-fat, low-starch diet. A Swiss family may get most of their protein from cows' milk and cheese, while normal adults of some other extractions can't even digest dairy products. Asians may be well adapted to a diet consisting largely of rice and greens, but this would not at all suit the personal chemistry of people of Scandinavian, seafaring ancestry. Although the government obligingly publishes RDA lists—Recommended Daily Allowances for dietary needs—it's important to remember that humans, like all other living things, come from varying genetic backgrounds, and biochemical needs are highly individual; nursing mothers need to meet their own individual needs.

There are no special foods that help or harm the milk supply. One often hears that chocolate is "binding" or that fruit has the opposite effect on the baby. In moderation, this is not the case; however, excessive intake of even the healthiest item can upset mother and baby both. One baby developed diarrhea when its mother started drinking eight to ten glasses of orange juice a day. Also, there seems to be no dietary element that increases the milk supply in a mother who is not dietarily deficient, although every culture has its own pet lactagogue, ranging from the powdered earthworms prescribed by Avicenna to innumerable herbal concoctions.

Babies don't mind what their mothers eat. Volatile oils, which give most spices their characteristic odor and flavor, pass through milk unchanged. This does not mean, however, that a nursing mother has to avoid spicy foods. While we adults may object to drinking the odorous milk of a cow that has been eating wild onions, there is no evidence that the breastfed baby objects in the slightest to garlic- or curry-flavored mother's milk.

CHANGES IN MILK PRODUCTION AND COMPOSITION AS THE BABY GROWS

The initial fluid in the lactating breast, colostrum, looks different from real milk and is much higher in some nutrients and in protective components. There are many ways in which the ingredients of colostrum reach the breast;

some are manufactured in the breast; some are transferred through the cell membranes. Researcher Margaret Neville, Ph.D., has found that some constituents of colostrum pass between cells of the tissues of the breast, through intracellular gaps. This "leakiness" is very high during the first few days after birth, when whole, huge antibody molecules can pass directly from the mother's bloodstream into the milk. After the fifth day, this "leakiness" seals up. Within a few days, the thick, yellowish colostrum gives way to thinner-looking, white, "mature milk"; in a mother who is nursing without restriction this may occur in twenty-four hours. Colostrum usually is no longer present by the end of the second week.

We used to think that once colostrum gave way to mature milk, the milk remained the same for the rest of lactation, however long that was. Now, researchers have found that the milk of a nursing mother changes gradually as her baby grows. Although the quantity of milk will increase substantially, some of the initial components increase and others level off or decrease. Living white cells, for example, which protect the baby against disease, become less abundant after the first few weeks. Meanwhile, however, the enzyme lysozyme, which is also antibacterial (and presumably "cheaper" to produce, metabolically), increases a hundredfold in the first three months, and stays at that high level throughout lactation.

In the first six months, the milk contains good levels of minerals and trace elements such as zinc, necessary for optimum muscle growth. But by the time the baby is six or seven months old, trace elements dwindle in the milk. Now, the baby is crawling around, stuffing things into its mouth, and taking in other foods besides breast milk. "The mammary gland is a marvelous machine," says trace element-researcher Michael Hambidge, M.D. As the baby begins to get some of its trace elements from other sources, the mammary gland gradually reserves the mother's supply once again for her own needs.

That marvelous machinery of the breast even produces special milk for premature babies. Researchers have found that the milk from mothers whose babies were born one to three months early has twice as many of some fatty acids, necessary for nerve and brain growth, as the milk of mothers of full-term babies, and 70 percent more of certain easily digested lipids for energy and general growth. Preterm milk also contains more protein and higher levels of some vitamins and minerals than full-term milk. In the past, research had seemed to indicate that preterm babies gain faster on formula than on mother's milk; but apart from other flaws, these studies were usually based on pooled milk from *full-term* mothers. Preterm babies who are fed their *own* mothers' milk tend to grow well, even if they are too immature to suckle and must be tube-fed the milk pumped by the mother.

Many human babies continue to nurse well into their second year, or even longer. As nursing intensity dwindles, the milk reduces in quantity and changes in content to "weaning milk." Weaning milk is lower in sugar and thus in calories, and higher in salt content, than the mature milk of full lactation. Some babies lose interest in the breast and wean themselves when this change occurs. In other cases, lactation may continue long after this transition in the milk begins; mother and baby may still enjoy bedtime nursings, early-morning nursings, and occasional "comfort nursing," for many months before the baby is completely weaned from the breast.

BREASTFEEDING AND MENSTRUATION

Throughout pregnancy, the menstrual cycle can be thought of as being suspended at a point just before menstruation would have taken place, had conception not occurred. Once the baby and the hormone-producing placenta are removed, the menstrual cycle in effect takes up at the point where it left off. Progesterone production falls off, the uterine lining is discarded through menstruation, and the cycle resumes.

However, if the mother nurses her baby, this event may be postponed. Prolactin is the pituitary hormone that triggers the production of progesterone in the menstrual cycle. Its role in the menstrual cycle is brief; it appears as a result of high estrogen levels caused by the release of an egg from the ovaries, and disappears as estrogen levels fall. But prolactin can be produced in two cases: when estrogen levels are high, or when the breasts are stimulated by the sucking of a baby. When a mother nurses her baby, this action in itself produces the prolactin that keeps her ovaries secreting progesterone. The menstrual cycle continues to be suspended, and ovulation does not take place. Menstruation will resume promptly if the baby is abruptly weaned.

It is thought that the menstrual cycle usually resumes with menstruation rather than with ovulation, and that usually two or three periods take place before the mother ovulates. By delaying the menstrual cycles and ovulation, breastfeeding tends to provide a natural contraceptive. The system is by no means foolproof, however. An episode of fatigue and overwork may interfere with lactation sufficiently to let ovulation take place without a period. More than one nursing mother has gone through an unusually strenuous week—running a big Thanksgiving family reunion, say, or working overtime to meet a deadline—and a few weeks later found herself to be pregnant again. For the nursing mother who is interested in the contraceptive value of breastfeeding, a fuller discussion is available in *Breast Feeding and Natural Child Spacing,* by Sheila K. Kippley (see References).

It takes a lot of sucking stimulation to hold the menstrual cycles at bay, especially in the first months. Breastfeeding-researcher Niles Newton, Ph.D., states that the key to cessation of menstruation is *unrestricted* nursing. In Newton's definition, unrestricted nursing means that: (1) the baby is near or with the mother night and day, and nursing occurs frequently (at least twelve times a day in the first month) without regard to the clock; (2) the baby nurses for a total of eighty minutes a day, in at least six to eight nursing episodes; and (3) at least one of these nursings occurs at night, between 9 P.M. and 6 A.M. Under these conditions, each feeding releases a new supply of prolactin, and the menses will remain in abeyance. This normal pattern of unrestricted nursing typically results in approximately eighteen months of amenorrhea, or total absence of menstrual periods.

Unfortunately, many mothers accept or are taught what some refer to as the standard-care system, in which nursing is artificially governed by rules: the baby is shoehorned into some kind of schedule as soon as possible; suckling is delayed, withheld, kept to minimum time periods, or interrupted, according to various instructions. Even when a mother under this kind of restricted regimen produces adequate milk, the hormonal impact on her body is minimized and menses resume more quickly.

Some medical care providers tell women that they should stop breastfeeding when they resume menstruating, especially if they have prolonged or "breakthrough" bleeding, because the baby will be getting too much estrogen in the milk; there is no evidence to support this notion. The resumption of the menstrual cycle does not decrease milk production, and a woman may and often does continue to feed her baby at the breast long after her periods have started up again. Some mothers find that for a day or two at the start of each period the milk may change in the direction of weaning milk, becoming less sweet and more salty. Some babies object to this change in flavor and may balk or fuss at the breast, while others don't appear to care.

ORAL CONTRACEPTIVES

Oral contraceptives work by maintaining levels of estrogen and progesterone so that ovulation does not occur. During lactation, the level of estrogen, even in a low-dose "mini-pill," may reduce the milk supply. While oral contraceptives do not have any obvious effect on the baby, research shows that taking them speeds the change to weaning milk and shortens the lactation period. Milk banks do not accept mothers as donors if they are taking oral contraceptives, partly because the effects of the hormones on the babies who receive the milk are unknown, and more pragmatically, because experience has indicated that mothers taking "the pill" have a hard time producing enough surplus milk to be able to donate.

BREASTFEEDING AND SEX

In the medical literature, breastfeeding is sometimes regarded as a source of sexual satisfaction to nursing mothers. In reality, although nursing is physically enjoyable, sexual pleasure is not the usual experience. Although the nipple itself is erogenous, during lactation it does not respond with the same sensations as during sex play. Furthermore, when the baby is latched on properly (see chapter 4, p. 106, and chapter 10, pp. 233–34), the nipple itself receives no sustained physical stimulation; most contact falls upon the areola, which is relatively insensitive to the touch. A few women have reported finding nursing sexually stimulating, even to the point of orgasm, but this level of stimulation is usually transitory and may in fact indicate poor positioning of the baby, with a risk of developing soreness.

The hormones of breastfeeding, prolactin and oxytocin, have demonstrably calming, soothing effects. The nursing mother's bloodstream is flooded with these hormones repeatedly and daily; no wonder some women always remember their nursing months as a happy, tranquil period. Some mothers find that their interest in sex is somewhat lower during lactation, perhaps because of low estrogen levels during the absence of menstruation; low estrogen levels may also lead to vaginal dryness and a need for added lubrication for comfort during intercourse. Others find that their general good mood and relaxed state intensify their interest in sex (for further discussion, see pp. 296–98).

Prolactin and oxytocin are also the hormones of lovemaking. Not only does prolactin stimulate affectionate behavior, but it is produced more abundantly under conditions of intimate affection, in men as well as in women. Oxytocin is released during orgasm in both sexes; many men are aware of and enjoy the sense of peace and ease, at least partly oxytocin-induced, that follows sexual climax. Nursing mothers may find that their letdown reflex functions strongly during orgasm, sometimes sending sprays of milk into a surprised partner's face; there is no harm in this or any other involvement of the breasts in lovemaking, and any milk that comes into the picture will not be missed by the baby.

BREASTFEEDING AND PREGNANCY

What happens to the nursing mother and her milk if she gets pregnant? For the first few weeks, very little. Then, as the placenta develops and produces high estrogen levels, milk production is once again suppressed. The mother's nipples may become tender and sore, and the taste of the milk changes to saltier weaning milk.

How long a pregnant mother should continue to nurse the baby is dictated partly by custom. In some cultures, the baby is weaned as soon as the mother realizes she is pregnant again. If other good food is available, the baby may spontaneously wean himself as the breast becomes less productive. Golopan's and Belevady's studies in India, where village mothers may nurse the "old" baby until the arrival of the new one, show that the quantity of milk diminishes greatly as pregnancy advances, no matter how much the baby nurses, but that such milk as is produced is extremely rich in fats and vitamins, and it may continue to form an important source of nutrition.

In Western cultures where standard-care, restricted nursing patterns prevail, the opposite circumstances can arise: the mother's menses may return so early that she becomes pregnant not when her child is a toddler but while her infant is still very young, two or three months old. In this circumstance, exclusive breastfeeding may result in the child's poor growth or failure to thrive, because of changes in milk production and composition; supplementation may be needed.

There is no doubt that lactation, especially during the second half of pregnancy, is a physical drag on the mother. In each six months or so of lactation, a woman may produce a hundred pounds or more of milk, which makes greater demands on her bodily reserves than the six or eight pounds of baby produced and nourished during the nine months of pregnancy. Where living conditions are poor and diet is inadequate, the mother's health suffers more severely when she is breastfeeding a baby than when she is pregnant with one. If she is doing both at once, the developing fetus may suffer, too.

In some cultures, mothers may nurse the infant through a subsequent pregnancy and right along with the new baby afterward. In the United States, this is called tandem nursing. There are mothers highly in favor of tandem nursing, usually because they feel that the older child continues to need the reassurance and emotional closeness of the breastfeeding relationship. There are some drawbacks, however, besides public criticism and the physical drain on the mother. Nursing in early pregnancy may be very uncomfortable for the mother. Not only may nipple soreness be a problem, but nipple stimulation may actually induce labor in some mothers; nursing should be discontinued if a woman has a history of miscarriage. And, finally, the milk of a mother who has just given birth is tailored to the newborn's needs; one has to consider whether components that are important to the infant are at risk of being usurped by the older child.

WEANING AND SUPPRESSION OF LACTATION

The process of breast involution (the breast returning to its former condition) and the cessation of milk production begin, imperceptibly, when the baby starts taking in nourishment other than breast milk, at six months or later; but substantial amounts of milk may continue to be produced for another year or two or three. In unrestricted breastfeeding, weaning occurs gradually and is largely initiated and governed by the baby, a process called "baby-led weaning." Typically, sooner or later nursing episodes become fewer, until the baby is nursing only at bedtime, or when in need of comforting; one day the mother may realize the baby has not nursed lately, and is in fact weaned. In cultures where breastfeeding is not socially restricted, complete weaning usually takes place somewhere between eighteen months and three years, but never before the end of the first year.

Mothers who have to go back to work sometimes worry that sudden weaning will be traumatic for the baby, and may decide not to breastfeed, rather than risk the upset. In fact, there is no real reason to wean the baby just because one has to return to work. Nursing babies readily adapt to this change, quickly shifting their own schedules so they can nurse more when the mother is back, and nap more while she's away. Babies are usually willing to take a cup or bottle from somebody else when the mother is gone (for more information, see chapter 13, The Working Mother: How Breastfeeding Can Help, pp. 329–52).

Even if one's work conditions require such long absences —the multiday absences of flight attendants, for example— that sustaining lactation will not be feasible, it is certainly worthwhile to breastfeed, however briefly. Even a single nursing, giving the baby all-important colostrum, is statistically extremely beneficial; in one Central American hospital all newborns were given a "colostrum cocktail" at birth, whether their mothers breastfed them or not; the reduction in illness in the nursery was dramatic. And the protection continues with each feeding; so nursing for a month or six weeks or two months is important, too. Longer maternity leaves can sometimes be arranged.

If one has to return to a job that will keep one away from home eight or ten hours a day, there is usually no real need to wean the baby. The mother can keep herself comfortable and maintain her milk supply by using one of the many manual or electric breast pumps now on the market, while she is away; pumps can be bought from drugstores, bought or rented from lactation consultants, or obtained through La Leche League International (see Appendix, p. 391). Many working mothers pump and store their milk once or twice a day, leaving it with the care giver for the baby's next feeding. (For a detailed discussion of manual expression, pumps, pumping, and breastfeeding schedules for the working mother, see chapter 13, The Working Mother: How Breastfeeding Can Help.)

Suppressing lactation is straightforward: if the mother does not put the baby to the breast, milk production will cease. Mothers who decide from birth that they do not want to breastfeed are sometimes subjected to needless medical regimens to "dry up the milk." Hormones, or "dry-up pills," are unnecessary. The old custom of binding the breasts tightly not only is terribly uncomfortable, but supplies tactile stimulation that may prolong milk production. A drug, Bromocriptine, suppresses lactation completely, but only while it is being taken; once the drug is stopped, a rebound effect may occur, with heavy milk production causing painful engorgement. One obstetrician routinely gave all his non-nursing mothers Bromocriptine because he could see how beautifully it stopped lactation in the hospital. Not until one mother, ten days after giving birth, phoned him at home at 3 A.M. and cursed him vigorously for the condition she was then in, did he rethink his routine.

RELACTATION AND INDUCED LACTATION

Sometimes a mother weans her baby, either by choice or unavoidably, and then wants to return to breastfeeding. Relactation is the term for reestablishing the milk supply in a mother who for some reason has stopped nursing. Common situations that call for relactation are: the separation of mother and baby, for example, because of hospitalization of one or the other (car accidents are the most usual cause); a mother's need to return to breastfeeding because the baby has turned out to be allergic to synthetic milks; the desire of a preterm baby's mother to establish her milk supply before the baby comes home.

In the 1940s and 1950s few people even considered trying to reestablish a milk supply once it had dwindled or stopped; if you "lost your milk," that was that. Mothers who wished they could go on nursing after they had been given "dry-up pills," or who were separated from their babies for whatever reason, were out of luck. Probably the biggest single factor in the popularization of relactation has been La Leche League International, a grassroots organization of nursing mothers that originated in Chicago in the early 1960s. Shortly after the organization was started, Lillian Bormet, the mother of a highly allergic baby, managed to redevelop her milk supply with the help of other nursing mothers from La Leche League; the story was widely publicized, and many thousands have emulated her successfully, since.

Relactation is usually accomplished by frequent nursing and good management: rest and nutrition for the mother, emotional support and encouragement, a lactation consultant or experienced nursing mother to teach good technique. (For details on how to reestablish or increase a milk supply while avoiding making the baby too hungry, see chapter 12, pp. 308–10.) Some mothers find a breast pump helpful. As a rule, a mother who was already nursing before the interruption or weaning is able to recover something close to the level of milk she was producing before the interruption. Mothers of preterm babies can develop ample milk supplies when the baby becomes able to nurse (see chapter 3, p. 60, and chapter 10, p. 230).

Success, however, does not depend just on the mother; since suckling stimulation is needed to bring in the milk, relactation is partly up to the baby. Breastfeeding-researcher Kathleen Auerbach, Ph.D., points out that you cannot predict which baby will "enthusiastically embrace" the reestablishment of breastfeeding. Some babies and mothers don't get along, and nursing has good days and bad days. Some babies wait contentedly for a long time between nursings, instead of nursing often and stimulating production. "Some babies," Dr. Auerbach jokes, "would get milk out of doorknobs, but many babies don't nurse that way and never will."

Sometimes a mother wants to relactate because she is adopting a new baby shortly after weaning her own, or while still nursing her own toddler. We used to think that a bounteous milk supply could be easily redeveloped for the new nursling. We now know that since the constituents of milk change over time, without the "jump-start" of pregnancy, there may be a physiological limit to the duration of the ability to relactate. One can continue to lactate, but it may be difficult to reverse the course of lactation. When one is nursing an older baby or toddler, the baby may be nursing often, but these feedings are apt to be "a lick and a promise" nursing, and rather undemanding. And the milk is now tailor-made to be the "old baby's milk." The new baby may need more in the way of calories than this milk can provide, and more sheer volume, too. Supplementation becomes unavoidable. In a study by Auerbach of 240 women who attempted to establish a milk supply to feed an adopted child, eighteen were still nursing a "birth baby" when the adopted baby came along. Of these, two were able to eliminate supplements within the first month. Eight others eliminated supplements at some point, but in some cases not until well into the second year; and the rest could never give up the supplement, in spite of experience, expectations, and the head start of a well-established lactation.

If relactation is still a new idea to some people, induced lactation may seem almost unimaginable. Induced lactation is the establishment of lactation in women who have never given birth and perhaps have never even been pregnant. Given enough sucking stimulation, such women experience additional alveolar development; they do produce milk, without the hormones of pregnancy. In induced lactation, the milk does not go through a colostral phase; the baby, however, does receive whatever antibodies and disease protection would be in mature milk (chapter 2, p. 40).

Induced lactation depends on the use of a mechanical device that trickles milk into the baby's mouth as it nurses, thus reinforcing the behavior of suckling and of feeding the baby at the breast if not *from* the breast. The first such device, the Lactaid, was invented by an adoptive mother who had never given birth, Jimmie Lynne Avery, and her engineer husband. Another such device, the Supplemental Nutrition System, or SNS, is marketed nationally and is available through La Leche League, the manufacturers, or from lactation consultants.

The aim of inducing lactation for an adopted child is not to produce a full milk supply, and indeed most babies need synthetic milk supplements throughout. The purpose is to facilitate attachment between mother and child, and to make the newcomer a member of the family. Some mothers and some babies do not take to the experience, which differs considerably (especially for the mother) from the experience of nursing a biological child; others just love it (see chapter 14, p. 353).

BREASTFEEDING UNDER SPECIAL CONDITIONS

There are several conditions under which mothers are sometimes told they cannot breastfeed, when in fact breastfeeding not only is possible but can be of real benefit to the mother. The blind mother, for example, is much better off breastfeeding; it is infinitely easier than coping with bottles, and it affords the closest possible relationship with the baby. Other physically handicapped mothers also may find that breastfeeding is really simpler than any alternative. Adolescent mothers are sometimes discouraged from breastfeeding on the grounds that they are still growing, themselves. As long as the very young mother gets enough to eat, she can lactate without harm to herself, and she may benefit from the calming and maturing effects of breastfeeding.

Some systemic diseases may interfere with the mother's health sufficiently to make breastfeeding an undesirable extra drain; but the mother's wishes should be taken into account. Diabetes, for example, need not preclude breastfeeding. The mother's blood sugar needs careful management both in pregnancy and during lactation, but diabetics have breastfed their babies, and information on how they did it is available (see Appendix). In fact, insulin-dependent diabetics may benefit from breastfeeding; blood sugar levels are likely to be closer to "normal" during lactation than they are at any other time. At the same time, the breastfed baby is receiving important protection against the future development of certain kinds of diabetes. A useful source of further information on diabetes and breastfeeding is the La Leche League publication, *Maternal*

Diabetes and Diabetes in Young Children: Their Relationship to Breastfeeding, which includes an updated list of medical references and a glossary (see Appendix, p. 391).

Mothers with cystic fibrosis are often told they can't breastfeed, because their milk will be too salty. This conclusion is based on a single study in which milk was sampled from the breasts of cystic fibrosis patients who had given birth, none of whom was actually breastfeeding. That milk was salty, not because of their metabolic disorder, but because their breasts were "drying up" and producing weaning milk; in fact, with good health management, mothers with cystic fibrosis can and do breastfeed. Babies with cystic fibrosis (a genetic disorder that, among other things, interferes with digestion) used to be weaned immediately and put on high-calorie synthetics, with the justification that they needed extra nutrition; now, the other benefits of human milk have been recognized, and breastfeeding is encouraged, sometimes with a regimen of added enzymes. It is not unusual for a breastfed CF patient to be doing so well that the condition is not recognized until the baby is weaned.

Mothers with developmental disabilities or mental illness need to be evaluated individually. Mothers taking long-term medications such as Lithium, or toxic drugs such as some immune system suppressants, may be able to breastfeed if the dosages are modified or replaced temporarily; drugs and medications are more fully discussed, and sources of detailed information given, in chapter 3. Breastfeeding is often forbidden or terminated if a mother must be exposed to the radioactive isotopes used in some diagnostic processes; often, however, the cessation can be minimal and temporary if an isotope with a short half-life is used (see chapter 3 reference section, p. 374). Some viral diseases, such as herpes, hepatitis, and AIDS, pose dangers to the baby but the risk can sometimes be circumvented on a case-by-case basis (chapter 3, pp. 96–100).

A special breastfeeding problem is the mother who has had breast surgery, especially breast reduction surgery. Cosmetic or plastic surgeons who "resculpt" women's breasts are almost always oblivious of the possible future use of those breasts to feed a baby. It is routine to slice through the milk ducts, rendering the nipple nonfunctional; in fact, circum-areolar cuts are favored, as the scar is thought to be less conspicuous than the scar from a lateral incision. Oncologists and general surgeons, not just plastic surgeons, are also guilty of performing biopsies with cosmetics in mind rather than function, resulting in unnecessary damage to the duct system of the breast. Even when performing a simple biopsy to check a suspicious lump, the surgeon is apt to place the incision cosmetically, without thought of having ruined the potential of that breast for nursing.

Usually the functioning aspect of the breast can be retained, in spite of surgery, if the owner of the breast is insistent. Sometimes, too, the severed ducts actually rejoin, and some milk can be extruded. All too often, however, a post-surgical breast cannot function fully as a lactating breast. Yet it is perfectly possible to nurse a baby successfully from a single breast; if only one breast has been damaged, breastfeeding can be done entirely from the other. Production will soon cease in the unsuckled breast.

WORKING MOTHERS

Working mothers sometimes assume they will have to stop breastfeeding when they go back to work. Edward Cerrutti, M.D., a pediatrician with a large practice of working nursing mothers, says he doesn't differentiate between working and at-home mothers; they are all nursing mothers, some of whom have to go to work. There is no need to "do something different or change your attitude."

Some working mothers express or pump their milk once or twice during the working day—for their own comfort, to keep up the milk supply, and sometimes to save that milk for the care giver to feed to the baby by bottle the next day. One large urban hospital maintains a "pumping room," with electric breast pumps, sink, refrigerator, comfortable chairs, and a television set, for use by nurses and other staff members, medical and nursing students, and office workers in the surrounding area who are nursing mothers and want to pump their milk during their work hours. A large clothing factory in the Midwest installed a similar room for the use of all employees, with "pumping breaks" permitted for factory line workers, after an executive mother in the personnel department experienced for herself what a problem it was to find privacy to pump during the working day.

OLDER MOTHERS

It used to be that an "older" mother was someone having her first baby after the age of thirty-five. Now, some women are having their first baby at forty or later. Does this make any difference in breastfeeding? No. The standard view in the medical literature is that older mothers are apt to have more physical problems, making all aspects of child care, including breastfeeding, more of an effort. But one pediatrician with many professional women and older mothers in his practice points out that the medical texts we use today are often based on research and experience from thirty or forty years ago, when a woman of forty or more might be sedentary, overweight, and a smoker. Today's older mothers are active, strong, and healthy, and they present a clinical picture "that doesn't fit the literature."

In fact, breastfeeding may be a bit easier for the older mother: Life teaches us judgment; and she may be more apt to do what seems right to her rather than to obey poor or inappropriate instructions. Life teaches us skills with people; she is likely to be more noticing and tactful with her baby than she would have been some years earlier; she is adroit at getting the nursing relationship off to a good start. And she may be eager to enjoy her baby fully because she has already proven herself to be a capable adult in other areas.

What about fatigue? Young mothers get tired, too; bottle-feeding mothers get tired, for that matter. The older mother with more life experience may be more likely to take responsibility for her fatigue and to do something about it, from improving her nutrition to changing her schedule. Also, she may be less likely to take her little one for granted, more likely to treat him with attention and thoughtfulness. Karen Osterlund, a La Leche League group leader who has been conducting breastfeeding meetings in the San Francisco area for twenty-five years, reports that she has begun to see many older mothers coming to meetings. "And I can't help noticing one thing right off the bat," she says. "They're *much* better mothers."

BREAST AILMENTS

A few physical problems are directly associated with breastfeeding. Most of them are a result of mismanagement of the process of breastfeeding, and can be avoided with common sense and enlightened rather than standard medical care.

ENGORGEMENT:

Engorgement is a clinical condition sometimes seen in hospitals. The breasts become so full of milk that they are taut, swollen, and extremely painful, while the areolar area is stretched so flat that the baby cannot latch on at all. The mother may run a fever. Engorgement is caused by separating mother and baby and unduly restricting nursing frequency and duration during the first days after birth. Medication for pain should be provided; relief can be achieved by gentle massage in a warm shower, getting the milk to flow, followed by frequent nursings. Engorgement can be prevented by frequent and unrestricted nursing from birth onward.

NIPPLE SORENESS:

Nipple soreness can range from mild tenderness to open, bleeding cracks, and is usually a byproduct of a poor nursing position that brings the baby's tongue incorrectly in contact with the nipple itself; repositioning the baby properly will alleviate the problem (see chapters 4 and 10). A baby with sucking difficulties can also cause sore nipples, as can the baby who is trying to suckle the breast with bottle-feeding motions; techniques exist for surmounting these problems (see chapters 4 and 11). Breast shields, salves, and ointments, all commonly offered in hospitals, do not ease nipple soreness and may make it worse; exposure to air between nursings, avoidance of moist cloth or padding over the nipple, and shifting the baby's position at each feeding will help more.

YEAST INFECTIONS:

Infection of the nipple surface and the interior of the breast by yeast organisms, usually *Candida albicans,* is not uncommon and can be extremely painful. Typically, the soreness increases during the feeding, rather than fading as mechanically caused soreness does. Pain may be felt deep within the breast. *Candida* infections often get their start when the baby is given antibiotics, which wipe out the normal bacteria of the mouth and allow the yeast to grow. The baby may or may not have the white patches in the mouth that are signs of thrush, or oral candidiasis. Treatment usually consists of a drug, Nystatin, painted on the mother's nipples and given orally to the baby. Both partners must be treated, or the baby will simply reinfect the mother; if the mother is the only patient presenting symptoms and the baby shows no sign of infection, some pediatricians refuse to prescribe for the child, making it almost impossible to clear up the mother's case.

MASTITIS:

Mastitis, sometimes called "milk fever," is a bacterial infection within the breast, typically localized in one duct or duct system. The symptoms are fever and flulike aching, with a place on one breast that is sore to the touch. A duct blocked by secretions or swelling is a common genesis of mastitis. Nursing the baby in different positions, so that different ducts are drained on each feeding, can relieve a blockage; it's helpful to position the baby on alternate feedings so its nose is right over the sore place, "even if you have to stand on your head to do it," says one lactation consultant. Hot compresses and frequent nursings are often sufficient treatment; if the infection persists, antibiotics are called for.

The standard medical information is that mastitis occurs in about 5 percent of nursing mothers, and that it usually develops in the first two weeks. Jan Riordan, Ph.D., one of the initial leaders of La Leche League and now a lactation researcher, is studying mastitis. In a survey of 400 or so experienced nursing mothers, she found that over 30 percent developed a breast infection at some time during a long lactation. Half of these treated themselves by applying heat to the affected breast and increasing the frequency of nursing, and so never entered the medical system. The other half used antibiotics. None developed serious infections or abscesses, which used to be hideously common in hospitals in the days when any infection was met with orders to wean the baby.

The precipitating cause in a large number of cases in Dr. Riordan's study was stress and fatigue, although a smaller study suggested that illness in another family member is a factor, perhaps because virulent staphylococcus or streptococcus bacteria have been brought into the house.

BREASTFEEDING AND BREAST CANCER

We often hear that one woman in eleven will develop breast cancer. It's misleading; the chances are one in eleven only for eighty-five-year-old women. The chances of developing breast cancer by age forty are more like one in a thousand; even by age sixty the chances are fewer than one in twenty-five. For years the standard medical opinion was that breastfeeding offers no particular protection against breast cancer. As usual, this conclusion was based on studies in which no attention was paid to duration of breastfeeding, and no distinction was made between real breastfeeding and token breastfeeding. Now, research has shown that many aspects of reproduction have a protective effect against your developing breast cancer; lactation is high on the list, and the protection offered is "dose-related," that is, the more and longer you breastfeed, the better protection you get.

The likelihood of developing breast cancer appears to increase as the length of time increases in which a woman has high levels of estrogen in her system. Thus, having children in your early years, or having an early menopause, protect you somewhat by reducing the lifetime exposure to estrogen. But lactation itself suppresses estrogen production. This appears to be one basis of the conspicuous protective effect of breastfeeding against the development of breast cancer in the childbearing years. Broad-scale epidemiological studies by the Centers for Disease Control show that premenopausal breast cancer is *twice* as likely to occur in women who have never lactated as in women who have, regardless of their family history, the number of children they have borne, their age at first pregnancy, or other factors. Furthermore, the longer the lactation, the greater the protection. According to one study, fully breastfeeding one baby for six months reduces a woman's chances of getting breast cancer (by age 85, if she lives that long) from one in eleven to one in 125. And researchers looking at effects of duration of breastfeeding have found that women who have lactated for a two-year period are strikingly less likely to develop cancer of the ovaries than women who did not lactate!

While the protective effects of breastfeeding are most apparent in premenopausal women, statistics indicate that even after menopause, a history of long-duration lactation continues to offer some protection against breast cancer. It is difficult to understand why this simple method of reducing breast cancer risk is ignored while methods of detecting breast cancer and treating it surgically receive such wide publicity.

How this protection takes place is not yet fully understood. Certainly many factors such as lifetime estrogen levels and genetic susceptibility are involved; but stasis and blockage of natural function may contribute to subsequent pathology. Riordan's research shows that plugged ducts, milk stoppage, and ensuing mastitis occur most commonly in nursing mothers in the outside upper quadrant of the breast. This is also the commonest site of breast cancer. In a study of women who for one reason or another lactated unilaterally, that is, breastfed their baby on one side only, breast cancer occurred three times as often in the "unused" breast. Perhaps suppressing lactation is a real factor in the causes of breast cancer. When you have experienced the changes lactation brings to the breasts, it seems sensible to suppose that these glands were meant to function and are healthier when they do.

CHAPTER 3

Human Milk

THE NATURE OF MILK

Giving milk is a characteristic of all mammals, including humans. Huge whales, shrews weighing less than an ounce, fast-growing rabbits and slow-growing elephants, herbivores, carnivores, insectivores, all give their babies recognizable milk. Whatever species of mother a sample of milk comes from, it still looks like milk, smells like milk, tastes like milk. It is still made of four basic ingredients: water, fat, special milk proteins, and milk sugars. It will contain at least some of each important vitamin and mineral. If it is let stand, the cream will rise. Be it the milk of a human, cow, or rabbit, it is capable of being made into cheese or butter and will go sour in the same way. Whatever the source, milk is milk.

On closer inspection, however, milk differs remarkably from species to species. Making milk is a rather expensive process for the mother, biologically. She has to find and consume extra calories to put into the milk and to run the elaborate machinery of the mammary glands. Complex molecules such as antibodies must be created for special purposes. Nothing should be wasted. In consequence, each species' milk is carefully tailored to provide exactly what that sort of newborn creature needs to grow well. The milk of seals and whales is almost 50 percent fat, to enable the baby to double its size in a few weeks. Horses and cows provide milk that grows bone and muscle in a hurry, for a baby that needs to be able to run fast from the day of its birth. The milk of primates, including ourselves, is specialized for, among other things, rapid growth of the brain.

While babies can often survive on the milk of other species—dogs can nurse kittens, and goats feed lambs—substitutions are often far from optimum. This is especially true if the species are very different. The problems are great when you must modify the milk of hooved animals for infant human beings—if you wanted a really good match for us, you'd have to milk gorillas.

Mothers' milk is for babies; cows' milk is for calves—people have been saying that for years. Feeding cows' milk to newborn babies used to involve an elaborate business of adjusting the differences between the two kinds of milk—differences that cause real problems for the immature digestive system—by adding water to dilute the protein content, adding sugar to raise the calorie content, and so on, according to various medical recipes. Mothers had to make this "formula" in their kitchens, and then sterilize the concoction by boiling it. Nowadays, corporations make up these doctored versions of cows' milk for baby food, and you can buy them ready-mixed and sterilized in the drugstore. In fact, we know so much about chemistry and nutrition that some of these synthetic foods for babies are not based on animal milk at all, but are made completely from other ingredients such as soy beans. These ingredients supply enough calories for a baby, and all the necessary nutritional components such as protein and vitamins (at least all those that have been proven necessary so far).

So what's the difference between these foods and the real thing, human milk? Plenty, starting with taste and smell, and including specific nutritional features, and constituents which affect the baby's physiology and behavior and protect against disease. Many of the components of human milk are substances that are destroyed by heating; thus they cannot be powdered or canned or even pasteurized. In some cases, they are factors that cannot be synthesized or duplicated in a chemistry lab, period—ingredients no artificial milk will ever contain.

UNIQUE PROPERTIES OF BREAST MILK

As researchers like to point out, the big difference between human milk and synthetic milks is that human milk is alive. Like blood or skin or any other tissue, it is a living substance, full of healthy cells, and it is designed to stay alive for a long time. Human milk fresh from the breast contains an average of one million living cells per milliliter (one cubic centimeter, or roughly one-third of a teaspoon). Colostrum, the first milk after birth, contains up to seven million living cells per milliliter.

Most of the living cells in human milk are leukocytes, or white cells, similar but not identical to those in our blood. White cells attack foreign bacteria wherever they find them. The white cells in human milk are primarily neutrophils, which take action on the surface of the baby's insides, and macrophages, which can penetrate into tissues and attack bacteria there. They can kill pathogens—disease-causing organisms—by engulfing and digesting them, or by releasing toxins into or around the enemy cells and in effect stinging them to death.

These living cells in human milk are extraordinarily vigorous. In one now-famous experiment, which has been successfully duplicated several times, biologists took a sample of fresh human milk and counted the bacteria in a portion of it, finding a fair representation of harmless skin flora (bacteria from the nipple and breast) and a few pathogens. They then left the milk sample, uncovered, on a table in a warm room for thirty-six hours—a perfect setting for culturing prolific bacterial growth, one would imagine. When they came back and tested the milk again, the bacteria count had actually gone down. The macrophages and other protective mechanisms in the milk had been doing their job.

The macrophages in human milk provide protection in the stomach and throughout the intestine. It's as if every swallow of mothers' milk contained a tiny PacMan army, gobbling the germs in its path. (And if the baby happens to sputter and get some milk up its nose, these protectors do their work there, too.) While peak production of macrophages occurs right after birth, they continue to be produced in useful quantities for at least four to five months. These macrophages can survive freezing; properly stored frozen breast milk continues to offer this cellular front-line disease protection when thawed. The macrophages of course cannot survive heating, including microwaving or pasteurization; thus they are not available in cows' milk-based products. And there's no way they can be created artificially; living cells come only from a mother.

ANTIBODIES AND IMMUNITIES

When *Nursing Your Baby* was first published, in 1963, we could not say outright that human milk, or even colostrum, *definitely* provided immune factors protecting the baby against disease. That had been proven, scientifically, only for goats and cows. There were in fact medical experts who argued that factors providing immunities or disease protection could not be possible in human milk; that antibodies would be digested, or that they weren't there anyway, and that humans, in any case, were not cattle.

Now, the evidence is in. With the advances in molecular biology, and a panoply of new laboratory techniques, researchers have demonstrated that human milk is laced with immunity-inducing factors, including antibodies to many common infectious agents. We now know that these antibodies are indeed absorbed and utilized by the baby. And the newest evidence shows that these and other immune factors offer protection not just in the first days or weeks of life—when the baby's immune system is immature and needs all the help it can get—but throughout lactation, from the first sip to the last swallow of human milk, and in some cases even after weaning and into adulthood.

The first feedings of colostrum, a yellowish, ultra-nourishing milk produced immediately after birth, are especially vital. Colostrum protects babies against specific diseases, including polio, coxsackie B virus, several staphylococci, and *Escherichia coli,* the adult intestinal bacteria that can cause particularly vicious intestinal, urinary, and other infections in newborns. They are present in colostrum in much higher concentrations than they are in the mother's blood serum. Leonard Mata, Ph.D., a breastfeeding-researcher working in Central America, starts off all newborns in his hospital with a "colostrum cocktail," from donor mothers if necessary. Mata reports that the reduction of illnesses, particularly in preterm infants, has been dramatic, even if the babies are subsequently artificially fed. Of course, dairy farmers have been doing this for years; all new calves are given colostrum for their first feeding, not milk.

The principal immunity-inducing compound in human milk, including colostrum, is secretory IgA (the letters stand for immunoglobulin A). Many of us have heard of gamma globulin, most of which consists of IgG, an immunity-conferring compound found in blood, which offers broad, short-term protection against many infections; it is sometimes given to people who have been exposed to or who might become exposed to hepatitis or other dangerous viruses. IgA is a slightly different protein, manufactured in the mammary gland and secreted into the milk by chemical pathways that were simply unknown in 1963. Secretory IgA offers protection against foreign molecules that might induce allergic reactions in the baby. Secretory IgA also provides antibodies to many bacteria and other organisms that cause infant diarrhea and respiratory ailments, not just in third-world countries but wherever mothers and babies may be.

The secretory IgA antibodies work not by destroying enemy cells, but by binding to them and preventing them from attaching themselves to the mucosae (the linings) of the digestive or respiratory tracts, where they could multiply and cause illness. Each pathogen, whether a polio virus or a pneumonia bacterium, has specific attachment points that the antibody can recognize and plug up, so to speak, to render the pathogen harmless.

A new pattern of antibody must be created for each new enemy encountered, but once the system has made that kind of antibody, it can quickly crank out more; that is why many specific diseases can be caught only once. Immunizations protect us against infection by presenting dead pathogens and tricking the system into making antibodies that fit those particular infectors—typhoid bacteria, say, or the mumps virus. Then when the real thing comes along, the antibodies swarm out and shut down the initial invaders before a major infection has a chance to get going.

A nursing mother can provide her baby, through her milk, with antibodies to many organisms to which she has been exposed in the past. If she happens to be exposed to a new pathogen during lactation—a new variety of cold virus, say—antibody production sites in her lungs and intestines go into action. The new antibody types are packed into special white cells that actually home in on the mammary glands, where they start secreting the new antibody into the milk, within two or three days of the mother's exposure. By the time the mother is coming down with the cold, the baby is already getting protection. That is one reason for a phenomenon many nursing mothers have noticed: when everyone in the family catches a cold, the baby often has the lightest case or escapes altogether.

Of course if the mother and baby are separated, and the baby picks up a cold away from home, the mother has no antibodies for that pathogen until after she catches the cold from the child. Children in day-care programs are often exposed to the germs of other households, for which they have no specific antibody protection; even if breastfed, they can catch colds. Other protective factors in the mother's milk, however, will operate to make the cold briefer and less severe than it otherwise might be.

The antibodies in mother's milk do not necessarily trigger production in the baby of the same antibodies; their protection works only as long as the baby is breastfeeding. However, breastfeeding shelters the baby long enough for the baby's own immune system to get into gear. By the time of weaning, the baby's body has usually encountered most of the common pathogens in its environment, and has developed a constellation of antibodies of its own.

LYSOZYME

An important antibacterial ingredient in human milk is lysozyme, an enzyme that is also abundant in saliva and in tears. Lysozyme is harmless to human tissue; in fact it is actually soothing, and reduces inflammation and redness. When it comes in contact with certain bacteria, however, it "lyses" or dissolves their cell walls, which kills them. Lysozyme is a sort of natural disinfectant; it performs that function in our eyes and noses, as well as inside the mammary gland, where it is produced in quantity; human milk contains 300 times as much lysozyme, per milliliter, as does cows' milk. Unlike some other protective elements in human milk, after an initial dip during the first month of lactation, the proportion of lysozyme per milliliter of milk actually increases, and remains at that higher level throughout lactation.

Lysozyme, like secretory IgA and other defense agents in human milk, is also designed to withstand the hostile environment of the acids of the stomach, and to act throughout the baby's digestive system. Lysozyme is one of the proteins that can be constructed artificially; it cannot be added effectively to synthetic milks, however, because like most enzymes it is destroyed by the heat necessary for canning and sterilization.

THE BIFIDUS FACTOR AND OTHER NUTRITIOUS PROTECTORS

Foraging white cells, immunity-inducing antibodies, and natural antiseptic enzymes constitute only part of the protective system in human milk. Many of the substances in human milk—fats, sugars, proteins, vitamins—that are perfectly good nutrients, also do double duty as protectors. The first of these to come to scientific attention was the *bifidus* factor.

Many bacteria cannot survive in an acid medium: a favorite formula of the past for combating diarrhea was made from buttermilk or sour milk. The artificially fed baby develops an alkaline environment in the intestinal tract that supports the growth of many organisms, including harmful and putrefactive bacteria; consequently, the intestines are often irritated, and the stool of the artificially fed baby has the usual fecal stench. Some of the sugars in breast milk, however, when digested, produce an acid environment in the intestines, in which harmful bacteria can't survive. As a result, the predominant intestinal bacteria of nursing babies are a harmless species called *Lactobacillus bifidus*. The stool of the breastfed baby has no unpleasant smell, but only a faint odor, something like yoghurt. Nobel laureate Paul Gyorgy, discoverer of vitamin B_6 and a pioneering researcher in the values of human milk, discovered a growth factor for lactobacilli in human milk and found it is virtually absent in cows' milk.

Waste products of *bifidus* metabolism make the breastfed infant's intestinal tract even more resistant to the growth of other, invading organisms. Manufacturers of synthetic milks have been working to develop "humanized" milks that contain something similar to the *bifidus* factor, but so far no one has succeeded in manufacturing a product that can maintain *L. bifidus* in the intestines of a bottle-fed baby.

Another nutritive ingredient of human milk that modifies the environment inside the baby is lactoferrin, a protein. The principal protein in cows' milk is casein; in human milk, lactoferrin makes up at least a third of the protein. Lactoferrin not only is much more digestible than casein, it also has the unusual property of being highly absorbent of iron molecules. Many pathogens, such as *E. coli* (the common indicator of sewage contamination in public water supplies) and the bacteria that cause infectious diarrhea, require free iron molecules for their own metabolism. With lactoferrin mopping up all the loose iron in the baby's intestines, these pathogens simply cannot grow.

Special groups of sugars in human milk, the oligosaccharides, fight pathogens in the way that antibodies do, by interfering with their attachment sites. These sugars are particularly effective against certain pneumonia bacteria and *E. coli* and their toxins. Some lipids, or fats, can disrupt and kill many kinds of viruses, including polio. There is evidence that fatty acids, produced during the digestion of lipids, protect the infant against intestinal parasites such as *Giardia lamblia* and amoebic dysentery. We may think of such parasites as being a serious problem only in the tropics; but *Giardia,* which causes chronic cramps and diarrhea, is spread by dogs and wildlife, and is found in brooks, streams, and some wells throughout the United States; it has also become widespread in day-care centers.

THE SOOTHERS: ANTI-INFLAMMATORY AGENTS

Infectious illness is usually accompanied by inflammation. If you get a scratch on your skin, and *Staphylococcus* organisms move in, your body's defense system will rush to attack them, but in the process the scratch may rapidly become red and swollen. The very tools of the fight, such as toxins that kill bacteria and free oxygen atoms to burn up the invaders, can irritate normal cells and cause painful inflammation. Sore throats, earaches, and diarrhea are all manifestations of inflammation caused by the body's attempts to battle pathogens.

The protective mechanisms in human milk, however, appear to be cunningly designed to do their work without causing unpleasant symptoms or pain. This happens in two ways: some ingredients fight germs without causing inflammation, and some ingredients directly negate or reduce inflammatory agents that do occur. For example, the kinds of white cells that cause inflammation and swelling while defending the body, such as basal cells that release histamines, are not the kinds found in human milk. The macrophages and neutrophils in human milk can kill bacteria without making trouble.

Other agents in human milk, including several vitamins, are antioxidants; they can combine with loose oxygen atoms that are part of the body's disease-fighting process but that could injure healthy tissue. Many fragments of sugar and fat molecules that appear during the digestive process are also antioxidants. Like secretory IgA, lysozyme, and lactoferrin, they can persist throughout the digestive tract and protect the baby from inflammation from one end to the other.

These components of human milk, and others still to be explored, do not directly fight disease. Instead, when a pathogen does get into the baby's system, these agents deter the process of disease control from causing the baby to feel pain or sickness as a side effect. Armond Goldman, M.D., of the University of Texas Medical School, was perhaps the first lactation researcher to deduce, in the early 1980s, the existence and importance of this new class of protectors in human milk. Investigation of anti-inflammatory agents is a burgeoning new area of research in human milk.

BREASTFEEDING AND ALLERGIES

One benefit of breastfeeding is that breastfed babies on the whole have far fewer skin ailments and other allergic reactions than do artificially fed babies. Allergies can be caused by proteins that are unfamiliar to the body's chemistry. New babies are less tolerant of alien proteins than are older babies, partly because their immune system is not operating fully yet. Some researchers have suggested that the intestines of newborns are highly permeable, and admit the passage of large molecules into the bloodstream. This permeable condition might facilitate the early transfer of antibodies from human milk to the infant's bloodstream; but it also might make the infant vulnerable if fed cows' milk or some other alien substance.

Initial feedings of colostrum are thought to protect the infant from allergic reactions through a phenomenon known as gut closure; theoretically, the lipids and secretory IgA in colostrum coat the linings of the infant's intestines, sealing the intestinal mucosae and making them impermeable to large molecules, thus making the subject less susceptible to invasion of disease organisms. A single feeding of colostrum might reduce intestinal permeability and render the infant capable of digesting such molecules rather than absorbing them unchanged. The bottle-fed infant, on the other hand, may continue to absorb whole proteins, and develop reactions to them, well into the second year of life.

Even in the fully breastfed baby, supplementation with solid foods in the first four months of life may set off allergic reactions, especially when the supplement contains complex proteins such as those in eggs. The protein in cow's milk is among the worst offenders in causing allergic reactions, and this protein can be transferred from the mother's diet to the baby through the breast milk. One mother found that her baby developed an allergic reaction if she herself drank too much cow's milk in a day. By experimenting, she narrowed it down: incredibly, if she drank twelve ounces of cow's milk, the baby showed no discomfort; if she drank thirteen ounces or more, the baby was upset and developed diarrhea and a rash.

Several studies have shown that infants who are susceptible to cow's milk protein allergy can be sensitized by a single feeding of a cow's milk-based formula, sometimes given in the hospital nursery as a routine "extra" feeding. An infant who reacts to cow's milk in the mother's diet may well have been "triggered" by a feeding the mother wasn't told about, during the first day or two of life. Thereafter, some researchers suspect, cow's milk antigens in her milk act like booster shots, causing allergic reactions.

A tendency to allergy is inheritable. If either parent has a family history of allergies such as recurring asthma, eczema, or hives; severe reactions to bee stings, or to cats or other animals; sensitivities to certain foods; or, if either parent had such problems as a baby or child, their children may be vulnerable to allergies, too. Breastfeeding is perhaps the single best step one can take to mitigate a child's risk of these annoying and in some cases life-threatening allergic reactions.

The tendency to develop allergic reactions decreases with age. Babies who might become allergic should be kept on a diet consisting solely of breast milk for five or six months. A mother who knows she herself is allergic to specific foods should avoid them during lactation, while finding substitutes to make sure that she doesn't compromise good nutrition in the process. Foods that a mother is sensitive to might also be avoided during pregnancy; there is some evidence that very susceptible babies can become sensitized to allergens, especially cow's milk protein, in the uterus. Surreptitious or routine supplementation with cows' milk formula in the hospital nursery, or in the first few months of life, should be guarded against. By six months of age, when nature intended a baby to be sampling new foods, most babies have passed the danger point when allergic reactions become established.

NOURISHMENT

The direct protection breast milk offers against disease is perhaps the most dramatic aspect of the benefits of breastfeeding. But the principal function of milk, after all, is to *feed* the baby. How well does mother's milk do that? It should not be a surprise to learn that the nutritive components of human milk are tailored precisely to our babies' needs, and that these components are not easy to duplicate precisely.

Human milk is not designed to produce the biggest baby possible in the shortest amount of time, as some medical practitioners crave, but to foster neural and brain development and behavioral growth along with healthy body growth. The special nutritional mix in human milk keeps babies growing at the most desirable rate for humans, while maintaining beneficial activity levels. Breastfed babies are physically active and show growth curves that differ in several ways from artificially fed babies (chapter 4). And the nutritional contents of human milk are geared to those growth needs. Here are some specifics:

PROTEIN:
The protein in cows' milk is mostly casein. Casein is not very digestible and forms a large, tough curd when it is mixed with digestive juices. The infant with a stomach full of the solid curds of raw cows' milk can be in real trouble. Diluting the milk helps; heating also makes the curds

smaller and softer. But they still tend to linger in the infant's stomach, so that he feels full for about four hours after a feeding. In human milk, casein forms only about a third of the protein content, and the remaining proteins, such as lactoferrin, are easier for the human baby to digest. The curd of human milk, produced from this different balance of proteins, is soft and fine, almost liquid. The stomach of the breastfed baby empties rapidly and easily. Consequently, the baby wants to eat more often, at least every two or three hours during the daytime, for the first two or three months of life. This in turn stimulates the mother's milk supply.

Human milk also contains a significant proportion of essential amino acids, the "building blocks" of protein, which can be absorbed and used by the infant just as they are. Colostrum is especially high in amino acids. According to Drs. Icie Macy and Harriet Kelly, authorities on infant nutrition, this bonus of nutrients probably forms a splendid basis for the rapid growth and profound changes taking place in the body of the newborn.

The human infant uses the protein in breast milk with nearly 100 percent efficiency. After the first few days of life, virtually all the protein in breast milk becomes part of the baby; little or none is excreted. The baby fed on cows' milk-based or vegetable-based synthetic milk, on the other hand, may waste about half the protein in his diet. Some of it passes undigested through his system and is excreted in the feces. Some is digested, but cannot be utilized by the cells of the body and is excreted in the urine. To get enough protein that is usable, the bottle-fed baby must drink a much larger volume of liquid than the breastfed baby. In taking aboard extra fluid to get the protein he needs, the synthetically fed baby may also get extra carbohydrates, which may make him obese.

The mother who has bottle-fed one baby, and watched him tuck away eight or ten ounces or even more on occasion, may worry because her subsequent breastfed baby couldn't possibly be getting a similar volume of milk. But, because he absorbs nearly all of every drop from the breast, the breastfed baby doesn't need to take in nearly as much. In fact, while bottle-fed babies vastly increase their volume intake of synthetic milk as they grow, the volume intake of breastfed babies levels off long before the babies begin taking other food, without affecting growth rates at all.

WATER:

Eliminating unusable protein is largely the job of the kidneys. This may place quite a strain on a function that is as yet immature. For years, it was widely believed that premature babies gained better on certain synthetic milks than they did on breast milk. Finally, investigators found that the weight gain was due not to growth but to retention of fluid in the tissues. This is the result of strain on the immature kidneys, which are not yet properly equipped to eliminate unsuitable proteins and mineral salts.

Human infants get plenty of water in their mothers' milk for their metabolic needs. Although an occasional baby seems to enjoy drinking water, during hot weather it is the mother who needs extra water, not her breastfed baby. The baby fed on cows' milk, on the other hand, needs water not only to regulate her own metabolism but to enable her kidneys to eliminate the unusable proteins and salts. Thus, she needs water by bottle in addition to the water in her synthetic milk, especially in hot weather.

FAT:

The total fat content of human milk is about the same as, if not higher than, that of undiluted cows' milk. (In diluted cows' milk formulas, the fat content is drastically reduced, and consequently, so is the amount of fat-soluble vitamins.) But human milk is much lower in saturated fats than is cows' milk; the possible long-term benefits of this are now being studied. Most of the fat in human milk is passed out toward the end of a feeding (chapter 2). When lactation is in full flow, the midmorning meal usually has the highest fat content. This is because the breast produces more fat particles overnight than the infant consumes at the early morning feeding. So the next feeding *begins* not with the thin fore milk but with the fat-filled hind milk left over from breakfast, and includes a second amount of hind milk after letdown.

If both breasts are used at a feeding, hind milk and fore milk will mix, during letdown, in the second breast, resulting in rather high-calorie milk being quickly available to the infant. Thus, a mother may offer both breasts at each feeding, and perhaps switch back to the first breast for a final "dessert," especially if the infant is ill or gaining slowly; it is important, however, to let the baby nurse as long as it likes on at least one breast, so that the richest hind milk is available.

At one time, the idea that a mother's milk should be measured for fat content was very popular. Medical professionals were not aware of the difference between fore milk and hind milk in each feeding. They did not take into account that there might also be variations in the overall fat content of feedings during the course of the day. Many women were told, on the basis of one sample of an ounce or two of milk drawn off in a doctor's office, that their milk was "too thin."

The overall percentage of fat in a mother's milk is an inherited characteristic, not affected by how much fat there is in her diet. Richard Applebaum, M.D., author of a medical text on the management of breastfeeding, states that in an individual mother, fore milk may have 1.5 calories per ounce and hind milk 30 calories per ounce, with some mothers averaging out to 25 calories per ounce, or about the equivalent of the light cream sold in supermarkets as "half and half." Babies compensate for the genetic variations in their mothers' milk by varying the duration and frequency of nursings. For example, while a typical three-month-old baby in our culture nurses about eight to ten times in twenty-four hours, a lactation survey turned up one mother whose three-month-old was nursing every four to six hours, for a mere fifteen minutes or so—and yet the baby was gaining well. The mother turned out to be producing milk with a fat content about as high as Haagen-Dazs ice cream.

Diet has no effect on the percentage of fat in the milk but it can affect the kinds of fats present. Studies in Africa and India have shown that a diet high in coconut oils, say, will produce a different mix of lipids from a diet in which most of the fats come from peanut or fish oils. Studies in the United States have also shown that manipulation of dietary fats is reflected in variation in lipid types in human milk. All the fat sources, however, produce suitable nutrition for the baby.

CHOLESTEROL:

A conspicuous exception to the rule that milk fats reflect dietary fats is cholesterol, the animal fat associated with clogged arteries and heart attacks in middle-aged men and postmenopausal women. Human milk is notably high in cholesterol compounds (about 2.4 milligrams per deciliter). Most of the compounds are the so-called "good" cholesterol, which is thought to benefit circulatory health and to combat the harmful effects of the "bad" cholesterol.

Furthermore, the cholesterol level is unrelated to the mother's diet. In one experiment, a group of lactating women spent four weeks on a high-cholesterol diet and four weeks on a low-cholesterol diet; their own blood levels of cholesterol rose and fell depending on diet, but the levels in their milk (and in their babies' blood plasma) remained the same. It appears that some cholesterol compounds in human milk are actually manufactured in the breast, to make up any deficiency in dietary supply. In other words, the breast monitors both the amounts and kinds of cholesterol in human milk, and keeps the "good" level high, possibly facilitating brain growth, since the brain is rich in cholesterol.

Very possibly babies need and benefit from this cholesterol in several ways; one theory is that these lipid concentrations in early nutrition influence the mechanisms that will regulate cholesterol levels in later life. Incidentally, researchers are finding that during lactation most women have surprisingly high levels of cholesterol in their blood, even if they are consciously avoiding high-cholesterol foods; we can only guess, at present, that Mother Nature has her reasons for this as well.

Some synthetic milk manufacturers advertise that their products are free of cholesterol, which they are, because the products are made with vegetable oils instead of animal milk fats. These vegetable oils, however, include a cholesterol-like substance called phytosterol ("phyto" means "plant"). Babies fed on vegetable oil-based synthetic milks have phytosterol levels roughly twenty times as high as that of breastfed babies, even the breastfed babies of mothers eating a vegetarian diet high in phytosterols. Apparently, the breast also monitors the amount of plant-source sterols in human milk and keeps that level low. We don't know what the long-term effects of reversing these sterol levels might be.

SUGAR:

The principal sugar in human milk is lactose, which, like the sugars in cows' milk, includes galactose, glucose, and other compounds. Sugar-related compounds are important in the maintenance of safe intestinal flora, as we have seen, and serve numerous other protective functions, in addition to providing calories and making human milk taste sweet, an inducement to feeding that even newborn babies can perceive and enjoy.

VITAMINS:

Even when the mother's nutrition is not ideal, breast milk normally supplies all the vitamins babies need until around the age of five or six months. And breast milk continues to be a good source of vitamins thereafter. Vitamins can be divided into two groups: those that dissolve in fat, which can be stored in the body, and those that dissolve in water, which must be supplied daily by the diet. Except in very peculiar circumstances, breast milk contains plenty of the fat-soluble vitamins A and E, which are supplied from the liver and other storehouses in the mother's body even when they are low or absent in her diet. Both of these vitamins are especially plentiful in colostrum, where they are undoubtedly valuable to the newborn, whose supplies of A and E are very low at birth. At the age of one week, the breastfed newborn has more than five times the amount of vitamin E in his system than does his bottle-fed counterpart. So far, breastfeeding is the only way we know of to establish this high, virtually adult level of vitamin E, a powerful anti-inflammatory agent, in the newborn.

The third fat-soluble vitamin, vitamin D, does not normally come from diet except in Northern and Arctic climates where the diet is rich in fish oils and fish liver. In the rest of the world, vitamin D is synthesized in the body through exposure to sunlight. Both breastfed babies and nursing mothers synthesize their own vitamin D in the sun. Some vitamin D is also supplied to the baby through his mother's milk.

Vitamin D controls the body's ability to absorb calcium. When it is not provided by the diet, and if exposure to sunlight is curtailed, children have rickets. The baby gets first claim on whatever vitamin D is available; in areas where this problem is chronic, babies often do not develop rickets until they are weaned; their nursing mothers, however, are susceptible to osteomalacia, or brittle-bone disease. The problem is endemic in Moslem cities where women are confined or veiled, but it can occur in Western cities, too. Vitamin D deficiency has been diagnosed in fully breastfed children in several U.S. urban areas, especially in families with genetically dark skin. Under a combination of cloudy skies, urban customs, and resistant pigmentation, some babies (some mothers, too) do not get enough sunlight. The antidote is simple: take the baby outside, under the open sky, at least fifteen minutes a day, preferably without a hat (except in the coldest of weather or in the tropics where sunburn is a possibility). Open skies are beneficial for mothers, too, especially during dark winters, because bright daylight can lift low spirits.

The water-soluble vitamins, vitamin C and the B complex, must be supplied in the diet. Cows' milk contains almost no vitamin C, since calves can manufacture their own. Human milk, on the other hand, contains quite a lot. The vitamin C content of human milk increases immediately if the vitamin is added to the diet. The milk of a mother who is eating plenty of vitamin C-bearing foods may have ten times as much vitamin C as whole cow's milk.

The nursing baby has first claim to whatever vitamin C is

present. Dr. F. E. Hytten found that, immediately after a feeding, when milk production is presumably at its peak, there is a sharp drop in the maternal serum levels of vitamin C as the active mammary glands corral all the available supply. This mechanism is so effective that scurvy, the disease caused by lack of vitamin C, has never been seen in a breastfed baby, even in parts of the world where it is common among adults, including nursing mothers.

The B complex vitamins, a mysterious and extensive group, play a role in human and animal nutrition that is not yet entirely understood. Some are supplied by the diet. Some are synthesized in the body. In most parts of the world, at least enough B complex vitamins for survival are supplied to breastfed babies by their mothers, whatever the diet. The notable exception is parts of Asia where polished rice is the main item of food. Polishing removes the thiamine, and whole populations may be deficient in that B vitamin, with breastfed babies dying of beriberi, the thiamine deficiency disease. D. B. Jelliffe, M.D., World Health Organization infant nutrition expert, comments that it is almost the only disease that we know how to prevent but which is nevertheless increasing. Polished rice has more snob appeal than unpolished rice, and unpolished rice cannot be stored as long in warm climates; it is difficult to persuade manufacturers not to polish rice when polishing is to their economic advantage.

Deficiency of other B vitamins in breastfed babies does not normally arise, even under conditions of deprivation, with the exception of vitamin B_{12} deficiency in vegetarians. If a vegetarian mother is breastfeeding, the baby may have symptoms before the mother does. In synthetic milks, B vitamin supplies may not be sufficient for the needs of individual babies. Some babies have had convulsions, found to be caused by insufficient vitamin B, when they were fed sterilized products in which parts of this vitamin complex were destroyed by heating.

MINERALS—CALCIUM:

Human milk contains less than a quarter as much calcium as cows' milk; this appears to be all the calcium a human baby needs, with the exception of extremely premature babies. Babies on cows' milk-based synthetic diets grow larger and heavier skeletons than breastfed babies, in the first year of life. However, they also have to excrete a lot of unused calcium and phosphorus, whereas breastfed babies excrete very little. At present, our understanding of calcium needs is inadequate. One authority sees a need to investigate the "poor calcification" of the breastfed baby, to see if long-term or immediate disadvantages result. Another accepts the breastfed baby as normal, and deplores the distorted growth curve of the baby on "too highly mineralized" cows' milk. We do know that babies absorb calcium from human milk much more efficiently than they do from synthetic sources, and that the calcium content of human milk remains stable even in the malnourished mother, since calcium can be drawn from her bones. In healthy mothers, this calcium is replaced after weaning.

MINERALS—IRON:

Iron is needed to make red blood cells. The baby is born with a good supply of iron and with a high concentration of red blood cells, which is presumably diluted to normal over a period of growth. It used to be thought that human milk contains "no" iron. In fact, it contains more iron than cows' milk, and the iron is in a form that is much more easily absorbed by the baby. High levels of vitamins C and E in breast milk function in making iron available to the baby's system, and lactoferrin in mother's milk binds and recycles iron molecules that in the bottle-fed baby may be usurped by bacteria. If the mother is not anemic during pregnancy, the baby's stores of iron are adequate for the first six months or more, even on an exclusively milk diet; additional dietary iron becomes available from grains, some vegetables, meat, and so on, when a baby starts eating solid food at six or seven months or so.

A breastfed baby may actually absorb more iron than a bottle-fed baby getting an iron supplement. Thus, the breastfed baby is not normally anemic. The high bioavailability of iron in human milk disappears, however, when supplemental feedings are added; the breastfed baby who is getting bottles of artificial milk as well should have additional iron in the diet.

If the mother is extremely anemic during pregnancy, as is the case in many parts of the world, fetal stores of iron may become inadequate within two or three months, and suckling anemia results. Suckling anemia is seen even in the children of healthy mothers when solid foods are withheld for an unusually long time. In Renaissance Italy, it was customary to give babies nothing but breast milk for up to two years. The results are illustrated in many paintings of the period: representations of the Madonna and Child frequently show the Infant Christ as a flabby, pasty-white, anemic older baby.

Babies on cow's milk–based synthetics receive even less iron from their diet than do breastfed babies. Some bottle-fed babies have been found to be anemic, also, due to covert (or hidden) bleeding from chronic irritation caused by bacteria in the intestinal tract. Since artifically fed babies are more subject to anemia, an effort is usually made to have them eating iron-rich foods, such as egg yolks, as soon as possible. This early exposure to eggs and other high-protein foods, however, may cause allergic reactions.

Breastfed babies usually signal when they are ready for solid foods by trying to help themselves to the foods on a parent's plate. The eventual necessity of adding iron to the diet and the desirability, around the middle of the first year, of introducing the baby to new foods ("A little bagel, a piece salami, he should know what good food tastes like" as one cookbook author puts it) should not be used as an argument to promote feeding solids to an already well-nourished breastfed baby before the fifth month.

MINERALS—TRACE ELEMENTS:

Trace elements are minerals—such as copper, manganese, sulfur, zinc, and many others—that occur in minute quantities and yet are necessary for healthy metabolism. Mothers deliver trace elements to their infants in their milk; for example, the breastfed baby shares the benefits when his mother drinks fluoridated water. Gradually, we are learning some of the roles played by these "micronutrients." Human milk is much higher in copper than is cow's milk; copper seems to be associated with iron metabolism. Zinc is involved in the growth of muscle tissue. Selenium, once considered to be unnecessary and in fact a poison, turns out to be important in the functioning of the immune system.

The diets of even well-fed mothers may or may not provide adequate supplies of all trace elements: trace element-researcher Michael Hambidge, M.D., states that the diet of the African Bushman mother is better supplied with zinc, for example, than the diet of an urban American woman. Suppose that a slightly inadequate zinc supply reduces a baby's rate of muscle growth by a few percentage points; the baby is still healthy and normal, and the growth reduction would be hard for a scientist to prove—but that is not optimum nutrition. Does this matter? Perhaps only to parents.

A mother can improve her trace element intake by eating a wider variety of foods (chapter 2, p. 37). The provision of trace elements in synthetic milks, however, is not in the mother's control, and is somewhat uneven. Where the nutritional need for a specific micronutrient has been proven, it is added as a supplement, unless it is part of some protein or other compound already in the mix; thus, infant synthetic milks and even some adult breakfast cereals are now fortified with zinc. Where the need is not known, however, synthetic milks may or may not be adequate. There have been some serious episodes of deficiency diseases in infants fed exclusively on one brand or another of synthetic milk, before the necessary but absent nutrient was identified and added.

Breast milk, while providing at least some of *all* the necessary nutrients, is also guaranteed not to contain trace elements at levels that are unnaturally or dangerously high. Synthetic feeds, however, may contain too much of a trace element, especially when research has not yet been directed at that specific substance. For example: the role of manganese in human nutrition is not known, although it is present in our bodies and in breast milk. Manganese amounts in human milk vary somewhat. Manganese amounts in artificial feeds, however, are not controlled at all. Cows' milk-based synthetic feeds typically contain ten times as much manganese as human milk, and soy bean–based milks up to a hundred times. That is enough so that the baby's excretion system can be overtaxed. Manganese that cannot be excreted is stored in the brain. In high doses, manganese is a neurotoxin.

PEPTIDES, ENZYMES, HORMONES, AND OTHER MYSTERIES

On close examination, human milk is full of other complex substances whose functions and roles have not yet been fully determined. Some aid the infant's immature system in digestion. Amylase, for instance, is an enzyme that promotes digestion of starches. Infants do not manufacture their own amylase until about six months of age. Cow's milk and synthetic milks do not contain amylase (which would in any case be destroyed by heating) but breast milk does; as a result, breastfed babies who are old enough for other foods actually tolerate and digest solid foods better than bottle-fed babies. Children with the genetic disease cystic fibrosis provide a striking example; among other symptoms, the child's ability to digest food is affected by this disease. If the child is breastfed, the ailment may not show up until the child is totally weaned, at eighteen months or more, as even small amounts of breast milk contribute at least some of the needed digestive enzymes.

Some of the compounds in human milk appear to promote the development of the baby's own immune system. Some apparently stimulate growth and development of the intestines. Harvard Medical School research on growth factors suggests that the first few feedings of colostrum and early breast milk may contain specific growth-inducing hormones that play a major role in stimulating the maturation of the intestines of the newborn. The result is improved food absorption and protection against allergies, infections, and serious intestinal disorders. These growth factors may be of particular importance in premature babies.

Breast milk carries with it many of the hormones that are found in the mother's bloodstream. The prolactin and oxytocin of lactation that are present in our milk presumably have the same calming, relaxing effect on the baby that they do on the mother. Another hormone, insulin, occurs in a mother's milk in higher levels than in her blood serum; we don't at present know why. The hormonal changes accompanying resumption of the menstrual cycle, and a subsequent pregnancy, do not appear to affect the still-nursing baby, but may alter the composition of the milk temporarily (chapter 2).

LONG-TERM BENEFITS OF BREAST MILK

It seems reasonable to suppose that breast milk confers benefits while the baby is receiving it; surprisingly, some studies are beginning to show health benefits after weaning. At Oregon State University, a study of dental caries in two well-matched communities, one with fluoridated water and one without, turned up a surprising side issue. As it happened, both towns had high percentages of breastfed children, so there were many in the study. Children who had been breastfed for three months or longer had 45 percent fewer cavities than their bottle-fed counterparts in the nonflouridated community, and 59 percent fewer cavities in the fluoridated community. The three-month period seemed to be a significant factor; children who had been breastfed only two months showed lessened protection (10 percent and 20 percent fewer cavities, respectively). Never mind the toothpaste ads—if you want good checkups, start life as a nursing baby!

A well-recognized, long-term drawback of bottle-feeding as opposed to breastfeeding is the bottle-caused distortion of the infant's use of the facial muscles and the pressure on his mouth, jaws, and palate. This is considered to be a major cause of malocclusions and other facial development problems in some children, including, typically, crooked or crowded teeth that require braces and orthodontia in later life. One large study shows that the effect of breastfeeding on malocclusions is dose-related: that is, the longer the baby is breastfed (past six months, into the second year, or more) the greater the benefit to his jaw and facial development.

One study of the relationship between infant feeding methods and obesity compared the height, weight, and skinfold thickness of 907 teenagers with their infant feeding histories. The authors concluded that breastfeeding, even if for less than two months, provided significant protection against obesity, with indications of increased protection with longer duration. Early or late introduction of solids made no difference and neither did race, birth order, or socioeconomic status. Other researchers, however, have contested the findings, and long-term studies beginning in infancy remain to be done.

Epidemiological studies (statistical surveys of large chunks of the population) in Sweden and the United States have shown that fully breastfed babies have less chance than bottle-fed babies of developing diabetes in childhood. When the incidence of breastfeeding fell, early-onset, insulin-dependent diabetes cases rose. When breastfeeding increased, the diabetes cases fell, and the onset was delayed where the disease did occur.

A British study has demonstrated that ulcerative colitis in adults is 100 percent more common in patients whose medical history includes weaning from the breast before two weeks than in patients who were breastfed for longer periods. Similar statistical studies have shown that breastfeeding, even for short periods, reduces the likelihood of contracting several other adult diseases related to immune-system problems, including celiac disease.

Perhaps most startling, two recent studies have shown that as the incidence and duration of breastfeeding goes up, the incidence of childhood leukemia and other lymphomas —white cell-related cancers—goes down. We do not yet understand the mechanism for this protection, and the evidence at present is only statistical, which means there is no guarantee in the case of any one individual. But people with a family history of immune-system disorders might wish to give the matter some consideration.

The discovery that preventive effects of breastfeeding continue far into adult life has occurred largely by accident; in the cases of the Oregon dental caries investigation and the British study of ulcerative colitis, the investigators had no idea in advance that any such correlations would show up. One wonders how many "modern" diseases, generally supposed to be byproducts of pollution or of the tensions of civilized life, are physiologically related to our widespread unnatural system for feeding infants.

KOOLAID AND KARMA: ENVIRONMENTAL CONTAMINANTS IN HUMAN MILK

Whatever we eat, breathe, or touch—wood smoke, hair spray, soapy water, bubble gum, the smell of pine needles—anything that can be absorbed into the human system may show up in human milk. An occasional mother has been startled to discover that drinking grape-flavored Koolaid tints her milk purple. Gatorade, another popular drink, gives some women pale green milk, and health-food store vitamins with powdered alfalfa in them can do the same. Volatile oils, which give most spices their characteristic odor and flavors, pass through milk unchanged. Babies don't usually care (although the *Journal of Human Lactation* reports one baby who refused the breast temporarily when his mother ate ten ounces of mint candies in two days).

That's all very well for harmless food ingredients, but what about substances passing through the milk that might be bad for the baby? These fall into two categories: substances mothers ingest knowingly, such as medicines, tobacco, alcohol, and other drugs, which we will discuss shortly; and contaminants we are fated to ingest unavoidably from the environment.

"Report of Dioxin in Human Milk!" "Breastfeeding may not be safe, authorities say." "Nursing mothers to test milk for PCBs." Headlines like these give everyone the jitters. We feel horrified at the very idea of any such contaminant in mothers' milk. Is this a real problem? How serious is it?

Of course anything can be bad for you in large enough quantities; people have been poisoned by carrot juice. But most of the substances we acquire from our environment are trivial in quantity and harmless in effect. A few compounds, however, have become public concerns: organochlorine pesticides such as DDT, which generally reach us through the food chain; dioxin-related compounds, which are sometimes a product of burning and thus can be airborne; and polychlorinated biphenyls, or PCBs, oil-like substances used in industry, which may reach us in many ways.

These substances are toxic. They don't degrade into harmless substances quickly. They are fat-soluble, and tend to be stored in the fat cells and accumulate in the food chain; they are found in the highest concentrations in carnivores. Female mammals who have such contaminants stored in their body fat may transfer a percentage of them into milk fats, during lactation. By the time the persistence of such compounds was understood, these complicated molecules had been manufactured in enormous quantities and distributed all over the world. They can now be found almost everywhere on the planet, and in all forms of animals, including us.

Almost certainly, we have all had *some* lifetime exposure to these compounds, from our food, from the ground we walk on, from the air we breathe; how much, and what, depends on where we live. World Health Organization surveys show that people in industrial nations have less exposure to DDT-related compounds, and more to PCBs, than people in third-world countries, who in turn might show more traces of agricultural chemicals in their body fat, but no PCBs at all.

What does this mean to nursing babies? Except in the case of some hideous industrial accident or overexposure, nothing. The quantities of pollutants received through mothers' milk are so minute as to be biologically trivial. According to a published statement by Jean Lockhart, M.D., president of the American Academy of Pediatrics, "The amount of harmful chemicals present in human milk makes a very minor contribution to the overall lifetime exposure to humans. Infants should not be deprived of breast milk from fear of contamination with trace amounts of toxin."

Of course, it is outrageous that we have contaminated the planet to *any* measurable extent; cleaning up our act, on individual, corporate, and governmental levels, has become a major popular movement. The idea of contamination in mothers' milk, however, as opposed to the contamination in, say, skin creams, or coffee beans, has grabbed a giant share of media attention for several reasons. First, it has headline-getting shock value; second, the fat in mothers' milk is easy to get and easy to measure, compared to human body fat or fat from carnivorous animals; in fact, mothers' milk is so easy to use that it has actually become a tool for estimating worldwide pollution. Third, we can now measure such infinitesimal quantities of chemical substances that we can identify molecular-level traces of substances, not in parts per thousand or million, but in parts per billion or even trillion. What we often cannot do, because of our general ignorance about numbers, is to put that information into perspective.

When the headline reads "Mothers' milk contaminated with . . ." the important question is not "Is this true?" but "How much contamination are we talking about?" It used to be that to isolate or identify a substance you had to obtain enough of it to weigh it. Now, using a variety of elegant new methods, tiny quantities of complex substances can be identified in an instant. For example, in *one* short experiment, using mass spectrometry and a capillary gas chromatograph, scientists identified over two hundred compounds in the *smell* of a cup of coffee. Theoretically, a mother could probably absorb all kinds of things into her milk—in "trace" quantities—just from walking past a coffee machine.

Using these techniques, someone looking for, say, hexachloro-1, 3-butadiene in a few ounces of human milk may find trace amounts. But is this harmful? It's like coffee: drink ten cups of coffee a day, and the caffeine in your milk will without a doubt be bad for your baby. Walk past the coffee machine, and one can hardly suppose the baby will suffer, even though parts per billion of measurable chemicals might indeed enter your blood and show up in your milk.

This hasn't stopped irresponsible people from stating that *everyone* should get her milk tested (test results, depending on the amount of fat in the sample, are highly variable and subject to gross overinterpretation); that babies should be fed cows' milk-based fluids because cows eat only grass, not meat, and so have accumulated fewer pesticides in their milk; and even that women shouldn't breastfeed at all.

Perhaps the most poorly founded of these scare-tactic arguments is that synthetic milks, based on cow's milk or plant material, contain fewer contaminants than our own milk. They just contain different contaminants, many of which are *not* screened for, and none of which is continually tested for (the Food and Drug Administration explains that it is too understaffed to perform such tests). Cow's milk-based fluids, for example, can contain amounts of antibiotics and hormones high above the government's allowable levels, and contaminants, such as aflatoxins from spoiled grain, that are almost never found in human milk. The water used to mix synthetic milk powders may not be safe; the water from some farm wells, for example, is laden with chemicals from fertilizers. The nitrates in well water proved fatal to at least one baby when mixed with synthetic milk powder, although the adults in the family were apparently not affected. Even the feeding equipment is not necessarily safe. Some rubber bottle nipples can leach a preservative, sodium nitrite, at such levels that one should really boil them in several changes of water before use. Avoiding human milk in favor of synthetic milks is definitely *not* the way to avoid feeding your baby environmental contaminants.

We are learning more about how and when contaminants appear in human milk. Australian and European studies demonstrate that pollutants stored in the mother's body fat are *not* transmitted to the milk fat at the same levels that they are found in body fat (as some have speculated), even if the mother is losing weight while nursing. According to long-term Australian studies, accumulations of pollutants in the body slowly decline over the years, and in nursing mothers, whose contaminant load can so easily be measured, the contaminants decrease across lactation and in subsequent lactations.

Most of the transfer of pollutants from a mother's body to the baby's occurs during pregnancy, not during breastfeeding. Once born, the infant is subjected to the same environmental sources of contamination as is the mother, for the rest of its life, of which the nursing period is a very small segment. With the exception of gross environmental insult—a PCB factory in Japan, for example, where pregnant and nursing employees virtually bathed their arms in the stuff all day—the actual risk of some possible future harm to babies from contaminants accumulated via breastfeeding is usually hypothetical. In South Vietnam, for example, where the herbicide content of mothers' milk was once found to be 30,000 times higher than that in U.S. mothers' milk, people who were breastfed have shown no observable or long-term effects; and current research suggests that the milk of Vietnamese mothers breastfeeding now will reflect recent levels of environmental contamination rather than the much higher levels prevailing in their own infancy.

Some situations may actually be improving; in Canada, the United States, and Europe, the levels of DDT and similar compounds in human beings were much higher in the 1970s than in the 1980s, suggesting that for these countries the peak of those contaminations is past. An Australian study found that younger people carried smaller traces of contaminants than older people, presumably because of the passage of environmental laws.

In the United States, statisticians currently think that the breast milk contribution to an infant's lifetime load of contaminants might theoretically increase the likelihood of that individual developing cancer at some time during his lifetime by 1 in 100,000. Remember that the general chance of developing cancer in a long lifetime is now about 1 in 4! The hypothetical additional risk from a year or two of breastfeeding is not much, compared to the very real risks—ranging from malocclusions to allergies—associated with synthetic milks, which in any case also include contaminants and lack a lot of beneficial substances.

There are always going to be new "scare stories." The press makes money from them, and researchers get headlines with them (see chapter 8, pp. 201–02). As well as taking common-sense precautions with their own environment and diet, parents can and should evaluate new alarms for themselves, remembering that statistics need to be examined carefully, and that while some people stand to benefit from scare stories, our babies are not among them.

DRUGS, ALCOHOL, AND CONTAMINANTS YOU CAN AVOID

Most things a mother ingests can appear in her milk, and this especially includes the mood-altering substances we take for pleasure: nicotine, caffeine, alcohol, legal drugs such as sedatives and tranquilizers, and illegal drugs from marijuana to cocaine. The rule of thumb with prescription medications is that the baby gets 1 percent of the dose the mother takes, but many of the mood-altering chemicals have a very long half-life in the adult body. That means they circulate in a mother's bloodstream not just once, but hour after hour. The breastfed baby accumulates a new dose at each feeding, and the baby may take much longer to eliminate the drug, so levels can build up fast.

Caffeine is a particular villain. An adult will eliminate caffeine from a single dose—one cup of coffee, for example—in four hours. A newborn baby, however, may take up to three days to get rid of a single dose, so subsequent doses rapidly add up to toxic levels. One mother reported that her first-born baby was irritable from birth, and became absolutely frantic, twenty-four hours a day, when she brought it home. Her doctor was unable to find anything wrong, decided the baby was "allergic to breast milk" (which never happens) and told her to put the baby on the bottle, whereupon the baby calmed right down. It took the mother years to realize that no one had asked her what *she* was doing—and she'd been drinking six or eight (or even more) cups of coffee a day, to soothe herself while trying to cope with her increasingly miserable breastfed baby, who was probably suffering from a caffeine overdose.

If a mother smokes, there will be nicotine in her milk. One nursing mother who smoked heavily found that her baby was not gaining well. She recalled that she herself never gained weight while smoking, so she quit, and the baby began gaining at once. Mothers should be aware that smoking is definitely one of those things that has an effect upon the baby before birth. On the average, babies born to smokers are smaller at birth than babies born to nonsmokers, and they may suffer other problems as well. The safest course is to stop smoking before you get pregnant, or certainly during pregnancy. Babies are susceptible to allergic and other reactions from being in smoky rooms, not just from ingesting nicotine, and a smoking mother always runs the unpleasant risk of accidentally burning her child.

Alcohol is so volatile, and passes so easily through the placenta, that women nowadays are advised to avoid all alcohol scrupulously during pregnancy. The babies of heavy drinkers may be born with a set of developmental disabilities called Fetal Alcohol Syndrome, with lifelong consequences. Alcohol appears in breast milk at roughly the same levels that it occurs in the bloodstream. Once born, the nursing baby is digesting these molecules, rather than receiving them straight into the bloodstream via the placenta. The net effect on the baby is negligible unless the mother drinks alcohol in enormous quantities. The classic case is of a mother who drank a quart of port at a sitting: both she and her baby passed out.

Some researchers feel that mothers should avoid all alcohol, even small amounts, while breastfeeding, but the general medical opinion is that alcohol in small quantities during breastfeeding does not appear to be a cause for concern. Some physicians recommend a glass of wine or beer a day for new mothers, as a relatively safe analgesic. Too much alcohol, of course, can affect one's judgment and care giving. No mother who has read it could ever forget the scene in John Updike's *Rabbit, Run* in which a young mother absent-mindedly drinks too much scotch and lets the baby slip under the bath water.

Marijuana stays in the system for several days, rather than several hours like alcohol. Smoking pot may result in cumulative doses for the breastfed baby; it may also affect one's mothering. Drugs that affect the mental processes may also be especially bad for babies, even in small quantities, since their brains and nervous systems are in a state of rapid growth. The stronger psychedelic drugs such as LSD may powerfully affect a mother's behavior and will reach the baby in utero; if taken in sufficient quantities, they will reach the nursing baby. The same goes for amphetamines and barbiturates (uppers and downers) and for all the grotesque mixtures of hash and strychnine, Sparine (animal tranquilizer) and other chemicals that are available on the streets of every major city. Opium and heroin pass through the placenta and also into the breast milk. The baby of a mother who is addicted to morphine or heroin is born an addict; playwright Eugene O'Neill is thought to have been a victim of this misfortune.

Cocaine is in a class by itself. Cocaine is extremely dangerous to the fetus and to the breastfed baby. It passes through the milk with ease. Babies have died from a single dose of cocaine-laced breast milk, and from breathing cocaine smoke. Even the smallest remnant of cocaine in the mother's system can damage a nursing baby. Medical researchers feel that a "clean" nursing mother who breaks down and takes one hit of cocaine should refrain from breastfeeding for at least three days. Babies cannot handle cocaine, period.

MEDICATIONS: WHAT'S SAFE FOR THE NURSING MOTHER?

Prescription drugs, like anything else ingested, can appear in trace quantities in a nursing mother's milk. Usually the amounts are so trivial that they make absolutely no difference to the nursing baby. Nevertheless, every time a new drug is introduced into the medical repertoire, somebody worries about what effect it will have on nursing babies. Doctors whose specialties have nothing to do with mothers and babies—surgeons, ophthalmologists, cardiologists, and so on—may prescribe drugs and forbid further breastfeeding without understanding its importance or the problems involved in stopping even temporarily. And most medical care providers are not up to date on drugs and breast milk; nursing mothers can be mercilessly forbidden to breastfeed upon being prescribed anything from antibiotics to aspirin, including, one expert points out, drugs that the same physician wouldn't hesitate to prescribe in oral doses for the infant itself!

In general, all the medications that people are normally given for transitory illnesses are safe for nursing mothers and their babies; this includes antibiotics (except for tetracycline, which can stain the baby's newly forming teeth) and pain relievers. Anesthetics given to a mother during the birth may inhibit her baby's sucking reflex at first, but anesthetics and analgesics given to a mother afterward, or postoperatively, will not affect her nursing baby; she should be free to nurse as soon as she wants to. Vitamins, even in megadoses, are harmless, as are single doses of most drugs.

Mothers usually excrete in their milk 1 percent or less of their own dosage of any medication. The mammary glands do not "store" drugs. A medication that a mother takes in the evening will be gone from her bloodstream and therefore from her milk by morning, whether she nurses the baby in the night or not. Most prescribed drugs, such as antibiotics, are gone from the system in two to four hours—that's why you have to take them every four hours. In the case of many common medications such as aspirin, the amount of drug in the mother's milk peaks ten or twenty minutes after the dose is taken, and then rapidly disappears.

Sometimes a doctor tells a mother to stop nursing "just to be on the safe side," although the drug in question is not really dangerous. Sometimes the doctor takes the easy way out by relying on the manufacturer's insert in the medication box—in these inserts manufacturers usually lean over backward, to keep out of legal trouble—or the *Physicians' Desk Reference,* or *PDR,* a manual on prescription drugs. The medical advisory board of La Leche League International, the breastfeeding educational organization, states that in discussing drugs that are safe for nursing mothers, the *PDR* "tends to be needlessly disparaging when information is lacking." Often the medical recommendations on a given medication and its effect on mothers' milk are based on a study of one or two cases, which simply indicated that the drug showed up in the milk, without making any attempt to estimate the quantity, much less the duration, of its presence; or to find out if it did indeed show up in the baby's blood or urine; or to find out if it was present in a form that the baby could even absorb.

A blossoming area of lactation-related research is pharmacokinetics, the study of how a drug moves through the system, or, in this case, two systems, mother's and baby's both. Cheston Berlin, M.D., chairman of the department of pediatrics at Pennsylvania State University's Milton Hershey School of Medicine, is a leading researcher on transmission of drugs through breast milk. As primary author of the 1989 American Academy of Pediatrics' Statement on Drugs he has helped see to it that all of the recommendations on that list are based on good research data, not on personal opinions, advertising circulars, or other unfounded sources that have crept into the medical literature over the years. Gradually, such efforts are correcting many old misconceptions.

Dr. Berlin, who is the father of several breastfed children, points out that separating the time of nursing from the ingestion of any drug will minimize the amount of drug that's delivered to the baby. One easy way to do this is to nurse just before taking the medication, and then wait "as long as is convenient" before nursing again. Two hours is plenty, but less time is okay if the baby is fussing.

The drugs likeliest to be passed along into milk are those with low molecular weight, those easily dissolved in fats, those that do not bind to proteins, and those with long half-lives. Thus alcohol, with a molecular weight of 100, zips into the milk almost instantaneously, while a diabetic mother's dose of insulin, with a molecular weight of 5,000, won't appear in the milk at all. Some drugs that might seem dangerous, such as the anticoagulant warfarin, bind to blood proteins and never get into the milk. Drugs that can't be absorbed in oral doses, and must be given to the mother by injection, are not a problem, naturally, since they can't be absorbed in the baby's stomach, either. Drugs that are routinely prescribed for sick babies are not going to hurt healthy babies in tiny quantities in the milk.

One not uncommon medical supposition is that antibiotics given to a nursing mother will "wipe out the baby's intestinal flora," as it is commonly phrased, and give the baby diarrhea. Dr. Berlin states that there are absolutely no data to support this notion, and of course, as we have seen, the current intestinal flora would certainly be wiped out by a switch to synthetic milk.

If a lactating woman is on chronic drug therapy, repetitive doses do build up. After a single dose of Tylenol, a mother might secrete less than .8 milligram in twenty-four hours. If she takes two pills every four hours, however, she would secrete 10.8 milligrams in twenty-four hours. One ten-day-old nursing baby was brought to the hospital with severe aspirin intoxication, because the mother was taking two aspirin every four hours for arthritis; the mother was switched to other arthritis treatments and the baby recovered.

Long-term medications that may offer some risks to nursing infants include lithium and other antidepressants, which over many months could affect the baby's developing nervous system; cyclosporines and other immunosuppressant drugs; and antituberculosis drugs (although many third-world mothers take these medications and nurse successfully). Radioisotopes necessary for diagnosis or treatment need not be cause for weaning. One can select the isotope with the shortest half-life, and suspend nursing for, say, thirty-six hours, to allow the drug to clear the mother's system.

Each case is different, however; some mothers, for example, apparently do not transmit lithium in their milk. When in doubt, the milk or the baby's urine can be sampled. The age of the baby is also an important factor in making a drug decision; a drug that might present difficulties to a preterm baby may be no problem at all to a nursing toddler. Sometimes a drug for a nursing mother on long-term therapy can be safely suspended for a week or a month, while the baby is very small. Some drugs—antiparasite drugs, for example—are safer for the nursing couple if given in a single dose rather than in smaller, repeated doses.

In general, when considering medication during lactation, one should select the least toxic drug, the drug with the shortest half-life, the smallest effective dose, and the dose that can be given least frequently. It's also important to consider whether the drug is necessary at all; why take anti-ulcer medication if you could get by with bicarbonate of soda, or why take tranquilizers if exercise and diet improvement might be just as good?

We have not included in this book a list of specific drugs and their effects on mothers and babies. New drugs come along all the time, old drugs are taken *off* the danger list as we learn more about lactation, and such a list would soon be out of date. La Leche League International in Franklin Park, Illinois, refers callers to their Breastfeeding Information Center. Another good source at the time of writing is the 1989 American Academy of Pediatrics' Statement on Drugs (any drug listing compiled before 1987 is no longer current). The nursing mother faced with a physician who is being intransigent about drug selection can enlist the help of La Leche League's Medical Advisory Board, by telephone.

VIRUSES

Several viral diseases in nursing mothers are apt to cause concern, and make people order the mother to wean because of fears for the baby. As with medications, weaning is often not appropriate or necessary. Viruses, like bacteria, can be found in breast milk; and, like bacteria, in the milk they are generally harmless to the baby. Some antiviral components exist in the milk itself. Others, such as fatty acids that dissolve the coatings of viruses, are produced in the baby's stomach during digestion. Some kinds of viruses—respiratory infections, for instance—may appear in the mother's milk but are not infectious while in the baby's stomach or intestines. In any case, a mother who has a viral infection is usually protecting her baby by producing antibodies to that very infection, in her milk.

Some viruses are dangerous for a fetus, but not for a nursing baby; an example is rubella, or German measles, which may cause birth defects if passed to a fetus through the placenta in early pregnancy, but which produces only mild illness in a baby. Another teratogenic, or birth defect-causing, virus is a common infection called cytomegalovirus, or CMV. In some parts of the United States, more than half the population has antibodies to this virus, which causes a mild, flulike illness. Full-term babies who pick up the virus from breast milk usually develop antibodies without any symptoms of illness at all, and thus become immune to that infection for life. In a population where this virus is widespread, girl babies especially benefit from being thus protected from possible later infection in pregnancy. We do know that CMV *is* dangerous to the fetus in early pregnancy, and also dangerous for preterm babies *if* they receive it in blood transfusions. We don't know what the effects of this virus might be from banked human milk given to preterm babies; hospital human milk banks test the milk and their donors stringently for this virus.

A serious virus for the newborn is genital herpes, so much so that babies born to women with active cases are usually delivered by Caesarean section, to prevent the infant from coming into contact with open lesions. Such babies may be safely breastfed, provided the mother keeps her hands clean and follows sanitary practices; in one known case, a baby was infected with herpes by breastfeeding, not from the milk but from highly unusual open herpes lesions on the mother's breasts.

Hepatitis B is another dangerous, infectious virus—commoner than it used to be because of intravenous drug use—that has been identified in mothers' milk. Sometimes people are carriers of this virus even though they are not ill with it themselves. Sometimes a mother who has already nursed her new baby for two or three days is told to give up breastfeeding, because a blood test taken from the umbilical cord at birth has come back from the laboratory and is hepatitis-positive, even though there is at present no evidence that the hepatitus B virus is *transmitted* via breastfeeding. A wiser course is to treat the mother with gamma globulin and the baby with hepatitis vaccine and to encourage breastfeeding. Often any actual illness is completely avoided, and the baby continues to get the protection of its mother's milk. (Birthing room personnel should also be notified and tested.)

A virus called human T-cell lymphotropic virus, or HTLV, which can cause a type of leukemia as well as central nervous system disorders, has become endemic in some parts of Japan and Africa. As with hepatitis, some people can be carriers after they themselves have recovered. This is perhaps the first virus that has been demonstrated definitely to have the capacity to infect a baby via mother's milk, although it is not yet known whether or not the baby will develop problems in adulthood as a result. The virus is not found in most parts of the world, but presents a concern for which we have no clear answer at present.

The big scare on the virus scene is, of course, AIDS. There are mothers who have received contaminated blood transfusions, or who have used drugs or are associated with at-risk men, who may not be ill themselves but who test positive for the human immunodeficiency virus (HIV), which causes AIDS, when they give birth. Should they breastfeed?

Women who are actively ill with AIDS usually do not have the strength to consider breastfeeding, and in this country are often separated from their babies at birth. The same is true for women who are confirmed intravenous drug users. Women who develop an active case of AIDS while breastfeeding are probably most infectious at that point and should not nurse. What about that mother who tests HIV-positive but is not ill herself? Presumably the likeliest opportunity for infection of the infant is during pregnancy, through the placenta. Even then, it is not automatic. An HIV-positive mother has a 1 in 4 chance of giving birth to an HIV-positive baby. Some of these babies develop AIDS and die; others appear to have only the antibodies—which is what the tests detect—and not the virus itself; they will be fine. It takes time to determine what the antibody presence means in an individual child.

As to whether an HIV-positive woman could infect her apparently uncontaminated baby by breastfeeding, although she is not ill herself, the evidence at present is not conclusive. One laboratory in Belgium claims to have found the AIDS virus in the milk of a few mothers; many other labs have tried and failed to duplicate that finding. Half a dozen cases exist in which a mother appears to have been infected with the AIDS virus after giving birth but while breastfeeding (typically through a blood transfusion during the birth, before the present screening methods were developed), and the baby was then infected. Although infection through the milk has not been proven at time of writing, an HIV-positive mother with an HIV-negative baby would want to consider that the possibility of infection may exist.

The World Health Organization has taken the position that in developing countries the benefits of breast milk far outweigh any putative risk from an HIV-positive mother, and that all such mothers should be encouraged to breastfeed. In the United States, however, the Centers for Disease Control, our national epidemic disease laboratory, has taken the position that the protective aspects of breast milk may be crucial for survival in third-world countries, but that in the United States, where "acceptable substitutes" for breast milk are available, HIV-positive mothers should *not* breastfeed.

This government position has put our health-care givers on the spot; you can't advise a mother to follow a course of action that the government recommends against. And the CDC stand has had the side effect of forcing all human milk banks to pasteurize their donated milk, which action destroys many of the anti-infectious components that newborns, and especially preterm babies, need so much. This measure has been necessary to protect milk-bank insurers from possible litigation.

BREAST MILK AND INFANT HEALTH: A SUMMARY

The protections offered by breast milk are valuable to any child. They are of course particularly vital in poverty-stricken or underdeveloped areas, where rampant disease as well as inadequate supplies and circumstances for artificial feeding mean that a baby taken off the breast may very well die. Increasing awareness of this circumstance, however, has lead to two popular misconceptions in the United States—especially, oddly enough, in the medical community. The first is that the *main* value of breastfeeding in third-world countries is that it protects the baby against contaminated bottles. That premise leads to the second misconception, that breastfeeding is not important in disease protection in developed countries, because we have sanitary alternative foods. A well-known report by Yale University researchers even purported to prove, as recently as 1986, that breastfeeding didn't make a significant health difference to U.S. babies. (That conclusion was made possible, in part, by failure to differentiate between briefly and fully breastfed babies; see chapter 8, p. 200.)

In fact, while a healthy American baby is certainly not likely to die if switched to artificial foods, the multitude of protective elements in its mother's milk will no longer be available; in our crowded urban world, where a baby has many chances to be exposed to new pathogens, that may make quite a difference.

At Mary Imogene Bassett Hospital in upstate New York, researcher Allan Cunningham, M.D., noticed in his own pediatric practice that breastfed babies seemed to be healthier. Some people said, however, that since it was the well-educated and well-off mothers who tended to breastfeed, those babies could be expected to be healthier anyway. Cunningham decided to study the healthy, normal babies born in the hospital in a two-year period, 1974 and 1975, to see if there were any other significant factors.

He limited the study to the 503 babies who had made regular "well-baby" clinic visits during their first year of life, and so were seen regularly by the same pediatricians. He divided them into three groups: breastfed babies, whom he defined as babies at least partially breastfed for longer than four and one-half months (there were 135 of these); limited breastfed babies, meaning that lactation was maintained for at least six weeks (80 babies); and artificially fed babies, which included babies who might have been breastfed in the hospital but were weaned shortly thereafter (288). Then he tabulated in all the babies the incidence of common illnesses requiring a doctor's care, such as chest colds, ear infections, vomiting, and diarrhea.

The results were published in the *Journal of Pediatrics.* During the first four months, when all of the "breastfed" cohort were still on the breast, the artificially fed babies were four times as likely to be sick, and during the first two months, sixteen times as likely. In the course of the first year, even though some of the breastfed babies were receiving mixed feedings, and nearly two-thirds of them had been weaned by six months, the wholly artificially fed babies still had twice as many of these common illnesses.

Perhaps the breastfed babies were simply doing better because their families were better off. Choosing education as an indicator, Cunningham took a look only at families in which the fathers had had at least three years of college. Of the breastfed group of babies in those families, the rate of illness worked out to 62 illnesses per 100 children, compared to 91 per 100 for the limited breastfed babies and 126 per 100 for the artificially fed babies (that is, some babies had more than one illness). How about families with smokers in them? How about families with babies in day care? Same kinds of numbers: In each of those circumstances, the babies breastfed for at least four and one-half months had fewer illnesses than babies breastfed for six weeks, and about half as many as babies raised on artificial milk.

As for the seriousness of the illnesses, babies on artificial diets were *fifteen* times more likely to wind up back in Mary Imogene Bassett Hospital than were the babies still receiving some breast milk. Over the whole year, only six of the babies who had been breastfed for at least six weeks were hospitalized for various infections, compared to 60 of the artificially fed babies (33 for common illnesses, 14 with bronchitis or pneumonia, and the rest with major ailments ranging from meningitis to allergy attacks; there was also one crib death in this group). In general, Cunningham's figures suggest that breastfeeding protects babies strikingly against serious illnesses, and somewhat against all illnesses, and that the protection increases in proportion to the extent and duration of breastfeeding.

The author points out that his study is still too small, statistically, to provide more than a "crude" indication of the protective aspects of breastfeeding. Large-scale studies, collecting data from birth on, rather than retrospectively, properly corrected for outside factors, and focused on long-duration, fully breastfed babies, remain to be done. Still, as Dr. Cunningham remarked to an audience of health professionals, "Breastfeeding is no panacea. It will not prevent all illnesses. But you are far less likely to see a breastfed baby than an artificially fed baby in the hospital or on the autopsy table. That is true in New Delhi and Nairobi, and it's true in Scarsdale and in Valley Forge."

A baby's illness, whether major or not, disrupts its parents' life, causes anxiety and wakeful nights, and most of all is no fun for the baby. What parents wouldn't prefer their child to have a short case of sniffles instead of a full-blown cold, a low fever rather than a high one, diarrhea once in a year instead of five or ten times? Parents of nursing babies can be sure that the protection the baby is getting from his mother's milk is making their life a little easier, too.

CONCLUSION

The human baby is remarkably adaptable. Most babies do well on almost any kind of diet that is anywhere near adequate; islanders in the South Pacific have raised orphaned newborn babies on a diet of ripe banana, green coconut, and water. However, while most babies survive on synthetic milks, there are many who, without being actually allergic, are never entirely suited to artificial feeding. The gradient of intolerance probably runs all the way from what is accepted as "normal" crankiness to the obvious cases of convulsions and the progressive emaciation called marasmus. There is the baby with rashes, and the baby with gas; the baby who vomits sour milk all over the house, and the baby who cries inconsolably by the hour. There is the baby who screams as he evacuates his bowels. There is the "colicky" baby. There is the baby who perpetually has a runny stool and diaper rash. Some people argue that these imperfect adjustments to an imperfect diet are not in themselves harmful—although the long-term evidence of the bottle-fed child's eventual susceptibility to colitis and other adult diseases suggests otherwise. In any case, these babies do gain weight and grow. In most cases their maladjustments are eventually outgrown. But while the problems are occurring, they may be distinctly unpleasant for the parents, and they are undoubtedly unpleasant for the baby.

There are a few babies, even today, who can tolerate only human milk. These babies, if put on synthetic milk, do badly from birth, and eventually are back in the hospital receiving fluids intravenously while one brand after another is tried in the hope of finding something the baby will tolerate. Sometimes the missing factor or the intolerable ingredient can be pinpointed. The baby cannot use cows' milk proteins, so a soybean-based milk is substituted; or it is the sugar, or the fat, that the baby cannot adjust to. Sometimes the fact that a particular baby is more sensitive than the average does not appear at first, because he is breastfed; he thrives until a routine supplement is introduced, or until he is prematurely weaned, at three or four months perhaps, when mother and doctor have serious difficulty in finding a synthetic milk that the baby can take without ill effects. All such babies, however, can tolerate human milk, and in some cases when no synthetic milk can be found that seems to fill the bill for a particular infant, the baby's life is saved only when a source of human milk is located.

As far as infant nutrition goes, we can say with complete

certainty that human milk is the only completely adequate food for human infants in the first six months, and forms a splendid addition to the diet thereafter. Even in undernourished mothers, breast milk has all the needed nutrients. Unless lactation is inhibited so that the baby does not get enough milk, he will thrive. Such individual variations as occur are easily adapted to by the baby, and the marvelous flexibility of lactation almost always insures a good and abundant supply of milk, whatever the vicissitudes of the mother's physical environment. There are still many questions to be answered about human milk. The one question that we can answer assuredly now is whether the best food for a human baby is its mother's milk: It is.

CHAPTER 4

How the Baby Functions: The Body

THE BABY'S EQUIPMENT FOR BREASTFEEDING

The newborn baby arrives in the world specially equipped for feeding at the breast. His nose is short, and tilts upward at the tip because the nostril openings are wider than in an adult. His cheeks are plumped up with two firm pads of fat that keep them from collapsing inward as he suckles. The combination of the baby's little nose and the fat pads in the cheeks form two channels on either side of the nose, quite obvious when you look for them; these channels deliver air right into the nostrils even if the baby's nose is close to the mother's breast. (In addition, if the baby's nose *isn't* very close to the breast or touching it, the nipple is likely to be in the front of the baby's mouth, rather than the back, which causes nipple soreness.)

The inside of the newborn baby's mouth is likewise designed for breastfeeding. The palate is shaped like a smooth dome, to make room for the nipple in the back of the mouth during nursing. The tongue protrudes if touched, which facilitates latching on to the breast. The protruding tongue response, however, makes it almost impossible to spoon solids into the newborn, as the tongue reflex just thrusts them out again. (This reflex probably also protects the infant against choking on objects or substances that enter the mouth accidentally.) Finally, in breastfed newborns a "sucking blister" usually forms in the center of the upper lip, and may persist for weeks. This blister is not an injury but an adaptation to the activity of nursing.

LATCHING ON

In order to breastfeed, the baby must first "latch on" to the breast. "Latching on" is the term for taking a grasp on the areola behind the nipple, with the nipple well back in the mouth, and with lips and tongue forming a seal to prevent swallowing air. In this position, the baby can milk the breast effectively.

To latch on well, the baby needs to be facing the breast directly, with the mouth wide open. Kittie Frantz, R.N., a pediatric nurse practitioner and an authority on positioning and breastfeeding, advises mothers to turn the baby on its side so that the mouth is level with the nipple; the baby's face, chest, stomach, genitals, and knees are all facing the mother's body, with the area from the chest to the knees flat against her. This brings the baby into the contact he was designed to maintain; and whether one is sitting up, lying down, or even walking around, the baby can be drawn close with the "baby-holding" arm by keeping one's hand on the baby's rump or the upper thigh.

SUCKLING BEHAVIOR

The mechanism by which a baby milks the breast is remarkably powerful; if you want to be impressed by a new baby's strength, just put a clean finger, pad upward, into the baby's mouth, against the roof of the mouth; you'll feel that mechanism go to work (it is an informative experience for new fathers). Suction, per se, is not, however, the main action. The baby may use the tongue and some suction to draw the nipple back into the mouth; then a combination of systems takes over. At the breast, the baby's mouth opens very wide, as wide as possible. The lips are everted, or turned outward, against the breast, forming a seal all around the areola; thus the baby can nurse without swallowing air

The baby compresses the areola horizontally between the upper and lower jaws, forming that whole part of the breast into a teat. The tongue comes out over the gum of the lower jaw, completing the air seal and incidentally padding the lower gum ridge, which protects the mother's areola and nipple. As the milk begins to flow, the lower jaw moves up and down, compressing the milk sinuses, or widened ducts, which are behind the nipple, under the areola (the milk sinuses are about the same distance from the nipple in all women no matter what the size of the areola). The tongue, meanwhile, in a wavelike motion from front to back, gently reaches forward, massages the ducts, and moves the milk out through the nipple and down the baby's throat. This tongue action also forms the areola and nipple into a teat shape, which puts the nipple deep into the baby's mouth, out of harm's way (see illustration on next page).

THE SUCKLING PATTERN

When the milk lets down, every suck is accompanied by a swallow and a breath; one can hear this: "suck-hah, suck-hah, suck-hah." Episodes of letting-down and rhythmic swallowing may occur several times during a single feeding, often without the mother even being aware of the ebb and flow of her milk. The baby typically nurses in a burst of four to ten or so suckling movements, followed by a short rest, and then another burst of suckling.

From time to time during feedings the baby may engage in bouts of what is called "nonnutritive" sucking, in which the jaw moves rapidly, almost in a quiver, and no swallowing occurs. Nonnutritive sucking is most likely to occur before the milk has let down, toward the end of the feeding, and when the baby is resting. Providers of standard medical care sometimes regard this as unimportant or even undesirable behavior, a sign that the baby is "not interested in the breast," or "just fooling around," or has "finished feeding." In fact, nonnutritive sucking is a normal component of breastfeeding and has several important functions: it stimulates the breast into letting down; it rests some of the baby's

The breastfeeding baby nurses with wide-open jaws, lower lip flanged outward, and the breast tissue drawn well back in the mouth. The nipple is in the arch of the palate, out of harm's way. The tongue and gum ridges compress the milk sinuses.

facial muscles while strengthening others; and it seems to soothe the baby without causing drowsiness. Most of the feeding is swallowing behavior, however; babies who swallow initially for a few minutes and then spend long periods —twenty, thirty, forty minutes—in nonnutritive sucking can tire themselves and make the breast sore. Changing to the other side and then back again may help.

BREAST VS. BOTTLE: EVENTS DURING FEEDING

One widespread misconception about breastfeeding is that it is somehow more difficult for the infant than bottle-feeding; that the baby has to "work" to nurse. For example, the conventional wisdom and standard medical care in neonatal intensive care facilities is that preterm babies, once they are able to suck and swallow—and thus no longer need to be fed by stomach tube—should be given the bottle until they have mastered that, because the bottle is "easier" than the breast. Additional justifications for starting the baby on the bottle are that taking babies from the incubator will chill them—the bottle can be given in the incubator, but the breast cannot; and that breastfeeding takes a long time, so the babies will get tired.

Paula Meier, D.N.Sc., professor of perinatal nursing at the University of Illinois College of Nursing, found sound scientific evidence to contradict all of these tradition-hallowed assumptions. While she was still a graduate student, Dr. Meier watched mothers breastfeeding tiny preterm babies in the neonatal intensive care unit and realized that these mothers and babies appeared to be disproving the conventional wisdom. One baby who had been fed his maximum estimated capacity of two ounces of milk, by stomach tube, at every meal, took five ounces the first time he was put on the breast. Other babies were coordinating sucking and swallowing on the breast before reaching the gestational age when they were "supposed" to be able to do that, and often long before they could cope with the bottle effectively.

Meier set out to discover whether babies really get chilled while breastfeeding. It was a straightforward task, since accurate instruments exist for measuring a baby's temperature externally. Meanwhile, Meier also used an external sensor, laid harmlessly on the baby's skin, to monitor the percentage of oxygen in the baby's bloodstream. This would provide a clear indication of how hard the baby might or might not be "working." Because Meier and her co-workers took measurements from the same babies, over and over, as they went back and forth between breast and bottle feeds, each baby acted as his or her own research "control," or opposite number.

On the question of chilling, the researchers found that preterm babies actually got warmer while they were out of the incubator and breastfeeding. Additional research has suggested some of the reasons. First, no matter how adroitly one warms the bottle, its contents will cool throughout the feeding; the baby is receiving cool liquid right into the middle of the body, which must then be warmed to blood heat by the baby itself, a costly expenditure of calories. Breast milk, on the other hand, stays at the baby's core temperature from start to finish. Second, we all tend to heat up a little while taking in nourishment; Dr. Meier's tiny subjects heated up more, on the breast, than those same babies did on the bottle. Finally, measurements of mother's skin temperatures showed that the breast the baby is nursing from actually heats up during the feeding. When mother and baby are in skin contact, the mother's body is actively warming the baby. This mechanism is interactive: if the baby's skin temperature is cooler than the mother's, the breast will heat; if the baby feels hot, the breast will cool. Nursing mothers constitute a reciprocal system for stabilizing the body heat of babies.

The standard assumption that babies are too weak to breastfeed until they reach 1500 grams (about 3½ pounds) also came in for scrutiny. In Meier's studies, which began with babies of about 1300 grams (or 3 pounds), oxygen levels in babies actively nursing on the breast remained at the same levels the babies showed when at rest. On the bottle, measurements of oxygen pressure fell: the babies were, in effect, getting out of breath. The differences were most dramatic for the very smallest babies; they burned up a lot of oxygen while bottle-feeding, but breastfeeding didn't cost them any extra effort.

Subsequent studies have unraveled some of the contributing factors. On the breast, sucking, swallowing, and breathing can be coordinated. Babies typically suck, swallow, and breathe four to ten times in a row, followed by a brief rest. On the bottle, because the milk flows continuously, resting, and even breathing itself, become problems. In fact, newborns, whether premature or not, tend to have episodes of apnea or breath-holding on the bottle. Holding the breath certainly contributes to the reduction in oxygen.

Mathew and Bhatia, at the University of Texas, have shown that normal, full-term babies, not just preterm babies, exhibit apnea while bottle-feeding. Worse, roughly one in five full-term newborns develops brachycardia on the bottle. Brachycardia, also called the diving reflex, is a physiological response to oxygen deprivation in which the heartbeat slows markedly, and blood is shunted away from the limbs and digestive organs toward the lungs and brain. It is a useful, oxygen-conserving response for seals and otters, no doubt, and perhaps for scuba divers, but hardly desirable, one would think, in a newborn human. In the University of Texas studies, brachycardia never occurred in the newborns while breastfeeding.

Length of feeding has also traditionally been considered a cause of fatigue in the newborn. Breastfeeding typically takes longer than bottle-feeding; does this mean it is more stressful? Meier's studies, and others, again indicate the opposite. In the comparatively short ten- or fifteen-minute bottle-feeding, the newborn receives a whole meal more or less at once. At the breast, on the other hand, a newborn may take thirty or forty minutes or more to ingest the same amount of nourishment. A feeding at the breast proceeds at the baby's pace, and may start and stop repeatedly, giving the baby a chance to rest. Preterm babies, especially, engage in lots of nonnutritive behavior at the breast, such as looking at the breast, pausing, nonnutritive sucking, and resting (the baby may actually open her eyes more when resting; while nursing, the eyes are usually shut tight in concentration). The baby signals clearly when the feeding is actually over, usually by pulling away; but the whole feeding may last fifty minutes—far longer than a bottle-feeding takes (and much longer than a busy nursery staffer would have time for). And yet, levels of oxygen in the blood show that even small, preterm babies are less fatigued on the breast than they are by more rapid tube- or bottle-feedings.

Furthermore, research shows that, at any age, rapid filling of the stomach, as occurs in bottle-feeding, is in itself physiologically stressful. Digestive processes may even shut down temporarily—if your grandmother scolded you, "Don't bolt your food, you'll get indigestion!" she was right. The pace set by the baby may allow the easily digested breast milk to begin passing into the intestines, so the stomach never overfills. When breastfeeding babies choose their own rate of filling, they experience no stress, even if they take a large amount of milk.

What is true for the tiny, preterm baby is also, of course, true for the full-term infant. Mother's milk comes at core temperature. The mother's body helps regulate the baby's temperature, winter or summer. Oxygen levels stay normal. The baby can use periods of nonnutritive behavior to rest, without relinquishing the breast. Breastfeeding is easier because babies can modify it for distress-free, organized feeding; they can't modify the behavior of the bottle.

CHANGES WITH AGE

By the time a baby is six months old, her physical adaptations for breastfeeding are beginning to be replaced by adaptations for eating solid foods. The sucking pads diminish, to be largely gone by the end of the first year Incoming teeth (rather than the gum ridge) form the "leading edge" of each jaw, although the gum ridge may persist below and in front of the lower teeth for a while. (The baby's incoming teeth do not interfere with nursing, nor do they constitute a hazard for the mother; during feedings, the tongue continues to cover the lower jaw so that the baby cannot bite and nurse at the same time.)

The action of the tongue and jaws also changes. The tongue no longer protrudes automatically, so the baby no longer shoves solid food out of her mouth in an effort to swallow it. As the baby's hands come under control enough so that she can pick up a cracker or a piece of meat, her eating equipment develops enough to make use of such items. Even though the baby loses her infantile breastfeeding specializations, she can of course continue to feed at the breast. By six months, she has considerable know-how; she does not need special equipment to nurse efficiently and comfortably. And as long as she nurses, the breasts can function, too.

BABIES WITH DIFFICULTIES: NEUROLOGICAL IMPAIRMENT

Some babies come into the world with an immature nervous system or other developmental problem that affects their ability to suckle. A baby may suckle weakly and tire easily, or the sucking response may be less vigorous than normal. Some babies may have difficulty coordinating sucking and swallowing, at first. Many techniques now exist for improving these motor patterns and in effect teaching the baby how to suck. Nursing supplementer devices (see p. 365) can be helpful. One can expect improvement as the central nervous system matures further, muscles get stronger, and the baby learns compensatory movements. Developing breastfeeding skills in a neurologically immature baby or one with a neurological deficit is of special benefit, as the organizing of the mouth movement patterns stimulates reorganization of the rest of the nervous system. These babies profit from patient, consistent assistance by the mother and from ongoing encouragement of the mother and her family by the health-care providers.

Some neurological deficits show up as behavioral difficulties. An example is the baby who persistently arches his back and rears away from the breast after latching on. This aggravating wrenching can be forestalled if the mother holds the child under one arm "football style" to nurse, and meanwhile sits in a chair with a firm back and puts the baby's rump against the chair, with his legs vertical and at right angles to his body (see illustration on p. 238); in this position he *can't* arch his back. He is also apt to become calm because, in this position, he feels his body supported, just as it was in the uterus.

Many babies with developmental deficits, including Down's syndrome, can breastfeed very well; these babies especially need the closeness and the physical benefits breastfeeding can give (see chapter 10, p. 276).

BREASTFEEDING THE BABY WITH A CLEFT PALATE

The baby born with a cleft lip or palate may or may not present special breastfeeding problems (see *You Can Breastfeed Your Baby,* by Dorothy Brewster). Unfortunately, most physicians who specialize in cleft lip problems have no experience with fully breastfed babies. Standard medical care dictates postponing repair surgery for weeks or months after birth, by which time, if the defect has caused problems in nursing, the mother may have long ago given up trying to breastfeed. After surgery, cup- or spoon-feeding is usually recommended for a month or more, until the repair has healed. To quote specialist R. C. A. Weatherly-White, M.D., of the Children's Hospital in Denver, in the plastic surgery textbooks, bottle-feeding is universally discouraged, and breastfeeding nowhere mentioned.

Dr. Weatherly-White's work, however, suggests that there are no disadvantages and many benefits to doing the repair surgery immediately, in the first week after birth, and then breastfeeding. He and his team undertook research to test the conventional prohibition against breastfeeding after they had made the initially disconcerting discovery that some of the mothers of babies who had been operated on in the first week of life had breastfed their postoperative babies without discussing it, and without problems. Their studies demonstrated that the baby with a cleft palate or lip may breastfeed immediately after surgery without endangering the sutures. A touching photograph in one research paper shows a nursing, postoperative newborn who is clearly in some pain but also clearly avid for the comfort of the breast. The Denver researchers found that the baby will recover faster on the breast, and cry less than it would otherwise— and crying does endanger the repair.

THE TONGUE-TIED BABY

A little recognized but by no means rare problem is the tongue-tied baby, born with a tongue that cannot be easily extruded from the mouth. All of us have a thin strip of tissue between the underside of the tongue and the floor of the mouth, called the frenulum. As a rule, the frenulum is attached about halfway back on the underside of the tongue. In some people, however, the frenulum is either very short or attached close to the tip of the tongue, holding the tip down. This tongue-tied condition makes it impossible for such a person to stick the tongue out, and may cause speech impediments. Since the tongue cannot protrude properly over the lower jaw, being tongue-tied also makes it hard for a baby to latch on to the breast and make a good seal.

A tongue-tied baby has trouble staying on the breast. He may have to clamp on ferociously, just to stay in place—making the baby tired and the mother's nipples sore. Tongue-tied babies tend to be noisy nursers, gasping and grunting, and sometimes messy, too, with milk leaking out of the mouth throughout the feeding. They also take a long time to get a meal down, and may either nurse extremely frequently, for long periods, or give up from fatigue before they're really full, and thus gain weight poorly.

Fifty or a hundred years ago, doctors and midwives routinely inspected babies' tongues at birth and clipped the frenulum with sterile scissors if it was too short, or situated too far forward, and thus apt to interfere with the baby's nursing. Now, since bottle-feeding is the norm, and being tongue-tied makes no difference to bottle-feeding, medical students are not taught to clip the frenulum. Indeed, it can be difficult to find a pediatrician who is even aware of the problem, and some medical care givers treat clipping the frenulum as if it were major surgery, requiring total anesthesia.

In fact, the procedure is easily done in the physician's office; it produces only a drop or two of blood and almost no pain, especially if the baby is nursed immediately afterward. Parents with a tongue-tied baby can sometimes locate a dentist or an oral surgeon familiar with the problem and willing to treat it. For the mother, the instant change from fierce to gentle nurser can be nothing short of amazing. For the baby, life becomes a lot easier, right away.

Tongue-tiedness is genetic; it runs in families. If you or your mate, as an adult, cannot protrude the tip of your tongue beyond your lips, it is something to watch for in your babies. A giveaway occurs when the baby tries to protrude her tongue; the tongue tip will dip into a vee in the middle, like the top of a valentine heart, instead of coming to a point. (You can sometimes get even a tiny baby to stick out her tongue by sticking out your own at her, since most new babies, when alert, will mimic this behavior.)

One nurse practitioner who accepts many referrals of tongue-tied babies was asked by the parents of one if she would mind also clipping the frenulum of their six-year-old son. When she did so, the boy cheered, stuck out his newly liberated tongue, and danced up and down—now he could eat an ice cream cone without being ridiculed by his friends. In another case, a tongue-tied father asked for the same treatment. At the instant freeing of his tongue, he also announced that he was heading for the nearest ice cream shop—and then he was going to go home, and for the first time, properly kiss his wife.

JAUNDICE

In many medical environments, one essentially normal event in newborns can create special problems for the breastfeeding family: jaundice. In the late 1960s, the pediatric community became very interested in the question of neonatal hyperbilirubinemia, or newborn jaundice. Most babies, breastfed or bottle-fed, become slightly jaundiced during the first week of life. Sometimes the skin and eye whites temporarily take on a yellowish, or jaundiced tinge. The jaundice usually appears on or around the third day and is gone within a week or so. The majority of these babies are perfectly healthy, are experiencing a normal physiological process, and need no medical therapy.

Unfortunately, misunderstandings of the nature of this process and its relationship to breastfeeding have led to customs of medical intervention that can be distressing to parents and babies, and that also can seriously compromise lactation. Parents can't tell in advance when they might run into pressure for overtreatment; to make sound decisions, it is wise to understand what goes on in the newborn, and why the fashion for intervention has arisen.

Red blood cells are constantly being created and reabsorbed in the body. As the red cells die and deteriorate, a waste product called bilirubin is formed. Until birth, the mother's body clears the fetal blood of most of the bilirubin via the placenta. After birth, bilirubin is excreted through the baby's liver into the intestines, and is evacuated along with the stool. Initially, the excretion is not complete; some bilirubin is reabsorbed from the intestines into the blood. There may, in fact, be some evolutionary advantage to this transitory reabsorption, as bilirubin has an antibacterial effect in the bloodstream.

At birth, the baby's bowel contains a black, sticky stool called meconium, which is loaded with bilirubin, giving it that blackish color. Normally, the laxative effects of colostrum start the intestinal tract moving in the right direction, and the meconium is eliminated. Although bilirubin continues to be excreted into the lower intestines, frequent feedings during the baby's first hours and days create more feces; the color of the feces changes to tan or yellow, indicating that the meconium is gone, and the frequent stooling continues to empty the intestines and to reduce the reabsorption of any bilirubin that might be there.

If the meconium is not eliminated, the bilirubin within it is reabsorbed by the bloodstream. This creates a temporary overload of bilirubin in the baby's system. Other contributing sources of bilirubin in the newborn include bruising during birth, which creates pockets of red blood cells that must be broken down by the liver; vacuum extraction, a birth intervention, is particularly culpable in creating this condition. Medications given to the mother during late pregnancy or labor may also contribute, by passing through the placenta and temporarily overloading the waste processing capabilities of the baby's liver.

Jaundice caused by this unexcreted bilirubin is called *physiologic* jaundice, meaning that it is a normal process, part of the baby's maturing. By way of comparison, if you felt very tired for no particular reason, you might be infected with a virus, or you might have anemia, causing pathological or unhealthy fatigue; something would definitely be wrong with you. If, however, you felt very tired *and* you had just run a ten-kilometer race, you would not be ill, you would be experiencing *physiologic* fatigue, a normal and transitory condition that will go away by itself.

In infants, the duration of this post-birth period of physiologic jaundice, and the peak levels of bilirubin in the bloodstream, depend on one thing only: how often the baby's bowels empty, which is in itself a result of how soon and how often the baby is fed. In a landmark study on the genesis of neonatal jaundice, researcher M. deCarvalho and his associates found that the bilirubin levels of breastfed babies could be cut in half, bringing them lower than the levels typical of bottle-fed babies, by feeding the babies every two hours instead of every four.

In hospitals, unfortunately, breastfed babies are apt to be more jaundiced than bottle-fed babies, not because of any flaw in breast milk, but because the hospital regimen interferes with breastfeeding. The mother and baby are not encouraged, and perhaps not even permitted, to nurse early enough and often enough, in the first three days, for the baby to make and pass sufficient stools. Since the visibly jaundiced babies in those hospitals are so apt to be the breastfed babies, some health-care givers refer to normal physiologic jaundice incorrectly as "breast milk jaundice." Babies who are, by nature, "sippers and tasters," and like to linger over feedings, are at a particular disadvantage.

Common jaundice associated with breastfeeding, really just hospital-aggravated physiologic jaundice, is visible by the third day after birth. There is a real, and relatively rare, genetic condition called breast milk jaundice, in which elements in the mother's milk produce a mild jaundice that appears later than the third day, peaks in the second or third week, and may last for weeks or months. It appears to be related to the fat content of the milk, and may not show up until the mature milk develops. It will usually occur in 70 percent of subsequent breastfed siblings. The researchers who identified this syndrome emphasized that it is "thoroughly benign," and no cause for weaning.

Real pathological jaundice, in any living organism, is a symptom of liver failure, and as such, is very serious indeed.

The resulting huge overload of bilirubin can damage any organ, including the brain. The most serious newborn pathological jaundice is caused by Rh or ABO blood incompatibility and is apparent at birth or soon after; other serious causes of jaundice include congenital conditions such as hypothyroidism. The bilirubin level in such cases is in general far higher than that of babies experiencing normal or benign jaundice.

The differences are important and should determine treatment options. More often than not, however, hospital staffs consider that jaundice is jaundice, and each case receives the same treatment regardless of the cause. One common treatment of the jaundiced newborn is to put the baby under special lights, the "bili lights," that contain some of the elements of sunshine. In the 1950s, an observant nurse noted that babies placed near the windows in the hospital nursery were less jaundiced than babies near the wall, a discovery that led to the present phototherapy. Of course, putting the baby under the lights usually means more separation from the mother, which is deleterious to breastfeeding; and babies can become dehydrated under the lights and thus be especially in need of frequent nursing.

The newborn breastfed baby should get at least twelve feedings in each twenty-four hours. Frequent feeding not only causes stooling but coats the infant's gut with milk fat, which protects against the reabsorption of bilirubin; to produce both stooling and gut coating, the frequency of the feedings is more important than the quantity ingested. In many hospitals, however, babies are still held to a biologically highly inappropriate four-hour schedule.

Furthermore, in some hospitals it is still customary to delay the first breastfeeding until twelve, twenty-four, or even forty-eight hours after birth; naturally the baby is going to have an elevated bilirubin level by the third day! Much of the published research about jaundice in breastfed babies was conducted in such hospitals. Lawrence Gartner, M.D., chairman of the department of pediatrics at the University of Chicago, is a leading researcher on neonatal jaundice; he points out that the babies in these studies were actually coping with problems caused not by breastfeeding, but by starvation.

Other hospital practices can contribute to elevated bilirubin levels, or hyperbilirubinemia. Sometimes water is given to breastfeeding babies in the nursery in the mistaken notion that it will "flush out" the jaundice. The mother may even be given a water bottle and told to give it to the baby. Water actually makes the situation worse, not better. Water may increase urination, but bilirubin is *not* eliminated via the kidneys; the water intake does not contribute to stooling and does not coat the gut. Water eliminates thirst and makes the baby feel full for a while; both reduce its nursing urge. The baby gets less milk, and the mother's breasts get less of the stimulation so vital to starting lactation. Researcher A. J. Nicolls, M.D., and others have shown in fact that water feeds in the hospital are directly correlated with *increases* in bilirubin levels. (Feeding water to nursing babies also contributes directly to problems of engorgement in mothers. A supervisory nurse who made this the topic of her master's thesis said that, in her opinion, "Any nurse caught giving water to a breastfeeding baby ought to be put on report.")

What constitutes a "safe" bilirubin level? The age of the baby is a factor. In very small preterm babies, bilirubin levels that would be acceptable in a more mature baby may be a justified worry. Babies differ genetically, too, in what is "normal." Caucasian and black babies, breastfed *or* bottlefed, tend to have bilirubin levels that peak on the third day, at perhaps 5 to 8 milligrams per deciliter of blood, gradually subsiding to the adult norm of about 1 milligram per deciliter by the fourteenth day. Children of Asian ancestry, on the other hand (including Native Americans and South American Indians), tend to have bilirubin levels that peak later (on the fifth day or so), peak higher (at 10 to 12 in at least 30 percent), and last longer than in black or Caucasian babies. A nurse or physician who doesn't understand this can panic at a bilirubin count that for this particular genetic group is standard.

The number that in a newborn is considered a "safe" level

of bilirubin also varies widely from hospital to hospital and doctor to doctor. When and whether a physician calls for the "bili lights" may depend on how recently he graduated from medical school. The older medical literature cautions concern when levels reach 10, 12, or 15 milligrams per deciliter; newer studies suggest 20 to 25 as the level indicating a need for intervention (see Maisels and Gifford, 1983). Some doctors have "pet" numbers; some, fearing malpractice suits, intervene in every possible case. Very few, at present, consider that disrupting lactation is the most severe intervention of all.

In fact, a very common treatment for jaundice is to tell the mother to stop breastfeeding for twenty-four or forty-eight hours, and to give the baby synthetic feeds during that time. Blood tests will usually show that the baby's bilirubin level falls as a result (which proves nothing except that breastfeeding was not yet well established). Of course, the effect on the mother and on her lactation can be devastating; one cannot just "stop nursing" for twenty-four hours, especially in the first days or weeks of lactation, and yet doctors make this request, to verify the diagnosis, as if they were asking the mother to stop driving, or avoid caffeine, or engage in some other minor inconvenience. As Jay Gordon, M.D., La Leche League medical board member, points out, a rise in bilirubin indicates a family with breastfeeding problems. The most important treatment is to help that mother and baby get the nursing going smoothly.

Some physicians defend the routine use of phototherapy on the grounds that it does the infant no harm. That is not entirely true. A study by Kathi Kemper, M.D., and others, at Yale-New Haven Hospital, found that after phototherapy for bilirubin not only were mothers twice as likely to stop breastfeeding, but also many drew the conclusion that the baby was extremely ill. This set the family up for what has been called the "vulnerable child" syndrome, a pattern of extremely anxious parenting—many doctor's visits, for example, and an unwillingness to let the child out of sight. This may continue for years, to the child's detriment.

Caught by this medical dilemma, what do mothers do?

Sometimes the "bili lights" can be brought to the mother's hospital room; having the baby near, despite the time he must spend under the lights, may make them both feel better. New lights have been designed for use in a special blanket that can be wrapped around the baby's torso so that she can nurse while being treated. Although not widespread, home phototherapy is allowed by some hospitals and covered by most insurance plans. Mothers who are forced to stop breastfeeding for a day or two need to pump their milk, and should be taught how, lent the equipment, and given the emotional support they will need. Kathleen Auerbach, Ph.D., while assistant professor of pediatrics at the University of Chicago Medical School, used a much simpler intervention in that university's large teaching hospital. When a baby was reported as jaundiced, Dr. Auerbach visited the mother during breastfeeding, and provided the baby with a little additional synthetic milk through a nursing supplementer tube slipped into his mouth while he was on the breast. Often this needed to be done only two or three times. The mother felt encouraged about breastfeeding, the baby was reinforced for suckling, and the mother's own milk supply soon increased. Meanwhile, the supplement usually improved the rate of stooling, which brought the bilirubin down; that, Dr. Auerbach points out, had the principal effect of reassuring the medical staff, thus forestalling less amiable intervention.

DIFFERENCES BETWEEN BREASTFED AND BOTTLE-FED BABIES

Lactation researchers such as Niles Newton, Ph.D., have pointed out that there are many obvious differences between the healthy breastfed baby and the healthy bottle-fed baby; one can learn to tell them apart at a glance (childbirth authority Doris Haire maintains she can tell the difference even when they're on television). The bottle-fed baby is apt to be pallid and plump, with soft muscles. The breastfed baby has a glowing skin, even in winter, and good muscle tone; her body feels resilient when you pick her up. Some of these differences are no doubt due to general health; the breastfed baby is less likely to be coming down with or recovering from some germ, and less likely to be washed-out-looking because of allergies and stomach upsets. But there are some fundamental physical differences, too.

For example, breastfed and bottle-fed babies smell different. An artificially fed baby may smell sour, like curdled formula; her diapers smell of urine and feces, and if she has spit up, her clothes will smell of sour milk or vomit. Breastfed babies smell positively sweet; it's not that they have no odor, they have a distinct and delightful odor (crudely imitated in scented talcum powder) that makes people want to cuddle them. Even the soiled diapers of breastfed babies have no unpleasant smell, and their spit-up milk smells like yoghurt.

Breastfed babies grow and gain weight differently from babies on artificial food. The breastfed babies often gain faster in the first three months and more slowly thereafter. Some babies in fact gain very fast on the breast and then slow down and grow into their weight; one nurse practitioner reports on a favorite (fully breastfed) patient, "Daniel the Porkchop," who weighed eight pounds at birth and twenty pounds at three months, but then eased up this galloping gain to grow taller and to reach a comfortable twenty-five pounds at one year. Often by the end of the first year, breastfed babies weigh less than bottle-fed babies, on the average; but typically the breastfed baby then follows a slow but steady growth curve that extends further into childhood. The bottle-fed baby is often actually overweight, since she may take in more calories than she needs in an effort to get adequate nutrition.

Breastfed babies are also more active than bottle-fed babies. They tend to sit, creep, and stand a little earlier, and they are livelier from the start. In one study, breastfed babies tested on the third or fourth day of life showed stronger arousal reactions than bottle-fed babies. Another test found more physical activity in general by the sixth day of life. Several studies have shown that on the whole breastfed babies sleep less than synthetically fed babies. From the first months, the length of maximum bouts of sleep tends to be shorter (since the baby must and should waken after four or five hours to be fed). From seven months on, the total number of hours that the baby spends asleep, per twenty-four-hour period, dwindles. In one study in which mothers kept daily diaries, bottlefed babies were sleeping fourteen hours out of twenty-four at thirteen months, and breastfed babies were sleeping only eleven.

This might sound like a disadvantage to the parents who want a little peace from a fussy baby and are glad when she goes down for a three-hour nap. But extra waking hours are valuable to the baby, giving her that much more time in the day to learn, to stretch muscles and mind, to socialize, to grow mentally as well as physically. Physicians who are more accustomed to phlegmatic and obese bottle-fed babies may find this normal picture deplorable; one doctor writing in the medical literature of the 1940s disdainfully compared the typical breastfed baby—friendly, lively, comparatively lean—to an orphan puppy, wiggling and ingratiating itself with everyone because it is looking for food.

The exception to the normal picture of the healthy breastfed baby is the baby who is not getting enough milk. In the United States, that is almost without exception due to mismanagement of lactation. The hungry baby is pale, and lacks the snap and cheeriness of the satisfied nursling. He may be fretful and cry often, or he may be lethargic, sleeping for longer and longer periods. His stool is scanty. Such a baby shows the need for investigation into breastfeeding problems that are leading to the insufficiency. In almost all cases, this kind of problem can be resolved without stopping breastfeeding.

GROWTH RATES

Officially, in most countries, the standard infant growth charts are based on the Caucasian, middle-class, synthetically fed baby, and they present an incorrect picture for breastfed babies and babies of other racial extraction. In Great Britain in 1986, R.G. Whitehead, Ph.D., and associates studied the growth and measurements of a wide number of long- and short-term breastfed infants, and concluded that "babies grow differently from the Child Health Service and Tanner Reference Curves, now that feeding practices have changed."

The fact remains, however, that overall, breastfed babies do not grow as fast or get as large throughout the first two years as bottle-fed babies do. They seem to catch up later; the height one ultimately reaches turns out to be dependent on one's genes, to some extent, but also on one's diet during the years after weaning. People grow taller if the available food supply is constant and abundant. For example, between 1920 and 1960 children of the second and third generations born to Japanese immigrants in Hawaii almost always grew much taller than their Japan-born parents and grandparents.

Still, during the nursing years, breastfed children are on the whole smaller than their bottle-fed counterparts. It seems to be nature's intention. Why? Researcher Margaret Neville, Ph.D., at the University of Colorado, asked a vital question: Is it indeed the mother's milk production that limits the breastfed baby's growth during the first year or is some other factor operating?

What Neville and her associates found, in an ingenious series of tests, is that breastfeeding mothers can almost always make more milk than their babies need (as we know). What limits the baby's growth is its own demand—its appetite. When one is giving a baby a bottle, there is always a temptation to get the baby to "finish the bottle" by jiggling the bottle until the last ounce or half ounce goes down. But on the breast, no one sees how much went in, and only the baby can tell exactly how much she wants; when she's satisfied, she takes no more. The breastfed baby thus takes the optimum amount of milk, not the maximum possible.

Dr. Neville says, "A little bit of frank speculation suggests that this adaptive mechanism would operate most efficiently in times of nutritional deprivation." In other words, in a primitive society the breastfed baby, making no more than moderate demands, survives well and also allows its mother to survive, even during times of scarcity. Contrary to our widespread assumption that bigger is better, evolution has perhaps developed human babies for whom "enough is as good as a feast." Our babies come into the world, it seems, as ecologically sound consumers.

CHAPTER 5

How the Baby Functions: Behavior

INNATE BEHAVIOR IN BABIES

Many of us were once taught that human beings, unlike animals, are not governed by instinct, but learn most of our traits and behavior through external events—as if we came into the world like blank chalkboards, waiting to be written on. The more dogmatic behaviorists even maintained that the only "instinct" in human babies was fear of falling. Babies certainly don't care for falling, and respond to any sense of imbalance by throwing out the arms and legs—the Moro reflex—and usually by yelling. We now know, however, that babies come into the world provided not only with suitable physical equipment but also with a wonderful assortment of innate, or inborn, behavioral skills, including a surprising amount of built-in social behavior, to help them survive and thrive in their new world.

There are several varieties of innate behavior. Simple motor patterns triggered by external stimuli—coughing and sneezing, for example—are called reflexes. The grasp of an infant's hand, which will close automatically on anything that touches the palm, is a reflex. A more complex level of innate behavior consists of motor patterns produced in response to internal or external stimuli. Facial expressions and some vocalizations, for example, are expressed automatically in response to feelings, and in turn are recognized as social signals by others. And much innate behavior

427

consists of combinations of reflexes and motor patterns into which a mix of learned behavior is quickly interwoven.

Some innate behavior shows up at birth; other innate patterns, such as those related to sexual activity, surface when they are needed, later in life. An example is the following response. Once the baby has learned to walk well, he is programmed to follow anyone moving suddenly away from him. If you move quickly away from a creeping baby, he will quietly watch you go. Move quickly away from the same child, now a runabout two-year-old, and he will make haste to follow you, and, if he cannot keep up, will burst into roars of protest. You need not be a parent to elicit this automatic response; one can sometimes see a toddler, frustrated by the sight of older children running past him in play, screaming furiously until someone picks him up. The utility of this inborn response is obvious. The toddler, old enough to stray but not old enough to keep up with adults on foot, is thus protected from being overlooked and abandoned if his elders suddenly decide to go somewhere else.

Biologists have found that behavior crucial to survival, such as reproductive behavior, is particularly likely to be innate. In mammals, that includes suckling. A newborn colt, for example (or any baby hooved animal) is programmed to get to its feet as soon after birth as possible. Innate mechanisms then dictate that it will move toward the nearest large object and make shoving motions with its nose. The nearest large object is likely to be its mother. Shoving along the mother's flank, the baby will shortly be blocked by a leg; if that is a front leg, the mother eventually will respond to the shoving by moving, and the baby will have to start over; if it is a hind leg, the shoving will bring the baby's lips in contact with the udder. Presto! Breakfast. It doesn't take long for the colt to *learn* to go straight to the udder, and to the right mother, as well. But the first motions that get it on the path to survival are dictated by its genes just as surely as are the color of its coat and the number of ears and legs it comes with.

Primate babies have a number of innate actions to help them to find food. When a baby chimpanzee is born, it immediately grasps whatever it can with its hand, and starts to crawl. Since it usually grasps the hair on its mother's abdomen, its crawl takes it up her body, with or without her help, to her breasts. A newborn human baby shares with other primates the habit of clenching his fists, especially when hungry, and of shoving his feet in a "neonate crawl." Like the baby chimp, he grasps tightly in his fists any part of his mother's clothes or anatomy he may come in contact with. This further insures that he will not lose contact with the breast. (Many a newborn baby seems to nurse more steadily and happily if he is holding something—his mother's finger, perhaps—in his fist.)

INNATE RESPONSES IN BREASTFEEDING

To locate the right place to suckle, the human baby, like other young mammals, has a "grope" reflex. In the newborn human, it consists of turning her head and "reaching" with her mouth in the direction of any touch on her cheek. When the mother picks her up, her head is apt to fall into the crook of her mother's arm, bringing the breast near her cheek. When the nipple touches her cheek, she swivels her head toward the touch. If the whole breast bumps her cheek, providing generalized stimulation, she may shake her head back and forth very fast as if to home in on the stimulus.

Once the baby has homed in on the breast, another reflex comes into play: a touch on the center of the lower lip makes the baby gape the jaw. Thus, even an accidental touch of the nipple in the center of the lip, as the baby gropes for the breast, produces exactly the right wide-open mouth for optimal latching on. The mother helping her newborn get started at the breast can lift her breast with her free hand and move the nipple to trigger the opening of the mouth on purpose.

Some lactation specialists teach new mothers to touch the nipple to the baby's lower lip so the baby opens wide, and then to quickly pull the baby in close, plopping that wide-open mouth right onto the breast; this helps forestall the baby's learning to latch on to the breast with mouth half open, or to grasp the nipple first and then "walk up" the breast into a proper wide-open position, both of which increase the chance of nipple soreness.

In our culture, women don't always have a chance to see other mothers nursing, and thus to learn from observation how to hold a baby in the best nursing position. An inexperienced mother may let the baby lie horizontally in her arms, as we do when we bottle-feed a baby; that is the position she has seen, after all. At the breast, though, a baby lying flat on its back has to turn its head to nurse; the result is a baby valiantly trying to nurse while looking over its shoulder, and inevitably tugging on the nipple itself, causing abrasion (see illustrations on p. 235). Or the mother may hold the baby too low, so that its head is tilted back, instead of facing the breast squarely. This is a highly awkward position in which to swallow—try it yourself—and again puts uneven and abrasive pressure on the areola and nipple. Medical care givers sometimes fail to recognize when a poor nursing position is causing problems, and some breast-feeding instruction pamphlets handed out in hospitals show very inappropriate positions in the illustrations.

Misunderstanding of the grope reflex can also lead to difficulties in the hospital, especially if the nursery staff is not trained in breastfeeding management. Some nurses still try to force the baby's mouth open by pinching both cheeks; that does give one a chance to shove in a bottle, but on the breast, which the baby must grasp for itself, a sensitive baby will become frantic trying to respond both ways at once. Or the nurse might try to put a baby to the mother's breast by pushing his face toward the nipple; the baby gropes away from the breast, in the direction of the pushing fingers, and the nurse writes on the chart, "Baby refuses breast"!

THRESHOLDS

The strength of responses such as groping and latching on, and the ease with which they are produced, can vary. A hungry baby will respond to a touch on the cheek or mouth far more vigorously than a full one; psychologists say that his "threshold" to the stimulus of touch has been lowered. A really hungry and vigorous baby may suck anything that touches his lips, such as his father's arm. There are also individual differences in the strength of the suckling responses, which are subject to the same variations as are all the other hereditary features of living creatures. One baby never gropes or gapes very strongly, and the mother has to teach him to latch on. Another baby turns toward the slightest touch, from birth, and has problems with his bedclothes touching him on the cheek.

An accidental, unnoticed light touch on the cheek may continue to induce a groping response in such a child for years. One "Candid Camera" television program showed a pretty woman "accidentally" annoying a man sitting next to her by letting the long feathers on her hat brush his face. The man was trying to be polite, to ignore the tickling feathers, and make conversation; but every time a feather brushed his cheek, he unconsciously opened his mouth and turned his head toward the touch. It was the grope reflex, still operative in the grown man.

External circumstances can also alter a baby's response threshold temporarily. Babies, for example, whose mothers have been drugged during labor may be drowsy for many hours after birth; it can be next to impossible to trigger suckling responses until the medications have been excreted. A baby who has been allowed to wake and cry until she is really ravenous may have such a low threshold that she can't settle down and latch on. These babies do better if nursed at the first peep of wakefulness, or at early signs of hunger such as rooting around and thrusting the tongue out, before prolonged crying disorganizes the baby completely.

LEARNING IN THE NEWBORN

Babies arrive with a little advance information; they have done some learning in the womb. For example, researchers have shown that newborns can identify and recognize their own mother's—and sometimes father's—voices, from birth. They have learned, already, something about the cadences of their own language; newborns whose mothers read a particular story aloud, repeatedly, before birth, have been shown to recognize the familiar tale after birth, even if read by another voice. Babies in the uterus have also gotten used to other noises in their environment. Pregnant women who live near airports are apt to give birth to babies who are not wakened by jet planes.

A lot of what newborn babies do is, indeed, innate and spontaneously manifested, without any learning being necessary. Crying, startling, yawning, and squinting at bright lights are all responses that are programmed into the genes, or, in scientists' slang, are "hard-wired." A lot more behavior in human babies is partly innate and partly learned, and is capable of being modified or "soft-wired." The suckling pattern is a good example. Some elements of it are innate— groping, moving the tongue appropriately, and swallowing. Others—how wide to open the mouth, how the lips behave —must be learned, and for good reason. Mothers and breasts come in many sizes and shapes, and babies must be flexible enough to adapt their nursing behavior to their own mother's body. For the breastfed baby, this very first experience of life involves learning and discovering. This kind of active learning—finding out how to attain your own goals by your own efforts, how to make the world work for you, instead of just passively enduring events—is the beginning of a baby's cognitive development. The happily breastfed baby starts life with a huge experience of his own capacity for attaining life's joys.

NIPPLE CONFUSION

Some babies, especially the fast learners, can be in real trouble if their first feeding is from a rubber nipple on a bottle. To keep air out and milk in, the baby must purse its lips, rather than open the mouth wide. If the milk flows continuously and too fast, the baby must stop sucking in order to breathe. Many babies quickly learn to pull the tongue back into the mouth and plug up the nipple, to stop the constant flow. Having learned these skills, the baby may try, and fail, to latch on to the breast, and end up by refusing to try further because the mouth shape and movements, so quickly learned on the bottle, don't work for breastfeeding

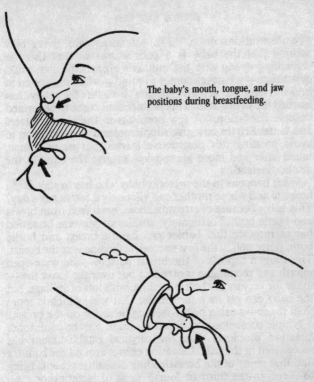

The baby's mouth, tongue, and jaw positions during breastfeeding.

The baby's mouth, tongue, and jaw positions during bottle-feeding.

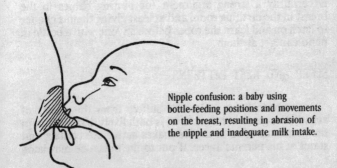

Nipple confusion: a baby using bottle-feeding positions and movements on the breast, resulting in abrasion of the nipple and inadequate milk intake.

(see illustrations on p. 133). Attending care givers may assume that the baby is a poor nurser or that there is something wrong with the mother's nipples, breasts, milk, or attitude—whatever comes to mind—when the apparent breast rejection actually occurs because the baby has learned the wrong skill. This problem has come to be termed "nipple confusion." A few hospitals in the United States and Great Britain now give supplements by cup or spoon to avoid creating this destructive learning; it is, of course, much safer and more appropriate to give the baby to the mother instead.

What happens to the preterm baby who has to stay in the hospital and whose mother can visit only a few hours a day? This baby, because of circumstances, *must* feed from breast and bottle both. Fortunately, studies of preterm breastfed babies indicate that babies can handle breast and bottle both, fairly well, *if* the first successful feeding is at the breast. The learned aspects of the breast pattern—the wide-open mouth and the tongue protruding out over the lower jaw—make for very messy bottle-feeding, with lots of spillage; but the baby can get its nourishment that way, which is more than it can do using bottle-feeding behavior on the breast.

Nipple confusion and breast rejection may be commoner lactation problems than the medical establishment has recognized in the past. Lactation clinics around the country find that many of the breastfeeding difficulties clients bring to them, in the third or fourth week of lactation or even later, can be identified as poor latch-on, originating in nipple confusion. The newborn's capacity for rapid learning is certainly a strong argument for putting babies to the breast in the birthing room and at least giving them a chance to latch on and learn the ropes before anyone with a bottle in hand can get at them.

SLEEP AND REST PATTERNS

A newborn baby, unless he suffers from the effects of anesthetics given to his mother, is both lively and wakeful in the first hour after birth. He makes active eye contact and stares at his parents' faces. If put to the breast he may latch on at once and with vigor, or he may lick and play, showing interest and beginning to learn. This wide-awake phase, in which the baby seems primed to explore his new world and meet his parents, is a sensitive period, comparable to the period in other mammals during which newborns are most capable of forming a bond. Failure to take advantage of this extremely receptive period may account for some of those hospital-born babies who are lethargic, apathetic, difficult feeders at the breast for days or even weeks.

This wakeful time is then followed by a sleepy period, in which both mother and baby can rest from the birth experience. This may last from two to twenty hours. The newborn may then begin to nurse every two hours or so. Research shows that parents can also expect one or more episodes of "cluster" feeding, in which six or seven feedings take place within a three-hour period. The baby may nurse twenty minutes, rest twenty to forty minutes, and then nurse again. In home births, one or more episodes of cluster feeding will occur soon after birth; in hospital births, where separation is likely, cluster feedings will occur somewhat later.

Cluster feedings tend to occur at night. After a bout of cluster feeding, the baby will go into a deep sleep, often for several hours. To the parents, it may seem that the baby "was up all night and wanted to nurse constantly." The baby's several hours of deep sleep may then coincide with the hours when the parents have to be up and doing.

These nocturnal tendencies may be attributed to the fact that the newborn comes into the world with a well-established temporal pattern of activity and rest periods, based on maternal activity before birth. During the daylight, when the mother is walking about, her movements gently lull the baby to sleep. At night, when the mother is still, the baby wakes up and moves around; nighttime kicking bouts are a legitimate gripe of pregnant women. When the baby is born, for the first few days or weeks it may stay on "uterine time," to the inconvenience of the rest of the family.

Most babies are quick, however, to pick up on the cues of light and dark that govern the rest of us, as long as they are roused often for feeding during the day. One mother, a nurse who worked the night shift, had the perfect solution. From the very beginning, her newborn slept at night (when it was accustomed to being rocked in the uterus) and was active during the day. When the mother went back to work, again on the night shift, it was easy to breastfeed, because the baby slept while she was away and was awake to nurse when she was at home.

STATES OF AWARENESS

It seems obvious that one can tell at a glance whether a baby is awake or asleep. Researchers, however, have found that newborns actually exhibit many states of awareness. Marshall Klaus, M.D., has named these states "quiet alert," "active alert," drowsy, crying, light sleep, and deep sleep. Parents soon learn the difference between light sleep and deep sleep, because if you put down a dozing baby too soon, it will cry. The alert states are less obvious. During the quietly alert phase, babies are content to look and listen, absorbing the universe; the actively alert stage is good for socializing and play. Family members can find themselves at odds with the baby, playing too vigorously when she is drowsy, or leaving her to cry when she is in a quietly alert state and would be calmed not by food or sleep but by a chance to see what's going on around her.

Finally, while some babies relish all kinds of stimulation right from birth, others seem to be swamped by receiving too many intense sensations at once; these are the babies who nurse better in a dark room, who cry at loud noises, who don't like being jostled or passed around. Such babies may simply "shut down" if the world becomes too eventful; they may appear to be asleep when in fact they have withdrawn temporarily from sensory overload. It is as if the baby himself were controlling his level of alertness, in the interest of self-preservation.

INDIVIDUALITY

The behavioral doctrine, which still governs some institutional thinking, held that human personality and social behavior were largely developed through life experience, an idea that certainly put an unfair burden on parents. Now, partly from studies of separated identical twins, scientists have determined that babies differ, from birth, in what you might call their approach to life and that children will continue to reveal those same tendencies as they grow. The consensus among developmental psychologists today is that individual temperament is largely a product of genetic inheritance, even though the ways in which that temperament shows up can be very much affected by life experience.

Mothers, of course, have known this all along. Every baby manifests its own individual style, from birth. Some get angry and are frustrated easily; others are usually calm. Some meet adversity head on, and others seem to pull back and think things over. Some seem to love lights and noise and activity, while others get upset if the world is too stimulating.

Nowhere are these newborn differences more apparent than in the breastfeeding interaction. Some babies are very businesslike; others—the "gourmets"—taste and play between small bouts of more focused activity at the breast. Some are impatient and can't wait for even an instant to start nursing, while others dawdle. Each baby will interact with its mother differently, and personality clashes are possible. A patient mother and an impatient baby make a workable combination, for example, but an impatient mother with a procrastinating baby may have some learning of her own to do.

EXPRESSING EMOTION

The newborn baby communicates in many ways besides crying. Facial expressions, for example, are present from birth. Once again, psychologists used to presume that human facial expressions are learned, not innate; if that were true, a newborn's facial expressions could not possibly "mean" anything. Now, ethologists, who study the evolution of behavior in its natural setting, have demonstrated that human facial expressions are genetically governed signals, conveying our feelings and emotional state; the great majority of these facial "gestures" are common to all humanity. Cultural fashions and learned behavior may be an added overlay, of course. For example, among the New Zealand Maoris, sticking your tongue out is a warrior's threat; in parts of China, that same gesture indicates surprise; and in the United States, a tongue thrust expresses derision. But in any country and in all human tribes, most facial expressions are the same. An angry man scowls, a frightened child widens the eyes, people who are joking raise their eyebrows, and so on.

Because of the old assumptions about human behavior, we still try not to credit what our eyes and instincts tell us. Seeing a tiny smile crease a newborn's lips, a mother may say, "Look! She's smiling!" and then quickly correct herself—"I know, it's just gas . . ." But it's not fair to babies to maintain that these fleeting changes "don't mean anything." The newborn smile is not yet an intentional *social* smile, but it is triggered by pleasure—a smile of satiety. Similarly, the expressions of perplexity, wonder, curiosity, misery, and bliss that flick across the newborn face are innate responses to the baby's feelings of the instant, and convey the same meanings that they would in any person. Mothers and fathers can see the baby's tiny expressions and respond to them; when the baby's face suggests emotions of interest and friendliness, it's "only natural"—an innate tendency—for parents to feel interest and friendliness right back. Researchers Marshall and Phyllis Klaus write, "The facial expressions of newborns are strikingly similar across all cultures. It seems that when expressing the common emotions of fear, sadness, joy, disgust, and anger, the human face speaks a universal language."

THE SENSES: WHAT BABIES SEE

The authorities used to assume that babies saw very poorly and were born into a world that made very little sense to them—in the phrase of psychologist William James, "a vast, buzzing, blooming confusion." Now, psychologists have demonstrated that babies can in fact see fairly well from the moment of birth, although they can focus easily only on objects in the close-in range of eight to ten inches (about the distance of the mother's face while they breastfeed). In looking, they are more interested in patterns than in plain surfaces; they are especially interested in patterns (two dots and a line) resembling a human face. They will look longer at a smiling pattern than at a frowning pattern. They are most interested in real faces, and they recognize eyes and can make eye contact from birth.

Until studies were made using slow-motion film, scientists did not realize that babies not only see their care givers' eyes and facial expressions, but respond to them. And they respond with mimicry. If, in talking to a small baby (less than a month old, say), you open your mouth wide, after a short pause the baby will open her mouth wide, too. Raised eyebrows, a smile, a squinched-up nose—all these will produce tiny but strenuous efforts in the same direction. Perhaps the easiest facial mimicry to demonstrate is sticking the tongue out; do this to a small baby, and, if the baby is watching you and is in the mood, the baby will do it back, often after visible false tries. The baby may become still and transfixed with fascination, or she may wriggle all over in her effort to create what she is seeing. You can observe, in action, a hard-wired response—that is, looking at faces and imitating them—combined with learning. Yes, but *how* do I get my face to do that?

WHAT BABIES HEAR

Babies begin hearing sound long before they are actually born; just ask anyone who has been to a rock concert when more than five months pregnant—some babies kick so hard at the amplified sound that the mother has to leave. Of course, the primary sound in the baby's uterine world is her mother's heartbeat. It has been found that a low tone, broadcast at a rate of about eighty beats per minute, is soothing to babies in hospital nurseries; the tone simulates the maternal heartbeat, which has dominated each infant's experience for nine months, and which would still be present were she lying next to or near her mother.

High-pitched sounds are easier for babies to hear than low sounds. That may be one reason why we tend to talk to babies in a high-pitched voice (see chapter 5). Slow-motion filming has shown researchers that babies do more than listen to our voices. They dance. One can easily observe that a wide-awake, comfortable baby will wriggle and wave his arms when his mother talks to him. What only the camera can show is that these movements occur in time with the mother's speech and follow the tempo of her stresses and pauses as if that chat were music—which, to the baby's ears, it probably is: the most beautiful music in the world.

SMELL AND TASTE

There's not much chance for a baby to learn to smell before it is born. Within a week of birth, however, a breastfeeding baby has learned to recognize his own mother's scent and to tell it from that of all other women. Experimenting with newborns in hospital nurseries, researchers have found that if one lays a nursing pad soaked with mother's milk on either side of a baby's head—one pad from his own mother and the other from someone else—the baby will turn toward the pad from its own mother. It is not the scent of the milk that appeals, however, but the scent of the mother. Given a choice between a sterile pad with his own mother's milk on it, and a pad that she has worn but which is milkless, the baby will prefer the pad with her body scent. By six weeks of age, babies respond to the scent of their own mother's milk, but not that of other mothers— and when they are exposed to the scent of cows' milk they often look disgusted.

Presumably the baby quickly learns the scent, as well as the voice and look, of other people around him besides his mother; this ability helps the baby feel at home among familiar people in his new world. The baby who must spend his first days in a hospital nursery, with changing shifts and many care givers, has a right to be confused or even dismayed by the unnaturally high demands on his memorizing faculties.

THE SENSE OF TOUCH

The continued experience of being touched and held is an important part of normal development in mammals. Rats that receive no handling from infancy become savage, while rats that are handled daily are placid and tame, even when the daily handling is followed by an electric shock. Baby monkeys have been experimentally raised with surrogate mothers. The monkey raised in the company of a "mother" made of bare chicken wire with a bottle attached will go to "her" for food, but spend the rest of his time cowering in a corner and scream with fear at any change in his environment. The monkey raised with a "mother" made of padded chicken wire that *doesn't* supply food nevertheless clings to the soft padding, like any baby monkey to his mother, investigates new objects with normal monkey curiosity, and shows fairly normal development. The only difference is in stimulus to the sense of touch.

The skin of a new human baby is far more sensitive than that of an adult. It flushes and mottles at every sensation. The whole skin is a sense organ, especially aware of contact with someone else's body. A fretful newborn can often be soothed if one merely holds him, naked, against one's own bare skin. For many months after birth, furthermore, a baby's mouth also functions as a primary organ for sensing by touch, as if it were an extra hand. Any new object to be investigated is not only held and looked at, but mouthed. And the infant's mouth has been described as the center of his neurological functioning; as the oral patterns of behavior come into synchrony, the rest of the nervous system follows.

The sense of touch also tells the baby about his position relative to gravity, whether he is still or moving, and whether he is being held tightly or loosely: this is called the kinesthetic sense. It is through the baby's kinesthetic awareness, through being touched and moved and handled, that a baby first locates himself and makes contact with reality. It may be that the need for physical contact is especially acute during the critical period of the first hours and days after birth, when we so often isolate babies. To replace the warmth of body contact and the snugness of uterine existence, babies in hospital nurseries are often swaddled, or wrapped tightly in blankets, so that their arm and leg movements are restrained. Indeed, swaddled babies cry less than unwrapped babies, a convenience for care givers. Mothers, however, tend to let their newborns sleep at their side or on their chest or abdomen, in full body contact, where they are apt not to cry at all.

Breastfeeding, of course, necessitates a great deal of simple physical contact between mother and child. Carrying the baby in a backpack, front pack, or sling also contributes calming body contact, with the additional benefit that the baby gets to see and learn about the world from an adult's height and viewpoint, rather than from the knee-level viewpoint of the stroller—a level from which the baby's experience is uninformative at best and at which the baby is somewhat vulnerable, as well. Prolonged and frequent body contact with adults may also contribute to self-regulation of the baby's body functions. We have seen that body heat is affected by close contact; the infant's heart rate and breathing may also be stimulated and regulated by body contact with others. Breastfed babies, for example, are much less likely to show periods of apnea while sleeping than are artificially fed babies.

It may be, also, as is indicated by the raising of baby monkeys with surrogate mothers, that physical contact with the mother is just as important as social attention in behavioral development. Psychologist James Clark Moloney, M.D., has proposed that the baby who is breastfed and backpacked develops more normally, and becomes a more secure individual, than the baby who gets plenty of social attention but less physical contact. Possibly the anxiety that marks our culture is in part owing to the custom of depriving our infants of body contact, leaving them in firm-surfaced cribs, feeding them with a cool, rigid rubber nipple and glass bottle, picking them up as little as possible, and pushing them about in plastic or metal chairs rather than carrying them against a parent's body.

BABIES NEED LOVE TO SURVIVE

Social attention is life itself to the human baby. Institutionalized babies who receive splendid physical and medical care but who have no social contact with other people begin to show altered development before two months of age. They are listless and underweight. They do not smile or babble or crawl at the appropriate ages; by six months they are visibly retarded, both mentally and physically. They have fevers for no apparent reason and are extremely susceptible to infection. Frequently, they die before the age of two or three years.

In *Child Care and the Growth of Love*, John Bowlby, M.D., points out that these symptoms of abnormality disappear with amazing speed if the infant is placed in a home and receives maternal care. However, there appear to be critical periods in the development of social responses that, once past, cannot be recaptured. Complete deprivation of social contact during the first or second six months of life produces a permanently abnormal personality. Deprivation for periods during the next two years may or may not result in permanent harm.

THE STANDARD-CARE BABY: A CULTURAL COMPROMISE

Some physicians and other medical care providers differentiate between "unrestricted" breastfed babies, who are breastfed in a biologically appropriate manner, and "standard-care" babies, who may be breastfed or partially breastfed, but who are subject to many cultural restrictions. Pioneering breastfeeding researcher Dr. Niles Newton identifies unrestricted, biologically normal breastfeeding as the technique "practiced by traditional and preliterate cultures and, in the United States, by . . . members of La Leche League" (and, of course, by many other parents).

Unrestricted breastfed babies are put to the breast whenever they want, for as long as they want. They are given no bottles. They are never left alone to cry. They are carried about, and held in laps and arms, whether awake or asleep, for many hours in the day. They sleep with or near the parents at night, which facilitates night feedings, for at least the first year. They receive solid foods only after six or seven months; breastfeeding continues well into or through the second year.

Standard-care babies, on the other hand, are breastfed according to a predetermined schedule. Instead of an average of ten or twelve nursings a day in the first month, they are limited to eight (a three-hour schedule) or six (a four-hour schedule) as soon as possible. Feedings are terminated as soon as the baby is deemed to be "finished"; nonnutritive sucking, playing at the breast, and falling asleep on the breast are discouraged; nursing purely for comfort is not considered desirable.

Standard-care babies sleep alone, often in their own room, from birth. They are allowed to cry for long periods. They are put down in a crib or some other baby-holding device whenever they are not being actively fed or tended to. Bottle feedings are introduced regularly, from the first weeks, and strained baby foods by four months or so. Breastfeeding may be terminated entirely by six or eight months if not earlier, and feedings are routinely delayed or curtailed for reasons such as, "She just ate—she can't be hungry again," "I'll wait until she really means it," "It's not time yet," "She's nursed long enough, she couldn't be getting anything now," or "She's just fooling around." These adult assumptions may not represent what is actually going on with the baby, at all; the baby, however, is not allowed to make the decision to nurse or not.

Standard-care babies, while receiving the nutritional and immunological advantages of breastfeeding, at least in the early weeks, are somewhat deprived of the comforting aspects. One study compared sixteen mother-baby pairs practicing unrestricted nursing with sixteen fully breastfed standard-care pairs. While weight gains and general health were similar in the two sets of babies, the standard-care babies, at two months, cried 35 percent more than the unrestricted nursing babies. Statistical analysis demonstrated what would seem to be common sense: the infants who were fed more frequently cried less, and infants who were fed less frequently fussed and cried more.

THE OLDER BREASTFED BABY

Behavior at the breast changes as the baby grows. A newborn may take half an hour or longer to reach satiety; the older baby is finished in a few minutes. The newborn concentrates entirely on suckling during nursings; by four months, the baby can nurse and be aware of the rest of the world at the same time; in fact, he may turn his head or interrupt himself at any strange noise or voice.

From three months on, the baby smiles and plays at the breast, letting his mother know how much he enjoys nursing. By four or five months, the baby often wants to play with his mother's face while nursing, and may like to feel her teeth and mouth with his free hand. For many babies, nursing continues to be an important source of nutrition, with four or more nursings per day, including at least one night feeding, through the first year. And long after nursing ceases to be a major source of calories, it continues to be a comfort—at bedtime, when a child is ill or frightened, and whenever a little love and cuddling seem to be in order.

How long do babies "naturally" breastfeed? Is there a biologically normal time for weaning? The matter appears to be highly variable; individual babies differ, and adult expectations vary from culture to culture. The general food supply is a factor, as well; weaning can be a calamitous event in a community with a protein-poor diet, or in the case of another pregnancy precipitating an abrupt end to nursing.

In most preliterate societies, babies are breastfed for two years or more. Presently in the United States, lactation consultants and others favoring unrestricted breastfeeding recommend "baby-led" weaning, in which the child's own choice dictates the end of breastfeeding. These babies wean themselves anywhere from early in the second year of life to late in the third year.

Although the earliest age at which babies spontaneously wean themselves—refusing the breast and preferring other food—seems to be about nine months, this early self-weaning may in fact be induced by breastfeeding practices that cause the milk supply to dwindle until it is no longer of interest; some mothers find that their first baby weans himself well before his first birthday, but subsequent babies wean themselves much later. Only one preliterate culture, in New Guinea, is on record as weaning all babies from the breast at nine months; it is reportedly a very restrictive and unpleasant culture in other ways as well.

Mothers sometimes get tired of nursing before babies do. The mother's feelings, a subsequent pregnancy, or social pressures may all contribute to the weaning process and the time weaning takes place. Some medical professionals still protest violently against nursing longer than a year; the standard-care bias that babies should be taught "independence" from birth is sorely flouted by breastfeeding any longer than is absolutely necessary. In reality there has been, to date, little published research on the results or effects of long-duration breastfeeding on children. Subjectively, a mother is likely to feel that the closeness she shares with her baby while breastfeeding is even more enjoyable and complete as the baby grows old enough to be a sociable companion as well as a nursling. Perhaps a nursing mother's love, lap, and milk provide our exploring, experimenting toddlers with a home base, a firm foundation of security, that makes them all the more confident as the time for independence approaches.

CHAPTER 6

Parents and Innate Behavior

INSTINCT AND THE NEW INSECURITY

In 1850, a new mother learning to take care of her first baby might have felt nervous, but she was bolstered by the firm conviction that whatever she did was right. Only a mother knew what to do for her infant, and she—by the grace of God, having become a mother—would be able to feed and care for her infant, thanks to her "mother instinct." Today, however, parents feel a distinct insecurity about child-rearing in general, as shown by the proliferation of parenting advice columns, books, magazines, talk shows, and famous experts. The more experts, the more confusion. Today, many parents are uneasy about the job. Parenting authorities (who, after all, see and address themselves to the most confused of us) seem to take for granted that the primary parental emotion is not affection, or satisfaction, or enjoyment, but "inadequacy." What ever happened to mother instinct?

We are coming to understand that instinct is not a blind, inflexible force but a series of nudges, of small reflexive responses to internal or external stimuli that, added together, tend to produce certain patterns of behavior. There is room for lots of variation, however. Innate behavior does not operate mechanically in every animal, every time; even ants have been found to display individuality in their behavior. It is only by long and careful observation of many individuals that the patterns of innate behavior can be seen.

We know now that unrestricted breastfeeding elicits and promotes appropriate mothering behavior. So it is perplexing to read the current medical research literature in which breastfeeding is seen as an *outcome* of a mother's nurturing feelings when it is in fact a cause. The psychological literature is even more astonishing. Whole schools of thought and research on parent-child "attachment" have arisen in which breastfeeding is completely ignored. A recent monograph titled "Growing Points in Attachment Theory and Research," supposedly a review of all significant new research on parent-child attachment, includes not one reference on breastfeeding. It's as if one were to study the marriage bond without considering sex.

LEARNED AND INNATE MOTHERING

It seems infuriating that humans, with all their advantages of brainpower, face the care of an infant with minimal instructions from Mother Nature, while any cat or cow or rabbit has the genetic programming to raise fine babies, knowing exactly what to do from start to finish. But is that really true? Do animals have a real advantage over us? The truth is that with animals, as with people, experience is a factor in successful mothering.

Every person who has raised horses or dogs or any other animal knows that mammal mothers do not do a perfect job the first time. Some horses are so nervous with their first foal that they must be restrained by force before they will let it nurse. Laboratory rats may lose some or all of their first litter through inexperience—letting the babies get chilled, or go hungry too long, or stray from the nest.

Many dogs are quite incompetent with their first litter. When puppies are born, they, like other animal babies, move toward the nearest large object; when their noses make contact with fur, they grope around until they eventually find the nipples. An inexperienced female may get up and down a lot at first, giving her babies no chance to start sucking. As one kennel owner put it, "It looks as though the bitch is puzzled. There they are, ten babies, and she thinks she ought to do something about them, but she isn't sure what. Finally she gives up, and lies down to rest—and it happens!"

Experimenters have found that animals have a chance to practice some aspects of baby care before the babies arrive. If a female rat is made to wear a collar throughout life, so that she cannot reach her body and never has a chance to lick herself, she does not know how to lick her babies as they are born. Then they have a hard time functioning normally and making contact with her; generally they do not survive. If a rat is deprived of the experience of carrying things in her mouth, she will not know how to build a proper nest, nor how to retrieve her babies if they stray. It is possible that some house cats arrive at maturity without good carrying experience. A new mother cat, for all her aplomb, may not know how to pick up a kitten. She may spend half an hour taking it by a paw, by the nose, by the tail, before she discovers the scruff-of-the-neck hold. The cat that has had a chance to hunt and kill and carry mice will pick up a kitten properly on the first try.

Observation can be important, too. A chimpanzee that was reared in the London Zoo and had never seen a baby of her own species was so horrified at the sudden appearance of her first baby in her hitherto private cage that she leapt backward with a shriek of terror, and could never thereafter be persuaded to have anything to do with it. Her second, born a year later, she accepted only after her friend the keeper demonstrated its harmlessness and showed her how to hold it. Gorillas are even more susceptible to problems of inexperience. For many years, gorillas born in captivity had to be taken from their mothers and hand-raised if they were to survive. Zoos have now learned that captive gorillas should be kept in compatible groups instead of alone or in pairs. In these colonies, when a young and inexperienced female gives birth, older females not only watch her and the baby, but tend to coach or reprimand her if she does something hazardous, such as holding the baby by one limb or upside down. One zoo had success in breeding a solitary female gorilla when a keeper persuaded a woman friend to bring her nursing baby to the zoo after hours and breastfeed in the aisle of the gorilla house, so the pregnant female could see how it was done. The gorilla watched with every evidence of interest, and was indeed able to feed and raise her own baby when it arrived.

THE BONDING PERIOD

Marshall Klaus, M.D., and John Kennell, M.D., were the first, in 1972, to publish research demonstrating the existence of a special period, in humans, for mother-infant bonding. Scientists knew that such periods existed in animals. In 1935, ethologist Konrad Lorenz, M.D., had demonstrated in geese a phenomenon known as imprinting, in which the newly hatched bird recognizes as its parent whatever it sees and hears on first hatching, whether that is an adult goose or a professor making gooselike honks. The subtle detail was that imprinting can occur only in a brief, critical period after hatching; subsequently, the gosling can never learn to recognize or follow a parent or parent substitute. Helen Blauvelt, Ph.D., demonstrated the existence of a similar critical period in goats. Ordinarily, right after the birth of a kid, the mother smells and licks it, lets it nurse, and from then on recognizes this infant as her own, and will accept no other. This instant formation of attachment is called bonding. If the mother, however, is separated from her offspring immediately after birth for as short a period as one hour, she may never accept it; the critical period has passed.

Obviously, matters are not as critical with humans; we are often (and in the past were routinely) unconscious or separated from our babies at birth, and yet we accept and love them. We can bond to adopted babies and to older children as well. But Klaus and his associates began to look closely at what happens when mothers and babies are not separated at birth. They compared a group of women who first saw and held their babies briefly six to twelve hours after birth to a group of women who were given their babies, nude, to hold (and breastfeed, if they liked) for an hour, soon after birth. A month later, a year later, even *two* years later, the "early contact" mothers behaved differently from the separated mothers toward their babies, fondling them more, holding them more, comforting them more in the doctor's office, and giving them fewer orders and instructions. This study, and work that followed, demonstrated a sensitive period in humans. And it became obvious that mothers in a hospital setting were being denied an interaction that the 1850s mother, whose children were born at home, experienced as a matter of course.

Other researchers have also investigated this phenomenon; the studies have come up with some surprisingly uniform results. Mothers who get some time with their newborns in the first hour of life, *and* have long and frequent contact with them thereafter, show long-term differences in behavior from mothers who are separated for hours and then restricted to six or eight twenty-minute feedings a day, the standard-care hospital routine. Furthermore, the babies of early-contact mothers laugh and smile more and cry less than those of delayed-contact mothers. One study of more than three hundred mothers examined parenting disorders: seventeen months after birth, ten of the delayed-contact, standard-care children had experienced abuse or neglect vs. two of the early-contact group. One study found that the effect of early and extra contact with their newborns was greatest on women who had "low social support." These differences were measurable whether or not the mothers were breastfeeding.

Among those mothers who were breastfeeding, the long-term patterns also showed differences. Mothers who had early contact were about three times more likely still to be breastfeeding when the baby was two months old than were hospital-routine mothers. Early-contact mothers on the average also continued breastfeeding for more months than the control-group mothers, and touched and looked at their babies more during feedings. And at twelve months, the babies of early-contact mothers weighed more.

The "bonding" evidence seems to be catching on. To quote T. Berry Brazelton, M.D., Harvard Medical School pediatrician, "One marvelous effect of Klaus and Kennell's elegant research has been that most hospitals are sensitized to the fact that they must change to be most effective for new parents." Now, many hospitals are routinely giving mothers —and fathers, too—a quiet hour immediately after birth in which to play with and get to know their baby. Many medical care givers also now delay giving the baby the legally required disease-preventing silver nitrate eyedrops (which sting), until after the first hour, so the baby can keep his eyes open and see his parents' smitten faces.

INNATE TENDENCIES IN NEW MOTHERS

One need not conjure up elaborate explanations to understand at least partly why contact in the hour of birth can have critical and long-term effects. The completion of the birth process is a tremendous thrill and relief in itself. Parents' emotions are heightened already by the dramatic birth experience; they begin a series of interactions with the baby, who is also wide-awake and responsive in this hour, in a flood of euphoric feelings. It is the perfect setup for love at first sight.

The standard-care mother, on the other hand, may meet her baby, a wrapped-up, somnolent stranger, a day or more after the birth, when triumphant feelings are long gone, a sore bottom remains, and she has been worrying for hours about whether the baby is normal or even breathing. The father may see the baby at first only through the glass window of the nursery. In the first case, the baby is a powerful reinforcer of nurturing behavior; in the second, a neutral or even a negative presence.

Parents, of course, can become attached to their children without this instantaneous experience, just as one can fall in love at any time during a relationship; happiness does not require love at first sight. Mothers and fathers come equipped with many innate tendencies that help to bridge the distance and to form an attachment to the newcomer, whenever the opportunity finally arises. For example, in light of the evidence that babies are soothed by a sound simulating the maternal heartbeat, researcher I. Salk made a startling observation in 1960. Out of 287 newly delivered mothers the great majority, regardless of past experience or right- and left-handedness, held their babies on the left side, over the heart. This observation has proved to be so sound that care providers can use it diagnostically. The mother who does *not* hold her new baby on the left (like the mother who does not look at her baby while discussing it) may be at risk for what are called parenting disorders: child neglect or abuse.

Another example is the almost irresistible tendency mothers have to unwrap their new baby and look at it all over when it is first brought from the nursery. If the nurses, in the interests of protecting the baby from exposure to germs, are particularly fierce about not permitting this, the mother may do it secretively, and try to wrap the baby up again exactly as it was. But do it she will, with the inevitability with which a little girl of two or three will strip the clothes off a new doll.

Many of the ways we touch babies have innate components. If a newborn is lying on its back, mothers tend to put a hand flat on the baby's chest, middle finger aimed at the baby's chin, and rock it slightly, in a gentle, rousing gesture. Holding the baby vertically against the shoulder and patting it between the shoulder blades is also a mildly stimulating or rousing behavior. A new mother tends to orient herself so that the baby is looking straight at her, and their heads are angled the same way, or face to face; researchers call this position *en face*. Mothers of preterm babies in incubators may bend over to put themselves *en face* to the baby lying on its side.

It's common for a new mother to place the baby in her lap, facing up, and spend long periods—many minutes, even hours—face to face, looking into the baby's eyes, talking, and touching the baby. One lactation consultant who works with many single teenage mothers teaches them to breastfeed in the so-called "football" hold, with the baby under one arm, looking up, so that the baby's eyes look straight into the mother's. This position tends to make the mother laugh, talk, and play with her baby, bolstering her sense of attachment, a crucial benefit in an environment where infant neglect can be a real risk.

FATHERS AND INNATE BEHAVIOR

Fathers exhibit innate behavior in many of the same ways mothers do. Fathers, like mothers, respond to infant vocalizing by vocalizing themselves. Both tend to begin contact with a new baby by touching the arms and legs, then by touching the body with the fingertips, then with the whole hand (men then tend to stroke the baby with the back of the fingers, which women do not). Men also tend to regard the baby *en face* and will twist themselves around to do so, if the baby is lying down, and they make regular and continuing eye contact.

Men are also susceptible to instant bonding to an infant at birth (although, of course, like women, they can also develop equally strong bonds through later exposure). In many hospitals, it has become customary to use the father as a labor coach and companion and to let him be present at delivery. The hour of birth can be an emotionally intense period for fathers. Yale University psychiatrist Kyle Pruett, M.D., in his book *The Nurturing Father,* quotes a man who had been present for his daughter's birth: ". . . she opened her eyes and looked at me—*right at me* . . . Perfect! Just perfect! . . . the doc cut the cord and put her on my wife's belly, and I touched her. I was sort of afraid because she was so small and soft . . . but she opened her eyes again when I touched her—like she liked it! A shiver went up my back." Dr. Pruett comments, "What a lucky little girl and mother. There appears to be no turning back from such experiences. This father seems hooked for good." With men, as with women, nurturing behavior, once elicited, flourishes.

Irinaus Eibl-Eibesfeldt, in his landmark book *Human Ethology,* looks at human behavior as it occurs in the natural setting in preliterate cultures. His studies show that even in the most warlike tribes it is not considered unmanly for a warrior to play with an infant; men as well as women spend a lot of time with babies and toddlers, and find them amusing. Fathers share food with babies and toddlers, cuddle, fondle, and kiss them, respond to them in sensible and competent ways, and feel and display affection from the first days on. Studies have been made, also, of middle-class American fathers who take a strongly nurturing role with their babies and small children. Interestingly, both sons and daughters of these nurturing fathers tend to exhibit high levels of nurturing behavior (toward pets and smaller children, for example) themselves.

There are differences, however, between the ways in which men and women interact with babies that are consistent across cultures, whether the parents are primitive Eipos in New Guinea or upper-middle-class Americans. Fathers play with babies more often than mothers, but clean them far less; mothers feeding toddlers, for example, are far more likely than fathers to wipe the baby's face and hands during the process. If a baby chokes, coughs, sneezes, or starts crying, the father is apt to draw back and wait for order to restore itself, while the mother is more apt to intervene. And fathers interact with babies far more actively than mothers, initiating games and motor activity as mothers never do. Fathers are much more likely than mothers to hold babies high in the air, shake them, spin around with them, and, as they grow older, engage in roughhousing and physical scuffles. Babies learn to expect this; as early as eight weeks, an awake and alert baby will respond to the father's approach with hunched shoulders and evident excitement. The world over, mommies are a comfort, and take care of you, but daddies are *fun!*

BABY TALK

One phenomenon in parents that is hard to explain without reference to innate behavior is baby talk. Every mother and father in the world—every grandparent, too—speaks two languages: their own language, be it English, German, Russian, Tagalog, or Yanomami, and baby talk. Baby talk has absolutely universal characteristics: it is high-pitched, singsong, repetitive, and often ends sentences with a rising tone, "Are you a pretty baby? Hmm? Pretty baby?" It is also apt to contain diminutives, slips or elisions, and grammatical errors, as if a small child were speaking. "Is um a pwetty baby?"

Like all innate behaviors, baby talk has purpose and value. Babies hear high-pitched sounds more easily than low-pitched tones; so both men and women raise their voices just about an octave when they talk to babies. Repetitions and questioning probably help babies to focus on the sounds more easily than they can on sounds in many-worded sentences; baby talk is actually a prelude to the way we talk to toddlers—"See the doggie? Look, there's a doggie. Can you say doggie?"—and part of the path of learning language. And perhaps most important, baby talk signals to the baby that this voice is directed at *him*. Out of the sea of voices around him, even a small baby knows, from the tone and tempo, when he personally is being addressed, and should respond. And this awareness does not depend on eye contact: a three-month-old can be made to laugh and wriggle by the sound of a grandmother's voice speaking baby talk on the telephone. Baby talk, in fact, is a powerful behavior for looping even very small babies into the social circle.

In the 1930s and 1940s, with the advent of "scientific" child rearing, baby talk was denigrated, even forbidden. It was "silly"; it was thought to set the baby a bad example; mothers were told, "Don't talk like that, the baby will never learn to talk properly!" The prejudice continues; in 1990, a syndicated newspaper cartoonist devoted several strips to the amusement afforded by father and grandfather secretly giving way to forbidden baby talk whenever they were alone with the baby. In fact, the almost irresistible strength of the urge to coax response from a baby in this "undignified" manner is evidence for the innate nature of the behavior.

Baby talk surfaces again in adult life during courtship and in affectionate exchange between lovers. Similar infantile exchanges are common in many species of birds and animals during courtship. In house sparrows, for instance, when a pair is being formed, the female chirps and flutters her wings like a begging chick, and the male offers food.

While lovers might be embarrassed to have their pet names and baby talk broadcast in public, this undignified behavior is by no means trivial; the use of baby talk, signaling intimacy and dependency, is quite appropriate to courtship and pair bonding.

ADULT RESPONSES TO BABY SIGNALS

Regardless of presence or absence of early bonding experiences, we grow attached to babies; and to facilitate this hold on adult emotions, babies have a large armory of attributes that function as social signals for eliciting attachment. All animals give and receive social signals, with ears, tail, posture, vocalizations: "Get off my hunting ground!" "Don't hurt me, I'm a harmless subordinate." "Look out! Danger!" "Hey, I found something to eat!" "Shall we dance?" Konrad Lorenz called this kind of signal a "social releaser," a stimulus automatically supplied by one animal that triggers or releases a specific mood or emotion, often leading to action, on the part of other animals in the same species.

A social releaser can be a sound, such as the wailing cry given by a chicken when a hawk passes overhead, making every chicken within earshot run for cover. It can be a scent—the odor of the urine of a female fox, mink, or dog in heat that arouses mating behavior in the male. It can be a gesture—the way a puppy rolls on its back, exposing its vulnerable throat and belly, to plead for mercy. It can be a pattern, such as black or white markings on the tails of many birds, or the phosphorescent array of lights on the sides of some deep-sea fishes, conveying the message to others of the species, "Come with me, we are the same kind."

Human babies automatically present many social releasing stimuli, to which all other humans are programmed to respond. Lorenz pointed out that the whole appearance of a human baby is a social releaser. For basic anatomical reasons, babies are born with disproportionately large heads, bulging foreheads, and large eyes, compared to adults. The very features that adapt the baby for breastfeeding—the fat pads that round the cheeks, the short nose and chin, the small mouth with elevated upper lip—also contribute to a characteristic look that makes us say, "Oh, how cute!" whether we are male or female, old or young, and whether the possessor of these attributes is a baby human, calf, raccoon, or even a duckling.

Soft cuddly contours and very short limbs complete the picture that seems to us innately adorable; this combination of characteristics may be seen in dolls, stuffed animals, and many cartoon characters. Think of Mickey Mouse, or Alvin the Chipmunk, or Bambi: big head, big eyes, button nose, no chin, short legs and arms, tubby tummy—all baby signs. At least two well-known artists have built careers on painting pictures of children and adults that are appealing solely because the eyes are about five times normal size, triggering the "cute" response.

Interestingly, human babies are not born with this full display of "cuteness" but develop it from about eight weeks on; people unfamiliar with newborns are sometimes taken aback by their appearance. The newborn, perhaps, has enough other things going for it to appeal to the crucial people, its parents. Only as the baby grows older does it need to be able to promote affection and forestall aggression from all the other people in the community, no matter what age and sex.

Social releaser stimuli often consist of behavior. The baby's grasp reflex, besides helping him hang on to the mother, serves as a social releaser. At the Yerkes Laboratory in Florida, where chimpanzees have been carefully raised and studied for years, it has been noted that a female that has just given birth is apparently very impressed when her baby reaches out with its little hands and takes hold of her. It is this touch of hands that tells her the baby is one of her own kind. In humans, touching of hands conveys friendship in a simple, universal—and therefore instinctive—way. The firm, responsive way a newborn baby grasps one's finger is a moving experience for both parents. It triggers affectionate behavior.

One easily observed social stimulus presented by all young animals is the infant distress call. This is the cheep,

cheep, cheep of a hungry chick, the earsplitting ki-yi-yi of a puppy caught in a fence, the bawling of a strayed calf, the wail of a newborn child. The infant distress call is usually loud, rhythmic, and distinctive. It is not easily ignored. All animals, including humans, react to the distress call of their own species by exhibiting anxiety and distress of their own. As Benjamin Spock, M.D., has said, "The cry of a young baby is like no other sound. It makes parents want to come to the rescue—fast!" It does indeed. It also makes unrelated people highly irritated, adding social pressure to a parent's desire to stop the noise. That is what a distress call is meant to do: to get on your nerves, to make you feel distracted and upset until you can put a stop to it.

An interesting social releaser in very small babies is sound other than crying. From the first weeks of life, breastfed babies murmur as they nurse. Little coos and hums that seem to express pleasure and relaxation can be heard throughout the feeding. A toddler may make the same little singing sounds when he is happily playing by himself, and one can hear the same class of sound—little sighs and murmurs of comfort—from an adult who is enjoying, for example, a good back rub. Richard Applebaum, M.D., points out that bottle-fed babies do not vocalize during feedings, or, if they do, that the sound is apt to be sputtering and grunting rather than cooing, melodious murmuring. Furthermore, a breastfed baby who is switched to the bottle will stop cooing within a few feedings. If she is switched back to the breast, the vocalizing begins again. Probably the artificial configuration of mouth and throat during bottle-feeding hampers the baby's ability to vocalize and eat at the same time. Possibly, however, the baby does not feel the same sublime enjoyment at the bottle as she did at the breast, and so has no emotions of comfort and pleasure to be expressed in pleasant sighs and murmurs. Certainly the nursing baby's little song is received by the mother as a message of comfort, contentment, and love, even if she is not consciously aware of it, and thus serves to strengthen the nursing bond.

Smiling is a social releaser. A newborn baby, when his stomach is full, often smiles—a fleeting grimace—as he falls asleep. While the baby is still very small, four to eight weeks old, this smile of satiety becomes a true social smile. At first, the releasing stimulus for this smile is a pair of human eyes. When the baby sees you looking at him, he smiles. Smiling as he catches your eye is a very valuable instinctive response, and it in turn acts as a releaser for social behavior from the parent, or indeed from almost any human, even another child or a grouchy old man; in fact, siblings and grandparents are often especially elated when smiled at by their baby relatives.

PHEROMONES

One special class of social releasers is scent. Scents used as social signals in lower animals are called pheromones. In insects, these scents are single compounds giving single messages; in mammals, both the compounds and the messages are more complex, but the phenomenon of scent-triggered behavior is very widespread. Dogs, for instance, use scents to mark their territories and advertise their own presence, and recognize instantly the odor of a female in season. We humans are less aware of our pheromonelike messages—in fact, in crowded cities, we do all we can to erase them, with cosmetics, bathing, deodorants, and laundering. Still, you may have noticed "good" scent markers— the enjoyable scent of the room or the clothes of a much-loved person—and "bad" scent markers, such as the sharp, sour smell of a shirt you wore to a frightening interview.

Scent signals are particularly profuse in the crucial area of reproductive behavior, even when we are not consciously aware of them. Researchers have found that when women of reproductive age live together as roommates or house mates, after a few months their menstrual cycles fall into synchrony; the evolutionary advantage of having your period at the same time as everyone else is not obvious, but the phenomenon is easy to demonstrate, and unconsciously recognized scent signals appear to be the mechanism. Women who live in close association with a man tend to reach menopause later than single women, not, the researchers say, because of sexual relations but of exposure to male body scent. In both sexes, pubic hair and underarm hair are scent traps, concentrating these reproduction-related messages; we recognize that a woman clasping her hands behind her head is in a provocative pose but we don't usually stop to think that she is also sending a scent message.

The fact that the nursing baby smells good is probably more important than we think; it is not just that smelling nice reinforces close contact from adults. Some working mothers who must pump their milk while they are away from home find that the letdown reflex can be triggered by smelling a nightie the baby has worn. Nursing babies put down to sleep in a crib drop off more easily if they are lying on a nightgown the mother has worn. These old, old signals of scent appear to be crucial in every stage of the reproductive cycle; lactation and care-giving behavior are certainly among them.

KINSHIP

All of the releasing stimuli presented by babies send the same messages to all related humans, not just mothers and fathers. The intensity of the response one feels increases with familiarity, of course; one's own child becomes heart-wrenchingly adorable, while the children of strangers are merely cute. However, if people are hard-wired to like babies, how can one explain cruelty to children? Distorted behavior can arise from disruption of an individual's development, of course, or to individual pathology; and it may also be that humans, like other social animals, tend to favor known kin over unrelated people.

In recognizing relatives, personal experience may be augmented by the nonverbal behavior and attitudes of others. For example, if you are a member of a large family that goes in for reunions, you will be well-acquainted with the phenomenon that children who are cousins, meeting for the first time, may take to each other and start playing together more rapidly than they would with any new school-mate. Babies and small children can form close relationships with grandparents and aunts and uncles, climbing all over them with the confidence of ownership from the first meeting, when they ordinarily would flee from a stranger. Adults may find themselves bonding strongly to a distant and seldom-seen niece or grandson, in a way they might never do to a neighbor's child. Intellectual awareness of the relationship plays a part, to be sure; but the genes murmur strongly in the background: Kinfolk are more important than strangers.

The absence of kinship, in contrast, can disrupt parenting or care-giving behavior; an unrelated child may be seen as a liability or even a competitor. European and U.S. folklore abounds in wicked stepmothers who are good to their own children but mistreat their stepchildren. Cruel stepfathers do not show up as often in legend, but they are not infrequently found in real life. As the newspapers and police blotter testify, no one is more likely to abuse an infant than the mother's "boyfriend"—a male resident of the house who is not the infant's father. Perhaps the innate anxiety aroused by a crying infant causes anger in an adult who has no parenting skills and in whom the absence of kinship takes off the brakes. A more subtle mechanism may be at work, as well; in many mammalian species, including lions, horses, and quite a few primates, a new dominant male moving into a group of females is highly likely to kill or try to kill any present young (which have been sired by some previous male) and replace them with his own. Humans usually control such antisocial behavior, but the genetic incentive is still there.

BREASTFEEDING—THE GREAT TEACHER

Both on the inborn and the learned levels, breastfeeding teaches new mothers what good mothering is. The innate needs and urges of the mother are met by breastfeeding. The frequent close bodily contact reassures mother as well as child—we all need hugs and cuddling, and babies can give this comfort as well as get it. Breastfeeding requires and creates attentiveness to and interest in the baby's moods and signals. The baby becomes easier for the nursing mother to understand; the comfortable interaction in a well-established lactation builds up a mutual communication, not dependent on words, that lasts long beyond weaning.

The hormones of lactation have a powerful effect on behavior. If prolactin is injected into male rats, they will retrieve baby rats and lick them. In humans, men as well as women have prolactin in their systems; researchers have found that prolactin levels increase in men who are nurturing small children. Prolactin levels are high during pregnancy, and in a breastfeeding mother will continue to be high for as long as a year.

The hormone that triggers mothering behavior most powerfully, however, is oxytocin. Dr. Niles Newton and her husband, Michael Newton, M.D., were the pioneering research couple who first demonstrated that humans have a letdown response triggered by oxytocin, and that the release of oxytocin and the letting down of milk could be inhibited by emotional disturbance. (They demonstrated this in a famous experiment, by tying a string to Niles's big toe as she nursed one of their four babies; if Michael, in the next room, unpredictably jerked the string during feedings—an annoying though not painful event—weighings showed that the baby got less milk.)

Oxytocin production can be reduced by emotional disturbance, but the reverse is also true, and very important for the nursing mother. Oxytocin release in itself triggers emotional tranquility and strong nurturing feelings—and, unlike prolactin, which has a long-term, slow effect, oxytocin works its magic instantaneously. Laboratory animals that have never had litters will exhibit mothering behavior within one minute of receiving a dose of oxytocin directly into the nervous system. No matter what her species, every time a mother's milk lets down, she is being primed on a very fundamental evolutionary level to cuddle and nurture. (Oxytocin is also the hormone of lovemaking, released during sexual climax in both men and women, although twice as much of the hormone is released in women.)

Many mothers are conscious of the soothing, almost euphoric side effects of oxytocin release during breastfeeding; it can be the working mother's daily high point, on reuniting with her child. A nursing mother is also sometimes conscious of how much she adores this particular baby, as the baby is nestled up to the breast; we now know that the flood of oxytocin, as the milk lets down, contributes significantly to that emotion.

Niles Newton, now an international authority on the psychophysiology of lactation, points out that the survival of the human race depends on reproduction, and that the continuance of reproductive behavior depends on the "voluntary satisfaction" to be gained from those largely self-initiated behaviors, coitus and breastfeeding. "Sexual intercourse," Niles Newton has said, "is well-known to foster bonding and care-giving behavior, especially if frequently repeated with the same individual." The same, of course, is true of breastfeeding.

Newton has also pointed out that women who practice unrestricted breastfeeding become physically different from bottle-feeding mothers, not only in hormonal levels, but in galvanic skin response (they are calmer), heart rate (which alters, as the baby cries or is soothed, strikingly more than the heart rate of bottle-feeders), and thermal skin responses, as the mother's breast heats and cools in response to the baby.

If lactation is suppressed, prolactin levels fall abruptly after delivery, and breastfeeding's multiple daily flushes of oxytocin don't occur at all. This hormonal "crash" may be a major factor (in addition to separation from the infant and other loved ones) in immediate postpartum depression, the so-called "baby blues." Not only are all innate urges being frustrated, but the sustaining, love-and-tenderness-inducing hormones are rapidly draining from the system.

The mother who breastfeeds feels this hormonal deprivation much later—on weaning—and much more slowly; as the baby gradually nurses less and less often, the mother's body is weaned from lactation, too. Even so, many women feel some sadness on weaning, especially those who do not plan to have another child. This is not just hormonal; as Newton says, it's only natural: "We *like* to breastfeed."

We are just beginning to see some of the results of changes

that have been occurring over the past decades. Long-term studies of cognitive growth, and social and family interactions, as related to duration of breastfeeding, are now in progress. Perhaps, as we come to understand more about genetically controlled patterns in humans and the biological advantages of these patterns, we can remove some of the strict rules that our society imposes on such functions as childbirth and child care, and give the natural patterns freedom in which to emerge. Then, one part of the pattern can lead smoothly to another as nature intended. Biologically normal labor can result in appropriate parental responses to the baby; successful early contacts can contribute to bonding and nurturing in both parents; and successful lactation can lead to continued good mothering and healthy and happy children.

CHAPTER 7

Helping and Hindering

STATUS AND BREASTFEEDING

During most of human existence all mothers have breastfed their babies; they have had to, if they wanted the baby to survive. Only the rich could afford to hire wet nurses, women who made their living by feeding another person's baby as well as their own. To abstain from breastfeeding, therefore, was a luxury, and even a rather ostentatious privilege: witness this grandmother, observed by Aulus Gellius in Rome in 600 A.D.:

"When he had asked how long the labor had been, and how severe, and had learned that the young woman, overcome with fatigue, was sleeping, he . . . said, 'I have no doubt she will suckle her son herself.' But the young woman's mother said to him that she must spare her daughter and provide nurses for the child in order that to the other pains which she had suffered in childbirth might not be added the wearisome and difficult task of nursing."

Task or pleasure, until this century, breastfeeding was necessarily the only safe way to feed babies. Artificial or substitute foods often spoiled or were contaminated with bacteria, especially in hot weather; the resulting diarrhea—the dreaded "summer flux"—killed babies who were not breastfed.

When safe artificial feeding of babies was first developed in the United States, it quickly became a status symbol. The baby bottle looked like tangible evidence of the modern

166

woman's liberation from drudgery. Feeding a baby by clock and scale was "scientific" and therefore superior to old-fashioned methods. It was the middle class that took up bottle-feeding first—the ones who could afford the paraphernalia and the expensive doctors' advice. As hospitalization for childbirth became customary throughout the nation, the accompanying systematized care of the newborn made breastfeeding physically less feasible. The medical profession began to assume a position of authority in all matters of infant care and feeding. Soon bottle-feeding was not only fashionable and medically approved but seemed to be the only method possible for most women. The people who continued to breastfeed were those too poor to buy ingredients and bottles—rural women, or recent immigrants who "didn't know any better."

After World War II, a medical reformation began in the whole area of maternity care. Individuals and organizations began promoting and developing programs for natural childbirth, rooming-in, and less structured systems of infant care. This more natural approach to childbirth was accompanied by a new focus on breastfeeding. Once again, the parents who were quick to espouse these improvements were the well-educated and affluent middle and upper-middle classes—what one hospital administrator called the top 10 percent. Today the middle-class woman is quite likely to breastfeed at least for a few weeks, while the very poor are still apt to regard the baby bottle as an important status symbol, visible evidence that one has money to spend.

PREJUDICE AGAINST BREASTFEEDING

The mother who breastfeeds today may well expect to be not only accepted but respected for doing so. So it's apt to be a shock to her the first time she discovers herself being criticized, subtly or openly, for nursing her baby. Anti-breastfeeding prejudice may be expressed in old wives' tales, subtle threats, pointed jokes, or open hostility. Criticism may come from such unexpected sources as one's family, medical care providers, or close friends. Perhaps a woman's obstetrician, who she had assumed would heartily endorse her intentions, is skeptical or even derogatory about her plans to breastfeed. Or a nurse in the hospital, who has theoretically come to help her at feeding time, tells her that her milk is no good or hasn't "come in" yet so there's no point in nursing, or her nipples are wrong, or even that her personality is unsuited to nursing. Or perhaps her own mother constantly questions whether the baby is "getting enough," or a woman friend reveals that she finds the idea of breastfeeding repugnant.

Nobody ever gets used to being a target for prejudice. Such an attitude can undermine the confidence of even an experienced nursing mother. How does this unreasoning attitude arise? Like all prejudices, it is based on fear and ignorance. The fear of loss of status still affects some people. One mother, herself a childbirth instructor, was astonished to find that her army officer father firmly held the view that nursing a baby is a sign of ignorance and poverty, and he felt ashamed that she was breastfeeding.

In some social groups, on the other hand, a curious reversal of prejudice has arisen; while bottle-feeding mothers are assumed simply to be misguided—more to be pitied than censured—breastfeeding mothers who don't take the job sufficiently seriously are looked down on. Working mothers are denigrated even when they breastfeed, because they are away from their babies during the work period. Breastfeeding itself can become competitive; the mother who nursed for two years feels superior to the mother who nursed for nine months, and women may publicly brag of nursing a child five or six years or more, as a matter of prestige. This fashion for breastfeeding, often branded by others as fanaticism, has sometimes caused a prejudicial backlash of its own.

The main cause of prejudice against breastfeeding, however, has to do with sex. We have come to regard the female breast as a sexual object, and an exclusively sexual object. Breastfeeding an infant is therefore seen as prurient or obscene. This sexual association has many repercussions. A husband can feel ambivalent, if he had thought of his wife's breasts as his possessions, and now they are so visibly the baby's. Women may feel shy about nursing, and men may find the whole idea embarrassing. Physicians are not immune; one mother who had just given birth reported that her obstetrician—who, after all, probably knew more about her private parts than she did—happened to come into her hospital room while she was breastfeeding and he blushed.

The assumption that the breast is a sexual organ pervades the community in general. It is taboo to expose sexual organs in public; therefore nursing where people can see you is shocking. A New York writer reported that he and his family were thrown out of a restaurant, amidst the chef's angry cries about "having sex in public," because his wife was breastfeeding the baby. People have been kicked off buses and even fired from their jobs for breastfeeding. Defending nursing mothers in court has become a small but active forensic specialty; problems range from charges of obscene behavior to judges who cannot understand why the divorced father of a breastfeeding infant cannot have custody for the weekends.

If the breast is comparable to the genitals, then the substance that comes out of it must be the equivalent of semen or urine; so breastfeeding becomes an unclean act, and spots from leaking milk are embarrassing. Again, medical personnel are not immune. In one infant intensive care nursery, when a baby developed a nasty rash, the attending physician instructed the head nurse to treat the rash by putting a little fresh mother's milk on it; she recoiled in horror, saying that she didn't like the idea of putting her hands in "that stuff."

Many people simply try to deal with the conflict by acting as if breastfeeding doesn't exist. Pediatricians give lectures and write books on infant feeding in which breastfeeding is not mentioned. A booklet on sexual development and reproduction, printed by the New York State Department of Health for use in high schools, described and illustrated such details as the growth of axillary and pubic hair, and the development of a human embryo, but never mentioned the female breast, as if even the New York State Department of Health did not know what breasts are for. A nursing mother may run into this blind spot about breastfeeding at home.

Relatives, seeing her holding the baby closely, may repeatedly try to look at the baby's face, or even to take it from her arms, without seeming to realize the baby is nursing. One mother finally forced her family and in-laws to stop "forgetting" she was nursing by pinning a sign to her sweater reading "Lunchtime" when she fed the baby.

Europeans sometimes think that we in the United States have very unusual ideas about milk in general. Many other countries make use of animal milk, especially in cooking or as a source of butter and cheese. But Americans are virtually alone in considering that animal milk is indispensable for growing children or that it is even a suitable food for adults. Certainly no other species of mammal includes milk in the adult diet; from a biological standpoint, the idea is quite impractical. Possibly our reverence for cow's milk is an offshoot of our breast taboos.

MEDICAL ATTITUDES

Between 1950 and 1980, the incidence of mothers in the United States who breastfed at least for a few weeks rose from next to none, to more than 50 percent. In part, this improvement reflected the efforts of individual doctors crusading to teach and promote breastfeeding. It paid off for their patients.

"I could never have nursed my baby without my wonderful doctor."

"My pediatrician talked me into trying breastfeeding, and am I glad she did!"

"My doctor really believes in breastfeeding."

"My doctor has six breastfed children of his own, and *all* his patients breastfeed."

These mothers found medical care providers who not only showed enthusiasm for breastfeeding but also understood its management. Sometimes a male physician became a fan of breastfeeding because his own wife successfully breastfed their children. Sometimes both the enthusiasm and understanding were acquired through shrewd observation over years of practice, seeing women whose milk supply seemed to be dwindling but who redeveloped their lactation, women who breastfed twins, or weathered illnesses without giving up breastfeeding, or women who held down demanding jobs and fully breastfed their babies, too. These object lessons enable doctors to encourage other mothers in the same circumstances, rather than just prescribe synthetic milk at any sign of difficulty. Now, most towns have at least one physician with breastfeeding expertise. And as parents in general have become more sophisticated about breastfeeding, physicians who solve problems by telling the mother to switch to the bottle may find her switching to another doctor instead.

Sophisticated enthusiasm for breastfeeding, however, by no means characterizes the medical profession as a whole, even today. Partly, this is because of lack of training. Medical schools by and large ignore the topic of lactation. One student in a large and famous medical school reported that her anatomy professor devoted two days to the penis and its functions, and ten minutes to the breast, most of which was spent on jokes. At present in 1990, many medical schools in the United States offer no instruction about breastfeeding. Very few medical schools *require* students to learn the basics of lactation management, and when they do, the requirement is apt to be for potential obstetric and pediatric specialists only, and the instruction may be a few hours or even less time.

In contrast, the topic of infant feeding, by which is meant artificial feeding, is often given weeks of attention. The natural result is that budding physicians graduate with a feeling that breastfeeding is not very interesting, complicated, or important, or they would have had to spend more time on it; and, simultaneously, that they have been taught all they need to know about it, and are now certified experts.

Most of the physicians presently in practice received this kind of preparation. Furthermore, they live and work in a climate of opinion that downgrades breastfeeding to just one of many suitable options, in a hospital system that frustrates normal lactation, and in an absolute blizzard of propaganda from the manufacturers of synthetic milk formulas for babies. Personal experience and prejudices also creep in. Some physicians, male or female, may be squeamish about the breasts and their role in sex. A man whose wife refused to breastfeed, or tried and failed, will have a different attitude from the man whose wife breastfed several children. A woman M.D. who breastfed her own babies for two months may feel that two months is adequate.

All too often what support such practitioners give to breastfeeding is in recognition of its emotional benefits. If the mother is having any difficulty in breastfeeding, or if the baby is not gaining according to the charts, then the doctor presumes that neither she nor the baby is reaping those emotional benefits, so there is no good reason not to switch to a bottle. The result is that, while most practitioners are aware that the medical societies and the federal government have all pronounced that "Breast is best," in their own practices many still either fail to help mothers breastfeed, or actually hinder them inadvertently. Obstetricians ignore the need to inform inexperienced mothers. Pediatricians order their favorite formulas for every patient whether the mother wishes to breastfeed or not. Hospital staff physicians allow harmful systems and practices to persist. And breastfeeding mothers continue to be ordered to wean babies for trivial or even fallacious reasons.

A MEDICAL NO-MAN'S-LAND

In this day of specialists, the nursing mother is in a medical no-man's-land. Her breasts are the concern of the obstetrician. The milk within them is the concern of the pediatrician. The pediatrician prescribes for the baby; the obstetrician treats the infected breast. If the milk supply should be increased, call the pediatrician. If the milk supply should be dried up, that's the obstetrician's job. Many a nursing mother has spent a worried day just wondering which doctor she ought to call this time.

Fear of malpractice suits complicates this separation. A

male pediatrician, for example, may not even be willing to look at a cracked nipple, lest he be sued for sexual harrassment, even though the condition of the mother's nipples is often a vital clue to a baby's suckling problems. And since breastfeeding is the pediatrician's bailiwick, the obstetrician may be unwilling and unable to discuss the topic. Many a mother has found herself furious at the OB who was so solicitous of her a week earlier, when she was about to give birth, and is now impatient, even rude, on the telephone, when she calls for breastfeeding help.

Sometimes the division between specialties is really harmful, as in the case of yeast infections. Unless both mother and baby are treated, the infection returns; yet doctors may be very resistant to prescribing a drug for whichever one of the nursing couple is not actually exhibiting symptoms (see chapter 2, p. 56).

MEDICINE AND BEHAVIOR

Some medical attitudes toward breastfeeding, such as the viewpoint of that anatomy professor mentioned earlier in this chapter, are just old-fashioned sexism. But a historical rationale also exists. Until very recently, Western medical education has been geared toward identifying and if possible curing pathology, not toward maintaining normal processes such as lactation. Also, medical education has traditionally stayed away from areas involving *behavior* of any kind: what the patient does, when not ill, has not been medicine's concern. (In fact the whole profession is tellingly called "medicine," which means pills, shots, and doses, not "health care" or some more general term.)

Medical education omits giving attention not only to breastfeeding but also to similar topics related to well-being, such as nutrition, physiotherapy, and body conditioning. (The recognition that diet and exercise are important in controlling heart attacks in adult men is a recent exception.) Medical care givers have in a way been forced to become lactation coaches not because it is their traditional province

173

but only because the culture itself no longer provides women with what they need to know.

LA LECHE LEAGUE: THE BEGINNINGS

Perhaps a correction for this situation needed to begin with women themselves. In 1956, two nursing mothers in Franklin Park, a suburb of Chicago, took their babies to a picnic. They were ordinary young mothers, the kind you might meet in church or pass in any supermarket. They were unusual in those days, however, because they were both breastfeeding. As often happens when a nursing mother takes her baby out in public, other mothers at the picnic began to talk about their own attempts and failures to breastfeed. The two nursing mothers were very sympathetic. Like many nursing mothers in that era, they had each had real difficulty in nursing their first babies, and had not been truly successful until subsequent babies came along. They agreed that they might have been successful from the beginning if they had known another more experienced nursing mother to go to for encouragement and advice.

From that picnic conversation came the idea for an organization to enable nursing mothers to get together and help each other. Its name, La Leche League, was taken from a poetic Spanish title for the Madonna: *Nuestra Señora de la Leche y Buen Parto* (Our Lady of Bountiful Milk and Easy Delivery). Seven nursing mothers were the founders of La Leche League. They started out by reading all they could find about lactation, and by discussing breastfeeding with interested doctors. Then, armed with facts and the experience of nursing their own babies, they held a series of four meetings for those friends of theirs who were expecting babies. Discussions were led by nursing mothers on various topics: the advantages of breastfeeding, the art of breastfeeding and overcoming difficulties, childbirth, the family and the breastfed baby, nutrition, and weaning.

By the time the third series of meetings was under way, and La Leche League was a year old, there were three groups. One physician, Caroline Rawlins, M.D., filled her car with expectant patients and drove sixty miles for the monthly meetings. The young organization began receiving national publicity. Hundreds of phone calls and letters from nursing mothers came in every month. An article about La Leche League, excerpted from the first edition of *Nursing Your Baby,* was published in *Reader's Digest.* Membership grew by the thousands.

Much of the work of this expansion fell on the shoulders of the original seven mothers. Most of the founding mothers, who constituted the league's first board of directors, had big families. President Marian Tompson had seven children, librarian-researcher Mary White had ten, and Viola Lennon also reared ten, including breastfed twins. For years La Leche League work was sandwiched in and around housework and family life. Mothers stapled newsletters together in the evenings instead of doing housework, and answered correspondence instead of watching television. One mother had a thirteen-foot telephone cord so she could counsel a nervous nursing mother and load the washing machine or make corn muffins at the same time.

In the second year of La Leche League's existence, Edwina Froehlich and other founders put together a manual, *The Womanly Art of Breast Feeding,* to convey in writing some of the things they had learned about breastfeeding. The League also began publishing a collection of information sheets and pamphlets on special topics, such as breastfeeding and diabetes, and breastfeeding and drugs.

Gradually, with the increasing scale of the work, enough money was raised through sales of the manual and other sources to set up a full-time office with salaried employees. A network of state and regional coordinators was established to facilitate new group formation. The League devised a leader development program to screen and train new group leaders and to insure that a basic emphasis on home and family, and on good mothering through breastfeeding, would remain unchanged.

A growing group of physicians became champions of La Leche League: pediatricians and family practitioners Richard Applebaum, Robert Mendelsohn, Herbert Ratner, Gregory White, E. Robbins Kimball, Robert Jackson, and

Paul Fleiss; psychiatrists Frank Countryman and Hugh Riordan. With Niles and Michael Newton and others they formed a medical advisory board on breastfeeding that by 1990 had educated and inspired two generations of medical practitioners. Eventually the Medical Advisory Board would include many leading researchers and specialists in human lactation, from the United States and the rest of the world as well.

In 1964, La Leche League held its first three-day conferences presenting panels and lectures on parenting and human lactation for league leaders, members, and healthcare providers. The conferences are now held every two years in a different city in the United States or Canada, and are usually preceded by A.M.A.-accredited seminars for medical professionals. A conference may draw more than 2,000 attendees; many of them, of course, are nursing mothers, so that means at least 1,500 nursing babies come along, as well as fathers and hundreds of other children from toddlers to teens. The babies, being breastfed, are apt to be remarkably easygoing about a hotel visit—all they need is mom, wherever they are; but an LLLI conference is quite an experience for a hotel staff. La Leche League International's professional conference manager Hope Melnick has learned what to tell them—turn off the escalators, they're an attractive hazard; warn the banquet waiters to watch out for children underfoot; be prepared for extremely crowded elevators at break times—but conferences still bring surprises. One year, the banquet manager phoned the Founding Mothers' Suite the night before the conference, crying, "We've got a problem! You've got my refrigerators full of oranges and bananas" (LLLI provides free snacks for parents and older children) "and we're expecting nearly a thousand babies! Where am I going to put all those bottles?"

By 1990, La Leche League, now called La Leche League International, had become a sizable business. The organization was now fielding nearly 10,000 active leaders in fifty states and forty-six foreign countries, and accrediting another 1,000 leaders yearly. They were directly counseling, by mail, phone, and in person, almost 100,000 nursing mothers a month—over a million a year. A free telephone hot line—1-800-LA LECHE—enables the league to put a worried new mother anywhere in the United States in touch with a leader in her town—often in her neighborhood—sometimes within hours.

Some league group leaders, because of the Peace Corps, corporate moves, or other travel, found themselves living in countries where local customs made the basic mother-to-mother league meetings unfeasible—but where the needs of new mothers for breastfeeding information and support was even greater than at home. One result was the development of LLLI's Breastfeeding Resource Centers, usually anchored by a local physician or health worker using LLLI literature, equipment, and teaching aids to promote and support breastfeeding. By 1990, there were more than six hundred centers in operation and a dozen being organized each month. The League had become affiliated with the World Health Organization, and in 1990 was using a $75,000 grant from UNESCO, with matching funds from Chicago foundations, in a new program developing and training rural women to be village breastfeeding advocates in Guatemala and Honduras.

Researchers interested in human lactation discovered La Leche League as a wonderful resource for information and research topics, as well as an enormous research population to draw on. For example, when Niles Newton wanted to study tandem nursing—women who are breastfeeding an older child and a new baby simultaneously—she asked LLLI for help in locating subjects. The league quickly came up with 506 tandem-nursing volunteers. By 1990, La Leche League was contributing volunteer subjects to fifteen research projects a year.

La Leche League had also become a publishing house. The central office had fifty paid employees. The newsletter, once mailed from Edwina Froehlich's garage, now went out from a league publications office, along with two other journals—one for leaders and another, *Breastfeeding Abstracts,* for medical professionals—and a series of research monographs on clinical problems for lactation consultants. La Leche League published and distributed dozens of books for mothers on subjects ranging from cooking to handling teenagers, some in partnership with medical authors. The league published a mail-order catalog, endorsing and selling selected breastfeeding-related products. A New York publisher, New American Library, licensed the rights to an updated edition of *The Womanly Art of Breastfeeding* and enjoyed steady sales.

The organization has retained its uniquely feminine style. Board meetings are attended by babies and grand-babies in a room full of toys. Major business conferences may be held around La Leche League's kitchen table. The kitchen, symbolically, occupies the very center of the Franklin Park offices' executive floor, and must be traversed to get to other rooms and offices; anyone passing through seems to be welcome to join any discussion taking place. Furthermore, business is not La Leche League's main interest. Manufacturers, publishers, and other business people sometimes tear out their hair trying to work with La Leche League. Decisions are not made in a hurry, and the bottom line is not always a consideration; for example, although teetering annually on the edge of going broke, until recent years La Leche League rejected the idea of charitable fund-raising of any kind.

In 1975, the coauthor of this book, Karen Pryor, told a league conference audience that it was the most successful subversive organization in the United States. The percentage of babies leaving U.S. hospitals breastfed had risen tremendously during its existence. La Leche League was undoubtedly a powerful factor in this widespread cultural change. By 1990, however, LLLI was no longer a fringe group, but in the mainstream.

LEADERS AND CHANGES

The experience of being a La Leche League leader is edifying. Many civic organizations are supposed to teach their members "leadership," but from the moment they pass their tests and run their first meeting, LLLI mothers have to *lead,* handling other mothers' crises, facing down authority if necessary, teaching, encouraging, defending.

Women who perhaps were once shy and uncertain become competent in a host of ways.

This is not always good for a marriage; sometimes a man whose self-esteem depends on feeling superior finds it hard when his once-subordinate wife is getting her picture in the newspaper and her way paid to national conferences. It is, however, good for the woman; as one leader, now an executive, put it, "I would never, never, have known the talents I have, much less learned to put them to use, if it hadn't been for the league."

As their children grow up, many league leaders have developed professions. Some, like conference director Hope Melnick and most of the founding mothers, are full-time salaried administrators at La Leche League. Other league leaders have become physicians, midwives, nurse-practitioners, lactation consultants, psychologists, and social workers. Kathleen Auerbach, Ph.D., and Jan Riordan, Ph.D., are among those who have become medical researchers specializing in lactation, and members of the faculty of medical and nursing schools. Diana Korte and Roberta Scaer turned their skills at tactful confrontation into a landmark book on the politics of childbirth, *A Good Birth, a Safe Birth*. Kittie Frantz, R.N., P.N.P. (Pediatric Nurse-Practitioner), who started the first inner-city league groups in riot-torn Watts in Los Angeles, is now an international authority on early management of breastfeeding, teaches at the University of Southern California Medical School, and has created and produced a series of breastfeeding instruction tapes, which are in use in hospitals and teaching centers all over the country.

Being a leader generates skills that work in any field. Several leaders, including founding mother Mary Ann Kerwin, have become attorneys. Former leader Leslie Hawkinson has been mayor of her hometown. Judy Sanders developed a successful professional acting career, going on stage for the first time at age forty-five. She finds that the qualities an actor needs—intuition, empathy, resourcefulness—were honed by being a leader, and her long experience of how people and families behave is an advantage that some lifelong performers completely lack.

LA LECHE LEAGUE AND WORKING MOTHERS

In spite of the professionalism of many former leaders, however, some mothers complain of an apparent prejudice, in parts of the organization, against working women. In some La Leche League groups, the LLLI beliefs that mothers and babies should be together, and that family comes first, has been taken a step further; mothers and babies should never be apart, and women who work "choose" to leave their babies—therefore are not good mothers. Of course, working outside the home has become necessary, indeed, unavoidable, for many present-day mothers; and the mother who works and breastfeeds is, after all, vigorously demonstrating her caring for and attachment to her baby. But many have felt rebuffed or condemned by what they perceive to be La Leche League's attitude.

Some now-professional women who were leaders in the early days of LLLI feel that the trend in leader selection and leader volunteers has changed. The league leader of the '60s and '70s was a path-finder, an innovator: she had to be, to teach breastfeeding in a bottle-feeding world. The leader of today is often a family-oriented traditionalist. She may oppose the women's movement and reject some of the ongoing changes in society. While her work and counseling are still sorely needed, they are not directed toward the women whose lives reflect those societal changes.

LACTATION CONSULTANTS

Other local organizations do exist, such as the Nursing Mothers Council in Philadelphia and several other cities, to support and advise breastfeeding mothers; some differ in policies and detail from the League, but most are avowedly volunteer and amateur. Now, however, a new kind of breastfeeding advisor has arisen, a trained and certified health professional: the lactation consultant.

By the 1980s, some women, in and out of nursing mothers' organizations, had spent decades studying lactation, identifying and assessing breastfeeding problems, and counseling nursing mothers. Women began to feel the need for an organization that would serve those whose skills and knowledge had reached the professional level. Furthermore, as breastfeeding became more popular, R.N.s, midwives, and other women of varied backgrounds were beginning to call themselves lactation consultants and to charge fees for advice; some were knowledgeable and some were not. Some form of licensing or testing also seemed to be needed, for the sake of the mothers, if for no other reason.

In the mid-1980s La Leche League funded the formation of a certification organization, the International Board of Lactation Consultant Examiners (IBLCE), to devise an exam by which one could become a certified lactation consultant. With the help of the National Commission of Health Certifying Agencies, the board located a psychometrician skilled in the design of certification exams, gathered a panel of fifty medical and breastfeeding experts, and used IBLCE, a nonprofit corporation, to manage the test design, administration, and grading.

Meanwhile, a group of women including nurses, physical therapists, league leaders, and others, formed the International Lactation Consultants Association, or ILCA (pronounced "ilk-a"). Some members of ILCA were board-certified and others were not. In addition to providing a forum for breastfeeding issues, ILCA publishes a research journal and holds annual accredited scientific meetings for medical professionals interested in lactation.

The IBLCE certification exam rapidly became a model of its kind. It is both difficult and fair; well-prepared people usually pass, but the top scores are seldom higher than 85 percent or so. The first half of the exam is four hours of multiple-choice questions on technical information: anatomy, child development, pharmacology, and so on. The second half is four hours of multiple-choice questions based on slides. "That's what separates the sheep from the goats," says one ILCA member. "A pediatrician who takes the exam may know all about the significance of a *Candida* infection, but if he can't identify a thrush-infected nipple when he sees one, that won't do him much good."

Because the information in the field is increasing so fast, lactation consultants must be recertified every five years (that might not be a bad idea in some other health-related specialties, too, but so far it has usually been resisted by current practitioners).

At the time of writing, in 1990, ILCA has over 1,800 voting members, 1,200 of whom are presently entitled to use the initials I.B.C.L.C.—International Board Certified Lactation Consultant—after their names. Perhaps half are onetime La Leche leaders; the rest are M.D.'s, nurses, physical therapists, nutritionists, midwives, mental health professionals, and others who have backgrounds in working with nursing mothers.

Lactation consultants earn their livings in a wide variety of ways. Some work full-time and on salary for private medical centers or a group of pediatricians, usually a happy situation for everyone, especially the clients. (Fees are comparable to the charges for other health-related services such as dental checkups or physical therapy, and are billable to health insurers and other third parties.) Some L.C.s are on the staffs of hospitals, helping new mothers and coaching nurses and interns. While hospital L.C.s are badly needed, they are not always used correctly; sometimes a staff simply dumps all breastfeeding instruction into an L.C.'s lap, which means that mothers who are not on her shift get the same uneven help as usual. Sometimes head nurses tend to look on the L.C. as merely an extra staff member who can be used for any nursing chore or called in whenever they are short-handed. A hospital lactation consultant may be strongly supported by some of the staff M.D.s and rigorously opposed by others. In that case she must think constantly about whose patient she is talking to, and what she is and is not allowed to say.

Some L.C.s are in private practice. They visit mothers and babies at home. There they observe the baby at the breast, looking for problems caused by poor positioning or sucking. They talk to the mother about her entire birth and nursing experience, spending two to four hours finding the exact cause of the problem and teaching the mother a way to fix it—time no physician can ever spend with a single patient. They follow up by phone and are available night and day for phone consultation. (See below and chapter 9, p. 213, for information on locating a lactation consultant.)

ILCA is a politically active organization, in contrast to La Leche League. Individually and as an organization, the members lobby for desirable legislation; in 1990, for example, they mounted a successful effort supporting Congressional appropriation of an additional $8,000,000 to the Women, Infants and Children (WIC) food supplementing program for breastfeeding information at WIC centers around the country. ILCA also attends conferences and actively presents itself as a source of breastfeeding information to other health-related professional associations such as organizations of public health officials, physical therapists, dieticians, and nutritionists.

A NETWORK OF SUPPORT FOR NURSING MOTHERS

What is beginning to evolve is an interactive network of support for the nursing mother, in which each level of assistance bolsters the others. The La Leche League leader provides friendship, accurate information, and practical guidance. When a problem arises that is out of her range of expertise, she can pass the mother on to a lactation consultant who provides trained expertise, specifically in breastfeeding. If the L.C. spots a medical problem—which may be anything from a neurological defect in the baby to a mother with walking pneumonia—she can refer the mother to a breastfeeding-oriented physician. And the medical care giver, ideally, provides good prenatal care, a good birth environment, and appropriate treatment for medical problems.

The system interacts, also, in reverse; busy practitioners who don't really have the time, the training, or the inclination to sort out a nursing mother's problems can refer her to a well-prepared and experienced certified lactation consultant, an alternative that many prefer to relying on a shifting pool of volunteer leaders. But lactation consultants are few, and nursing mothers are many. La Leche League, with its

10,000 leaders and telephone hot line can often supply exactly what is needed, and all that is needed: information and mother-to-mother contact. Often, lactation consultants recommend such contact to a mother even when her particular breastfeeding problem has been resolved.

HUMAN MILK BANKS

In spite of the help available to nursing mothers, there will always be situations in which breastfeeding is impossible—typically, when a sick newborn must remain in the hospital and the mother lives too far away to come in and nurse. And despite the continuing refinement of artificial foods, there have always been some babies who cannot tolerate anything but human milk. Furthermore, sick babies, traumatized babies, and babies with very low birth weights may also do much better on human milk than on even the most specialized synthetics. One answer is the human milk bank.

Operating like a blood bank, the milk bank collects milk from donor mothers, tests it, freezes it, and then dispenses it to hospitals on a doctor's prescription. Milk banks in the United States have ranged from small operations with a few donors, run out of somebody's kitchen freezer, to elaborate charities with many volunteers, to professional services set up within hospitals. Most present-day milk banks operate within a hospital and supply milk to neonatal intensive care units in their own and other institutions.

Donors, who are nursing mothers willing to express extra milk for sick babies, are recruited from maternity patients or located by word of mouth. Mothers are screened for health (no smokers, no one on medication or birth control pills, no one with active illness, no drug users) and trained in techniques for clean expression of milk and proper storage, in containers provided by the milk bank. In some communities, mothers deliver their own milk to the bank periodically; others use volunteer drivers to pick up the milk. Some mothers donate milk for a few months, others for a year or more; some come back with each new baby. Some women produce ten or twelve ounces of extra milk a week; others can donate by the quart. One California mother whose terribly ill baby was saved by 55 liters—almost 15 gallons, many months' supply—of human milk, went on to have two more healthy breastfed babies and paid the bank back by donating 150 liters of her own milk.

Human milk is paid for by insurance companies and various state agencies. Pediatricians prescribe it for newborns with problems of malabsorption, various kinds of intolerances, and a wide range of infections, including intractable diarrhea, gastroenteritis, and ulcerative colitis. Newborns who must undergo surgery, especially for problems such as intestinal obstructions, do better if they receive highly digestible human milk pre- and postoperatively, avoiding the added insult to the gut of the cows' milk proteins in commercial products.

Irritation of the gut walls by cows' milk protein can cause bleeding—a sometimes overlooked cause of anemia—in normal babies. In small preterm babies, artificial feeding can be accompanied by a highly dangerous condition of the intestinal walls, necrotizing enterocolitis, which can be prevented or ameliorated by human milk. And the immunizing and protective mechanisms in banked human milk are especially valuable for infants with immune system disorders; most of these protective components are unharmed by freezing the milk—although they are usually destroyed by heat sterilization.

In the early 1980s, milk banks were proliferating in the United States. The rising incidence of breastfeeding made more donors available, and more and more neonatologists were learning to use human milk for their tiny patients. Extremely small preterm babies, who, technically, should still be in utero, need more protein than full-term milk delivers; for these patients, synthetic milk manufacturers actually developed protein supplements that were designed specifically to be added to human milk. One large California health maintenance organization estimated that the use of human milk was reducing overall costs in its neonatal unit by 20 percent, owing to decreased severity of illnesses and length of hospitalization. One bank, the Mothers' Milk Bank of the California Institute for Medical Research, in

San Jose, typically collected up to 60,000 ounces of human milk a year, from approximately seventy-five donors, and regularly shipped milk to more than fifteen hospitals.

Then came the AIDS epidemic. Like many viruses, the HIV virus can be shed in human milk. Whether or not the virus can then infect the recipient of the milk is incidental —how could you be sure? The very idea was enough to panic medical administrators. And it would obviously be impossible to test every donor every week, or to look for the virus in every ounce of milk. Milk banks around the country had two choices: pasteurize the milk (which would reduce its benefits considerably) or close down. Many closed. By 1990, there were only seven milk banks in the United States in full operation.

In 1985, a group of U.S. and Canadian banks formed the Human Milk Banking Association of North America to set up specific guidelines for milk bank operation. The guidelines, designed with the advice of the Centers for Disease Control and British milk bank authority J. D. Baum, M.D., have since been endorsed by the American Academy of Pediatrics, the Canadian Paediatric Society, the Centers for Disease Control, and the Food and Drug Administration. They include pasteurization, but at 56° C instead of the higher temperatures that are more usual. Live-virus testing at the Centers for Disease Control demonstrated that this treatment is effective against the HIV virus, but destroys only 10 percent of the secretory IgA and leaves other protectors, such as lactoferrin and lysozyme, intact; this is the procedure milk banks now follow.

Milk banks are usually run by one energetic, dedicated woman, often with a single assistant and a handful of volunteers; a stellar example is Terry Asquith, chairman of the Milk Banking Association, who runs the Mothers' Milk Bank in San Jose, California. Asquith is currently working, with the blessing of the Surgeon-General, to establish broad-scale research in a promising area, the use of human milk in ameliorating the illnesses of babies born to HIV-positive mothers. Her milk bank survives, although, like all milk banks, the program is constantly in financial peril.

Use of human milk depends very much on the habits and

preferences of individual physicians. All too often, medical teams will try everything under the sun to help a sick baby except human milk, leaving that for the last-ditch effort. If the milk comes too late to help, it is easy to say that human milk "doesn't work." Asquith feels that milk banks will continue to struggle in a climate of indifference and opposition, "until the day when every medical school instills in every medical student a thorough understanding of the *wonders* of human milk."

CHAPTER 8

The Practical Politics of Breastfeeding

WORKING FROM WITHIN: TEACHING MEDICAL PROFESSIONALS

Helping mothers, one at a time, is important; but the fastest way to help a lot of mothers and babies is to change the behavior and point of view of the people who are currently practicing and learning medicine, and who in turn can reach thousands of mothers in a lifetime. La Leche League's physicians' seminars reach hundreds of practitioners each year. And at least three teaching hospitals in the United States have established breastfeeding teaching programs.

At Beth Israel Hospital in New York City, Marvin Eiger, M.D., coauthor of *The Complete Book of Breastfeeding,* has established a lactation clinic that serves to educate both patients and staff. Two full-time, board-certified lactation consultants counsel mothers before and after birth, and together with Dr. Eiger, maintain a breastfeeding clinic for nursing women. (Eiger states that his most important role is not in caring for patients but in defending his lactation consultants and the lactation program from pressures in his own institution.) The lactation consultants maintain a continuing in-service training in lactation for maternity and nursery nurses and staff. Finally, and perhaps most important, every six months the lactation program offers a series of one- and two-day teaching symposia to the medical profession at large on breastfeeding management and research.

The Medical School of the University of Southern California has a teaching clinic under the direction of pediatrician Laura Waxman, M.D., and pediatric nurse practitioner Kittie Frantz, that is *required* for all pediatric and family practice interns, residents, medical students during pediatric rotation, and physician assistant students. It is also attended voluntarily by midwifery and nursing students, and by medical students and residents in other fields. The program is only one morning long, but in that time Waxman and Frantz instill in perhaps a dozen budding M.D.s a week an understanding of hands-on management of breastfeeding mothers and babies. It's an unsentimental program. Young male students blanch to see Frantz demonstrate good and bad positioning with a teddy bear and her own (clothed) breasts. The students must interact immediately with mothers, usually low-income and Hispanic, who have come to the hospital's outpatient clinic for breastfeeding help. Many medical students in this clinic are actually seeing a woman breastfeeding for the first time. The class is a crash course in things these students have never thought of before.

"What's the single most important reason for helping these mothers breastfeed?" Frantz asks.

"The bonding thing?" one med student ventures.

"Immunities?" asks another.

"Yes," Frantz says. "But breastfeeding is especially vital to these mothers because it costs no money." She also explains some of the things that can go wrong if the mother is not taught what to do. Everyone is properly horrified, for example, at the warning to a woman intern working in the emergency room, to watch out for babies who show up in dire straits because their mothers fed them a bottle of something from the drugstore that was white and said "milk" on the label—it was milk of magnesia.

Frantz has worked as a pediatric nurse practitioner for private physicians serving the spectrum from street people and welfare cases to Hollywood's richest. Even the most indifferent students start concentrating on breastfeeding information when she tells them from her own experience, "Mothers know a lot about breastfeeding, now. And mothers talk to mothers. If you are going into pediatrics, no matter where you end up practicing medicine, well-informed support of breastfeeding is the single best practice-builder going."

WELLSTART

The San Diego Lactation Program, Wellstart, began as a teaching service at the University of California's San Diego Medical Center. Various medical school departments put their heads together to set up a lactation program that would not only make things easier for nursing mothers and babies, but, more significantly, would teach health-care students how to promote and manage breastfeeding well. The program began with such straightforward steps as throwing out promotional literature for synthetic milk in clinic waiting rooms and replacing it with good breastfeeding information. Soon the program was expanded to a large nearby hospital; it included staff training, prenatal education for parents, and the institution of such practices as delivery-room breastfeeding, routine rooming-in, and the routine use of human milk for all ill and preterm infants in intensive care. An outpatient lactation clinic was started, initially just one day a week, not to serve all the mothers possible but to provide teaching opportunities for medical personnel interested in learning the management of breastfeeding.

UCSD medical and nursing students rotate through the lactation program as they would through any other specialty, receiving at least sixteen hours of classroom instruction and extensive clinical exposure to breastfeeding management techniques. Pediatrician Audrey Naylor, M.D., director of Wellstart, and other faculty members offer training programs for professionals in other cities and work hard to maintain cordial and, when feasible, instructional interactions with private physicians in the area.

In 1983, with a grant from the U.S. Agency for International Development (AID), Wellstart began a training program for health professionals from teaching hospitals in developing nations. Physician-nurse teams come to San Diego in small groups for an intensive multiweek course in lactation services. Their travel costs and personal expenses are paid for. In return, participant hospitals must commit themselves to support the development of each team's plan in their own country; Wellstart provides them with follow-up technical services and, as a goodbye present, their choice from a huge collection of teaching slides and references.

By 1987, Wellstart had trained more than eighty professionals from thirteen countries in Asia, Africa, and Latin America. Follow-up surveys indicate that harmful practices are being supplanted by vigorous lactation programs wherever graduates go, and that many are giving workshops and courses of their own, thus reaching hundreds of other health professionals in a powerful contribution to much-needed change.

Professionals can instruct other professionals. But all nursing mothers can be teachers. Karen Pryor recalls appearing on a panel about breastfeeding, with a nursing mother and her baby, and the chief pediatrician from the biggest hospital in that city. The M.D. monopolized the discussion with inappropriate, even harmful misinformation about breastfeeding. After the program Karen, seething, shared a cab with the mother and baby. "Well," the mother remarked, "I just moved here with four kids, and I've been looking for a pediatrician. I think I'll go to that one."

"Why?" Karen asked, astonished.

"I know he doesn't know anything about breastfeeding," the mother went on, "but I don't need help with that. And he's probably very good with ear infections and things."

"Probably."

"So he'll get to know me, and my nursing baby, and he'll *learn* about breastfeeding. And he'll change."

"You're a saint."

"Oh no . . . I've done it to three other doctors already."

RESEARCH AND RESEARCHERS

Helping mothers breastfeed—and teaching medical care providers to help them, too—solves part of the problem of effecting change in the system. Just as fundamental is the need to improve our scientific understanding of the process and relationship—to demonstrate why and how breast-feeding works, so that it can no longer be treated as just another medical fad. This is the province of basic research.

Whenever a new field of research opens up, in *any* branch of science, the establishment views it with traditional preju-dice: as "an unimportant field for research" and, contrarily, as a field in which "everything of importance is already known." Human lactation has long been thus dismissed as an unsuitable area for research. Now, however, the increase in the number of women who breastfeed has enlarged both the client population—breastfeeding patients—and, per-haps even more important, the sources of funding for professionals who want to work with nursing couples. A small but growing cadre of physicians and researchers doesn't have to be convinced that human milk and breast-feeding are important; these professionals are dedicating their lives to expanding our knowledge of lactation. They are committed; they are crusaders; one writer has dubbed them "lactophiles." And they are plunging down investiga-tive trails in all directions.

Human lactation research is occurring not just in medi-cine but also in fields such as biochemistry, immunology, psychology, pharmacology, and public health. As the quan-tity of research increases, the quality does, too. Heightened interest and rapid computer access to scientific abstracts mean that superficial or slanted research is eyed by more colleagues and jumped on more quickly than in the past. People ask better questions and plan their studies more competently. A body of good scientific work now exists for new researchers to build on.

This explosion of good information is not a national phenomenon; it is planetary. As this book was being written, a brief computer scan of a single, recent two-month period turned up dozens of brand-new research reports on human milk, of which at least twenty were real news. The finds included an important paper from China on virus transmission in milk; papers from Guatemala, Canada, and Gambia on yet more newly discovered immunity-enhancing factors in human milk; a startling article from Hong Kong about contaminants in the milk of mothers who eat seafood from Hong Kong Harbor; and from the United States a study, reported in a genetics journal, demonstrating that a sense of humor about breastfeeding—what the authors call "coping humor"—increases the secretory IgA in mothers' saliva and breast milk, and is statistically related to a lower incidence of colds in mothers and babies alike.

BREASTFEEDING ECONOMICS

When we read newspaper accounts of great medical advances and new discoveries, we may think of medicine as a field that changes with startling rapidity. In fact, some areas of medicine are strongly traditional and accept change slowly, even in the face of good research and scientific evidence. One state director of public health has said that a new drug is accepted in three months, but effecting a change in childbirth and newborn care takes at least ten years. The power of tradition has been a potent force in the continuation of artificial feeding as the norm. Another and perhaps even more potent force has also been at work in maintaining obstacles to breastfeeding: the natural human desire to make money, leading to the active efforts of corporations and individuals that benefit financially from artificial feeding.

The development of comparatively safe artificial feeding was soon followed by production of commercially manufactured artificial milks. Why should a mother go to all the trouble of mixing ingredients and sterilizing the results, when she could buy a ready-made product? And what a product! Anyone who starts using it is probably going to have to go on using it. Doctors recommend it. And every new human being on the planet is a potential customer. "Infant formula" rapidly became big business. By 1950, nearly every baby in the United States was being reared on synthetic milk of one brand or another. The competition was between brands, not for the market; the manufacturers *had* the market. Furthermore, a worldwide market existed, just waiting to be tapped.

By the mid-1950s several multinational corporations undertook aggressive marketing of bottle-feeding and synthetic milks in underdeveloped countries. Milk company advertisements plastered buildings and decorated roadsides from Guam to Guatemala, picturing enormous healthy babies—who owed their health to the use of this or that canned or powdered substance. From this ubiquitous propaganda mothers gained the impression that breast milk is not good enough. In fact, some companies dressed their village sales representatives in nurses' white uniforms, to underscore the presumed health benefits of their products.

The immediate results of artificial feeding in a destitute environment are often disastrous. Families making seventy-five cents a day can hardly spend ten dollars a week on baby food, so a mother may use a spoonful of precious powdered milk in each bottle rather than a cupful, diluting it so thinly that the baby is starving. Furthermore, one cannot make up a sterile or even a clean baby bottle in a sewage-strewn slum, without clean water or even a pot to boil it in. A single contaminated feeding is sometimes enough to send a baby on the downward spiral of infections, diarrhea, and dehydration that ends in death.

From South Africa to Singapore, hospitals and clinics began to build rehydration centers, designed to treat the ever-growing overflow of infants dangerously dehydrated by diarrhea, brought on by artificial feeding. They were treating the victims, not of poverty and tropical diseases (since the breastfed baby is well-protected against both hunger and infection) but of a highly successful marketing plan. By 1960, D.B. Jelliffe, M.D., and his wife, Patrice Jelliffe, United Nations trailblazers in the area of maternal and child health, were pointing out in World Health Organization meetings and publications that this disastrous scenario was occurring all over the world, and with ever-increasing frequency.

By 1970, the health consequences of corporate promotion of synthetic feeds were becoming obvious in many underdeveloped countries. Public opposition to these practices also arose in the Western nations. Crusaders in Great Britain published an investigative report—with a life-size baby bottle on the front—called "The Baby Killer." Swiss activists took one of their own big companies, Nestlé, to court, charging it with irresponsible marketing practices; a group of Canadian nuns sued Bristol-Myers, a major manufacturer of synthetic milks, for misstatements. In the United States, opposition to Nestlé's marketing practices led to an organized Nestlé boycott that gradually spread to ten countries.

In 1981, the U.N.'s World Health Organization adopted an International Code of Marketing of Breast-Milk Substitutes, limiting or prohibiting such practices as inaccurate advertising, gifts to mothers or health-care providers, and the giving of free samples of products to new mothers. Although the international corporations lobbied vigorously against it, the resolution, now generally known as the WHO Code, was ratified by all of the participating nations with the exception, to our shame, of the United States. Since then, some nations have independently passed even stricter codes of their own. In the Philippines, for example, as a result of new legislation, a mother has a hard time even getting a bottle in the hospital. Combined with reeducation, and eradication of the central nursery, such programs go far to reinstate breastfeeding as the standard. This in turn not only reduces infant mortality but eliminates a serious national and individual cash outflow and contributes markedly to both public health and population control.

MARKETING SYNTHETIC MILKS IN THE UNITED STATES

In the United States, the major manufacturers of synthetic milks are drug companies, such as Abbott Laboratories (Similac), Squibb and Bristol-Myers (Enfamil), and Mead Johnson; food companies such as Gerber's and Nestlé have at present only a minor share of the market. Since the United States up to the time of writing has not ratified the WHO Code, these manufacturers of synthetic baby foods have continued to be free, in this country, to go on promoting their products as they see fit; now, for example, several companies are advertising directly to mothers, a practice forbidden by the WHO Code.

Synthetic milk promotion has always included, and continues to include, heavy advertising in medical journals and direct promotion to physicians. The manufacturers present themselves as helpful friends to the physician, supplying not only free milk and bottles to hospitals, but free tape measures, parent information pamphlets, M.D. educational seminars, pencils, notepads, all-expenses-paid trips to medical conferences, and so on. No one in these companies does any of this without the well-founded expectation that it will add to the bottom line. Marketing executives know very well, and must prove it at year's end, what the financial return will be on all their "helpfulness" to physicians.

Pediatricians, however, who seldom have much exposure to big business procedures, are by and large unaware of the effect these promotions will have on their decision making and patient care. Doctors are just as susceptible as the rest of us to Madison Avenue techniques. Individual practitioners usually don't have time to review new research personally and must rely on responsible outside sources. This leaves them wide open to propaganda. If a company has sufficient prestige and dignity, if it presents information in such a way that it seems to be entirely confirmed by good scientific research, and if the information is endorsed by enough brilliant names, a doctor will probably accept it as reliable.

The drug companies that manufacture synthetic milks also fund much of the research on infant feeding. Unsurprisingly, a lot of this research is in areas where it is possible to minimize or denigrate the advantages of human milk; for example, just looking through the titles of research reports on human milk since 1980, one can surmise that it is a lot easier at present to get funds, say, for a study of contaminants in human milk than it is for a study of contaminants in synthetic milk. And of course the research that gets funded is the research on which doctors base their decisions.

Along with the information on new research, the doctor is also bombarded with promotional materials. Just look around any pediatric clinic. The names of brands of synthetic milk are everywhere, on notepads, telephone-book covers, pencils, growth charts, and so on—not only reminders to the physician but subtle suggestions to the mother that their medical care givers approve of and encourage the use of those products.

One particularly insidious promotional practice, which also utilizes the medical environment's aura of approval to influence mothers, is the free "baby kit," containing pamphlets on infant care, baby clothes, and small toys, given to mothers as they leave the hospital. In addition, the kit contains a product sample, which may amount to as much as five days' supply of synthetic milk (enough, once it has been put into the baby, to make lactation hard to reestablish). Research shows that mothers, in a moment of insecurity, are likely to use the samples, and that use of the samples is directly related to early cessation of breastfeeding. The mother is now a customer.

Once a mother starts using a given brand—tacitly recommended by the hospital, after all—she is highly likely to stay with that brand. One is not surprised to learn that manufacturers compete to get their kits into hospitals. A common ploy, and one that financially hard-pressed hospitals have trouble refusing, is that the corporation will provide, free, all the synthetic milk used by the hospital nursery all year long, if the hospital will distribute its gift pack rather than some other manufacturer's. Hospital usage of a particular brand is such a successful promotional device that recently, according to the *Journal of Human Lactation,* a bidding war broke out in Vancouver, B.C., for the favor of one particular large hospital; the winning manufacturer ended up not only giving the hospital a three years' supply of free synthetic milk, but paying $500,000 for the guarantee that the hospital would use *only* its product during the three years.

With the increasing restrictions on foreign marketing, a lot of high-priced talent has been turned loose on the promotion of synthetic milk in the U.S. market, and with some success. The federal WIC program, which supplies free food to mothers and babies, rapidly became the biggest single customer for synthetic milks in the world. And physicians, parents, and WIC managers have also reacted compliantly to the marketing suggestion that synthetic milk is not just for the small infant. Medical personnel began recommending as a general rule that people should use brand-name synthetic milk for the entire first year instead of switching to much less expensive cows' milk after the first six months, as mothers used to do.

Still, many women don't use the product at all. The industry in fact apparently began to notice that breastfeeding was sufficiently widespread in the United States to have become a financial threat. Only a handful of tiny corporations benefit from breastfeeding financially—the makers of nursing bras, for example. On the other hand, in 1990, a family feeding their baby synthetic milk for a year spent a minimum of $600 on this commercial product, not to mention what they spent on bottles, nipples, and auxiliary equipment (and perhaps on medication for allergies, infections, and so on—but surely the drug companies don't consider their synthetic milk products as profit centers in that way).

Breastfeeding mothers, on the other hand, spend nothing. Every time another mother breastfeeds, she is costing some corporation hundreds of dollars in lost sales, an alarming blow to the corporate bottom line. This very real competition can no longer be fought directly, as it has been in developing countries, with information suggesting that the product is better for your baby than plain old mother's milk. The advertising pitch has become more subtle; "of course you want to breastfeed, but when breastfeeding fails or it's time to wean . . . our product is best."

Sometimes the propaganda is truly ingenious. The *Journal of Human Lactation* reports on breastfeeding advice pamphlets, published by milk manufacturers and distributed free to mothers, that purport to teach breastfeeding, but that stress difficulties and drawbacks, and treat hospital-generated problems, such as engorgement, as the expected norm, and pamphlets with bland and more or less accurate texts, but with illustrations in which breastfeeding mothers look unhappy and impoverished, and bottle-feeding mothers look radiant and upscale. Other illustrations show mothers holding babies in positions guaranteed to cause sore nipples (positions that the new mother is likely to emulate, consciously or not). Free educational videos have been created with the same kinds of hidden agendas: an emphasis on the difficulties of breastfeeding, and visuals that, if used as examples, might well bring about such difficulties.

Another countermeasure to the popularity of breastfeeding has been the deliberate funneling of sizable amounts of corporate funding to programs that do *not* further the cause of breastfeeding. The message can be quite blunt; at the 1989 La Leche League International Conference, an executive of a major synthetic milk manufacturer told the attending representative of UNESCO (the United Nations education agency), in front of bystanders, that if her agency continued to take it upon itself to promote breastfeeding, his corporation might have to rethink its annual donation.

Meanwhile, grants are being made toward professional-level workshops, programs, and publications that down grade the importance of breastfeeding. Professors, doctors and researchers are courted publicly and sent to drug company-sponsored meetings—at ski resorts, for instance —with all expenses paid. The proceedings of not necessarily impartial medical gatherings are published, sometimes at corporate expense. Studies with predetermined outcomes get funded. The sums of money involved can be impressive —and tempting—to professors and university administrations alike.

Good, solid, statistically sound research on breastfeeding is hard to do. For example, random sampling is fundamental to much medical research procedure, but one cannot establish a *real* random sample of nursing couples by, say, telling all mothers in even-numbered rooms to breastfeed for a year and all mothers in odd-numbered rooms to bottle-feed. Aside from the built-in social difficulties, a lot of breastfeeding research is seriously flawed, even when undertaken in good faith. For example, numerous studies have been made concerning the occurrence of various illnesses in breastfed vs. artificially fed babies. But until recently, many investigators, as pointed out previously, did not differentiate between fully breastfed babies and token or partially breastfed babies. Some studies consider babies "breastfed" who were breastfed for only a few weeks or even a few days, or were getting one breastfeeding a day and the rest in bottles. Inevitably, results from such studies are ambiguous at best.

To see what can happen, let's look at one well-known study, by Bachner, Leventhal, and Shapiro, published in 1986 in the *Journal of the American Medical Association*. The authors sought to clarify the question of whether or not breastfeeding protects against infections, not by doing further research but by examining all the research that had been done (the technique, called meta-analysis, has become rather fashionable in the medical literature). The authors granted from the start that breastfeeding protects against infection in underdeveloped countries; but their personal position, stated at the beginning of their discussion, was that the evidence was conflicting for any protection in industrialized countries.

By establishing requirements concerning research methodology and statistical sampling, they narrowed their survey to twenty studies. (They did *not* exclude all the studies that commingled token or partially breastfed babies with fully breastfed babies.) Then, to their credit, they did a meticulous analysis of the design flaws in these studies, which anyone planning to do breastfeeding research would do well to peruse. The final conclusion of this review, however, which has come to be known as "the Yale study," was that breastfeeding "has at most a minimal protective effect against infections in industrialized countries."

The value of this kind of study depends, of course, on the validity of the assumptions made at the start; for example, lumping mixed-feed babies with breastfed babies is a biologically inappropriate assumption that will compromise your results. Other researchers in breastfeeding epidemiology were, however, taken aback by another aspect of the Yale study. After initial (and ambiguous) findings had been presented to the research community, the authors modified one selection requirement, permitting the admission of several more research studies, most of which had produced negative findings. The statistical evidence against the protective value of breastfeeding thus appeared to be strengthened. To many scientists, that is not fair play.

Finally, while one hesitates to compare publications of a distinguished university to the output of, say, the Tobacco Institute, it is hard even for a layman to overlook the fact that the authors of this survey have been supported in their work by awards and grants from a synthetic milk manufacturer.

MILK AND THE MEDIA

The Yale study had regrettable impact, especially in medical circles in underdeveloped nations; medical personnel will be coping with the repercussions for a long time. Unfortunately, this is likely to be true of any bad news about breastfeeding, simply because bad news *is* news. A story revealing something wrong with mother's milk is like a story about someone killing dolphins: it's irresistible. And the press and TV don't necessarily mind if the originator of the story is someone who knows next to nothing about lactation.

The "dioxin scare" is a good example. A group of chemists at an upper New York state university found dioxin in the body fat of autopsied cadavers; the cadavers were mostly those of elderly derelicts who had been living on the streets. The researchers speculated that women (healthy young women living normal lives) might have the same dioxin in their body fat. The chemists then speculated that if the women lost weight, the dioxin would simply be recycled in the body; that the only way fat could actually leave the body would be through breastfeeding (not true—we excrete skin oils, for example) and that all breast milk, therefore, could contain dioxin. They then *publicly announced,* at a meeting of the American Chemical Society. that mothers should breastfeed either not at all or "for just a short time," a wildly unscientific conclusion that, of course, was pounced on with joy by some members of the press.

This uninformed snap judgment was immediately refuted by the World Health Organization, the American Academy of Pediatrics, La Leche League International, the Center for Disease Control, and even a dioxin expert at the Environmental Protection Agency, but it scared people anyway. And this kind of scare is very much to the economic advantage of some organizations, and not just milk manufacturers, either.

One would think, for example, that nursing mothers and environmentalists should be on the same side—not just morally, but practically; *think* of all the energy squandered in making just one can of synthetic milk, including the laboratory-generated ingredients, the can and the label (and the advertising). Nevertheless, environmental groups are not always above using these breast milk scares to swing public opinion; after the dioxin uproar, one began to hear leading conservationists speaking of mothers "purging" pesticides out of their bodies into their milk. And most synthetic formulas no longer contain any animal fats, just because of the media-generated public fear of pesticides—although they may contain plant-based oils, such as high-cholesterol coconut oil, the effects of which on babies are not known.

PROMISE OF CHANGE

The forces opposing breastfeeding and other biologically normal parenting behavior seem substantial. Modern childbirth is all too often what Helene Deutsch, M.D., dryly calls "a miracle of masculine efficiency." The artificial feeding of infants, with its measurements and schedules, is also a typically male, technical procedure, not easily transferred to the ultrafeminine techniques of successful breastfeeding. Niles Newton writes, in her book, *Maternal Emotions:*

> Unfortunately it seems easier to help a woman express negative feelings than to re-educate her. It seems easier to suppress lactation than to teach the mother how to breast feed successfully. It seems easier to separate the mother and the baby at birth in the hospital than to teach her how to care for the baby.

It also has seemed easier, in the past, to shut the father out of the system entirely rather than to enable him to develop skills in caring for his infants and toddlers. If the medical care of the future, however, follows the trends exemplified by the best of current practices—in which parents and infants receive the help and consideration they need both from trained medical specialists and from a constellation of helpers—medicine may well become a potent force in making the tasks of parents more rewarding and successful.

Promising signs of enlightenment abound. Medical science is really solving some breastfeeding problems. For example, drugs have been found that can help mothers who are pumping milk for a preterm baby to keep a good supply going on pumping alone. Today, many more practitioners understand that it takes two to breastfeed. In the past, if a baby wasn't gaining, it was almost always blamed on the mother's "insufficiency"; now, practitioners, especially family-practice physicians and lactation consultants, look at the baby as well; quick recognition and treatment of latch-on and sucking problems is saving many breastfeeding experiences.

On the national scene, declarations have been made in support of breastfeeding by major medical associations in the United States and Canada, and by state, provincial, and both federal governments. Former U.S. Surgeon General Everett Koop made breastfeeding support a national policy in the 1980s, with specified goals. Gradually, the wheels of government bureaucracy are grinding to bring other policies and practices into line with that administrative decision.

On the international scene, growing support for breastfeeding is being manifested by everyone from crusading individuals to international agencies. Derrick and Patrice Jelliffe's 1988 book, *Programmes to Promote Breastfeeding,* contains forty-seven reports from lactation program leaders in more than forty countries, ranging from Sweden to Papua New Guinea. Dr. Derrick Jelliffe, now on the faculty of the UCLA medical school after having served nursing mothers across half the planet, is deeply involved in developing low-cost, interactive television instruction in breastfeeding management for health workers who can't afford textbooks and travel, with a pilot project in Kenya.

AN ENLIGHTENED SOCIETY

Ultimately, help for families must come from society at large. The workplaces of both parents play a critical role. The majority of American businesses are still far away from recognizing that the needs of the children of their employees cannot be overlooked. This, too, is part of the stereotypical masculine bent of America; it is not efficient to allow the needs of families to complicate the straightforward goal of turning a profit; it is easier to ignore the private lives of employees than to help them find creative solutions to balancing family and work.

But here and there, signs of change can be found, many of which have been brought about by nursing mothers. That is not surprising. Who else but the breastfeeding mother would be as strongly driven to work for changes that will allow her to put her baby's needs first? Who else but the breastfeeding mother understands so well that cooperative, feminine methods of bringing about change are more effective than confrontational, masculine tactics to force change? Who better than the nursing mother can see the drawbacks and harmfulness inherent in our masculinized medical care system of regulations and prohibitions, time limits, uniformity, hierarchies, and rationales?

Most hospital administrators now recognize the right and need for both parents to be with their hospitalized children of all ages, a right first brought to their attention by breastfeeding mothers who refused to be separated from their nursing babies when the baby was hospitalized and who worked to change hospital regulations. For some years, the University of Chicago medical school maintained a lactation station—a quiet room equipped with electric pumps, a bathroom, comfortable chairs, a television set, and privacy, where working nursing mothers could express their milk. It was open twenty-four hours a day for the use of nurses, students, and workers in the surrounding area. The idea spread to companies and office buildings; Chicago lactation consultants can now supply mothers with the address of the downtown lactation station nearest to their place of work. (Unfortunately, the university hospital's lactation station was closed after the lactation consultant who founded it left the staff.)

Working nursing mothers are beginning to prove to many companies that they are more reliable and harder workers if given the time and space to pump their milk and flexible work schedules so that they can coordinate their time with their babies' needs. The managements of enlightened companies are extending the rights demanded by nursing mothers to all the parents in their work forces, including such needs as extended maternity leaves, flexible hours, on-site day care, and sick-children care, and the choice of working at home. They have received in return deeply loyal and conscientious staff members.

Society remains, however, generally unenlightened about the benefits of helping families cope. The federal government, at this writing, refuses to pass the family leave bill, which would enable employees to care for newborns and sick family members without risking their jobs. The dispersal of families and the changing economic system mean that most new mothers come home to an empty house and full responsibilities during their recuperation from childbirth. But the need for a father to take even a brief leave from work after a baby is born often is considered downright ridiculous in the business community. American society sees motherhood as a role of negligible importance, neither valuing nor supporting the job of the mother who stays at home full time, nor recognizing the need for plentiful, quality day care for the children of the mother who works.

MAKING CHANGES

In *A Good Birth, a Safe Birth,* authors Diana Korte and Roberta Scaer point out that when one sets out to make a change—in organization, or institution, or society—the first thing that happens is one is ignored and told to go away. The change-maker who persists then receives promises and reassurances that changes will be made; but again, nothing happens. If one keeps on pressing, cosmetic changes occur; for example, hospitals establish rooming-in so that mothers can be with their babies—but the fundamentals are not changed; hospital schedules still prevail over patients' needs, and individual ignorance and prejudices still govern what a mother is told and what she is or is not permitted to do. (When Gale Pryor's son, Max, was born, as this book was being written, in the most "modern" of hospitals, nurses still came into the room and scolded her for holding the baby "too often" and "spoiling" him.)

When pressure for change continues, the next step is that the Establishment starts to get mad. Establishment representatives actively attack the change-maker and the changes she is trying to make; this is where we stand with the synthetic milk manufacturers and standard-care medical establishment at present. In this phase, all's fair—dirty tricks, personal insults, and bullying included: this is war. As Korte and Scaer point out, although this seems most unpleasant and unfair, one can regard it as a sign of progress; when lip service and token cooperation give way to open attack, it means you're getting somewhere. Perhaps in that sense we can regard the current breastfeeding backlash as a promising development.

The final step in making a change is that the change *is* made. Everyone accepts it, lives by the new system, and with amazing speed forgets that there was ever another way; the bad old days vanish as if they had never been. Let us hope that is where we now stand with breastfeeding and all the wiser ways of health care that it represents.

PART
II

CHAPTER 9

Before the Baby Comes

GETTING READY

The months when you are nursing your baby can be among the most pleasant of your whole life. However, it's up to you to make them so. Unfortunately, as we have seen, Western medical systems are not always set up to accommodate the needs of the nursing mother. It takes a little advance planning if you are to avoid some circumstances, common in our society, that make giving birth and breastfeeding less pleasant and less successful than they should be. Experienced nursing mothers, who have successfully breastfed several babies, generally make the kind of arrangements that are suggested here, so that they themselves are free to relax and enjoy the new nursing baby without unnecessary obstacles to their physical well-being or their peace of mind.

CHOOSING A HOSPITAL

It is possible to find competent medical care, even in a town where you are a stranger, by selecting an accredited hospital or health maintenance organization and going to the doctors on its staff; or you can ask your previous health-care provider to recommend someone in good standing at your new location. But how can you find the kind of care that not only is medically competent but will give you

211

the emotional support and practical help you want, in giving birth and in nursing your baby?

One place to start is with the hospitals. Medical attitudes and policies toward nursing couples have come a long way. Natural childbirth techniques are widely accepted, if sometimes more in theory than in practice. Comfortable birthing rooms, complete with rocking chairs, wallpaper, and draperies, can be found at many hospitals. If arrangements are made in advance, a midwife may attend you throughout your labor and birth. Your husband, too, may be able to stay with you throughout your labor and birth, even if you have a Caesarean section.

Hospitals have also learned to accommodate breastfeeding mothers and babies. Nurses are often knowledgeable and supportive. Frequently, there is a lactation consultant on the maternity ward to help nursing mothers. Many hospitals will encourage you to keep the baby in your room as much as you like during the day, and sometimes at night if you have a private room. That is an advantage to the nursing mother, since breastfeeding is much simpler if you have the baby near you all the time.

But there are differences among hospitals. You can find out by telephone what the hospitals in your area offer the nursing mother. Will you be allowed to nurse your baby immediately after the birth? Even if you end up having a Caesarean section? Can your baby stay with you as much as you like? Even at night? Are the babies routinely given sugar water in the nursery? Is there a lactation consultant on staff? Do they give breastfeeding classes or show videotapes? How much more will a private room cost? You may need to make special arrangements ahead of time to have everything go as you've planned. Then you won't have to be bothered with administrative details when the baby is born.

CHOOSING A DOCTOR

Many kinds of medical care givers can be of great help to a breastfeeding mother. Professional lactation consultants will evaluate and advise on breastfeeding problems. Some medical practices retain a lactation consultant or nurse practitioner who specializes in breastfeeding counseling. Family-practice physicians take care of mother and baby both, which not only is very convenient if you both happen to be sick, but can circumvent breastfeeding problems that may arise if only one of the nursing couple is treated. In one informal survey, mothers reported that family-practice physicians were actually more experienced and more helpful about breastfeeding than specialists in pediatrics or obstetrics. If you are planning to use specialists, however, here are some guidelines:

THE OBSTETRICIAN:

Your obstetrician's job is to keep you healthy during pregnancy and to help you give birth to your baby. Your obstetrician will not supervise your lactation, and indeed may not know much about how to nurse a baby. (It is the pediatrician who handles most questions on breastfeeding.) However, the obstetrician is responsible for any physical problems involving the breasts—infections, say—that may arise after the baby is born. Also, you will still be in your obstetrician's care while you are in the hospital, so her attitude can make a great difference to you in the first days of breastfeeding. She will help you put the baby to your breast as soon as ten minutes after birth, if you like. She will make sure you do not receive any drugs to suppress lactation and will prescribe mild pain relievers or anything else you may need to help you relax and be comfortable enough for your milk to flow easily. She will be capable of helping you if problems such as engorgement or nipple soreness arise.

The obstetrician who is not interested in breastfeeding and is not convinced of its importance will not be able to give you this kind of help, and is much more skillful at suppressing lactation than at keeping it going. The male obstetrician whose wife did not breastfeed, or worse, whose wife "failed" or weaned early, may actually be obstructive: you might be better off with an inexperienced but "educable" OB. Although you can probably lactate with perfect success without any help from your obstetrician, it will be at least a convenience for you if he or she is supportive, and it may save you a few arguments in those postpartum days when you will want to be peacefully getting to know your baby without having to argue with your care givers.

To find the kind of obstetrician you want, you may have to shop around a little. The most "brilliant" doctor, or the doctor all your friends go to, may not be the one for you. Look first for a doctor who has breastfed her own children or whose wife has happily done so, and who has a majority of patients who breastfeed. Find a doctor who believes in the principles of natural childbirth. While both you and the doctor may shy away from the term "natural childbirth" as smacking of faddism, nowadays every doctor with a real understanding of and consideration for maternity patients uses a great many natural childbirth techniques and gives the patient a vote in how the birth should be managed. Such an obstetrician is more likely to be helpful and experienced about breastfeeding.

While you may be restricted in your choice of doctors by the kind of health insurance you carry, you can expect that at least some of the doctors on the approved list will be the kind you are looking for. If you are not restricted, then locate a hospital that encourages breastfeeding. The maternity floor nurses may be able to tell you which doctors on the staff arrange prenatal classes for parents and which doctors have the most patients who breastfeed; these practices are associated with modern, enlightened childbirth techniques.

When you have a list of possibilities, make an appointment with each one for a consultation. If you later decide that this is not the doctor for you, the consultation will have cost you less than a full examination. (In addition, once a doctor has done a full pelvic exam on you, you may feel committed to asking that person to be your obstetrician.) Sometimes you can easily spot the obstetrician who is especially skilled with natural births; her outstanding characteristics are apt to be gentleness and endless patience. She seems interested in you as a person, not just as a pelvis; she listens to everything you ask, with no hint of intolerance. She is not in a hurry, no matter how full the waiting room is. She is gentle, never brisk or rough. She explains everything she does, at great length, without condescension. This care and patience may make the office visits longer, but may make the birth easier and will foster the development of mutual trust and respect between patient and physician.

Occasionally a physician will be very annoyed to find that you are "shopping" for medical care. This is not the obstetrician for you. The doctor who has had experience with spontaneous childbirth and who has seen many happy nursing mothers will understand very well why you are being careful to select a physician who appreciates these matters.

THE PEDIATRICIAN:

It is a good idea to pay at least one visit to your pediatrician before the baby comes. Your obstetrician will be glad to recommend one or two pediatricians and may be able to suggest someone who is especially interested in breastfed babies. The hospital nurses may be able to tell you which pediatricians in town are the greatest champions of mothers' milk for babies.

Pediatricians are more accustomed than obstetricians to mothers who shop for a doctor. They aren't apt to resent being questioned. However, don't start out by asking bluntly, "Are you in favor of breastfeeding?" You put the pediatrician on the spot; he doesn't know whether you want him to say yes or no and may feel defensive. You can tell him that you plan to breastfeed, and would like to have rooming-in (if it is available), and see what he says. If he tries to talk you out of both, you probably have the wrong doctor.

Ask him how many of his mothers breastfeed, and for how long. If he doesn't know how many, or gives a number lower than 50 percent, or starts explaining why so many mothers quit early these days, then you can suspect that he is not helpful to the breastfeeding mothers in his practice. If 60 percent or more of his mothers breastfeed, and if he seems proud of them, you can be fairly sure he gives them help and encouragement. Finally, you can ask if he has children himself, and if they were breastfed. If they were not, the doctor may regard the question as impertinent. If they were, he will enjoy telling you so; if his own children were breastfed a year or more, you will know that this doctor is personally acquainted with the normal course of lactation.

Suppose you already have a pediatrician you are satisfied with, but who does not encourage breastfeeding or is in favor of it but does not really understand how it works? His lack of interest in the management of lactation has nothing to do with his skill at preventing complications with measles or clearing up middle-ear infections. You need not feel obliged to change to some other doctor just because you two don't see eye to eye on breastfeeding. Don't let him shake your confidence. You can ignore misguided interference. You can nurse your baby satisfactorily on your own. He may even learn from your experience and be more helpful to his next nursing mother, especially if you are open with him. But tell him when you have not followed his advice (about giving solid foods early, for example) or he will assume the baby's good health is related to the advice you never in fact followed.

"CONTRAINDICATIONS"

You may nurse your baby if you have a cold or the flu or some other mild, contagious disease. Breastfed babies show remarkable immunity to such ailments and often escape getting sick even when the whole family comes down with a "bug." However, a mother with whooping cough or active tuberculosis (not just a positive skin test) should have no contact with her baby at all, since these very contagious diseases are dangerous for her newborn; in such a case she, of course, could not breastfeed.

It used to be thought that a mother with Rh factor incompatibility could not breastfeed. That is not true. Rh antibodies may exist in the milk of an Rh-negative mother, but they have no effect on the baby. Genital herpes, however, can be a serious threat to the newborn; nevertheless, even mothers with active herpes infections can usually breastfeed safely provided they take proper precautions (see chapter 10, p. 230). Hepatitis B is a viral disease that poses serious dangers to the newborn, but there is no sound evidence that it can be transmitted through breastfeeding. Evidence for the AIDS virus is conflicting. These infections should be handled on a case-by-case basis in consultation with one's doctor (see chapter 3, pp. 97–99, for details on both these viruses).

The diabetic mother can breastfeed successfully, with careful management. Breastfeeding, in fact, is less likely to cause problems than is pregnancy; some mothers find that their blood sugar is more stable and their need for insulin actually decreases during lactation (see pp. 51–52). Furthermore, there is significant evidence that breastfed children are less susceptible, themselves, to developing diabetes than are formula-fed children (see chapter 3, p. 84). Since diabetes has some genetic elements, the mother who is diabetic may be especially interested in this protective aspect of breastfeeding her babies (see Appendix).

Mothers receiving chemotherapy or radiation treatments may be asked not to breastfeed. However, in some cases, an alternate drug can be prescribed that does not endanger the nursing baby. When planning a diagnostic radiation procedure for a nursing mother, the physician and technicians may consider using a minimal radiopharmaceutical dose and a longer imaging time to protect her baby and their nursing relationship. Epileptic mothers sometimes have a medical conflict if they wish to breastfeed; some drugs prescribed for epilepsy do adversely affect the nursing baby. If you or your doctor are in any doubt about the safety of the medication you must take, send for La Leche League's publication on medications and breast milk, which is supervised by the League's medical board and is frequently updated to reflect current research, or refer to the American Academy of Pediatrics' most recent report (1989 or later) on drugs and breast milk (see References for chapter 3).

You should not be taking any illicit or "recreational" drugs during pregnancy, but if you are, now is the time to stop. All such drugs—including nicotine, caffeine, alcohol, and marijuana—pass through the milk and can affect the baby. Cocaine is especially dangerous to small infants; it passes through the milk, and it can be fatal even in a single dose (chapter 3).

If the mother is desperately ill from some chronic disease, her doctor may justifiably forbid her to breastfeed. However, the mother who is temporarily incapacitated after a difficult or surgical delivery is better off breastfeeding than not. Lactation gives her an excuse to get more rest during convalescence, and saves her from the multiple chores of bottle-feeding. Lactation can be of the same benefit to the mother with a heart condition or with many another chronic illness that can be well managed and monitored.

THE PHYSICALLY DISADVANTAGED MOTHER

The disabled mother deserves more than ever to breastfeed her baby. A mother who must live in a wheelchair or who is blind will find breastfeeding infinitely easier than trying to cope with bottles and synthetic milk. It is no more difficult for her than for any other new mother to learn to nurse, and she gains a sense of joy in her self-sufficiency that goes far to combat any feelings she might have that she cannot give her child as much as other mothers do. Kathy Beaudette, a blind La Leche League group leader, says that breastfeeding is "the only way to go" for a blind mother and her child, and that it offered for her, even after weaning, "the miraculous closeness to my son that only touch could bring." La Leche League International offers a variety of loan material about breastfeeding and child care, including its book *The Womanly Art of Breastfeeding*, on tape and in Braille.

CLOTHING

Wearing a well-fitting brassiere during pregnancy will help prevent loss of breast shape. In late pregnancy and during lactation you can expect to be about one full cup size larger than you used to be, with variations upward depending on the amount of milk present. If you started out as a skimpy A you will probably be no larger than an ample B, and will get adequate support from any well-fitting bra. If you started out as a B or C you will probably need the sturdy maternity bras. By six months after weaning your breasts will be back to their previous size and shape. Many mothers find their figures have actually improved.

Before you go to the hospital, pack two or more nursing bras in your suitcase. These are made with a flap that lowers, so you can feed the baby without losing support. Bras do get wet from milk, at first, so you will need at least one to wear and one to wash. Nursing bras may be bought at lingerie shops, maternity shops, department stores, or through mail-order catalogs. The plain cotton drop-cup type is generally affordable and comfortable. If you don't want such institutional-looking underwear, you can find very pretty nursing bras, costing slightly more, at some better stores.

When you are nursing, you need clothing that gives easy and discreet access to the breasts. One mother was given as a "welcome home" present a new dress that buttoned up the back! Not only did it have to be removed entirely to nurse the baby, but it took two people or a contortionist to get it off and on. Invest in nighties that open in the front and sweaters or shirts you can lift from the waist.

BREAST CARE

No breast care is necessary in the first six months of pregnancy. In the last three months, it is probably wise to stop using any soap on the breasts. The skin secretes protective oils that help to make the nipple and areola strong and supple. By scrubbing with soap, you remove this natural protection. The protective skin secretions are mildly antibacterial; it seems likely that nature is guarding your breasts and preparing them for the job of nursing.

The nipples are highly sensitive, right after you give birth, for good reason: to respond better to the stimulation of the baby's suckling, which triggers the hormones that make and release the milk. Proper positioning in the first days of nursing can help prevent sore nipples from developing. Despite common belief, fair-skinned women are not more likely to develop cracked nipples than others, but mothers who have had trouble with sore nipples with previous babies, may again. One theory is that our clothing overprotects our nipples so that they become sensitive. To desensitize the overprotected nipples, doctors sometimes recommend scrubbing with a rough towel or (horrors!) a brush; a Connecticut clinic has found that it is simpler and less uncomfortable to trim a circle of material from the cups of your brassieres so that the breast is supported but the nipple exposed, allowing some gentle chafing against clothing. You may wish to stitch around the openings to prevent unraveling. Better yet, if at all possible, simply expose your bare breasts to air and sunshine occasionally.

Some women have nipples that are flat or retracted. The hormones of pregnancy will tend to improve the shape of the nipples, without any other help. Truly *inverted* nipples will retract when pressed between thumb and forefinger; these are uncommon. The standard advice is to pull the nipple out daily with the fingers; however, research indicates that this does not improve the shape, and most women dislike doing it. Wearing bras that are open at the tips will help, as the edges of the cut-away circles push gently on the margins of the areolas, which makes the nipples more prominent. Once lactation begins, the nursing of the baby will soon draw the nipple out normally in any case; however, retraction will recur when the baby is weaned.

The mother whose nipples are so inverted that she fears she will never be able to nurse can achieve normalcy with breast shields or shells worn regularly during the last weeks of pregnancy. Once fitted, the shield will provide a constant pressure that causes the inverted nipple to press out. The Medela Breast Shell Kit and Breast Shields are inexpensive, and available through La Leche League. Be selective when purchasing a breast shield; some brands can be uncomfortable. Models with multiple air holes are preferable to models with one or just a few. (Breast shields are useful only to correct inverted nipples and can be damaging if used otherwise.) One experienced lactation consultant, a nurse working for a group of obstetricians, feels that retracted nipples are seldom seen in women whose love life involves a lot of breast play. Some couples tend to avoid the breasts, others make much of them. It is of course a matter of personal preference. However, it seems at least possible that the tender attentions of a man to this highly erogenous area are part of nature's way of preparing a woman's body for the task of nursing a baby.

Research indicates that it is unwise to put alcohol or other "hardening" agents on your nipples. These irritants, although sometimes recommended by health care personnel, are worse than useless because hard, dry skin cracks more easily than soft, supple skin. Anointing the nipples with oils and creams is apparently harmless, if the preparations are water-soluble and rinse off easily, but they don't do much good, either. After the baby is born, anything you put on your nipples is likely to enter the baby's body, so read the labels and package inserts; if a product is "not for internal use," don't use it.

HELP AT HOME

If you want to enjoy the first weeks of nursing your baby, instead of struggling through them exhausted, don't go home to a house in which you must do all the work alone. It is tempting to think that you can manage without any help. But you must protect your returning strength in these first weeks, or the baby's milk supply may suffer. And your husband, willing though he may be, will also be feeling the strain of new child-care responsibilities. Possibly he is not accustomed to housework and you may become impatient seeing how long it takes him to clean up the kitchen or prepare dinner. All too soon, you will find yourself helping out, and getting overtired, which is bad for your morale and your milk.

Anthropologist Dana Raphael promoted the term "doula" for the woman who traditionally helps a new mother in preliterate societies. While the mother recovers from childbirth and gets to know her new baby, the doula sees to the cooking and other household chores and looks after the mother. Often the doula is the new mother's own mother, but she might also be a sister, neighbor, or friend. Most cultures take it for granted that new mothers need this kind of support. Our culture seems to take it for granted that new mothers can sink or swim on their own, even if they have been sent home from the hospital with a newborn just hours after giving birth.

If your mother, mother-in-law, or some other relative offers to help out for the first few weeks, and is a truly helpful, nondisruptive presence, accept the offer gladly. However, if she must stay with you, you may feel called on to act as a hostess. And if spending time with her is ever a strain for you, consider making other arrangements. One grandmother customarily spends a week taking care of each new mother in the family—but she stays, not with the parents, but at a nearby motel. "Most of the work that needs to be done is daytime work," she points out, "and the parents need their privacy in the evening—and I need mine!"

Grandmothers who live far away often feel better about the separation from you and your children if they can be of help right after the birth. If personal help is not practical, probably one of the nicest baby presents a grandparent can give is the money for a few weeks of paid household help. But it really is your own responsibility to look out for yourself and line up a doula. In some cases, the baby's father can take paternity leave for two weeks or so, to help out. One new mother had her own mother visit and help out the first week and her husband's mother the second week. A single mother enlisted the volunteer services of her best friend's seventeen-year-old brother, who turned out to be a superlative errand runner and launderer, and a pretty good cook.

If you go to a health maintenance organization (HMO) for your health care, find out if they offer a home care service for new parents. Several do, and it is becoming more common. If the service is arranged before your baby is born, a mother's helper will come to your house for several days after you return home to help out in whatever way you wish, whether straightening the house, making a few meals, or doing the shopping. You may need help for longer than three days, however, and often this service is provided only if you leave the hospital within forty-eight hours of giving birth.

Independent services may exist in your area that provide the same kind of help for as long as you need it. Fees charged by private services vary from reasonable to extravagant. Although the cost may not be covered by your medical insurance, a crucial week or two of help may be well worth it. Look in the Yellow Pages under "Home Services." Some states provide state-funded "homemaker" services. Some retired La Leche League leaders have gone into business as doulas, and will provide you with not only tender loving care but good breastfeeding advice as well; they may advertise in the newsletter of the local diaper service.

Sometimes a neighborhood in which there are a lot of young families can organize to make things easier for a new mother. For instance, a neighbor can take the toddler or older children for the afternoon, so that the new mother can nap (it is wise to institute this as a routine before the baby is born). One Chicago neighborhood has organized a housewives' round robin in which each woman takes a turn doing the morning housework and providing a cooked dinner for the household where there is a new baby. Since there are some twenty families in on the arrangement, the mother who comes home with a new baby receives twenty days of having her housework done and her family's dinner prepared for her.

The one kind of help you don't need is a baby nurse. You may find yourself cleaning house and cooking meals for the nurse while she takes care of your baby. However, almost every city has a visiting nurse association, and you should certainly take advantage of this service. It may even be free in your area. Ask your doctor to arrange it, or ask the nurses at the hospital before you are discharged; sometimes the visiting nurse is part of the service normally provided for each new mother. The visiting nurse can tell at a glance how the baby is doing, can help you with baths and other new tasks, and will also keep a weather eye on your own state of health. She is a good source of advice about diaper services and other methods of saving your energy. In almost any city or suburb, you can look under "Nurses" or "Sitting Services" in the Yellow Pages for trained, experienced mother's helpers.

Professional couples in which both parents must work long hours sometimes rely on live-in help. Organizations exist in large cities that train and place European-style "nannies" or "au pairs" who care for children twenty-four hours a day. A nanny poses a risk for the nursing mother if she is not supportive of breastfeeding. One New York City mother warns from experience, "Some nannies hired through an agency actually charge more for taking care of a breastfed than a bottle-fed baby. Others will not be openly critical but will say things like 'The baby's not interested in nursing any more,' when it's obvious to the mother that's untrue. Ask during the interview if the person nursed her own children, and for how long; some older women believe two to three months is quite long enough, and after that will offer little support and possibly the reverse."

MATERNITY LEAVE

If you plan on returning to your job after the baby is born, arrange in advance for as much time at home on maternity leave as possible. Many women have returned to full- and part-time work as soon as six weeks after the birth and continued to nurse their babies successfully right into toddlerhood. Nevertheless, the longer you can manage to stay at home full time, the more relaxed you'll be, and the more secure you'll probably feel about your nursing relationship. Eight weeks of paid leave are *required by law* in many states (check with your state Department of Health to see if this is true in your state). Often an employer will agree to another four or more unpaid weeks. Save your vacation time and add it on to your maternity leave. If you can possibly manage it financially, take six months or more off. This time is for you and your new baby; the rest of the world will still be there when he's older.

If you cannot manage to take additional leave, don't despair. It is quite possible to return to work full time and continue nursing your baby, with or without synthetic milk supplements, for as long as you wish. You will find, in fact, that it helps to ease your conscience and your heart, making up somewhat for having to be away from the baby. Many mothers are working and nursing successfully now. (See chapter 13, "The Working Mother: How Breastfeeding Can Help")

SHORTCUTS

After you have arranged for help in the house for two weeks, and have set up a way for your older children to be away from home for a couple of hours a day, try to organize as many short cuts as you can to lighten your workload in the first month you are home. Here are some suggestions:

1. If you plan on using cloth diapers, arrange for diaper service for the first few weeks at least. This saves a tremendous amount of work. If you live in the country and cannot get diaper service, buy a few dozen disposable diapers for the first several days at home. (While many mothers continue to use disposables until their child is using the bathroom, other mothers use cloth diapers exclusively because they are more comfortable for the baby and less damaging to the environment.)

2. If you can possibly afford it, now is the time to purchase major appliances you don't have. A washer and a dryer are more important than living room furniture. A dishwasher or a microwave oven will be worth more to you than wall-to-wall carpet. There will be time for interior decorating again in years to come,

but while your children are very small, the most important purchases are those that reduce drudgery and give you more time and energy for your family, particularly if you plan on returning to work.

3. If you have a toddler already, a high school girl or boy can be a great help by coming in for an hour or two after school to supervise bath and supper and to play games.

4. Stock the cupboards with quick, nourishing foods, with the emphasis on proteins. If you are alone with the baby most of the day, you may not feel like going to the kitchen and cooking, but you need plenty of nourishing food, especially at the start of lactation, or you will feel tired and depressed. You're less likely to skimp, or to fill up on coffee and doughnuts, if something better for you is easily available. Stock up on high-protein foods such as quick-cooking oatmeal, cheese, canned tuna, sardines, salmon, baked or refried beans, and tofu. A blender can produce instant high-protein milk shakes, with an egg or two added, if you don't feel like cooking.

5. A microwave oven can be a godsend to a family with a newborn. Frozen dinners can be made piping hot in five minutes. These days, a huge variety of prepared foods for the microwave can be found. Look also for dinners in a pouch that can be heated quickly in boiling water. However, commercial TV dinners, whether for the microwave, oven, or stove, usually don't have enough food in them to satisfy a nursing mother's appetite. You can probably make less expensive and tastier dinners yourself before the baby is born and freeze them. The servings should be generous and should include your favorite meals and desserts; make the first days at home a time for treats. You can freeze meals for your other small children, too. Then, even if your husband is not comfortable in the kitchen, either of you can produce a hot meal quickly.

6. You and your husband may well find you simply don't have time to market in the first weeks. Even in these days of supermarkets, you might be able to find a neighborhood store that will take an order by phone

and either deliver it or hold it until it is picked up. This is a great timesaver. Or you could ask a neighbor to shop for you from a list you have prepared.

7. Address your birth announcements ahead of time.

8. Even if you have a washer and dryer, you may wish to cut their use down to a minimum for a few weeks by sending your sheets and towels out. Some laundries have a linen delivery service, which, just like a diaper service, will supply you with clean sheets and towels, pick them up weekly, and substitute new ones. That means you can have clean sheets and towels every day, if you wish, without doing any laundry or buying any extra sheets. These services are listed in the telephone book under "Linen Supply Services." If a nearby dry cleaner or laundromat offers wash-and-fold services, consider taking just the baby's things to be done. If the charge is by the pound, it will cost very little to do an entire layette of tiny shirts and sleepers; but check to make sure they do not use fabric softener, which can irritate the skin of some babies, and which reduces absorbency of the clothing. Whatever means you choose to reduce the laundering task, get the system in place and try it out before the baby comes.

DIET AND REST

Now, in late pregnancy, is a good time to learn to nap. Any book on natural childbirth, such as *Childbirth Without Fear,* by Grantly Dick-Read, one of the originators of the modern concept of natural childbirth, will teach you relaxation techniques that will help you fall asleep in the daytime. A nursing baby is usually less trouble at night than a bottle-fed baby. But he will be hungry, and only you can feed him, so you are bound to lose a little sleep. To keep your spirits up and your milk supply bountiful in the first weeks of lactation, it will help if you have practiced and learned the knack of napping—really sleeping—once or even two or three times during the day. Ideally, in the first few weeks, you'll be able to sleep whenever the baby sleeps.

Pregnancy is also a good time to improve your own eating habits. You may not feel like going to the trouble of changing your ways once you are preoccupied with the new baby. You don't need to change your diet radically, or eat things you hate, to eat right. You just need to concentrate on good nutrition, on getting the vitamins, minerals, proteins, and calories you need (see chapter 2). If you acquire the habit of eating well now, you will find that after giving birth you will have more energy and a better disposition, both of which are vital to the nursing mother. Clinics and HMOs sometimes offer nutritional counseling, which is worthwhile if you feel uncertain.

FITNESS

During pregnancy, during childbirth, and during lactation you will have an easier time of it, enjoy yourself more, and be more of a help and pleasure to those around you, if you are fit. Staying fit, strong, and supple can be fun, rather than a duty, and it is never the wrong time to start; the smallest effort will bring some improvement. Half an hour of fast walking outdoors, daily, will do a lot.

The benefits of looking after your body's well-being are many: You don't get as tired, you don't get winded, you feel more cheerful—all especially valuable during pregnancy, but definite benefits at any time. It's nice to know, too, that the fitter you are, the brighter your eyes, and the prettier you look.

A CHANGE OF PACE

A mother often has the feeling, especially with a first baby, that after the pregnancy is over everything will get back to normal. The housework will get done again; she will wear her normal clothes again, and return to normal life. The trouble is this doesn't exactly happen. As Jean Kerr says, "The thing about having a baby is, from then on, you have it." If you already have small children, one more may not make too much difference. But if this is the first baby or if it has been a number of years since you had an infant in the house, the usual tendency is to try to fit the baby's care and feeding into your life and still do all the things you used to do. You may especially look forward to doing the things that were difficult in the last months of pregnancy—keeping the floor waxed, going out at night often, entertaining, and volunteering for extra work on the job. This attempt to lead two conflicting lives at once, that of busy woman and that of new mother, is exhausting for anyone and frequently causes breastfeeding to fail. You will find your life is easier if you can postpone the return to "normal." In a way, you can look at these early months of nursing and "tuning in" to your baby as your reward for the hard job of pregnancy and childbirth.

Especially in the first weeks, your baby will want to nurse often and for long periods. This may be the first time in your adult life when you can legitimately sit down occasionally in the daytime, put your feet up, watch television, or read a mystery novel, because you are also feeding the baby. Perhaps this is nature's way of insuring not only that the baby gets enough milk but that you get enough rest for an easy convalescence. The housework and the world's work will always be there, but the nursing relationship is soon over. It is worth taking time off to see it well begun.

CHAPTER 10

In the Hospital

THE HOSPITAL

Hospitals' labor and birth policies have changed a great deal in recent years. Fathers may now stay with their laboring wives at all times, even during a Caesarean section. Lactation-suppressing drugs are no longer given routinely. And breastfeeding immediately after giving birth, even after a Caesarean section, is widely allowed. However, policies vary from hospital to hospital, and from doctor to doctor. Do not assume your desires and plans will fit in with the hospital's protocol. Discuss them with your obstetrician ahead of time; if necessary, make prior arrangements with the hospital administration. At every step, ask questions and make your preferences clearly known to all.

A widespread improvement in maternity care is the availability of birthing rooms in which you may both labor and give birth to the baby, rather than move to a sterile delivery room in the last stage of labor. These rooms typically have been designed to be as homelike as possible with pretty wallpaper, a comfortable chair for your husband or other labor companion, and a bed, rather than a delivery table, for you. An increasing number of hospitals offer labor-birth-recovery rooms in which you may labor, give birth, and rest with your baby for several hours. Birthing centers affiliated with hospitals may even have labor-birth-recovery-and-postpartum rooms so that you need never change rooms from the time you arrive until you go home

Although birthing rooms can signify a family-centered approach to childbirth and a supportive attitude toward breastfeeding, they can also be the result merely of the hospital's public relations department realizing they will attract patients. An attractively decorated labor and birth room doesn't guarantee a positive birth experience or a good start to breastfeeding. It is the education and the attitude of the staff and of your own family-practice physician or obstetrician *and* pediatrician that will make the difference. Of course, even women cared for by supportive and flexible obstetrics staffs may have difficult labors and Caesarean sections. The sensitivity of the staff, however, can lessen the trauma of a complicated labor and enhance the joy of an easy one.

In addition to discussing your labor and birth in advance, you should speak to your family-practice physician or your baby's pediatrician beforehand. Tell him you plan to breastfeed. Ask him to *write a note on your chart and the baby's chart* that you will be breastfeeding and that no bottles of water, sugar water, or synthetic milk are to be given to your baby at any time. He can also instruct the staff via the chart to let your baby room-in with you, or be brought to you as often and for as long as you wish, and not to skip nighttime feedings. If it is written on the chart, it is an order and has more force than verbal reminders.

GIVING BIRTH AND THE FIRST NURSING

When you first arrive at the hospital, a resident doctor or nurse will probably examine you to see how far along in labor you are. Tell him or her that you intend to nurse your baby as soon as he is born. Healthy newborns, unless sedated by medications given to their mothers during labor, are usually alert for an hour or so after birth. During this time, your baby will make eye contact, turn toward your voice, and enjoy being touched and held. This is the ideal time to begin breastfeeding.

While lactation-suppressing drugs are no longer given routinely, other drugs given to you during labor can cause your baby to be sleepy when born and weaken his sucking. When your own obstetrician arrives, remind him that you intend to nurse the baby as soon as it is born. Repeat that you wish to avoid taking any drugs that might make the baby too sleepy to nurse. However, if you feel the need for pain relief, don't feel that you must not take *any* drugs. Just ask the staff to keep in mind that you plan to nurse; your husband or birthing coach can continue to alert them as your labor progresses.

Most doctors and nurses are now aware of the many protective and nourishing qualities of colostrum, the "first milk," and will not suggest that water is preferable for the first feeding. Most doctors these days also will agree to delay putting silver nitrate drops in your baby's eyes for a few hours. Required by law in most states in case the mother has venereal disease, silver nitrate can cause the baby to squint and his eyelids to swell for a while, keeping him from making the eye-to-eye contact so important to you both the first time you nurse. But don't assume all doctors, nurses, or hospitals have changed their policies about giving water or administering silver nitrate drops. Ask ahead of time and make arrangements if necessary. If the hospital staff discourages you from nursing immediately after birth because the baby "might get cold," rely on your husband or birthing coach to remind them that one of the warmest places a newborn can be is skin-to-skin with his mother, her arms around him. A warm blanket around the mother's shoulders while she is holding the baby will warm them both. Your husband should also remind the health-care staff that your requests have been approved by your doctor, and he can remind your doctor to write his orders on your chart and the baby's chart (so all the nursing shifts will be following the same instructions).

When your baby is born, if all is well and you are feeling up to it, the doctor will probably place him on your chest or beside you so that you can have a good look at him. In the excitement after birth, you may have to ask to hold your baby. Your husband can be in charge of remembering to say that you want to hold your baby right away. The nurse will help you get comfortable and begin to breastfeed. If she doesn't, you can manage by yourself. If your husband is with you, he may already have had a chance to hold and get to know the baby; this first hour of life is exhilarating for all of you, and the perfect time to get acquainted.

PUTTING THE BABY TO THE BREAST

When you are given your baby, turn onto your side (if you can) so that you will face the baby with your whole body with his mouth directly in front of your nipple. He should be on his side, facing you, so that he doesn't have to turn his head to reach your nipple. Put your arm around him and bring him close. Babies' little snub noses are designed so that they may breathe even when pressed close to their mothers' breasts. Get as close as you can be (see illustration below).

Hold your breast with your other hand, thumb on top and

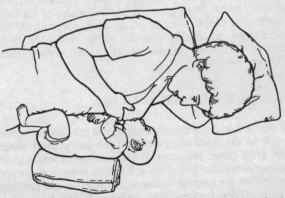

Nursing the newborn while lying down: The baby is propped on his side with a rolled-up towel behind his back; thus his body faces his mother so he does not have to turn his head to nurse. His head is level with the breast and free to move so that he can adjust himself comfortably. The mother has put a pillow behind her own back for extra support and comfort.

fingers below. Touch the center of the baby's lower lip with your nipple, and he will open his mouth wide. Then pull him in close so that he takes the nipple and all or most of the surrounding areola into his mouth. (Don't be concerned if you have a large areola; just let the baby take as much as he can into his mouth.) If the baby's lower lip has been drawn in along with the nipple and areola, gently pull down on the lip to draw it out, after he begins to nurse. For the first feeding, don't offer both breasts to the baby. Cuddle your baby and let him get to know your touch and scent and taste. Some babies don't want to actually nurse at this first feeding, but just to taste and be held and explore this new experience. That's fine; it's good practice.

To nurse sitting up, don't lay the baby on his back as if you were going to give him a bottle; instead, hold the baby on his side, across your midsection, so that he faces you with his whole body and does not have to turn his head to reach your nipple (see top illustration on facing page). Lay his head on your arm, with your hand holding his bottom or leg. You can put a pillow under your arm so you won't get tired from holding him. Support your breast from underneath with your other hand. Then gently tickle the center of his lower lip with your nipple until he opens wide, and quickly pull him in close, so that he gets the nipple well back in his mouth on the first try (see additional discussion on positioning on pp. 240–41).

IF YOU HAVE A CAESAREAN SECTION

If you've had a Caesarean section, you may not feel strong enough to do anything, even feed the baby, until several hours after birth. However, if you are awake while in the recovery room and feel up to it, you may wish to nurse your baby before the anesthesia has worn off. If so, ask the nurse to place pillows between your knees and behind your back so that your abdominal muscles will not be stressed. Once you are comfortably on your side, ask the nurse to put your baby right up next to you, facing you with his whole body and with his mouth directly in front of your nipple. If you

This, Not This

A good position for nursing while sitting up: The baby's body is flat against the mother's, rolled toward her and held close in. The mother supports the baby's head in the crook of her arm, and lifts her breast slightly with her other hand. The baby feels secure and does not have to strain to reach the breast.

A poor position, nursing sitting up: The baby is flat on her back, so she must nurse with her head turned, making it hard to swallow. The mother holds the baby's head in her hand, straining the neck and inhibiting the baby's head movements. The nipple will be too far forward in the baby's mouth, leading to soreness. Pinching the breast between two fingers interferes with a good latch-on and increases the chances of soreness.

wait to breastfeed until you are settled in your room and feeling a little better, the nurse will help you in the same way.

If you have active genital herpes at the time of the birth, you will probably have a Caesarean section to avoid exposing the baby to lesions in the birth canal. This doesn't mean you can't breastfeed; you just have to be careful, while the infection is active, not to carry the virus accidentally to your baby on your hands. Pediatricians advise that you scrub your hands before you hold the baby, and then avoid scratching yourself. A simple way to remind yourself to be careful is to spread a blanket over your lap from the waist down while you are nursing.

IN THE HOSPITAL NURSERY

If your baby must be in the hospital nursery at all, remind your doctor to leave orders in the nursery that your baby receive no synthetic milk, sugar water, or plain water. Your baby is born with extra fluids in the body, which will see him through until your milk supply is well established. He will lose a little weight as he gradually loses these fluids. This loss need not be made up with synthetic milk or sugar water, which will ruin his appetite for your milk. Sucking on a rubber nipple can alter the baby's normal mouth movements and may make him a poorer sucker at the breast (see chapter 4, pp. 132–34).

FIRST FEEDINGS

In the hours and first days following your baby's birth, try to use both breasts at each feeding, alternating the breast you start with, and letting the baby nurse as long as she wants. The nurses may give you other advice, but this really does seem to be the best system in the early weeks. You can change sides, if you want to, without sitting up, by hugging the baby to your chest and turning over with him. Use your leg muscles, rather than your abdomen, to shift yourself across the bed and over. You can attach a safety pin to your bra or move a ring from hand to hand to remember which side you started with last time. Later, you will want to nurse longer on one breast, and the baby may prefer to take one side only at a feeding; but for now, offer two. The sucking stimulation is good for you, and many small feedings are good for the baby.

If your baby doesn't want to stop nursing on the first breast, don't worry. Some babies hate being interrupted. Nursing on one breast at a feeding will work as long as feedings are *frequent* (every two hours or so) so that the unnursed breast doesn't overfill and become engorged. Hold the baby just as much as you like; nursing and cuddling, particularly in the simplicity of the first days, are inseparable and should flow undisrupted from one to the other. It's perfectly all right to keep the baby in your bed, or let him sleep on your chest. The baby *won't* be spoiled by this; after all, you've been cuddling him constantly for nine months.

Keeping the baby with you in bed most of the time is particularly handy if you have had a Caesarean section. You and the baby can doze together, and you won't have to rouse yourself and get up every time you nurse; you can nurse lying down, rolling the baby to the other side by hugging him to your chest as you turn (remember to use your leg muscles, not your stomach muscles to turn over) and thus get up and down far less often than if you were bottle-feeding.

If you feel like nursing sitting up, but the weight of the baby bothers your incision, try using the "football" hold (see illustration on p. 238). This position is fun, anyway, because it allows you to look right into your baby's eyes and talk to him while he's nursing.

If you feel self-conscious because your roommate can watch and hear you, ask the nurse to put a screen around your bed while you are feeding the baby. This is not false modesty. Most of us need time to get used to breaking a lifelong taboo against showing the breasts. Your baby will nurse better and get more and richer milk if you are not feeling embarrassed, and if that means you must have privacy, by all means ask for it. Or consider paying the extra

Nursing in the under-the-arm position, sometimes called the football hold: This mother has tucked her baby under her right arm while nursing on the right breast. Her right hand supports the baby's shoulders and neck while leaving the head free to move; her left hand lifts her full breast slightly. She has tucked the baby's legs up against the back of her chair, which puts the baby in the snug and calming fetal position.

cost for a private room. It may be well worth the benefits of nursing comfortably. It's also more likely your baby will be able to room-in with you twenty-four hours a day in a private room, while it may not be permitted in a shared room.

BREAST CARE

Remember: soap, alcohol, and most other medicines and ointments are actually harmful to your tender skin. If you keep your clothes clean, nature will keep your breasts clean. A daily bath with plain warm water is plenty. Unfortunately, some hospitals still have rules about scrubbing or sterilizing the nipples before nursing. You don't have to obey rules that you *know* are inappropriate; but you probably don't need to flood your body with adrenaline by arguing the case with nurses. You might follow up, later, with a note to the hospital concerning unsuitable breastfeeding advice you

238

received, so that the matter can be corrected for mothers coming after you.

SCHEDULES

Rooming-in mothers usually nurse a baby eight or nine times or more during the day, and often sleep with the baby at the breast each night. Each feeding may last half an hour or more, or just a few minutes. Such liberal nursing is the best way to avoid troubles such as breast soreness, engorgement, and infection, because it establishes an abundant, free-flowing milk supply from the beginning. In a few weeks, the baby will settle down to fewer feedings, but for now, ten to twelve nursings in twenty-four hours is appropriate; some of them hardly amount to full-fledged feedings, anyway.

CLUSTER FEEDINGS

Sometimes a new baby has periods of wanting to nurse over and over for a few hours, every twenty to forty minutes or so; researchers call this cluster feeding (see pp. 134–35). It usually happens at night, during the first week or two of life, and an episode of cluster feedings is usually followed by a period of profound sleep (for both of you) lasting several hours. These frequent feedings do not mean you don't have enough milk; the baby may be getting lots of milk. And she's growing, and showing a healthy appetite. Remember these episodes of frequent feedings help you lose weight, help the baby learn to breastfeed, and help your milk supply. This is nature's way to start breastfeeding.

NIGHT FEEDINGS

Newborn babies are often night owls, feeding more often during the night hours; perhaps that is because they are used to being lulled to sleep in the uterus by mom walking around in the daytime, they arrive still on "uterine time" (see p. 135). So your baby may be especially interested in nursing during the night, just at first. You need to plan on napping along with him during the day, as well as sleeping at night. If your baby is in the nursery, don't let the nurses talk you into skipping the 2 A.M. feeding. If they forget to bring the baby, ring the buzzer and remind them. Your breasts need this feeding as much as the baby needs it.

If you are not allowed to room-in and must leave the baby in the nursery all the time, ask to have him brought to you for an hour at each feeding. If this is impossible, ask that he be brought to you every two and a half to three hours. "May I have my baby?" should become a familiar refrain in your room.

TIME LIMITS, POSITIONING, AND PREVENTION OF SORE NIPPLES

It is a custom in many hospitals to tell nursing mothers to limit the amount of time the baby is on the breast. For example, the hospital staff may tell you to nurse only three minutes per side to begin with, then five minutes the next day, then seven and ten. They are trying to prevent your nipples becoming sore; sore nipples for the first week used to be considered by many an inevitable part of nursing a baby, so limiting nursing time to brief periods in the first days has been the standard advice for years. No one really took note of the fact that limiting nursing time doesn't seem to prevent soreness at all; in fact, it is a major cause of sore nipples. Time limits, for example, force mothers to take their babies on and off their nipples very frequently, sometimes just as things are going well; this upsets the baby and contributes to more soreness for the mother and less milk for the baby.

Let the baby make the decisions on how long he sucks. If your nipples are going to get sore at all, limiting sucking time to five minutes, or ten minutes, or worse yet, one minute, will simply postpone the peak of soreness. A sucking time limit will also keep the baby from getting as much milk as he needs.

Researchers have reexamined the problem of sore nipples to see what really does cause it and what can be done about it. Kittie Frantz, Director of the Breastfeeding Infant Clinic at the University of Southern California Medical Center, studied breastfeeding difficulties in the first days after birth. Her close observations and interactions with mothers and babies led her to conclude that sore nipples are usually caused not by too much nursing but by incorrect positioning of the baby at the breast. If the baby has to reach for the breast, or takes the nipple only partway into the mouth, abrasion occurs. Frantz found that when babies are properly positioned and allowed to nurse as long and as often as they wish, most new mothers experience discomfort only for a moment, when the baby first latches on, and even that discomfort is over with in two or three days. Sore nipples are a brief or nonexistent problem.

If you have acute discomfort when the baby first latches on, you can use the breathing exercises taught in childbirth classes to alleviate the pain; slow, deep breathing can also be helpful if your uterus is contracting uncomfortably during nursing. (Remember, those uterine contractions are helping to flatten your stomach and are also a sign that your letdown reflex is working—see p. 24 and pp. 29-35.)

If your nipples hurt and continue to be painful while the baby nurses, make sure that he is facing you with his whole body, that he does not have to turn his head to reach the breast, and that he has as much of your areola in his mouth as possible. Make sure his lower lip is flanged outward, not tucked in over his gum. Make sure the baby is high enough, in relation to your body, so he is not pulling down on the breast; look at your breast to see if there are "pull" lines toward the nipple as the baby nurses. You may want to put a pillow under your arm or under the baby to raise him a little; or, if you are lying down, just move him up the bed a little farther toward your head. Meanwhile, please look at the section on healing sore nipples, pp. 248-50.

GETTING THE BABY TO LET GO

A nursing baby can suck with remarkable strength. If you try to pull the breast away, he will just hang on harder. To get him off without hurting yourself, stick your finger into the corner of his mouth to break the suction. Then you can take him off without any trouble.

BURPING AND SPITTING UP

Doctors usually advise "burping" babies after feedings by patting them to bring up any air they may have swallowed. You can also burp the baby before you switch to the other breast. The idea is to coax any swallowed air up out of the stomach before it moves into the intestines and causes discomfort. The nurse will show you how if you don't know. You can hold the baby on your shoulder, with your shoulder gently pressing into her abdomen as you pat the small of the back. You can sit her up on your lap, supporting her with one hand across her chest, and pat her back; or you can lay her across a thigh, using the pressure of her stomach on your thigh to gently massage the stomach. Some babies never seem to have gas in their stomachs, and some often do; some are easy to burp and some hard—you'll just have to find out what kind of baby you have.

All babies spit up sometimes. In the first days, the baby may spit up a little of the yellowish colostrum. Occasionally, a baby burps so heartily that he spits up a great gush of milk. This is nothing to be alarmed about. To see if he wants to replace the milk he lost from a particularly juicy burp, just offer the breast again. If he doesn't want to nurse, he won't.

HOW TO TELL WHEN YOUR BABY IS HUNGRY

Already, your baby has many ways to show you how she feels and what's going on with her; by studying her you will learn to understand these communications. For example, try to notice when she is beginning to be hungry; you don't need to wait until she is actually crying to pick her up. Offer her the breast when you see signs of being ready, such as rooting, turning the head, sticking the tongue out; such movements signal that the baby is looking for the breast.

People sometimes talk about "demand" feeding, meaning that the baby should be fed whenever she wants; maybe a better term is "request" feeding, meaning that you don't need to wait for something as severe as a demand. Also, requests work both ways; you can wake the baby and request the baby to feed, too, if you are feeling full or uncomfortable; breastfeeding, after all, is a partnership.

HOW TO TELL WHEN YOUR BABY IS FULL

He signals satiety by relaxing his clenched fists, by a cute little grimace of a smile, sometimes by arching his back and growling in a gesture of refusal, and, of course, by falling asleep. You can burp him and offer the other side, but after that don't try to prod him into nursing longer. Sometimes a baby will wake up and nurse again when he is switched to the other breast. If not, take his word for it. He alone knows how hungry he was. If your letdown reflex was working well, he may have gotten a huge meal in four or five minutes. One researcher points out that the stomach of a newborn baby is about the size of the baby's fist—not very big—and holds only about an ounce. The baby may be hungry again in an hour, but he knows when he's full now.

THE "LAZY" BABY

Lots of babies are casual about nursing at first. If the baby does not seem to want to nurse, don't be discouraged. Don't try to force him into nursing or to keep him going once he's started, by tricks some nurses may use, such as shaking or prodding him, blowing in his face, tickling his feet or his cheek, and so on. Efficiency may be on your mind or the attending nurse's but it's not on his, and this kind of treatment just upsets and scares him. It may make him retreat even further into sleepiness and lack of interest. The sleepy baby needs and appreciates your warmth and voice and nearness, especially if he does not yet nurse vigorously. Let him doze on your chest or stomach, while you doze, too. Babies seem to love this, and perhaps he draws strength from being so near, and will wake up to nurse later on. The sleepy baby is a peaceful companion, warmer and dearer than any childhood teddy bear; if he spends some of his feeding periods just being held and cuddled, that's doing him good, too.

GETTING ACQUAINTED

It is amazing how much personality tiny babies have; each one is an individual, responding to his mother in his own way. Some babies are hearty nursers. When put to the breast, these babies vigorously and promptly latch on and energetically suck. Such babies are the easiest of all to breastfeed. Some babies procrastinate. These babies often show no particular interest in nursing, at first. It is important not to prod or force them when they seem disinclined. They do well, once they start. Some babies are "gourmets." They insist on mouthing the nipple, tasting a little milk and then smacking their lips, before starting to nurse. If this infant is hurried or prodded, she may become furious and start to scream. Otherwise, after a few minutes of mouthing, she settles down and nurses very well. (Mothers who have nursed gourmet babies seem to think that this early dallying and playfulness at the breast often turns out to be a sign of a lifelong humorous turn of mind.)

Some babies are "resters." These babies prefer to nurse a few minutes and then rest a few minutes. They often nurse well, but the procedure takes much longer than with a hearty feeder. Small and preterm babies may be resters, interspersing bouts of sucking with periods of remaining latched on but either resting or making the little jaw movements called nonnutritive sucking. These babies cannot and should not be hurried; they know what they need to do to gather strength.

There are many babies who fall among these groups and others who fall into groups not described because they are less common. The groupings serve merely to emphasize the fact that each baby nurses differently, and the course of the nursing will depend on the combination of the baby's nursing characteristics, the mother's personality, and the quality of the help the mother receives.

YOUR MILK SUPPLY

When you were eight or nine months pregnant, you may have begun to notice a pale yellow liquid secretion from your nipples. This is colostrum, the "first milk," and it is a wonderful substance. Colostrum, once thought to be worthless, is now known to be the ideal first food for babies (see chapter 3, pp. 63–64). When colostrum changes to mature milk, the breasts start producing more abundantly, sometimes too abundantly. Long and frequent nursing can bring this change about within twelve to twenty-four hours after giving birth, as is usual in many home births. Nursing on a hospital's four-hour schedule postpones this shift to mature milk and the rise in milk production to three to five days after the birth.

The baby's appetite usually increases wonderfully, along with the milk supply. Still, she may not be able to keep up with the burgeoning supply. Your breasts, in addition to being full of milk, may be swollen as blood circulation increases. Lumps, bumps, and swellings are to be expected as the glands fill up with Grade AA mother's milk. Some areas of the breast do not drain as freely as other areas at first, and may feel lumpy even after a feeding. All this fullness is an unusual feeling and may make you uncomfortable; don't worry, it is normal and it is only temporary. Rooming-in mothers have a real advantage during this initial phase of milk production. They can pick up the baby whenever they feel too full, and in any case the baby usually wants to nurse so often that the breasts don't get too overloaded.

If you find yourself getting too full for comfort, and you don't have your baby nearby, perhaps you can express milk manually (see Chapter 13, p. 329). Try to get the hang of this when the breast is not too full, perhaps just after a feeding. At first, the milk will come in drops, and then in a dribble, and then in a fine spray. Sometimes it is easier to do this while standing in a hot shower with the water hitting your back.

Sometimes it is hard for the baby to grasp the breast when it is very full, because the areola is distended and tense. It can hurt you like the dickens when he tries, too. If this happens, express some milk before the feeding to make the areola more flexible. When hospital rules enforce long separations, new mothers sometimes get so full of milk that they become engorged, with the breasts painfully distended, hot and hard to the touch; this should and can be avoided entirely with frequent nursings.

LEAKING, DRIPPING, AND SPRAYING MILK

When this happens, it is wonderful news. It means that your letdown reflex is starting to work. The letdown reflex must work if the baby is to get the milk he needs (see chapter 2, p. 19). Any female can secrete milk. Breastfeeding mothers establish a good letdown reflex; they not only have milk but can give milk. At first, unless you have nursed babies before, you probably won't feel the letdown reflex working. But you can recognize the signs of it: milk leaking or dripping in between nursings, or during nursing from the other breast; afterpains or uterine cramps while nursing (these are caused by the same hormones that make the milk let down); sore nipples just at the start of nursing, or a feeling that the baby is biting, which fades away as he nurses (the pain stops when the milk starts letting down). You may also feel a great sense of relaxation or sleepiness as the milk lets down, or even find yourself dozing off; that, too, is a good sign that the hormones are beginning to do their job.

The milk may let down several times during a single feeding. Some mothers are able to feel the letdown reflex as a sort of pins-and-needles sensation; other mothers never feel it. But you can tell when the milk lets down because you can hear the baby begin to swallow and breathe—"suck-hah"—with every suck. If you'd like good evidence that your milk is letting down, tuck the forefinger of your free hand under the baby's chin, and gently lay it on her throat. You will be able to feel her swallowing heartily, a very convincing demonstration that *something* is getting inside her, if you were wondering.

As your milk supply increases, you may be warned again by the nurses about sucking time limits. But it is bad for your letdown reflex to be fussing about how many minutes you nurse. Babies nurse in different ways, some in one long burst, some intermittently with little rest periods in between. Your breasts will actually adapt to the rhythm of your particular baby, with the milk letting down strongly at first, and then repeatedly or intermittently, adjusting to the baby's patterns. You can see that this kind of interaction could not easily be developed if you were trying to limit feeding durations according to the clock.

Besides, time limits often do not reflect what is actually going on. The baby may need a few minutes to settle down, you may need a few more to let down your milk, and the feeding may not really start until many minutes have passed. Even if every other mother in the ward is obediently taking her baby off the breast according to whatever system the hospital fancies, you must put your watch away in a drawer and continue to let the baby decide how long to nurse.

SAFEGUARDING YOUR COMFORT

If you feel sick, or uncomfortable from stitches, hemorrhoids, afterpains, or anything else, be sure to tell the doctor and the nurses. Any kind of discomfort makes it harder for you to relax while you are nursing the baby. You are justified in asking for something to relieve discomfort. Pain relievers will not pass through your milk in sufficient quantities to affect the baby (see chapter 3, p. 60). If you are being given antibiotics or other medications, these will not harm your baby. You can minimize the presence of all medications in your milk by taking them just after a feeding, not before.

HEALING SORE NIPPLES

Sometimes, even with proper positioning of the baby at the breast, mothers still have sore nipples. Usually, this soreness consists of a pain that makes you wince (or even brings tears to your eyes) as the baby first latches on, but that fades away as the milk lets down. Sometimes the nipple looks red and chafed. It may develop a pale crust or scab temporarily. Sometimes it looks very sore, or it cracks and even bleeds. The nipple will heal by itself, in spite of sucking, provided no harmful substances such as soap or alcohol are applied and any positioning difficulties are corrected.

Soreness generally starts around the twentieth feeding, gets worse for from twenty-four to forty-eight hours, and then rapidly disappears. Limiting sucking or skipping feedings only postpones the peak of soreness. Mothers who nurse every two or three hours will usually get better by the fourth day, while mothers on a four-hour schedule won't be over their soreness till the sixth day or later. Lots of medicaments and treatments, ranging from special lanolin creams to wet tea bags, get undeserved credit for miraculous cures that nature would have accomplished alone.

Keep a sore nipple dry and exposed to the air between feedings. This will help it to heal. Sunbathing or very cautious use of a sunlamp can help, too. If lack of privacy means you cannot go around with the flaps of your bra down to let the air reach your nipples, an old-fashioned but effective treatment is to have someone bring you a couple of little sieves from dime-store tea strainers. You can put these in your bra over the nipples, and they will allow the air to circulate and keep you dry. La Leche League International sells plastic breast shells that work the same way (see

Appendix). The worst thing you can do for sore nipples is to wear nursing pads or gauze pads, which get wet and stay wet; they keep your nipple moist and stick to the sore places so that you do more damage every time you remove them.

It is normal to favor a cracked nipple somewhat, but don't chicken out now! Too much skimping on nursing can make soreness worse or lead to other problems. To minimize discomfort and speed healing, you can start all feedings on the least sore side; once the milk has let down, you can switch. Wake the baby up and nurse him before you get too full, rather than wait until you are bursting, when it is harder for the baby to latch on. Make sure the baby's mouth is wide open before you pull him close; don't let him "walk up" the nipple. His lower lip should flare out; pull it down gently if you need to. Try not to let the baby chew on the nipple itself, or hang on, sucking but not swallowing, for prolonged periods.

One good way to minimize soreness is to nurse the baby in a different position each time; this distributes the stress more evenly, rather than letting pressure fall on the same part of the nipple at each feeding. You may hold him under your arm in the "football" hold at your side (see illustration on p. 238); you may lie down and let him lie across your chest to nurse. In all positions, make sure the baby comes straight onto the breast and that you are holding him close enough and high enough so that he doesn't drag the breast downward or have to tilt or twist his head to nurse, which will make you sore.

Nipple shields, which are very popular in some hospitals, are rubber or plastic shields that fit over the breasts, often with a rubber nipple on which the baby sucks. They keep your areolas from being touched by the baby, but ensure that the baby gets milk by suction alone and usually he gets very little. That is bad for your milk supply, discouraging for the baby, and no help to your nipples; it is better, in the long run, to endure the pain, knowing it is temporary. Above all, don't nurse for a brief period and then take the baby off before the milk lets down. It is the putting on and the taking off that do the damage, especially if the milk has not let down. If a nipple cracks and bleeds, you may see blood in the baby's mouth. That is an alarming sight but not too uncommon. Forget it. The nipple will heal by tomorrow or the next day, and the blood will not harm the baby.

JAUNDICE

Sometimes babies develop a little normal (physiological) jaundice while they are adapting to life outside the womb. The baby's eyes may look a little yellow for a few days. This is nothing to worry about; as soon as lactation is going well, the jaundice will clear up. However, some hospitals and some doctors insist on putting jaundiced babies under special lights and giving them synthetic milk supplements for a day or two. If this happens, keep in mind that you will soon be home where you can breastfeed without interference, and that your baby is *not sick* and will be fine; it's just that currently there exists a medical custom of overtreatment for this condition. If this happens to you, read the section on jaundice in chapter 4, pp. 116–22.

THE NURSES

A nurse who has happily breastfed her own babies can be a wonderful help to you and your baby. Some women today are trained as lactation consultants, specializing in helping the breastfeeding mother (see chapter 7, pp. 180–83). You are truly fortunate if one of these health professionals is employed by your hospital. However, many nurses are young and have not had children. They have never nursed a baby, and they really don't understand the kind of help you need. Some older nurses were trained in the times when almost all babies were bottle-fed and subjected to strict regimens; they may be critical of normal breastfeeding procedures. If you think a nurse is being particularly brisk, careless, or domineering with you, it often helps to ask her for advice, *not* necessarily about breastfeeding. "Please," "Thank you," and a friendly smile can coax indulgences such as a longer feeding time from even the strictest supervisor.

In many hospitals, the nurses cannot afford the time to coach nursing mothers, even if they would like to. Mealtimes are rushed, and they must sometimes take the baby back to the nursery just when he is getting started. This problem is compounded by early discharge; now, instead of having five days to get you off to a good start, they may have as little as twenty-four hours. Listen closely when knowledgeable nurses do have a minute to help you, and ask them to suggest resources for you to turn to when you go home.

Even when all the nurses are supportive and willing to help you, they are apt to have been trained at different schools, in different decades, so each nurse may have rules for managing breastfeeding which contradict what some previous nurse has told you. Also, different doctors may leave differing orders, so the poor nurses must tell one patient one set of rules and other patients another set. Stay calm; don't let the confusion bother you. Feel free to tell the nurse that you can manage alone, thank you. But don't get into arguments with the nurses—they have the upper hand! Luckily, nurses are busy, shifts change, and no one is going to have time to check up to see if you are following her particular brand of instructions. And sometimes you'll run into a wonderful nurse who really makes you feel at ease, and really knows how to help. Let her!

GOING HOME

The amount of time mothers and babies stay in the hospital has been dramatically reduced in recent years. Where a week was once considered a minimum for every mother, now only mothers recovering from a Caesarean section stay in the hospital four days or more. Mothers who give birth vaginally often go home the next day, or even a few hours after birth. Theoretically, one stays in the hospital to rest, but many women feel that the supposed "rest" you get in the hospital is a bad joke, especially in semiprivate rooms or wards. One mother, in a private room with her rooming-in baby, counted the number of times someone came into her room during the baby's second day of life. Nurses, dieticians, cleaning women, lab technicians—some stranger interrupted or woke her seventy-two times in one twenty-four-hour period. When a janitor came in to fix a broken closet rod, just as she was putting the baby on the breast, she called her husband and went home.

There are some advantages to going home early to escape this stressful environment; the comfort of your own home and the lack of interfering hospital policies can be a help in nursing. On the other hand, early discharge leaves you on your own in learning to breastfeed. If you go home twenty-four hours after giving birth, you may miss out on the careful teaching of knowledgeable nurses. Your baby may not really have done more than nuzzle your breast yet. If, once you are home, you stay in bed with your baby and nurse often and leisurely, the two of you will probably learn to nurse without any assistance. However, someone experienced in breastfeeding should be available to you during these early days to answer questions and support you.

If a midwife helped you through labor, she will probably be there to help you in the first days at home, too. A breastfeeding class may be offered during your prenatal instruction; be sure to attend it if you know you will be discharged early. Sometimes you can call the maternity floor of the hospital for breastfeeding advice after you get home. Some hospitals and clinics maintain a breastfeeding "help-line" for new mothers. If your hospital has a certified lactation consultant on the staff, you can of course rely on her for telephone advice and face-to-face visits either in your home or in the clinic.

Lactation consultants are professionals who teach breastfeeding and evaluate and advise on breastfeeding problems. Board-certified lactation consultants are qualified experts who may be found on the staff of your doctor's office or HMO, or in private practice. A lactation consultant may stop by your hospital room to help you the first few times the baby nurses. Lactation consultants offer phone consultation and also make home visits. Your medical insurance may or may not cover the cost of a lactation consultant (roughly the same as a visit to the dentist), but it is a wise investment.

Your medical care givers may be able to help you find a lactation consultant. Ask if there is an L.C. on the staff of the hospital where you will be having your baby. If there is not, or if you only find you need help later on, you can call either the International Lactation Consultants Association (see Appendix) or the Lactation Consultant department of La Leche League, for names of the consultants nearest you. Some cities and states have regional organizations of lactation consultants; look in the Yellow Pages under Social Service Organizations or under Breastfeeding.

La Leche League International has groups and leaders in many communities throughout the United States. An experienced LLLI leader can provide you with encouragement, information, and good advice by telephone. When the baby is crying, and you don't know why, and you are *sure* it's because of your milk, a friendly listener who's been through it all herself may be just what you need. You can locate the leader nearest you by a free phone call to La Leche League headquarters: dial 1-800-LA LECHE.

When you leave the hospital, you will probably be given a nice goodbye gift of baby care pamphlets, perhaps a pair of booties or a rattle, and a can of synthetic milk. Go through the package. Take the booties, leave the can. Giving "formula kits" to all new mothers, including breastfeeding mothers, is a widespread practice funded by the synthetic milk manufacturers. They are hoping that even if you start out breastfeeding, you will panic and use their product, thus beginning the cycle of supplementing with bottles that so often leads to early weaning. You don't need to let them do this to you. You won't be exposed to temptation if you leave the bait behind.

Some mothers find that the fatigue of going home causes a temporary drop in their milk supply, but that is no reason to stoke the baby with synthetic milk. Just let him nurse more often, and the milk supply will return. Other mothers find that they have much more milk available for the baby when they get home, probably because their milk lets down better in familiar surroundings. Home, where rooming-in and request feeding are yours for the asking—as well as privacy, good food, and the tender care of your loved ones—is the best place to establish lactation.

THANKS TO THE STAFF

Before you leave the hospital, take a minute to thank any nurse who was especially helpful to you. If the nurse who helped you is off duty, get her name and leave a note. Getting mother and baby off to a good start can be almost as rewarding for the dedicated nurse as it has been for you. She won't expect to be thanked for her kindness and skill—and probably hasn't been in years. But she will feel pleased. Maybe it will encourage her when the next nursing mother comes along needing her help.

CHAPTER 11

One to Six Weeks:
The Learning Period

HOMECOMING

It is surprising how tiring the trip home can be. Even if you feel more than ready to leave the hospital, you may be glad to lie down when you get home. Put the baby's bed next to your own, so you will be able to feed her or reach over and pat her without getting up. If you have other small children, arrange for them to be out of the house when you first get home. Then you and your new baby can be settled in bed before the welcoming tumult. You might want to make sure, before you leave the hospital, that there are enough groceries in the house to last a few days, so that you won't be obliged to plan meals and make lists right away.

THE "FORTY DAYS" RULE

Somehow we in the United States have gotten the idea that in primitive societies women give birth more easily, and recover at once. We imagine the peasant woman giving birth in the fields, tying the baby in her shawl, and going back to the plow. Lolling around in bed after giving birth will just weaken you, is the theory. Furthermore, our Puritan work ethic prods mothers to return to their normal activities and responsibilities as fast as possible; we feel guilty for every extra day we can't get that plowing done.

In fact, most cultures provide for a "lying-in" period after giving birth, in which the mother not only is relieved of her duties but is cared for by other women in the family. The typical duration of sequestration for mother and baby is forty days. Often the lying-in period is justified by superstition; the baby must wear certain clothes or amulets to be safe; mother and child must stay home to avoid the evil eye, and so on. The net effect, however, is that the mother has time to convalesce, her nourishment is guaranteed and provided by others, mother and infant can establish their breastfeeding relationship without hindrance, and neither of them is exposed to new sources of infection during this vulnerable time. A Chicago lactation consultant who works with recent immigrants from Asia, Malaysia, and India says that her mothers are flabbergasted, and their families are horrified, when the mother is expected to bathe the baby herself a day after giving birth, and when she is instructed upon discharge from the hospital to bring the baby back to the clinic for a checkup a week or two later, which may necessitate a long bus ride and exposure to many people.

Perhaps forty days of "doing nothing" seems a ridiculously long time to you, or an unattainable luxury. But there are many generations of experience behind that widespread tradition. People recover from childbirth at widely varying and quite unpredictable speeds. The hothouse flower who catches every cold that goes around, and never does anything more strenuous than put a tape in the VCR, may feel perfectly fit in two weeks, while the marathon runner is still feeling weak six months after giving birth. You may well find that you need a month or so of virtual idleness in order to convalesce completely from pregnancy and childbirth. The more work you do in that first month, the more time it will take you to feel strong again. Doing too much too soon is especially hard on the nursing mother, who is using her strength to make milk as well as to recuperate from pregnancy and delivery.

Even in our own culture this curtailment or even deletion of convalescent time is a relatively new idea. In the 1930s, mothers spent about two weeks in the hospital and then went home and spent another two weeks or so in their bedrooms, with orders not to go up or down stairs. (Certainly, forcing the mother to stay flat in bed all that time would have weakened her, but few mothers did that; a mother could care for her baby, and move around, but a "no stairs" rule effectively eliminated any chance that she would take over the housework too soon.)

Even a few years ago, mothers were kept in the hospital five days. Today, many hospitals send mothers and babies home in one day, and the typical hospital stay is two and a half days, even after a Caesarean section. While mothers have been persuaded that this is good for them, the main impetus has been cost reduction. As a result, it becomes the mother's own responsibility to see that she gets enough rest to convalesce quickly after going home.

Taking it easy is especially important if you have to go back to work fairly soon. If you overdo now, you may find yourself paying for it later, with weeks, even months of fatigue that could have been mitigated by a little more early rest. While home can and should be more restful than the hospital, to make that happen you must deliberately stay in bed and curtail your activities as much as you can. Don't worry about finishing the birth announcements. Don't read, however interesting the book, when you feel like sleeping and have a chance to do so. Limit your visitors to a few minutes. Don't drink too much caffeinated tea or coffee, which may make you restless so that you can't nap. (More than a cup or two a day can make your baby very jittery, too—see pp. 90–91)

Other people in the household, even the baby's father, may be so glad to have you back that they begin relying on you right away—to find the can opener or tell them if the chicken is cooked yet. Resist that urge to get up "just for a minute." Nursing the baby can be your best excuse to stay out of circulation for a while.

A FEW GOOD TIPS

Dr. E. Robbins Kimball, who has helped hundreds of mothers to nurse their babies successfully, sends each patient home with a list of three rules.

1. SPEND THE FIRST THREE DAYS IN BED.

This does not mean lying down whenever you get a chance; it means staying in bed, getting up only to go to the bathroom. Keep the baby near you or in your bed. Let your husband get breakfast and dinner and bring them to you; let whoever is helping you with your housework fix lunch. Don't even rinse out a diaper; use disposable diapers during this period if possible. Stock up on books and magazines, or move the TV into the bedroom. Remember, you don't have a baby every day, and when you do, you deserve to enjoy life for a little while. Naturally, when you come home from the hospital, you can see all sorts of things that have been neglected in your absence. But don't even straighten out a pillow; instead plan on doing it after your three days in bed. Three days from now, you may find that the things left undone don't seem quite so vital as they did at first.

Because you are in bed, visitors will not overstay their welcome, or expect you to serve coffee or drinks. Feel free to tell people that the doctor instructed you to stay in bed, even if he didn't. If you have another small child, and there are hours in the day when there is no one to watch him but you, just shut the bedroom door and keep him in your room with you. Even an eighteen-month-old can amuse himself with books and crayons, and likes to be read to, and he will soon learn to take his nap on your bed.

2. TAKE THREE ONE-HOUR NAPS A DAY.

During your first three days in bed, pull down the shades and sleep. For the rest of the month, use your ingenuity to get into bed and sleep for each one of these naps. Sleep while the children sleep, sleep before dinner while your husband takes the baby for a walk in the fresh air, sleep after breakfast while a neighbor watches the toddler. Don't read; don't write notes; you can do those things while you nurse the baby. *Sleep*. These three naps a day will do you more good, and do more to make breastfeeding a pleasure and a quick success than anything else you do in the first weeks.

3. REMEMBER THAT IT TAKES TWO OR THREE WEEKS TO LEARN HOW TO NURSE AND A COUPLE OF MONTHS TO BECOME AN EXPERT.

Don't regard every little event as a signal for panic. Sure, there will be days when you don't have enough milk. There will also be days when you have too much. There will be days when the baby seems to go on a four-hour schedule, and days when the baby wants to eat all the time, every two hours or oftener. These "frequency days" are nature's way of making your milk supply increase to keep up with your fast-growing baby's needs. You benefit, yourself, from these days. Research has shown that the more frequent the feedings, the faster the breastfeeding mother loses any extra weight she put on in pregnancy.

Researchers have found that the first two "frequency days" are apt to occur around the sixth and fourteenth days of life. The experienced mother hardly notices them but the mother who is still clock-watching and counting each feed is very conscious of them. All the events that take place in the early days of nursing your first baby loom very large, just like the events of your first pregnancy. Just remember that you (and your baby) are still learning. Breastfeeding will be easier and easier as you go along.

CONDITIONING THE LETDOWN REFLEX

Sometimes a new mother's letdown reflex doesn't work very reliably and she loses a lot of milk through leaking, or she may never seem to have quite enough, so that her baby does not gain very fast and sometimes cries at the breast. Such a mother needs to make a deliberate effort to induce her letdown reflex to function smoothly and reliably; nursing will be much more satisfactory once this happens. Here are some suggestions:

1. CONCENTRATE ON THE BABY WHILE YOU ARE NURSING.

Nursing "etiquette" means that you don't have to make conversation with someone else or answer the telephone while your newborn is at the breast. Go into another room, turn your back, and "retire" a little, mentally; while you are still learning to breastfeed, your body needs a chance to work without distraction.

2. CUT OUT EXTRANEOUS EFFORT, such as dinner parties (don't accept invitations yet, and don't extend them), the Late Late Show, and so on.

3. MONITOR YOUR OWN SCHEDULE: two or three one-hour naps, no skimping on meals or staying away from the house too long, no long car rides.

4. DURING THE DAY, WAKE THE BABY AND FEED HER, EVERY TWO TO THREE HOURS, rather than let her sleep for long periods; your breasts need regular stimulation to condition the letdown reflex. At night, wake the baby if you waken feeling full. Don't let her sleep five or six hours, while your milk production slows, or your milk leaks and goes to waste.

5. IF YOUR MILK SUDDENLY LETS DOWN, PICK UP THE BABY AND FEED HER, even if you just fed her. A sudden letdown after or between nursings doesn't mean that the milk didn't let down during the feeding—it may have let down several times, without your awareness. Extra letdowns just mean that your letdown is working *more* than enough; putting the baby to the breast even briefly will help condition your letdown reflex more specifically to your baby's sucking. Then feed her again in two to three hours, or sooner if she fusses.

6. IF YOU HAVE A CHANCE, TAKE FIVE MINUTES BEFORE FEEDING TO SIT DOWN, PUT YOUR FEET UP, CLOSE YOUR EYES, AND THINK ABOUT NOTHING.

7. NURSE IN THE SAME COMFORTABLE QUIET SPOT AT EACH MEAL; TAKE A DRINK OF WATER BEFORE YOU NURSE.

Your body responds well to routine. Your letdown reflex will associate itself with these habits.

8. REMOVE DISTRACTING INFLUENCES.

You can't let down your milk well if a neighbor is trying to chat with you at the same time, or if the phone is ringing, or if your three-year-old is getting into trouble in the kitchen. Later on, when you're an old hand at nursing, these things won't bother you. Now, while you're just beginning to get the hang of it, send the neighbor home, take the phone off the hook, and read a story to your three-year-old.

8. DON'T CHEAT YOURSELF THROUGH PERFECTIONISM.

A mother tends to feel that it is more important to get the laundry done, the house clean, the children well organized, the yard presentable, the errands caught up with, and the meals ready on time than to get enough rest or a good breakfast for herself. But none of these things is as important to your family—especially to your mate and to your nursing baby—as a relaxed, cheerful mother. Learn to look at taking care of yourself as your duty to your family, rather than as self-indulgence.

9. DON'T LET THE BABY SKIP NIGHT FEEDINGS, even though you need rest; get up at least once. And, although you may be fatigued, don't ask your husband to give the baby a bottle of formula in the night. At this point, you may have limited storage capacity; if your breasts get too full, milk production slows down. Don't go so long between feedings that your breasts feel lumpy. Your body actually produces more and richer milk at night, which helps the baby go longer on fewer feedings than during the day, and which also makes those night feedings especially important while the baby is still so small.

NURSING TRANQUILITY

One of nursing's greatest benefits to mothers is that it brings peace. Sitting down to nurse the baby allows you to withdraw, momentarily, from your other cares and duties. For a little while, all problems can be answered with the words, "I'm feeding the baby, I'll be there in a few minutes." The plumber on the doorstep, your mother-in-law wanting to know where to put the laundry, the phone ringing, the four-year-old insisting on a trip to the playground—all can wait. Behind the closed nursery door, curled in a rocking chair with the baby, you can restore yourself with the physical feelings of peace and tranquility that come with nursing. These moments of solitude are a simple but rare blessing in the lives of most mothers.

If you are in the habit of leading a high-geared, active life, you will especially come to enjoy these brief excursions into tranquility. Later on, at the end of a strenuous day, you'll absolutely crave getting home and sitting down with the baby. If you are sometimes overanxious, you can probably be an extremely successful nursing mother. (Dairymen say that the high-strung cows give the most milk; perhaps these are the cows that are most sensitive to their surroundings.) You will soon get into the swing of relaxing with the baby instead of struggling and fretting; and you have a great advantage, in so doing, over the bottle-feeding mother. The hormones of breastfeeding will help you, or even teach you, to be more easygoing.

One new mother, who all her life had suffered from a severe rash during periods of emotional stress, described an especially ghastly day that ended with her husband's being painfully cut by the lawn mower. True to experience, she broke out in the rash; then she sat down to nurse her twin babies, certain that she would produce no milk. Instead, the milk let down quickly. As she nursed the babies, she began to feel relaxed for the first time all day. By the time the meal was over, her rash was gone. These restorative moments of complete relief from stress are the reward that nature has always meant nursing to give to the mother.

FEEDING FREQUENCY

Dr. Niles Newton says, in an article on breastfeeding that was written primarily for doctors:

The advice given by Southworth in Carr's *Practice of Pediatrics,* published in 1906, is still worth remembering, since at that time successful breast feeding was the rule rather than the exception.

Southworth's schedule was:

First day: 4 nursings
Second day: 6 nursings
The rest of the first month: 10 nursings in 24 hrs.
Second and third months: 8 nursings in 24 hrs.
Fourth and fifth months: 7 nursings in 24 hrs.
Sixth through eleventh months: 6 nursings in 24 hrs.

He assumed the baby would have night feedings until six months old.

What a far cry this natural feeding schedule is from the four-hour schedule that modern formula-fed babies are put on. Even the baby fed synthetic milk "on demand" is expected to fall into roughly a four-hour schedule within a few weeks. But the nursing baby should not be expected to do so. Throughout the first four weeks, many a nursing baby eats ten times in twenty-four hours, which means an average two and a half hours between feedings. If he sometimes sleeps four or five hours at a stretch at night, he may well double up in the daytime, and take some meals at even shorter intervals. If it seems to you that your baby is "always hungry," keep track for one day to see if he doesn't fall into the standard ten-nursings-a-day pattern, and if his apparent insatiability isn't a result of your expecting him to go three or four hours between meals, as an adult would, and as a baby fed on slow-digesting cow's milk is expected to do.

We sometimes make a concession to a small synthetic milk-fed baby, and start him out on a three-hour schedule. But the breastfed baby may not work up to a three-hour schedule—one that averages out to eight meals a day—until the second or third month, and Dr. Southworth did not expect breastfed babies to cut down to six meals a day, or a four-hour schedule, until they were six months old! No wonder so many mothers in the previous generation could not nurse their babies, when a four-hour schedule was flatly insisted on from birth, and when it was customary to tell all mothers to nurse from one breast only at each feeding. The woman who produced so much milk that she could feed a baby adequately, despite the limited sucking stimulation given by offering each breast only once every eight hours, must have been rare indeed.

Suppose your new baby does not fit Southworth's description? The La Leche League manual, *The Womanly Art of Breastfeeding,* says:

> Occasionally, we see a baby who goes to extremes in one of two ways. One day he may seem to be exceptionally active, fussy and hungry all or most of the time. If we nurse him more often than every two hours, which is what he seems to want, he only gets fussier and more restless, but will go right on nursing! This type of baby is often getting more milk than he really wants. What he wants is more sucking, without the milk.

One possibility is to feed the baby on a two-to-three-hour schedule and use a pacifier in between; another is to use just one breast per feeding, and let him stay on for a while when the milk has slowed to a trickle, or return to that breast if he wants more suckling for comfort, even when he is probably full.

The other extreme is the too placid baby. This one will sleep peacefully for four, five, or more hours between feedings, be fairly quiet, and nurse rather leisurely. As time goes on, she may seem to get even quieter, and you think, "Such a good baby. She certainly is doing well." Then comes the shock, when you take her to the doctor for her first checkup and find out to your amazement that she has not gained an ounce, and may even have lost weight.

Here again, remember that the breastfed baby needs to be fed, as Dr. Southworth advises, about every two to three hours, with perhaps one longer stretch at night. The trouble in this case is not a lack of milk on your part nor a lack in its quality. It is the baby who needs to be encouraged. The exceptionally sleepy, placid baby must be awakened to be fed more often, and should be urged to take both breasts at each feeding. Sometimes a baby tires easily, and almost seems to lose interest; that baby needs to be given the opportunity to learn to nurse longer, as well as more often. Watch the baby; you can help her to settle down and nurse by reducing outside stimuli (noise, light), increasing the areas of contact between her skin and yours, rocking, singing, and letting the baby rest at the breast between bouts of active suckling.

By increasing the number of times a baby nurses in a day, and encouraging the baby to nurse longer, you will automatically increase your supply, and soon the baby will be gaining as she should. In this case, too, it is important to make sure the baby nurses a long time on the first breast—twenty or thirty minutes, say—to get the last few swallows of high-calorie, fat-rich hind milk into her before you offer the second breast (see chapter 2, p. 31). One side is all some babies will take, at first anyway. Research shows that babies who always take only one side get just as many calories as babies that almost always nurse on both breasts.

Some lactation consultants advise the mother of a slow-gaining newborn to massage the breast, gently, for a minute or two as the baby starts to nurse, using the free hand to make firm, soft strokes from the outermost perimeter of the breast tissue toward the areola. The theory is that doing this mechanically moves fat particles toward the milk ducts, and thus helps to increase the calorie count of a particular feeding. It may be, also, that massage relaxes the mother or stimulates the letdown reflex or both.

HOW TO TELL IF THE BABY IS GETTING ENOUGH MILK

1. WHAT GOES IN MUST COME OUT. Does the baby have good bowel movements? The feces of a breastfed baby are normally yellowish and rather liquid, with the odor and consistency of yoghurt. The new nursing baby may have several bowel movements a day; some may be just a stain on the diapers. Later, he will have one every two to four days, but it should be fairly big. The baby who is not getting enough to eat has consistently scanty, watery stools, which may be greenish in color.

2. DOES HE HAVE LOTS OF WET DIAPERS? If you are not giving him extra water, which he doesn't need anyway, those wet diapers are an indication that he is getting plenty of breast milk. (Be aware, however, that modern disposable diapers are remarkably absorbent and can sometimes seem dry even if your baby has wet them once or twice.)

3. IS HE CONTENT WITH EIGHT TO ELEVEN FEEDINGS PER DAY, the typical nursing schedule? If you are nursing him this often, and letting down your milk at feedings, he is probably well fed.

4. IS HE GAINING? There is a tremendous amount of emphasis these days on how much weight a baby gains; synthetic milk-fed babies sometimes put on a lot of weight, and the rate of gain has become the yardstick by which the baby's health is measured, by mothers and often by doctors, too. La Leche League says, "A good rule to follow, in a healthy baby, is that he should be gaining from four to seven ounces a week, but that less than this in a given week or two is not in itself cause for alarm." *More* than this is not cause for alarm either; some breastfed babies gain very fast in the first three months or so (see chapter 4, p. 105).

That does not mean you should rush off and buy a scale; home scales are usually quite inaccurate anyway. And weighing before and after feedings would be a great waste of time. It is the weight your baby gains over time, not day-to-day fluctuations, that matters. Don't be rattled if someone remarks that your baby "isn't gaining fast enough," as long as he is happy and healthy, his color is good, his arms and legs are getting plump, and you nurse him long and often. Try to put the question out of your mind until your baby's next checkup with the pediatrician. If you really want to weigh the baby, the scales in the supermarket are usually very accurate, and checkout personnel will probably let you weigh the baby if they are not too busy. Take duplicates of what the baby is wearing, weigh the baby, weigh the duplicate clothes, and subtract the clothing weight plus the baby's previous weight to see how much the baby has gained.

YOUR FOOD

Part of enjoying life in these first six weeks is eating heartily and well. This is not the time to diet; lactation is the best "diet" there is, anyway. A few months or a year of giving milk can strip unnecessary weight from you without the slightest effort on your part. Some mothers think that the most enjoyable thing about lactating is that for a few happy months they can dive into meals with gusto, and take two helpings of everything, yet never gain a pound.

Of course you will have plenty of high-quality breast milk no matter what you eat; milk is produced independently of diet. But while you can at this point safely eat more calories than you used to, this does not mean that you should fill up on "cheat foods" such as cake and sweet rolls. Sugary, starchy foods provide "empty calories," because they are nutritionally deficient. Meanwhile, the mammary glands raid your body for the vitamins, minerals, and protein missing from your diet but needed for milk production. You don't lose weight, and you tend to feel tired and "used up."

It's better to eat *something*, even if it is junk food, than to go hungry or try to eat unfamiliar food you don't like just because you think it's good for you. But right now, your own body needs extra protein and extra calcium (especially important for teenage mothers, who may still be growing themselves). Give yourself food such as beans, meat, chicken, cheese, eggs, and fish. You don't need to drink a lot of milk, or even any, especially if it doesn't agree with you. Canned fish such as salmon and sardines are a great source of calcium, and so are most green leafy foods such as lettuce and all the cabbage relatives. Don't concern yourself greatly about cholesterol; during lactation Mother Nature regulates the amount and kind of cholesterol in your body and in your milk, presumably doing exactly what is best for you and your baby (see chapter 3, pp. 75–76).

Try to make sure that whatever you consume is good, nutritionally. The whole-grain (dark) cereals and breads provide more protein than refined white bread, as well as extra flavor. Enriched or brown rice is more nutritious than polished rice. Fruit and fruit juices can give you as much "quick energy" from sugar as any soft drink can. Beans and tortillas and chilis are "real food"; candy bars aren't. And remember—the baby will be fine, whatever you eat, but you will feel better if you eat good food, and enough of it, during the first few weeks. It's your vacation. Enjoy it.

BABY'S REACTIONS TO YOUR DIET

A normal varied diet should have no harmful effects on your baby; people will tell you nursing mothers ought to avoid cabbage or chocolate or spicy foods, but in general babies don't care (see chapter 2, pp. 35–39, for a full discussion). Some babies, however, do develop "colic"—suffering stomach pains, passing lots of gas, and crying in obvious discomfort, often at the same time every day—in reaction to one substance common in mothers' diets: cows' milk protein. This is especially likely if you have any sensitivity to dairy products yourself, or if you consumed a lot of dairy products during pregnancy. If your baby has a lot of gastric discomfort, you can easily check out whether this sensitivity is the cause by eliminating all dairy products (milk, cheese, yoghurt, ice cream, and processed foods containing dried milk solids) from your own diet for one week, and observing whether the baby seems more comfortable. You can reintroduce small quantities of dairy products later, if you wish, to find out what the baby can and can't handle; usually, breastfed babies become less sensitive to such maternal diet effects as they get older.

Another cause of colic can be iron supplements you may have been taking during pregnancy. If you were taking iron pills in addition to vitamins, stop. You probably don't need them now, anyway. Some mothers feel that consuming sugar substitutes gives the baby diarrhea; soft drinks, especially, can contain large quantities of sugar substitutes, but they are also found in some ice creams and many "lite" or diet foods. Some mothers find that their babies get diarrhea if the mother drinks a lot of fruit juice (a quart or more in twenty-four hours). Occasionally, a baby seems to be gassy and uncomfortable if his mother consumes a lot of carbonated drinks.

LIQUIDS

You may not really be eating for two, but when you are lactating, you are certainly drinking for two. If you are tired or preoccupied, it is easy to forget about taking enough fluids. There is no need to force yourself to drink copious quantities of liquids, but you do not want to go thirsty. If you drink a glass of water or juice every time you nurse the baby, that will be plenty; taking that much liquid will also help to prevent constipation. You may feel intensely thirsty at the moment the milk lets down; nature is reminding you to drink that glass of water. Many women find it convenient to keep a pitcher of water handy where they nurse the baby.

You do not need to make a special effort to drink milk. In most parts of the world, nursing mothers drink no milk at all. Cheese, meats, and even salad greens provide you with calcium. Although you probably avoided alcohol during pregnancy, light use of alcohol—one glass of wine or beer before dinner, say—is not harmful for the nursing mother, or her child. One German baby nurse swore that all her maternity patients succeeded in breastfeeding because of her prescription: a big bowl of sugared and creamed oatmeal for breakfast, and a glass of port wine at 10 A.M. and 4 P.M.

LITTLE PROBLEMS

There are lots of little events in the early days of nursing that may seem like problems because they are new to you. Three months from now you probably won't even remember them. Here are some solutions:

LEAKING:

If you leak primarily during feedings, you can open both bra cups and hold a clean diaper to the fountaining breast while the baby drinks from the other. Or use handkerchiefs, cut-up cloth diapers, or the nursing pads you can buy at the drugstore, to wear inside your bra. (Take note: don't use nursing pads with plastic exteriors; they may cause soreness by keeping your nipples wet. Don't use cut-up disposable diapers; many of them are filled with a plastic gel and treated with chemicals that can irritate your skin.) Mild leaks can be controlled with the flannel liners that may sometimes be bought with nursing bras. Sometimes you can stop the milk from leaking out by pressing down flat on the nipples with your hands or forearms, when you feel the milk let down. Leaking will diminish as your letdown reflex becomes better established. If you *don't* leak, don't think you are strange; some women seldom or never leak milk.

LOW MILK SUPPLY AT SUPPERTIME:

The early evening meal does seem to be the scantiest. If you have nursed the baby a lot that day, your milk production may still be catching up to the baby's needs. Even newborns sometimes wake up and act hungry when they smell food cooking, so you can find yourself putting the baby to the breast again when you sit down to eat. Instead of feeding the baby, let your husband amuse her, or offer the pacifier. After a shower and a good dinner, you may find you have a surprisingly ample dividend of milk that will send the baby off to a good sleep.

TOO MUCH MILK:

In the early days of nursing, both your supply and the baby's needs fluctuate. It takes several weeks for your supply and the baby's appetite to synchronize, and even then there may be days when you have a little more or a little less milk than she wants.

BABY OVERSLEEPING:

If your baby is sleeping six or eight or ten hours at night, so that you wake up every morning groaningly full of milk, wake him in the night to feed him. The baby would probably feed off and on all night if he slept in your bed. Remember that your body produces milk more copiously, and with higher fat content, while you are sleeping. Sleeping separately, babies sometimes sleep through meals that you both need. Getting too full every morning tends to lower your total milk production. In another month or two, both you and the baby will be able to go longer between feeds.

A STRONG LETDOWN REFLEX:

If your milk lets down so vigorously that the baby sputters, chokes, and cries during feedings because he is getting flooded, try sitting him upright to nurse, and try nursing him on one side only, per feeding, but for as long as he wants. Sometimes when a mother has a strong letdown reflex, the baby gets full before he has had enough time to suck and be cuddled, and he frets for the comforting, rather than for extra milk. Try putting the baby back on the same breast, rather than switching him to the other side, so that he can satisfy his need to suckle, without getting more milk than he can handle.

NIGHT FEEDS:

Just take the baby in bed with you, and doze while he drinks. There's no danger of rolling on him, really. Mothers have slept with their babies since the beginning of humanity. You can put him back in his own bed, if and when you wake up.

CRITICISM:

If a friend or relative criticizes you for nursing, reread Chapter 7, the section on Prejudice Against Breastfeeding, pp. 167–70, to understand why they do it; then turn a deaf ear.

GOING OUT:

Don't go out socially yet, unless you feel very lively and the four walls of your bedroom are really beginning to get you down. If you do go, take the baby—a nursing baby is so portable! Pleasant adult company is sometimes a real tonic, if you are careful not to overexert yourself in new surroundings. Sometimes just a drive in the car is a welcome change of scene. Go to a movie—your baby gets in free and will probably just doze and nurse through the whole show.

GROWTH SPURTS

Many babies seem to go along comfortably for a time and then have a spurt of growth that makes them suddenly extra-hungry, wanting to eat all day long. These so-called frequency days don't mean that your milk supply has suddenly dropped, but just the opposite; the baby is growing and his needs have suddenly risen. Think of it this way: if a bottle-fed baby suddenly increased his intake, everyone would be exclaiming about his wonderful appetite, and bragging that he took a whole extra bottle today. When a breastfed baby's appetite increases, we tend to panic, sure that we are not satisfying his hunger, instead of just recognizing it as a healthy sign of growth.

Growth spurts are likely to occur sometime in the second week, at somewhere between three and six weeks, and at three months. If you suddenly find yourself "nursing night and day," check the calendar and see if this doesn't coincide with a likely growth spurt. Your production will adjust accordingly.

SPECIAL SITUATIONS: NURSING A "DIVIDEND" BABY

One mother who may have a hard time sticking to her decision to breastfeed is the mother who already has children, and who, when her youngest child is ten or twelve years old, has another baby. Somehow a baby born out of season is always at a disadvantage, whether it is a fall colt or a Christmas lamb, or a child who arrives as a dividend to the family that already seemed complete. Even if the mother breastfed her previous children with complete success, she may find that she doesn't seem to do well with this one. The baby nurses, but he just doesn't gain.

The problem is basically one of practicality. Once you get out of the habit of orienting your life around infants and toddlers, it is very difficult to get back into that habit. Life becomes so different for most families when the children are older that it is difficult to go back easily to a nursery world of long peaceful feedings, weekends at home, and neglected housework. Other responsibilities have intruded on the hours that were once free for sitting around with a baby. The result is that nursing time is curtailed so that the milk supply dwindles, or sometimes the letdown reflex is inhibited so that what milk the baby does get is simply rather low in calories.

If you are in this situation, and you want to continue to nurse, stop to think ahead a little about how many changes this is going to make, temporarily, in your household. This baby deserves his mother's milk just as much as the others did; but making it possible for him requires a special effort not only from you but from the rest of your household, too.

Even if you don't work outside your home, read chapter 13, The Working Mother, for hints on how busy women manage nursing and other responsibilities as well. Let older children (and your spouse) get into the habit of doing more of their own cleaning, cooking, transportation, and wardrobe management. Teach them to expect just as much from you in the way of love and kindness but perhaps a little less in the way of goods and services. Get into the habit, yourself, of resting more and doing less, so that you can enjoy this baby the way babies were meant to be enjoyed. All too soon this one, like the others, will be grown.

The mother who has her *first* baby rather late in life, perhaps after many years of marriage and of being a working woman, paradoxically may have a very easy time breastfeeding. Just having a baby in a childless household is such a big change that the adjustments necessitated by nursing can easily be accomplished simultaneously. The nursing relationship is a special blessing for an older mother, making this child doubly enjoyable and helping her to be casual and easygoing about motherhood.

NURSING TWINS

Lots of mothers have nursed twins. It is usually easier to breastfeed twins than it is to feed them sixteen or more bottles every day. It is also much better for the twins, who may be small at birth and need the extra boost of mother's milk. Benjamin Spock, M.D., surveying mothers of twins, found that mothers who breastfed twins were better organized and felt better than the mothers who bottle-fed twins. Several books by mothers of twins offer helpful advice not only for breastfeeding twins (and triplets!) but for managing their care (see Appendix).

Most mothers of twins nurse them simultaneously, at least when they are both awake at the same time. This seems clumsy at first, but the fact that both breasts are nursed at once when the milk lets down seems to benefit the necessary high rate of milk production. In the old days, professional wet nurses probably increased their production, in order to feed two or even more babies, by this method of simultaneous feedings. For comfort, try tucking one twin under each arm, supported by pillows or the arms of a big chair. Or put one twin in your lap and use its stomach as a pillow for the other twin. Most mothers have enough milk for twins without adding cereals or anything else, at least until the combined weight of the twins is twenty or twenty-five pounds. That is usually when they are around five or six months old, when one would begin adding solids anyway, but may occur earlier.

It is customary to advise mothers of twins to rotate the babies, that is, to nurse each baby on each breast, not to always keep the same baby on the same side. The theory is that the stronger sucker will then be able to stimulate both breasts to higher production. However, in all animals that have multiple young, scientists have found that each baby has its own favorite nipple, and after some confusion in the early days soon learns to go to the same place for every meal. In this way, each gland adjusts its secretion of milk to the needs of the particular baby that nurses on it. It may be that human twins can regulate their milk supplies individually and that keeping them always on the same breast would simplify matters. An extreme difference in needs may make you look a bit lopsided; on the other hand, production may differ without any difference in appearance. It is also possible that the production level and even milk content may differ on each side. One mother pumping milk for a sick twin produced thirteen ounces regularly from one breast, and seven from the other, each morning, and yet her breasts were the same size.

The mother nursing twins may have to make a special effort to get enough calories. With supermarket shelves full of unnourishing products, such as corn flakes and Jell-O, it is easy to eat a lot without actually getting much food. To nurse twins (or nurse one baby and give milk to a milk bank) without losing too much weight, a mother may need one or even two extra meals a day, with emphasis on meat and potatoes, beans, or rice, and perhaps some hearty snacks as well. Like any nursing mother, if she finds herself losing weight or feeling tired or depressed, she may need additional B-complex vitamins.

Mothers of multiples agree that one should hunt before birth for a cooperative pediatrician. As a rule, twins can gain just as well as singles on mother's milk; some, however, do need supplements as they grow, especially on days when the mother is overtired. A mother nursing twins or triplets runs a higher-than-normal risk of breast infection if she lets herself get overtired.

NURSING THE DISADVANTAGED BABY

The baby who is born with a serious abnormality, such as Down's syndrome or a cleft palate, can still be fed his mother's milk. Nursing a disadvantaged baby may take patience and dedication. The retarded or brain-damaged infant may have little or no sucking reflex. An ill or preterm baby may be separated from you by hospitalization. You will need the strong support of your health-care team. A board-certified lactation consultant can be very helpful in establishing and maintaining lactation under challenging circumstances.

The worried mother of a disadvantaged child is often exceptionally willing to make the extra effort. It is one thing she can clearly do to help, and it brings profound emotional relief to her. The mother of a Down's syndrome baby, healthy and nursing at eight months, said, "It is all I can do for her, to make her feel close and happy, and to give her the best start toward growing up that she can have. I often feel so thankful I can share this much, at least, with her." One mother who nursed a normal baby and simultaneously expressed enough milk for his cleft-palated twin put it this way: "I believe Steve needed the nutritional advantage of the milk, and thus I wanted very much to give it to him. The day I took him home from the hospital and began to express my milk for him, I experienced a great sense of relief and my anxiety over his condition seemed to dissipate. The act of providing breast milk for him in the unconventional way of a bottle provided me with great peace of mind and a feeling of usefulness. I felt I had climbed Mt. Everest when I succeeded."

THE PRETERM OR SERIOUSLY ILL BABY

It is always a shocking experience for both mother and child when a very small baby has to stay in the hospital while the mother goes home. Here again, the maintenance of a supply of breast milk is the most useful thing a mother can provide for the child. Small preterm babies do well on breast milk (see chapter 2, pp. 40–41).

Feeding of breast milk rapidly corrects the chemical chaos in the bodies of infants who have undergone surgery. Many mothers have expressed milk and carried or sent it to the hospital daily. In one case, an infant with a heart anomaly had to undergo major surgery in a military hospital; the mother's milk was picked up every day in an ice chest by an air force ambulance.

PUMPING MILK FOR THE HOSPITALIZED BABY

To develop or maintain a milk supply while you are separated from the baby, you should plan on pumping your milk; even if the milk cannot be given to your baby, as is sometimes the case if you live far from the hospital, pumping your milk will keep your own supply going until the baby can come home. Information about manual expression, pumping, and kinds of pumps is given in chapter 13, pp. 335–43.

To develop a milk supply or keep production going, you will need to pump an average of every three to four hours (most definitely, you must include night time), or six to eight times a day, with no interval longer than five or six hours between pumpings. You should also be prepared to pump in between if you suddenly feel the milk let down. Use the hints in Chapter 2 (p. 19) and Chapter 11 (p. 255) for conditioning your letdown reflex, which will help to develop and maintain your productivity.

If you need to pump or express milk for a week or more, there is a drug, metoclopramide, that can be taken by mothers of premature babies to increase milk production. This drug apparently increases the prolactin output (which is normally a byproduct of the suckling stimulation that the mother is not getting). In a study at the Yale University School of Medicine, twenty-three mothers of month-old hospitalized preterm babies experienced improvement, with production of fewer than 100 milliliters (less than $3\frac{1}{2}$ oz.) daily increasing to almost 200 (or 7 oz.) daily in many cases. Fifteen were able to take their babies home fully breastfeeding.

Some hospitals today allow parents, especially nursing mothers, to stay with their infants at all times, except, of course, during surgery. Many hospitals do not. Find out exactly what your hospital's policies allow you to do and not do. Can you stay overnight with your baby? Can you be with your baby in the recovery room? How soon will you be allowed to nurse your baby after surgery? If the hospital bars you from caring for your baby in ways you feel necessary for your baby's well-being, speak with your baby's doctor. Call the hospital administration. Find out what the laws are in your state regarding the treatment of families in hospitals. Some states require that parents have access to their hospitalized children at all times. And remember that all rules can be bent—and usually are, when the parents express their preferences clearly and forthrightly.

If you do run into a problem with hospital policies, call Children in Hospitals (see Appendix), an organization in Massachusetts dedicated to minimizing the trauma that hospitalization can cause children. Barbara Popper, the founder of CIH, and her team work to educate medical staffs about the need for children to have their parents with them at all times. They advise parents in choosing a hospital with family-oriented policies and a sympathetic doctor. They also publish the CIH *Consumer Directory of Hospitals,* a useful resource for anyone with a family member facing hospitalization.

La Leche League International is also experienced at supporting and advising mothers of seriously ill or disabled nursing babies. Nothing can help so much as talking to someone who has been in the same boat. La Leche League can also guide the mother in ways to get along with members of the hospital staff, and to enlist their support without harassing them. If, in the course of your baby's hospitalization, your milk production ceases, LLLI has several pamphlets on relactation, or reestablishing a milk supply.

THE NURSING MOTHER AND THE REST OF THE FAMILY: YOUR HUSBAND

One of the rewards of breastfeeding, for the married woman, is her husband's approval. Your husband's pride and confidence in you can keep you nursing while you are a novice at the job. Your husband can dispel your doubts, reassure you, and steady you. He can save you from rushing for the bottle just because the baby has had an extra-hungry day and your supply hasn't caught up with her need, or because your breasts seem soft, the baby is fussing, and someone remarks, "You can't just let that child starve!" Your husband can brighten the time you spend at home, with comments and anecdotes from the outside world. He can make you rest when your conscience is urging you to overwork. It is your husband who, in the middle of night, may bring the baby to you to nurse in bed, barely waking you or the baby.

What husbands need, in return, is appreciation. It's a shock for a man, too, to have this new person in the household—right in your bed, in fact—a person who occupies so much of your time and attention. You can reassure him by praise and verbal thanks, of course, but more effectively, by your attention, even passive attention. For example, if he is cooking dinner, or mowing the lawn, you can sit down and nurse the baby while watching him do it. You are still resting, and he feels appreciated. That feeling is a powerful reinforcement.

YOUR CHILDREN

If you have more than one child, but this is the first you've breastfed, you may feel strange initially about nursing in front of the others. But children soon get accustomed to the sight and take it for granted. The child closest in age to the baby sometimes wants special attention while you are nursing. Make the baby's mealtime a special time for your older child, too, in which you read to him and cuddle him. A nursing baby makes a very good book rest, and you can quite easily hold two children in your lap, or put your free arm around the older child. You can enjoy your peaceful private nursings alone with the baby now and then, when the other child is asleep or outside playing. Don't let yourself resent the older child's intrusion; if you seem to enjoy his company when you are nursing, and perhaps give him a special half-hour of play or attention at some other time, he won't think of nursing as disadvantageous to himself.

Of course, you don't have to let the older child tease or annoy you or the baby at feeding times; just tell him, firmly, that that is not acceptable behavior. After all, you have a right to breastfeed, and your new baby has a right to his mother's milk, regardless of how the older child feels about it. Most toddlers and older children learn to regard nursing as just what it is: a nice, friendly, and very convenient way to feed the baby.

An older child who sees the baby at the breast may want to try nursing, too. The best way to deal with such a request is to let the child try. He won't be very successful, and he'll find that after all, it's just milk, and not the ambrosia the baby seems to think it is.

GRANDMOTHERS

The sensitive grandmother is usually very pleased that her grandchild is being breastfed. Watching the new baby at the breast, she remembers her own days of new motherhood, and she feels fonder than ever of her daughter or daughter-in-law for being such a good mother to this new member of the family.

But it is not given to all of us, even grandmothers, to be mature all the time. Mingled with her pride is often a certain amount of jealousy. A grandmother may well be more skillful at first with the baby than is its inexperienced mother. She may be secretly anxious to have her son or son-in-law see what a good mother she is; but there is one thing she cannot do for the baby (in our culture, at least) and that is, nurse him. So she may be jealous because you are the only person who is really indispensable to the baby. At the same time, she may be jealous of the baby, because this little newcomer takes you away from her. Especially during nursing, the closed circle of rapport between mother and baby may make a grandmother feel excluded. In her anxiety to regain your attention, she may break in with remarks that are more thoughtless or even cruel than she realizes. The cure is simple; seek privacy during nursing, and at other times make a special effort, so that she feels welcome and appreciated. Ask for help you really need in areas where she excels, such as cooking your favorite foods, and be sure to show appreciation for this truly needed assistance.

GUARDING YOUR OWN WELL-BEING

Even if you have doting grandmothers and grandfathers and a loving husband and a great medical team, *you* must take responsibility for your own health; nobody else can do it for you. Your pediatrician may be primarily interested in your baby's health, and not in yours. Your obstetrician may be primarily interested in your pelvic organs, and not in the rest of you. All too often, a new mother drags on for weeks with anemia or bronchitis or some other ailment that neither her obstetrician nor her pediatrician notices, although she may see both of them during that time, and that she herself tries to ignore, often because she feels too tired to bother going to another doctor.

Seeing a family-practice physician may be more useful at this point than going to two specialists. Either way, you know your body best, and you need to take primary responsibility. Watch your nutrition. Get enough rest. If you are coughing, running a fever, bleeding vaginally more than slightly, or with fresh blood rather than a brownish discharge—if you are pale and have blue circles under your eyes—see someone. Get treatment; don't just try to tough it out if you are not well. Your baby needs you healthy.

IF SORE NIPPLES PERSIST

The likelihood of nipple soreness diminishes after you have left the hospital and the early days of nursing are past. Occasionally, however, a nipple can get sore once you are home. Check the baby's positioning, and make sure the baby is latched on well, with the lips flanged out and the nipple well back in the mouth, out of harm's way. Rotate positions you hold the baby in from feeding to feeding. Keep your nipples dry between feedings. Let a little breast milk dry on the sore nipple; it has healing properties. If these suggestions do not result in improvement, a certified lactation consultant can evaluate your situation, or, if there is a lactation clinic in your town, now's the time to pay a visit.

Sometimes a new nursing mother gets into trouble because she does not know how to treat a sore nipple and does not want to ask her doctor for fear that he will insist she wean the baby; so she goes on nursing despite the nipple's getting worse and worse, until it is really injured. Where damage is severe, you can nurse on one breast only and let the sore nipple heal, if you have to. Again, a lactation expert, whether L.C., experienced nurse practitioner, or midwife, can help.

Sore nipples that persist for many days may be caused not by poor positioning but by a yeast infection. Symptoms may include pain that persists or gets worse during the feeding rather than peaking at the beginning, red or weeping spots on the nipples and areolas, and pain within the breast. Typically, a yeast infection, or thrush, starts in the baby's mouth after the baby has been given antibiotics. You may see white patches on the baby's tongue or inside the mouth that look like milk but don't wipe off. The infection can be passed back and forth between mother and baby repeatedly. Even if one or the other doesn't have any overt symptoms, both need to be treated (see chapter 2, p. 56).

OTHER BREAST AILMENTS

Plugged ducts—little areas of the breast that don't drain milk well—are a not uncommon problem; a plugged duct can lead to a minor infection within the breast that may make you feel ill. If you discover yourself feeling feverish and miserable, check your breasts to see if you can find a "hot spot" that is tender to the touch and perhaps looks reddened. You can treat this yourself with hot moist compresses and frequent nursing; lactation consultants recommend positioning the baby so that his nose is pointing toward the sore spot, "even if you have to stand on your head to do it." That will help to drain the blocked area. Rotating the baby to a new quadrant of the breast at each feeding will drain all the ducts thoroughly. Plenty of rest and fluids are also vital. A plugged duct, if not tended to promptly, can lead to mastitis, or a breast infection.

If you do not feel better within twenty-four hours, or if you start running a higher fever, see a doctor immediately and get some antibiotics. Mastitis usually responds well to antibiotics. As a rule, antibiotics will not harm your baby through your milk; tetracycline, however, should not be taken by nursing mothers because it can stain the baby's newly forming teeth.

CONFIDENCE BUILDERS

All of us have doubts sometimes about our nursing ability, even if we have nursed babies before. When the baby is fussy, or the doctor is noncommittal about whether the baby's doing well, or a friend criticizes, it is hard not to worry. You can't see the milk going into the baby, so there's no way to tell exactly what he's getting. You start to concentrate so much on the fear that he's getting no milk that you become tense at feeding time, and lose the easygoing sense of teamwork and friendship with the baby. When these good feelings are there, the milk is there, too, automatically; you don't have to worry about it any more than your happy nursing baby does.

If you are having doubts, try these suggestions:

1. FIND ANOTHER NURSING MOTHER, past or present. If you don't know one, ask your neighbors and acquaintances. Now is the time to pack up your baby and visit someone who has had more experience. There may be a La Leche League group in your own town; LLLI will notify you of the nearest group leader if you call, free, 1–800–LA LECHE. Or you might ask your doctor for the name of some other patient who is an old hand at breastfeeding. One phone call to another, experienced, nursing mother can boost your morale for a week.

2. EVEN YOUR PETS CAN INSPIRE YOUR OWN CONFIDENCE.
One nursing mother wrote about her cat having kittens: "While the actual birth was a bit of a surprise to the cat (the first kitten was born on the back doorstep), by the time the others arrived, she was already confident in her new role of mother. During the first week, Domino was with her babies constantly. She didn't seem to mind their continual nursing.

No one suggested that the milk of Cindy Lou, the cocker spaniel next door, might be more nourishing for newborn kittens or at least would help them to sleep all night. And when Domino did leave them for a while, it took only the tiniest meow to bring her leaping back into the box. Watching Domino raise her family is a continuing delight and inspiration . . ."

3. LISTEN TO THE BABY SWALLOWING—"SUCK-HAH"—EACH TIME THE MILK LETS DOWN if you can't believe the invisible milk is there. Or you can tuck the forefinger of your free hand under the baby's chin, as she nurses, so you can feel her swallowing. Or try expressing a little milk manually, after a feeding (see chapter 13, p. 337) to reassure yourself that it exists.

4. REMEMBER THAT BREAST MILK IS AN EFFI-CIENT SOURCE OF NUTRIENTS tailored to the needs of your baby. One way you might look at it, is that *two* ounces of breast milk contains as much and more of the needed nutrients as *four* ounces of synthetic milk provides, even if your milk looks "thinner" and bluish. And when the fat-rich hind milk is added in, your milk probably has as many calories, per ounce, as light cream. So your baby is getting plenty of nourishment even when the amount of milk he takes seems meager compared to the bottleful after bottleful that a synthetic milk-fed baby may take.

5. DON'T JUDGE HOW MUCH MILK YOU HAVE BY HOW FULL YOUR BREASTS SEEM.
Often we feel very full in the hospital; then, when we get home, the breasts are no longer burstingly full, and it seems as if the milk has gone. But the fullness in the hospital is only partly caused by milk; some of it is due to increased circulation and some swelling in the tissues, which quickly dies down. The breast is never, in fact, really empty, but continually makes milk. And once the letdown reflex is working well, much of the fluid content of the milk is not drawn from the bloodstream into the breasts until it is needed. Thus, there may be several ounces of milk available

to the baby in a breast that feels quite soft nearly all the time.

6. REMEMBER: THE PRIMARY TREATMENT FOR A FUSSY BABY IS MORE REST FOR THE MOTHER.

Write that out in big letters and stick the note on the refrigerator, to keep it in front of others in the household as well as yourself. A nursing mother, especially in the first weeks and with her first baby, needs to cut back on anything else that takes energy, such as work, phone calls, conversations, reading, cooking, and whatever she may think she ought to be doing. She needs to persuade her loved ones to give her some peace, in whatever way she can manage. Leave the dinner table, and go to bed early. Take the rest you need.

7. GIVE YOUR BABY LOTS OF SKIN CONTACT IF HE CRIES OFTEN.

Sometimes babies need to be cuddled more than anything else, and feeling the warmth of your skin can have a magically calming effect. A rocking chair is also a great tool for relaxing mother as well as baby, not just during feedings, but between and after feedings when a little cosy time is in order. Some babies need extra suckling; if the baby will not nurse on the breast longer, you could offer a pacifier, but pacifiers are a nuisance and usually end up on the floor; try letting him suck on the tip of your little finger, the pad turned up against the roof of his mouth, instead. Sometimes a fretful baby is overstimulated by playful parents or siblings, by too much going on for his young nervous system to cope with; try skin contact and peace and quiet.

8. PRACTICE UNRESTRICTED BREASTFEEDING.

Read the section on unrestricted vs. standard-care babies in chapter 5 (pp. 143–44). By three months, standard-care babies on the average cry 35 percent *more* than unrestrictedly breastfed babies. Are you giving yourself (or is someone else giving you) a lot of reasons why feedings are being curtailed, delayed, or interrupted? Could you change some of that? Maybe your baby would like to have fewer rules in her young life.

9. ACCEPT THAT SOME BABIES ARE JUST FUSSIER THAN OTHERS. TAKE COMFORT FROM THE THOUGHT.

A pair of breastfed twins supplied a good example, reported in the La Leche League newsletter for mothers, *New Beginnings:*

> "Chatty Cathy," the smaller twin, is a little "fuss pot"—squirming and spitting, sleeping only in short hauls, and gaining rather slowly. Charlotte nurses peacefully, lives life in an easygoing way, and is gaining much faster than her sister."

The same mother, the same supply of milk—no supplement, no solids—and two very different babies.

10. DON'T PERMIT YOURSELF TO WORRY IN THE EVENING.

When you are tired, little worries become big ones. You are especially likely to worry about your milk in the evening, or in the middle of the night. Force yourself to think about something else, to put the milk question out of your mind until morning. Let your husband walk the baby or rock him. Take a shower, have a glass of wine, walk around the block. Call someone who can reassure you. Remember that the best prescription for a fussy baby is not a bottle— bottles bring problems of their own—but more rest for the mother.

11. REMEMBER THAT THE FIRST SIX WEEKS ARE THE LEARNING PERIOD.

Good, easy times are ahead of you, when you won't even remember how worried you once might have been. And if you ever get to feeling nursing "isn't worth the bother" of learning, try rereading chapters 1 and 3.

CHANGES AROUND FOUR TO SIX WEEKS

Some babies get weaned to a bottle around the age of one month to six weeks, not because their mothers don't have enough milk, but because the mothers *think* they don't. Why? First, a one-month-old baby is often a rather crabby soul. He is far more aware of things than he was at two weeks, and that means he is more aware of cold, heat, wet diapers, loneliness, and his not-very-grown-up insides. So he cries. Second, around a month or six weeks after delivery, you may begin feeling pretty good. You do more. You don't take those naps. You deal with all the housework, and you are more and more tempted to take up your social life and outside interests again. You may even be returning to your full-time job. So you get tired; and the immediate result of your fatigue is a fussy baby.

Once again, hang this rule up someplace where you can see it often: *The best treatment for a fussy baby is more rest for the mother.* When the baby is not happy or does not seem to be getting enough milk, you need to slow down and spend more time peacefully nursing him.

Many of the mothers who quit around the one-month mark do so simply because they are discouraged. They feel as if they are going to spend the rest of their lives with a baby at the breast, constantly nursing. There will never again be a time for getting the house clean or spending an evening out; they will never sleep through the night again; the idea of breastfeeding presents a picture of endless months of being tied to a constantly fussy baby, just as they've been tied in the past four or six weeks.

But this is no time to get discouraged. This is the turning point. From about six weeks onward, breastfeeding becomes quite different. The baby rather abruptly drops about two meals a day, so that he is nursing eight times in twenty-four hours, instead of ten or more. You begin getting one six-hour stretch of sleep at night, and your ever-improving letdown reflex works so well that some feedings are over in five or ten minutes; you hardly notice that you had to stop whatever you were doing to feed the baby. Going out becomes easy; you can take the baby, or leave him with a bottle of breast milk. The little problems such as leaking and overproduction are beginning to disappear. And you begin having the strength to come and go as you please, without detriment to your milk supply.

These first six weeks have been trying, in some ways. You and your baby have been learning to breastfeed; your baby has been adjusting to the strange and not always pleasant world she has been born into; you have been gradually recovering from the prolonged demands of pregnancy, and from the effort of childbirth; if this is the first baby, you have also been making the emotional change of becoming a mother. These have been demanding tasks, but most of the drudgery is behind you now. Now, at the six-week mark, you can expect a major change; now begins the "reward period" of nursing.

CHAPTER 12

The Reward Period Begins

TWO TO THREE MONTHS

A new baby is fascinating, but a two-month-old baby is more fun. By two months, a baby is pert and pretty, instead of blotchy and strange-looking. She can "talk" and smile her wonderful smile. She looks at people, takes an interest in colors, and obviously enjoys the company of her father and any brothers or sisters she is lucky enough to have. She is a lot easier to care for than she was a few weeks earlier; she is more content, and when she does want something, you can often "read" her cries and tell if she is hungry, or uncomfortable, or tired, or simply needs to be held close for a while.

By the time two months have passed, you probably feel pretty good yourself. Any physical discomforts of the early days after giving birth have passed. The little problems of the learning days of nursing—leaking, milk fluctuations, nipple soreness—no longer exist. You are beginning to take the reins of the household in your own hands again. You may be ready to go back to work, having learned to pump and store your milk for your baby's meals with the sitter (see pp. 334–44).

You are beginning, too, to sense the nature of the nursing relationship, the warm spirit of mutual affection that unites the nursing couple. A brand-new baby is having such a time trying to get fed that he hardly has attention for anything more. But a baby of two months looks at you with his bright eyes as he nurses; he knows you from all other people, and ne loves you. He enjoys your company; he waits trustingly for you to feed him, and he wants to be sociable before, during, and after meals. He is no longer a perplexing bundle of contrariness, or a cute but frighteningly helpless doll, to be dressed, undressed, bathed, and fussed over; he is your own little friend, and caring for him is second nature, like caring for yourself. Perhaps you used to feel a sense of relief whenever the baby went to sleep, and of apprehension when he stirred; now, you find you enjoy having him around and don't worry about him, whether he's asleep or awake. In fact, you may miss him, sometimes desperately, if you are away from him. You are becoming a happy nursing couple.

CONTINUING THE HOLIDAY

Ideally, a mother could comfortably go on staying home with her baby for as long as she wanted to after giving birth. Today, the demands of supporting a family and returning to work or school often cut short the time at home once considered every mother's due. Now, it seems as if women are expected to give birth and then continue with every activity exactly as before.

If you can possibly extend the time you stay at home without any responsibilities other than being a mother, to four months at the very least, you will find your return to the outside world much less taxing than at two months. Six months to a year is even better. Nursing can be the excuse you need in order to say, "No, my one and only responsibility right now is nursing and caring for my baby."

Even if you are not returning to work, you may continue to find yourself becoming overtired at this time. You are still convalescing, a fact that friends seem to forget. People who wouldn't dream of imposing on someone in late pregnancy, sometimes completely overlook a mother's need for rest after the baby is born. Once the two-month mark is past, you may find yourself being considered available again for business trips, volunteer work, baby-sitting swaps, and so on, and so on. One excuse—"I'm so sorry, the doctor has told me not to accept any additional commitments while

I'm still nursing the baby"—will take care of most of these demands.

If you absolutely cannot take more than two months away from your job, don't despair. Read Chapter 13, "The Working Mother: How Breastfeeding Can Help." Breastfeeding will maintain the special closeness between you and your baby as long as you nurse, whether you return to work or not.

PICKING UP THE BABY

Sometimes babies cry because they are lonely and frightened. Just because the baby stops crying when you pick her up doesn't mean she's "spoiled." That's an idea based on outdated theories, and many people, including some healthcare providers, still champion it. It's very unfair. Of course the baby stops crying when you pick her up, if picking her up was what she needed. She's not "testing" you at this age; she really needs comforting. Behavioral scientists have shown that plenty of human handling and body contact is as important to babies' emotional growth as plenty of good food is to their physical growth. Isn't it convenient that breastfeeding supplies both!

Grandmothers and husbands, and even, or perhaps especially, brothers and sisters, can carry and hold and rock a new baby when she needs comforting and you are busy; they don't have the pleasure of feeding her, so they like to share her in other ways. When you are all alone and your baby is fretful, and yet you are too busy to sit and rock her, you might try that time-honored device, the baby sling or backpack, that puts the baby in touch with your body, your heartbeat, your breathing, even while you continue doing whatever you need to accomplish.

NIGHT FEEDINGS

You can expect a breastfed baby to go on needing at least one night feeding, plus a late-evening or very early morning feeding, for five or six months; many babies (and mothers) cherish that predawn cuddle and nursing throughout the first year. Your milk supply may need this feeding, too.

The mother who at this point feels exhausted because she has to feed in the night isn't getting enough rest in the daytime. If you simply can't nap during the day, consider keeping the baby in bed with you, at least for the second half of the night, so that you can doze as he nurses.

CLOTHES

Depressing, isn't it? For months you looked forward to getting your waistline back so that you could wear your own clothes again; and now that your waistline is normal, you still can't get into any of your clothes because you are more bosomy than before. If there are one or two things in the closet that you can manage to get into, they probably button up the back or zip up the side and are very inconvenient for nursing. The woman who has been flat-chested all her life may enjoy this predicament; in fact, her clothes may fit and look better when she is lactating than when she is not. But even she may have the problem of finding something to wear that enables her to nurse the baby without getting completely undressed. This can be crucial when the baby suddenly decides in the middle of a morning of shopping that it is mealtime, and you then realize that you can't nurse him without taking your dress off. (Emergency solution: Find a dress shop and nurse him in the fitting room.)

The problem of finding clothes that can easily and discreetly give nursing access has always been with us. Paintings of madonnas and other mothers from various periods and countries show all kinds of solutions. Some simply take advantage of a rather low-necked dress, perhaps using a shawl for modesty. Others have been portrayed in dresses that unbutton or untie in the front, or that have slits concealed in drapery. The most elegant solution is perhaps that shown in a Flemish painting in which the Madonna wears an elaborate, high-necked gown with two rows of gold ornaments down the bodice that on close inspection are

293

found to be hooks and eyes holding closed an opening on each side.

Things are easier nowadays. It's easy to find clothes that pull up from the waist or button down the front: cardigans, skirts, shirts or overblouses, shirtwaist dresses. Since you'll be nursing for quite a while, you'll probably find it's worth buying a couple of unbuttoning drip-dry shirts or blouses to wear when you and the baby go out of the house. Pick print material that won't show dark wet spots if you should happen to leak. To nurse discreetly, unbutton the bottom buttons rather than those at the top.

The most convenient and least revealing kinds of tops are those that do not unbutton, but that can be lifted from the waist for nursing: overblouses, jerseys, sweaters, and so on. Some kind of pull-up-able top is invaluable if you want to nurse the baby while you have visitors—and hate to miss the conversation—or while traveling, or at a movie, or indeed anywhere away from home. The baby covers your slightly exposed midriff, your sweater or blouse conceals your breast, and you will find that no one can tell whether you are nursing the baby or just holding him. In fact, the more confidently and calmly you put your baby to the breast, the less likely people are to notice what you are doing.

You do not have to wear a nursing bra, although they are convenient. You can nurse in an ordinary bra by unhooking the back or slipping a strap off your shoulder. If you wear wireless bras, lifting up can be done almost as easily as with a nursing bra. In fact, you do not absolutely have to wear a bra at all, unless of course you are uncomfortable without one. A good bra can improve circulation by lifting a drooping breast and it can keep you comfortable when you are very full. But a bra that hikes up in back and sags in front doesn't do either, and the bra that is too tight may impede circulation and milk flow. How much a bra does to protect your figure is a matter of opinion, and perhaps heredity. One woman who wears bras night and day, massages the skin of her breasts with lanolin during pregnancy, and forgoes nursing lest she damage her figure, may still wind up with striations and loss of shape; while another mother who can't stand bras and never wears them may bear and nurse three or four babies without losing the upstanding bosom she started with. Most women, in fact, find the shape of their breasts to be fuller and firmer after nursing a baby or two. So it's up to you. If you really want to be cautious, then wear a well-fitting bra twenty-four hours a day while you are nursing and for six months after weaning.

FRESH AIR

Try to spend at least half an hour walking outdoors every day, even in the winter. Take the baby; it's good for him, too. Being indoors all day tends to make you concentrate too much on your indoor work and the imperfections of your surroundings. You actually need sunshine, in any case, for vitamin D. A short walk in the late afternoon improves your appetite for dinner and lifts your spirits, too. And it may help your milk supply. Dairymen say that cows give more milk at the evening milking if they are turned out of the barn for an hour or so in the afternoon.

NURSING AWAY FROM HOME

Many nursing mothers dislike leaving their small babies behind, no matter how competent the baby sitter; often the happy nursing couple hates to be separated, even briefly, during these early months. So take the baby along. It is just as easy to take a nursing baby with you as it is to leave him at home and then miss him all evening. All you need is a blanket and a couple of extra diapers; the bottle-feeding mother may have to portage half a drugstore. Nursing babies are usually cheery and quiet if they are near their mothers; you can take a small nursing baby on a camping trip, to a dinner party or a restaurant, a football game or even a formal dance, with complete aplomb. Feed him before you leave or in the car once you are there. (Please don't feed him while driving; he belongs in his car seat. If necessary, pull over and park to nurse—carry a shawl or blanket in the car, to put over the baby and your shoulder to insure privacy.) If you are out visiting and the baby is hungry again before it is time to leave, take him to some quiet corner such as your hostess' bedroom, and feed him again; that will usually hold him until you are back in your car or at home again.

To take the baby shopping or to the park, feed him just before you leave the house. (Plan on taking time to do it: don't hustle him, you might hurt his feelings.) Or you can feed him in the car after you get where you're going. That will give you a reasonable amount of time before he is hungry again.

If you must feed the baby before you get back to the car the most comfortable place to do so is in a ladies' lounge. Usually there is a chair or couch where you can sit. Buy or take something to read, if you don't want people to talk to you. Don't feel self-conscious about other women noticing you; you may find that most will go by without noticing, except for an occasional woman who will be delighted to see a mother nursing, and an occasional mother who will look at you longingly and then tell you how she tried and failed to nurse.

In emergencies, you will probably find that you can nurse quite unnoticed even in a public place such as a park bench or a restaurant booth. You will feel conspicuous but you won't be nearly as conspicuous as you would be with a screaming, hungry baby in your arms.

BREASTFEEDING AND SEX

The closeness of a mother and her nursing baby, while it brings joy to the father, sometimes partially eclipses the mother's need for other close relationships, including sex. That may be due in part to the temporary abeyance of the menstrual cycle, with its mood swings and peaks of desire, and its high levels of estrogen. The nursing mother may feel compliant about sexual relations without actually being eager. Perhaps, too, nursing a baby provides some of the fringe benefits of sex, such as closeness with another person and a feeling of being admired and wanted; so a mother may turn less often to her husband for the balm of touching and physical closeness. A mother who notices a reduced need for lovemaking in herself during lactation should take thought to be generous and affectionate to her lover; he needs to be touched and to feel wanted, too.

Some women on the other hand find that the experience of lactation intensifies their physical affection for their husband. The hormonal patterns of sex and lactation are very closely allied. One mother, having nursed her first child, found that from then on, when her husband kissed and fondled her breasts, she was swept by a palpable wave of deep affection, almost adoration, such as she had felt for her infant. The play of hormones can be downright startling. Oxytocin, the hormone responsible for the letdown reflex, is also released during orgasm; Niles Newton calls it "the hormone of love." Many a couple has been astonished to discover that, as the woman reaches climax, her milk may let down so sharply that it sprays into the air six inches or more in twin tiny-streamed fountains, sometimes catching her unwary mate full in the face. This phenomenon, like accidental letdown in other circumstances, generally abates as lactation becomes more fully established and the letdown reflex more controlled.

Some men, because of their own upbringing, feel conflict about a nursing mother's breasts. Some men worry that they shouldn't touch their wife's breasts as long as she is lactating. In fact, there is nothing in mutually agreeable love play that should be avoided during lactation; a couple can be as free with each other's bodies then as at any other time, and if a little milk comes into the picture one way or another, it's harmless, and the baby won't miss it. There's always more where that came from.

Babies seem to have an aggravating tendency to wake up and fuss and want attention precisely when their parents are making love. Letting the baby sleep in another room, with the door closed, at least some of the time, may help.

In our culture, some parents and more than a few grandparents feel a little uneasy about a boy baby nursing at his mother's breasts for more than a few months. Nursing is such an intense physical pleasure for a baby that it is not uncommon for boy babies to have erections as they nurse—they often do so before urinating, too—and the thought of a male child still nursing when he is "old enough to know what he is doing," (at whatever age that might be!) seems to have disquieting sexual overtones. While it is a rather difficult thing to demonstrate scientifically, the practical experience of many families suggests that male and female nursing babies alike take their mothers' bodies for granted in a healthy, accepting way, no matter how long they nurse. One might speculate that the fetishistic attitude of many American men toward the female breast is at least partly the result of having been deprived during infancy of the experience of long nursing, and of that natural awareness and acceptance of the female body.

DON'T RUSH SOLID FOODS

The American Academy of Pediatrics does not recommend introducing "solid" foods into breastfed babies' diets until they are four to six months old. Many mothers of artificially fed babies begin putting a little cereal in their bottles long before then. Your breastfed baby does not need cereal or any solid food to be "satisfied," no matter how big and husky he is. A pacifier will do just as well, or an extra nursing on a fussy day. Every mouthful of cereal or fruit you put into him simply substitutes for the more nutritious breast milk.

Young breastfed babies often act as if they know this. They cry and struggle when getting their solid foods, or they take only a mouthful or two. It is a sad sight to see a mother trying desperately to get two tablespoons of applesauce into a frantic, crying baby because someone told her he should be eating "real food by now."

So forget about solid foods right now, despite the brochures and free samples from baby food companies that are arriving in the mailbox. (Of course those companies are interested in seeing you start solids early!) At somewhere around five to seven months, your baby will let you know he is ready for solids, probably by grabbing a handful of mashed potato off your dinner plate and eating it! You can safely wait until then.

VITAMINS

Your healthy nursing baby does not really need vitamin drops, especially if you take vitamins yourself and eat a well-rounded diet. Most nursing babies hate the strong taste of vitamins; why make them suffer? The one exception is vitamin D, which is manufactured in the body upon exposure to sunlight. You and your baby should both get a little time outdoors every day, if you possibly can; even on cloudy days, ten or twenty minutes' exposure to the open sky will help. If you cannot get outdoors because of the climate, you should take a vitamin D supplement. If you live in the desert, near the equator, or in any area where sunlight is very strong, you should be careful the baby doesn't get sunburned (there are several sunscreens safe for children on the market; put a touch on his nose and cheeks as a precaution.) Several brief exposures to sunlight are safer than one long one. Also, be thoughtful about shading the baby's eyes; when you are holding him, he can't choose which way he is facing, as you can. Turn his back to the sun so he doesn't have to squint and fuss at the glare.

ALWAYS: FLUCTUATIONS

Babies grow and mothers recuperate somewhat in the style of the algebra problem involving the frog in the well that jumped up two feet and fell back one. Sometimes a three-month-old baby goes on a four-hour schedule for a day, like a much older baby; sometimes he falls back to eating like a much younger baby for a while. You, too, may find you gain strength in spurts, as it were, and occasionally fall back to needing that extra nap or rest period you had been doing without.

Your milk production will fluctuate to some degree in relation to sucking stimulus. If your baby is a steady, hearty eater who wants the same big meals day after day, you may experience very little fluctuation; with the gourmet type of baby who may want a banquet today and only hors d'oeuvres tomorrow, your milk supply may often be in a state of change. Also, you can continue to expect occasional frequency days, when your baby nurses extra hungrily, thus stimulating milk production to rise over a period of a day or two until supply again equals need.

At three months, your baby will probably get his first immunization shot, the DPT shot, which protects him against diphtheria, tetanus, and whooping cough (pertussis). This may make him fussy and feverish, and he may want to nurse off and on all day, purely for the comfort of it. The mother who has raised both bottle-fed and breastfed babies can really appreciate what a blessing it is to have such a surefire way of comforting a fretful baby.

MEDICATIONS AND ORDERS TO WEAN

Most nursing mothers need very little medication. And most of the drugs that are prescribed for transient illnesses are perfectly safe for a nursing couple. They include antibiotics and pain relievers. Occasionally, however, a mother whose lactation is going beautifully is ordered to stop breastfeeding because she must take some prescription drug that the prescribing physician says is not safe for the baby. What do you do if this happens to you?

It is difficult, of course, to confront or even question the physician on whose help you depend; but this may be the time to go politely toe-to-toe. Here are some things you can say: "I would prefer not to take this treatment, since I intend to keep breastfeeding my baby. Can you suggest an alternative that would be less of a problem? Can we postpone this for a few months?" One of the problem areas that perhaps can't be avoided or postponed is a radioisotope scan. Some of these chemicals have a very short half-life, and you get rid of them in four days or less; others hang around in the system for months and would definitely be hazardous. Request that isotopes with a short half-life be used so that you can pump for a few days, discarding the milk and giving synthetic milk or banked human milk (see pp. 184–87) to your baby, and then resume breastfeeding; both La Leche League and the *Journal of Human Lactation* have published reviews of these medications (see the References section for chapter 3).

Often the physician ordering you to wean is in a specialty that doesn't normally deal with nursing mothers or babies. If you are at odds with any physician over medication, try to find a board-certified lactation consultant in your area, or some other health-care provider specializing in lactation, to be an effective professional ally, one whom the physician can work with comfortably. If you must deal with the matter by yourself, here is a summary of the advice given by Jerry McKeagan, M.D., director of pharmacology at the Williamsport Hospital in Pennsylvania, who is the father of seven breastfed babies and an authority on medication and mother's milk:

First, explain that you intend to continue breastfeeding, as you feel that it is important. Ask if you might get along without that drug, or if some other, safer drug or therapy might be used instead. It's rare that there is no acceptable substitute. Second, ask how long you are going to have to take the drug. Drugs that will be administered only once, or for a few days, are a different matter from drugs that must be taken for months. Third, tell the doctor how old your baby is. If you are nursing a jaundiced newborn, your medication might add significantly to the baby's load of toxins; if you are nursing a lusty ten-month-old, it's quite a different matter. As for the newborn, even a drug that you must take for some chronic condition can often be safely suspended for two or three weeks, right after childbirth, so your infant gets off to a good start.

If the question remains unresolved, ask your physician to look up the drug in the *current* (no earlier than 1989, as of this writing) American Academy of Pediatrics' Statement on Drugs, which is very reassuring on drugs and breastfeeding. If an antibiotic is in question, ask if it is ever given orally to babies; if so, the 1 percent dose the baby might get through your milk is far lower than the baby would get directly. Refer your physician to the discussion in this book on what kinds of drugs can pass into the milk and what kinds cannot (chapter 3, pp. 92–96).

If none of this works, you can get a second opinion from another physician, perhaps one more in tune with lactation. Or you can call La Leche League's Board of Medical Advisors for the latest information [main offices: Franklin Park, IL, (708) 455-7730]. Be prepared. Write down the information they will want to know: the name of the drug, the size and frequency of the dose, and the condition you are being treated for; this last is very important. Sometimes the drug may not even be the right choice for you. And stay cool; this is not a hard one to win.

LUMPS AND BUMPS

It is unlikely that a woman who is lactating will develop breast cancer. However, the breast is apt to be full of strange lumps and bumps during nursing, especially in the first weeks. Usually, such lumps are simply enlarged lobes of alveoli that swell and dwindle and that feel very hard and distinct when the milk has just let down. A lump that does not change in any way is often a lacteal cyst, or milk-filled pocket within the breast. These cysts are harmless. If you are worried about such a lump, it's wise to have it checked out; but be sure to find a physician who is really familiar with lactating women. He is the only one who has the experience necessary to tell good from bad in these matters. General surgeons and obstetricians whose patients do not usually breastfeed have been known to recommend surgery for conditions that are actually part of the normal range of breast changes during lactation.

THREE TO FIVE MONTHS

While the growing baby can now get a full meal in five or ten minutes, he sometimes likes to nurse on and on until he falls asleep at the breast, now dozing, now and then sucking, until you finally lay him down, still dreaming of sweet milk, and sucking in his dreams. To get the baby to bed without wakening, take him off the breast, and if that partially wakens him, hold him until he subsides again. Then take him to his crib and lay him down, but keep your hand on his back, if he stirs, until he sleeps once more. It is sudden desertion that makes him roar. (Laying a nightgown you have worn across his crib sheet may work like a charm. Your scent is one of the things he knows best and finds most calming.)

Around four months, the baby develops a new trick. He interrupts himself. Suddenly he is very interested in noises. If someone in the room starts talking, or if you speak suddenly while nursing, the baby may drop the breast and jerk his head around to locate the voice. He may jerk his head around without letting go, too! The TV distracts him, and you may find you can't even read a magazine, because he is interrupted by the rustle of the turning pages. An exceptionally aware baby may be unable to start nursing again when interrupted by noises, or may cry at such interruptions.

Fortunately, in about two weeks the baby will have learned to nurse and listen at the same time. Meanwhile, keep your own voice down while nursing; put your hand over the baby's ear to keep sounds out; and sit so that the baby can see the source of any disturbance and continue nursing while studying the event. If he does break away from the breast, you can usually coax him back with soothing words and a gentle pat.

Once the baby has learned to look, listen, and drink at the same time, she takes a genuine interest in her surroundings, watching the faces of others as she nurses. By five months, if you cover her ear, she will reach up and pull your hand away; she wants to hear everything. She may also play at the breast, waving her free hand about and watching it, playing with your clothes, patting your face. A five-month-old baby is apt to get hold of a button on your blouse and try to put it in her mouth, while she is nursing. She loves to watch your mouth as you talk to her while she eats, and her biggest problem is trying to smile at you and nurse at the same time.

Another feature of the four- or five-month-old baby's awareness of the world is that she may refuse to take a bottle. Although you may have left her with a sitter before, and she may have taken bottles occasionally in the past, she suddenly refuses them. Now, apparently, she would rather wait for her own warm, good-smelling mother, and her sweet milk, than drink even that same milk from a cold plastic and rubber contraption in the arms of a baby sitter. Luckily, by this age she can wait three or four hours in the daytime, which is long enough for you to get errands done without her. And in the evenings, many babies are willing to eat at five or six, and then sleep through until one or two in the morning. This gives you enough span for an occasional night out. By contrast, mothers who work nine-to-five often find that the baby at this age shifts her own schedule so that she sleeps most of the time her mother is gone, and wakes to nurse and socialize in the evening when mom is home again.

If your baby is going through a spell of refusing the bottle, you may be able to get around a baby's persnicketiness by having the sitter offer milk in a spoon or a cup with a spout. In a month or two, the baby will accept the bottle again.

THE BABY SLING

The oldest labor-saving device in the world is probably the baby sling. Every human society seems to have some version of it, some way to carry a baby comfortably and safely on your body instead of in your arms. Psychologists point out that the backpacked baby, in addition to feeling loved and secure from body contact, meets the world at your eye level and facing forward, which is better for his confidence and morale than seeing everything from your knee level in a stroller.

Many families nowadays backpack the baby instead of using a stroller out in public. But have you ever thought of doing it at home, when you have a thousand things to do, and the baby is fussy and fretful with a stomachache or a tooth coming in, or plain lonesomeness? Mothers who have tried this are astonished at the tranquility it produces. There is something extremely soothing to a baby about being closely, snugly wrapped on his mother's warm, loving back, looking over her shoulder at the interesting things she is doing, or being lulled to sleep in a front pack simply by the rhythm of her breathing and moving. A half-hour of being carried may tranquilize the baby all day. One mother says that when she has company coming for dinner she always carries the baby for an hour or so while she is cleaning up and getting the meal started; then the baby is quite happy to be alone in the playpen or on a blanket with some toys while she cooks and talks with her guests.

Carrying your baby properly on your back (or on your chest, if it's a tiny baby) is far less tiring than carrying him in your arms. You can carry quite a heavy baby for hours and never notice it. Did you ever see pictures of children in India or China, with heavy baby brothers or sisters on their backs, and wonder how they do it? The answer is that the weight is properly located. Your legs are doing most of the work, rather than your easily fatigued back and arm muscles. Carrying the baby in a sling can actually make you feel better, because it improves your posture; the extra weight keeps you from slumping and slouching. Meanwhile, you have both hands free to scramble an egg, dial a telephone, or run the computer. And you can get more work done because you aren't being interrupted to soothe a fussy baby. Errands out of the house are easier (and safer) without wrestling a stroller in and out of stores and over curbs. Some working mothers find they can even sit at the computer or talk on the phone with the baby content and slumbering in a front or back pack.

Fathers can backpack babies, too, of course. This is especially handy if the family wants to go on a long excursion, sightseeing or hiking or cross-country skiing. A tall man who is backpacking a baby should try to position the load so the baby's head is no higher than his own; that way, he can judge more easily the height of doorways and other overhead obstacles, and duck low enough for both of them.

TRAVELING

Traveling is much, much easier with a nursing baby than with a bottle-fed baby. In the first place, your baby doesn't care where he is as long as he's with you. Nursing is such a comfort and reassurance to him that your lap and your arms make even the strangest places quite acceptable. He doesn't cry for his familiar crib, or get thrown off schedule because he happens to be on an airplane or in a car; you, not cribs and schedules, are the center of his world, so he is completely nonchalant about travel. You can go on a business trip, or take a hiking trip with your spouse or friends in the wilderness, and take your baby along—and all of you will enjoy yourselves.

Nursing is infinitely more practical than bottle-feeding while you are on the move. The logistics of supplying a baby with sterile synthetic milk during, say, a car trip from New York to California are formidable. Pity the poor bottle-feeding mother, with her insulated bottle of synthetic milk (How long will it stay cold, how long will it be safe to use?), heating a bottle under hot water in the motel sink, while the baby screams; or, several days from home, mixing dry milk powder with tap water in a far from sterile bottle and hoping the baby "won't mind." The breastfed baby is the only baby who can be safely taken traveling in Africa, rural Latin America, the South Pacific, or other spots where sanitation may be poor. If you or your husband is likely to be stationed abroad, or if you have a chance to travel for some other reason, this is a real point in favor of making breastfeeding a success.

If you plan to fly with your nursing baby, you may want to choose a night flight. Darkness, with fewer passengers moving up and down the aisles, means more privacy for you. Ask for a seat on the bulkhead row so that you have more room to put a bassinet or baby basket at your feet. Sit in the seat at the window or farthest from the aisle. Wear a two-piece outfit that can be lifted from the waist; even the flight attendants won't be able to tell that you are nursing, and they may be perplexed because you don't ask them to warm a bottle for the baby.

If you are traveling with your husband, let him do the work. Your baby depends on you not to get exhausted, and if you get overtired, your baby will respond by being fussy. You can keep rested if you stay cool, don't rush, and let your husband do all the driving and cope with tickets and baggage. If you must travel alone, plan your schedule reasonably, so that you will have adequate time between planes and before boarding to avoid stress and to relax. It's not impossible; one management consultant took her five-month-old nursing baby on a three-week lecture tour with complete success.

IF YOU EVER FEEL LIKE QUITTING

Sometimes when you are feeling tired or your milk seems skimpy or a relative is pressuring you to do things her way and put your baby on the bottle, it seems easy to say, "Well, I've nursed this baby three months—or four, or five—I'll put him on a bottle now, and perhaps I'll have better luck and be able to nurse the next one longer."

Don't kid yourself. First, you'll never again have as much time or leisure as you have with the first baby in which to learn this womanly art. Second, it is a common fallacy to assume that breastfeeding becomes less valuable as the baby grows older. From the nutritional standpoint, this may be so as the baby adds other foods to his diet. But breastfeeding continues to provide protection against illness for as long as it is continued; this can be extremely valuable for a baby of eight months or even eighteen months, just as it is for one of a few weeks. Nursing continues to be practical, too, saving time, easing stresses, and keeping the baby happy, healthy, and close, for as long as it continues. Don't let yourself be forced into a decision you're not ready for; unless you would really prefer to stop, keep on nursing; you'll be glad you did.

HOW TO UNWEAN A BABY

Suppose sometime in the last few weeks you lost your confidence, or your doctor came out strongly against continuing breastfeeding, or you suffered some discomfort such as mastitis, and you are now giving your baby supplementary synthetic milk. There is no reason why you cannot gradually build up your milk production until your baby is entirely breastfed, especially if your baby is still small—the younger the baby, the more cooperative he is likely to be—and not yet receiving a lot of solid foods. If you don't make the effort to eliminate synthetic milk-feeding entirely, your milk supply will almost certainly continue to dwindle until the baby is entirely bottle-fed.

Before you begin, take a couple of days to keep track of how many ounces of supplement your baby is actually taking in twenty-four hours. Write that down, and stick the note on the refrigerator or someplace where you won't lose it. Then pick a day when you can count on peace and quiet, nurse the baby as often as possible, and offer her one ounce less of synthetic milk than she has been getting. You may worry that she'll be hungry; you are more likely to discover that she doesn't even seem to miss it.

Wait a day—or two or three—and then drop another ounce out of the supplement feedings. Your milk supply will be increasing, meanwhile, especially if you increase the frequency of feedings; giving *more* feedings is more important than giving longer feedings. Nurse the baby several extra times during the twenty-four hours. (Extra feedings at night should be compensated for by an extra nap in the daytime if possible).

After a week, write down how much supplement the baby is still getting; see the difference from where you started? Depending on how much synthetic milk your baby was getting at the beginning, over a period of three weeks or more, you should be able to feed the baby all by yourself again. You will know you can trust your body, and that it is making enough milk, because the transition has been made without misery or hunger, and when the bottle was gone, the baby didn't miss it.

One circumstance can upset mothers no end, during a period of rebuilding a milk supply: a growth spurt. When a frequency day—a sudden increase in appetite—occurs during this period, instead of recognizing it for what it is, you're likely to despair and think your production is at fault. Stay calm! Remember a sudden increase in the baby's needs is something that happens repeatedly to any nursing mother, because the baby is growing. It happens to bottle-babies, too; we just notice it less when they're on the bottle—and remember, we take it differently; we don't say, "Oh no, the baby's hungry again." We say, "Wow, what a wonderful appetite." So take care of yourself; remember the first prescription for a fussy baby is more rest for the mother. Get some rest, nurse a lot, and the supply will keep on growing.

Sometimes a baby who is accustomed to a bottle can be very unpleasant about being asked to nurse when your milk production is still low. He sucks for a moment and then screams and wrenches away. Try squeezing a few drops of milk out so that he will taste it as soon as he latches on; once he is nursing, you can soothe him so that he stays on the breast, by rocking, patting him, and talking or singing to him. Don't put anything on your breasts to lure the baby to nurse; we suggested that in the old version of *Nursing Your Baby,* and we were wrong. Honey is particularly dangerous; it can give babies a form of botulism that makes them dreadfully ill.

If your baby is far along the road to being weaned to the

bottle, and you are nevertheless anxious to bring him back to the breast, you might find a nursing supplementer helpful. This is a device designed to speed up the process of relactation, or reestablishment of the milk supply; there are several on the market. The device has a container for synthetic milk—either a little bottle or a plastic bag—that hangs around your neck; a slender tube can be taped to your breast so that it fits in the baby's mouth as he nurses. Some supplementers drip milk in by gravity; some—the Medela company's SNS, for example—let the milk flow only when the baby actively nurses; that, of course, reinforces the suckling, so that milk production is stimulated even during supplementary feedings (see illustration on p. 365). A nursing supplementer can be obtained through any board-certified lactation consultant, who will also coach you in its use; or you can order one through La Leche League.

It is always worth making the effort to reestablish your milk production for a young baby, if only for the pleasure and convenience of being able to nurse him for as many months as he needs you to do so; but it is especially worthwhile if you have a family history of allergy, or if your baby is exposed to colds at a day-care center or baby sitter's home.

CHANGES BETWEEN FOUR AND SIX MONTHS

A five-month-old baby has probably settled down to two naps a day. He may sleep ten hours at night, especially if his mother is well rested so that daytime nursings are ample (with temporary exceptions: see "Sleep Changes," below). He has learned to anticipate, and he whimpers or calls for meals instead of crying. He is well aware of the difference between you dressed and you undressed, and will lie quietly in your arms while you uncover the breast. However, he will roar with indignation if you answer his whimper by picking him up, and then put him down again before you feed him! This is probably the peak of the nursing cycle. Soon your baby will be taking more and more nourishment from other sources. Now he is still growing fast, may already have reached twice his birth weight, and may be taking one and a half pints or even a quart of milk from you every day. You find this reflected in your own larger appetite and greater thirst. You may find, too, that some of your physical energy is definitely being given to milk-making. Even though you feel strong and are getting plenty of rest, new or recently resumed physical exercise—such as playing volleyball or attending an aerobics class—may leave you breathless and drenched with perspiration. If so, put off strenuous activity for a few more weeks; you will have more stamina when your nursing baby is seven or eight months old.

A baby of five or six months has a characteristic gesture in coming to the breast. The arms are raised and fists clenched; when he nurses, the baby hugs his mother, one arm on each side of the breast; he may or may not hold on to her clothes. This gesture enables him to home in on the breast almost without help from her, and is especially useful at night; it also helps to keep him in the nursing position even when his mother, carrying him on one arm, gets up to answer the phone or turn down the stove. You can see this gesture in a bottle-feeding baby of the same age who raises his clenched fists up on either side of his head while he drinks, but in his case the utility of this apparently instinctive gesture is lost.

Around five months, a baby may suddenly become extremely efficient at the breast. He hardly gets started before he's all through, and wants to get down and play; and you can't believe he got any milk in that brief time. Actually, the baby nurses so strongly and the milk lets down so well that he may easily nurse both breasts and get a full meal in five minutes or less. Don't interpret this speed as a sign that he is losing interest in the breast. It is still the source of all his nutrition and an important part of his emotional life.

SLEEP CHANGES AT FIVE MONTHS

Five to six months is a very exciting time in a baby's life; she is beginning to creep, to explore, to handle things; every day is full of discoveries. One result is the self-interruption of daytime nursings; the baby sometimes seems almost too busy to nurse, especially if there are older children around. As a consequence, babies at this age sometimes go back to wanting a *lot* of nursing at night; maybe that's the only time when they can relax and really concentrate on being close to mom.

For a week, or even several weeks, the baby may want to nurse longer or more often at night than she has been doing. If this happens to you, have patience; soon the baby will mature just a little more, and will be able to handle these event-filled days and his mealtimes, too; then she will go back to sleeping more soundly. One lactation consultant points out that at any age a sudden increase in nighttime nursing is often a signal that the baby is getting ready for a big developmental milestone. Watch her; within a week or two, chances are that she will do something she's never done before—crawl, sit, or stand, perhaps. When the change has been accomplished, the feeding pattern will revert to normal.

SOLID FOODS

You can tell that a baby who is nearing the six-month mark is ready for solid foods. Her first teeth are coming in and with them an urge to put everything she gets hold of into her mouth (this urge, of course, may begin much earlier). This mouthing and tasting is a baby's way to get to know the universe. It may soothe her gums, and it also serves to teach her the difference between food and nonfood. By five or six months, a baby can put finger and thumb together and pick up a crust of bread. She can creep about. If the adults of the family sat on the ground and ate with their hands, as our ancestors must have done, this baby would be ready to join right in and help herself. In preliterate societies, adults— men and women both—often share food with creeping and toddling babies, either by scooping up something soft on a fingertip and putting it in the baby's mouth, or by kiss-feeding (passing the baby a little food that has already been partly chewed); the idea is repugnant to us, perhaps, but sensible in a world without strained baby food— or spoons.

Doctors usually recommend that you start the baby on mashed bananas and cereal, which are both digestible and tasty. Since your baby is not used to spoons, he may bite down on the spoon or try to spit it out. Put a bit of food on his lips and let him lick it off. He'll catch on quickly, and will soon be leaning forward with his mouth open like a baby bird. You may have received free samples in the mail from baby food companies or your doctor's office may have passed on samples from the cartons sent there. Since your baby has been thriving on nature's menu alone, you have probably put all the little cans and jars on the shelf; now, when you do try them out, you may find that your baby regards these preparations as pretty insipid, and is much more interested in sitting at the family board and helping himself with his fingers to everything that looks good.

Fine. A baby of six or seven months can manage anything she can mash up with her tongue and gums, and will enjoy scrambled eggs, cottage cheese, ripe avocado, cooked carrot or sweet potato, pieces of soft pear or melon, bread, rice, and so on. One baby's very first solid food was a mouthful of blackberry pie; her face made it clear that this new sensation was a world-class thrill. Babies also like something fairly firm to hold in the hand and chew on. A cube of cheese will be relished, as well as a hard old heel of bread for trying out those teeth. A chicken bone with nothing left on it but the flavor is fun to chew. Some babies are crazy about dill pickles. In any case, you don't need to bother with the packaged teething biscuits; they make a sticky mess and contain a lot of sugar, to start your baby on the road to the dentist.

The most useful of the prepared baby foods are the meats, which provide the protein and iron your baby is beginning to need. Prepared "dinners" seem to be mostly starch; they are handy for traveling or other emergencies if your baby likes them, but are less nutritious and more expensive than good fresh food from your own table.

The principles to follow in choosing your baby's foods are the same principles of good nutrition that you follow in feeding the rest of the family. If you have a blender or a food processor, you can make your own baby foods from leftovers. His meals should be high in meats, vegetables, fruits, whole-grain bread or cereals, brown rice, beans, and potatoes, and low on sugar, fats, and calories-only foods such as puddings. If you have other small children, he can probably eat just about what they eat. Both he and your other children will enjoy being together at mealtime.

THE CUP

A baby of five or six months may enjoy drinking water and juice from a cup, or he may refuse it. If you offer regular cows' milk in a cup, chances are your baby won't take it. The breastfed baby's usual reaction to his first cup of milk is to taste it, and then laugh and push it away, as if that were the most ludicrous place to find milk. By nine or ten months, when he can manage a cup more or less by himself, he will take more pleasure in drinking from it.

BITING

About this time, your nursing baby may try out his teeth on you. Usually he will do this at the end of a meal; so if he shows an inclination to bite, don't let him dawdle, but take him off the breast as soon as he seems to be through. If he does bite, tell him firmly that he may not, and take him right off the breast. After one or two tries, he'll get the idea. Occasionally, a baby of six or eight months may bite deliberately, if you try to feed him—perhaps because you are planning to go out—when he isn't hungry.

REFUSING A BREAST

Occasionally, a baby will develop a predilection for nursing from one breast but not the other. A baby may reject one breast temporarily because his mother has tried to slip him vitamin drops or medicine while he was nursing on that breast. You can fool the baby into taking the "wrong" breast by holding him under your arm instead of across your lap, so that the breast he has been rejecting is on the same side of his face as the one he likes would normally be. Of course, you could nurse him on one breast only, if you had to.

Sometimes the baby is taking so much solid food, as well as milk in a cup, that he is actually weaning himself without your knowing it. One can, without noticing it, favor one breast for convenience, so that the baby nurses longer and more often on that side. Then the other breast will produce less and involute more rapidly. As the milk supply wanes, it changes, becoming less sweet and more salty; the baby may come to reject that breast because the milk in it really does taste different to him.

FATIGUE

Around five or six months is another vulnerable period similar to that around one month or six weeks, when a great many mothers wean their babies. The reasons are the same: the baby is bigger; the mother is going out more, doing more, and getting too tired. The baby responds by being fussy and wanting to nurse more often, and it seems as if the milk is going. Or the baby is doing well but the mother feels tired all the time and the convenience and pleasure of nursing no longer seem worthwhile.

Fatigue starts a vicious cycle. It is only when you are tired that dust clusters under the bed or dirty windows or cluttered toys seem unbearable. Perhaps your obligations at your job hang over you, so that you drive yourself to do more and more work just when you most need the rest. Poor nutrition also contributes to fatigue, and the fatigue kills your appetite, so that your nutritional state becomes worse and you lose weight; that, too, makes you feel tired.

VITAMINS AND FATIGUE

Look to your diet. Despite the wide availability of good food in this country, some women select very poorly balanced diets; mild vitamin deficiencies are common among pregnant American women. When you are lactating, you need calcium and you need protein. Vegetarians, especially, need to be very careful not to become protein-deficient. Remember, the baby will do fine if your diet is deficient. *You* are the one whose energy levels and resistance to infection will take a dive.

When the baby is over four months old, or when he reaches a weight of twenty pounds or more, your milk production may be at its peak. On a Western diet of refined flours and processed foods, some mothers begin to suffer from deficiencies in the B-complex vitamins. Again, vegetarians are particularly susceptible. One symptom seems to be fatigue. If you wake up in the morning as tired as you were when you went to bed, so tired that you feel like crying at the thought of having to get up at all, you may be suffering from a B vitamin deficiency. You may be so depleted that replenishing your B vitamins from food sources, such as liver and whole grains, would take quite a while. A natural supplementary source such as fenugreek herb tea or brewer's yeast (both available in health food stores) will give you the rapid boost you need.

Synthetic B-complex vitamin pills will also help, but in our experience don't seem to be as effective over a long period as is brewer's yeast, which you take by mixing it into milk or juice. Start with a tablespoon a day and work up to three or four; or, take natural-source vitamin tablets. Start with a normal day's dose and then double it in a day or so. (Too much, too fast, may give you diarrhea.) You may feel the difference after the very first dose. With a little experimenting, you will be able to tell, yourself, how much is ideal, and you may benefit from this daily supplement as long as you are nursing.

Tearful exhaustion in the nursing mother is often attributed to poor time management—"Stop trying to do too much!" she is told—or to psychological depression. The role of possible B-complex vitamin deficiency in lactation, which could also be related to thyroid activity, has not been the subject of extensive research, and extra B-complex–rich supplements are not needed by most nursing mothers. When the need is there, however, the supplement's effect is a blessing. Typically, the extremely exhausted nursing mother abruptly cheers up, gets her appetite and her energy back, and finds that her milk supply simultaneously increases from merely adequate to abundant. One surgeon husband said that he could tell when he walked in the door in the evening whether his lactating wife had remembered to take her brewer's yeast that day or not; if she had forgotten, she'd be fixing dinner in tears.

HOUSEKEEPING SHORTCUTS

It's not the dirt and dust that get us down, it's the mess and clutter and disorganization in the house. What we need are a few quick ways of producing the appearance of neatness; then we feel calmer about the state of the house, and there is more time and strength left for enjoying husbands and babies, working at your "other" job outside the home, or doing a few things for yourself.

Take a few tips from newspaper columnist Heloise Cruse: When you first get going in the morning, quickly make the bed; then at least something's done. Put the breakfast dishes (all right, and last night's dinner dishes, too) in the sink, and cover them with hot soapy water. That gets them out of sight, and meanwhile the grease and food are soaking loose. Then take a very big paper bag and walk around the living room and bedrooms, putting everything into the bag that needs to be disposed of: crumbs, newspapers, magazines, opened envelopes, bits of toys, and all the other clutter a room acquires in a day. You can put pillows back and gather up toys as you go. Don't put everything away separately; never walk down a hall or up the stairs with just one or two things in your hands. Put things that belong in other rooms in a pile at the door, then take them along when you're going there anyway.

Then take a pad of toilet tissue, wet it with alcohol, and quickly wipe the bathroom fixtures. Alcohol is cheap, disinfectant, leaves no odor, and makes chrome shine. (Diaper wipes work well, too.) Then with broom or carpet sweeper, quickly clean up the middle of the living room and kitchen.

You've worked for about fifteen minutes, and your house is clean and neat looking. If someone drops in, you won't be embarrassed. If you never get a chance to do another thing all day, you're still ahead because the depressing, overwhelming mess is gone. If you are heading off for the day at your job, you won't have to face a messy house when you return home in the evening; you can relax with your baby and husband instead. Later on, you or your husband can rinse off those dishes—that's about all they need, after all that soaking.

Now start the laundry. Then plan what you're going to have for dinner. That way, there will be no last-minute scramble in the cupboards at six o'clock, only to find out that you don't have some ingredients that you need, or that the dinner you do have available should have been started an hour ago.

To Heloise's advice, we would add: In the late afternoon, take a walk in the sunshine. Then just before the rest of the family comes home, go around the living room quickly, and set the table. Everything is nice and neat. If the table is set, everyone feels optimistic about the chances of getting dinner pretty soon—even if it won't be ready for an hour, or even if your husband or some other member of the household is going to cook it. Then you have time to sit down, nurse the baby, hear the day's news, and relax.

If you have returned from your own job, skip neatening the house and setting the table. Put your things down as soon as you walk in the door, pick up the baby, get something to eat and drink, and sit down. Nurse the baby and rest; let your husband set the table and get dinner started. You must attend to the baby and yourself before anything else.

Shortcut cleaning is more important than all the other housework, such as vacuuming under beds and washing windows, because that is what soothes your nerves and takes away that feeling of pressure and futility. To make it even easier:

1. Go through every room in the house and throw out or give away everything that you haven't used in a year. (Heloise Cruse suggests that you do this when you are mad; you'll be more ruthless.) That dress you were planning to make over but never will, that waffle iron that always burns the waffles, all the old clothes that no one is wearing (which fill up your closet and drawers and crowd and wrinkle the clothes that you do wear); that ugly chafing dish you don't use, and all that stuff in the kitchen drawer that you might want sometime. Have you wanted it in the past year? No! Then throw it out! Give it to the Salvation Army; they will be glad to have it. It's much easier to keep half-empty closets and shelves clean and orderly. Do you really use those hand towels? Will you ever mend that old sheet? The fewer linens and clothes and possessions you can get along with, the fewer things you will have to wash and clean and sweep around.

2. Before you acquire something in the way of furniture or interior decorations, stop and think: Will this make my life easier or harder? Will it have to be cleaned, or guarded from scratches? As La Leche League leaders suggest, before buying something for the house, ask yourself: Wouldn't I rather have that nice empty corner or bare tabletop?

3. Confine the children's toys to one room. Concentrate on toys that are discarded after use, such as paper dolls, or on activity toys that are sturdy and can be used

by several children, instead of clutter toys with a hundred parts for you to pick up. Big baskets or even cardboard boxes are good for keeping toys—and boots and sporting equipment—in one spot and out of sight. Convenience is more important than style. And by all means, give your children the message that their toys are their responsibility. Even a three-year-old can learn to put his own toys away.

4. As La Leche League leaders advise, order before prettiness, convenience before style, and above all, people before things. Sure, it would be great to have the floors waxed all the time, like those on the TV commercials, and to have interiors with that un-lived-in look, like the cover of a magazine. But it is far more vital that you get a nap and a walk in the sunshine, and time to nurse your baby. It is far more vital to do just a little jiffy top cleaning and save your strength and good humor for smiling at your family and listening to what they have to say. Your husband may care about a certain amount of neatness, but most of all he wants your good company. Your children need clean clothes and hot food, but most of all they need a cheerful loving mother. People—including yourself—before things.

BREASTFEEDING AND CREATIVITY

A creative woman, an artist or scientist, may find that he. work flourishes during lactation, or she may be inclined to give up creative work entirely during the months when she is breastfeeding. While loss of interest in one's work can be exasperating, it is only temporary. Psychiatrist Helene Deutsch suggests that breastfeeding can bring its greatest benefits to the woman who is usually immersed in serious creative work. Nine months or more of a happy nursing relationship can provide a rare interlude of peace and satisfaction in a demanding lifetime. In her classic *Psychology of Women,* Deutsch describes women who have set their creative work aside to nurse their babies, and then returned, reinspired, to their callings.

EMERGENCY SEPARATIONS

What can you do if you are suddenly separated from your nursing baby for a few days? What if one of you has to go to the hospital, or you must make a sudden trip to a dying relative, or keeping your job depends on your attending an out-of-town business meeting?

First, do what you can to prevent the separation. You can take your nursing baby with you, even to a distant funeral, and that will be less trouble to you than trying to dry up your milk, and worrying about your baby while you're away. If you have to go to an out-of-town meeting, perhaps you can hire a nanny when you get there to take care of the baby in your hotel room when you must work; or perhaps you can take a friend or relative with you to baby-sit—someone you trust, who will actually get pleasure from the trip.

When a nursing mother must be hospitalized, it is sometimes possible to let her baby go with her, if she is in a private room. If the baby is the patient, he needs his mother's milk more than ever. Many hospitals today allow parents to be with their hospitalized children twenty-four hours a day; in many cases, this relaxation in rules was first made so that nursing mothers could stay with their babies. If you or your baby is hospitalized and only the hospital's regulations separate you, call Children in Hospitals (see Appendix), the Boston organization that works as an advocate for families in hospitals. Its people will tell you how to negotiate with the hospital administration to change its policies or at least to make an exception for you.

If the separation is unavoidable, pump your milk while you are gone and discard it if you must. The important thing is to keep the supply going until you can be home again. If the separation takes place when the baby is at the stage where he likes mother's milk only from the breast and will not take a bottle, try having him fed with a cup or spoon. In emergencies, some nursing mothers have solved the problem by leaving the baby with another nursing mother who was willing, temporarily, to breastfeed two. Babies, of course, can tell the difference; some don't mind and some do. The baby who objects to nursing at the breast of a stranger can sometimes be induced to nurse if his face is covered with a handkerchief so he cannot see the unfamiliar mother's face.

SCHEDULE CHANGES AFTER SIX MONTHS

Your baby may drop the 2 A.M. feedings at six months, but chances are he may still want one very early morning feeding, around dawn. Some nursing babies never give up this feeding voluntarily until they are weaned. During the day, the baby of eight months or more will probably eat three meals of solid food with the rest of the family or just before they eat. But he may still want four or five nursings in each twenty-four hours; these feedings still provide a useful excuse for you to get off your feet for a while. Sometimes he'll be through with the breast in five or ten minutes. Sometimes he'll want to linger. When you can give him the time (perhaps after lunch, when both you and he are planning on a nap, or when you first come home from work, or at his bedtime), you can get a good deal of vicarious enjoyment out of letting him nurse half an hour or more until he nurses himself to sleep.

BEDTIME NURSING

Falling asleep at the breast would certainly appear to be one of life's most satisfying luxuries; just watching your baby as he blissfully relaxes is enough to make you fall asleep yourself. And it certainly makes it easier to put him down for the night without tears or fuss.

Bottle-feeding mothers use the bottle in the same way. But leaving the bottle in the baby's mouth means that he goes to sleep with the front of his mouth awash in a sugar solution;

this situation contributes to the development of cavities. Physicians, therefore, are apt to warn bottle-feeding mothers against letting the baby fall asleep on the bottle. On the same basis, they may tell the breastfeeding mother she should never let the baby fall asleep at the breast. What they often don't realize is that in breastfeeding the nipple is well back in the mouth, not near the teeth where the bottle-feeding baby holds it. Also, breast milk doesn't go on flowing after the baby falls asleep; the breastfed baby does *not* sleep with a mouth full of sugar solution, and you don't have to worry about cavities if you do the natural thing and nurse your baby to sleep.

Some physicians also forbid mothers to let the baby fall asleep on the breast because they believe it will cause a sleep disorder; the baby will wake in the night and be unable to fall back asleep on his own without nursing again. This theory, currently popular among pediatricians, is disputed by many mothers who sense that nursing their babies to sleep helps them sleep more peacefully than making them learn to fall asleep without the comfort of their mother's arms and breasts. In fact, the security you give your baby now will help him to be more confident and independent when he is older. Depriving him, right now, would upset both of you. If someone tries to lay down the law to you on this matter, be kind but firm, appreciative of the concern but unmoved. Don't let this misguided hypothesizing interfere with your family life.

THE PERSISTENT NIGHT FEEDER

By the time a baby is seven or eight months old, he doesn't need a night feeding as a rule, although he may still need a predawn snack. You are now lactating steadily without the stimulation of night feeds. If you feel you would like to give up feeding the baby at night, there are three methods to try. You can let him cry it out, which may be ghastly for everyone; for some babies, an abrupt desertion is very frightening, but for others, this works like a charm. You can try rocking or singing to him, without feeding him; sometimes company and reassurance are what he really wants, and forty minutes of singing the first night becomes twenty minutes the second, a back rub from cribside the third night, a called-out reassurance the fourth, and peace and quiet from then on. Or you can let the father take over. Amazingly enough, some babies will go right back to sleep because their fathers have told them to.

Don't think that you can have uninterrupted nights by weaning to a bottle. Your baby may give up his midnight snack if it no longer consists of breast milk, and then again he may not. There are plenty of bottle-fed babies who go on demanding a bottle in the night well into their second or third year. Several papers in pediatrics journals demonstrate that sleep patterns in infants are individual and utterly unrelated to whether they are breastfed or bottle-fed. This does not mean that you must tolerate the behavior of a fifteen-month-old baby who wakes you up for company once an hour all night; you have some rights, too. But some babies just can't bear to give up that last night feeding. If you can't break the habit, resign yourself. Something so terribly important to him isn't worth fighting over. Take a nap in the daytime, if you are able, and try again in a month or two.

CHANGES AT EIGHT MONTHS

By now the reassuring nature of breastfeeding as a sign of love is almost more important to your baby than the fact that it satisfies her hunger. She may want to nurse for comfort, if she bumps her head or has been very frightened. A baby of this age can be very bossy about feedings. When the flow from one breast has slackened, she may fling herself across your lap and indicate that you should make the other available, and pronto. If you are carrying her, and she decides to eat, she may pull at your clothes, wriggle and wrench down to breast level, and all but help herself. Her purposefulness is hilarious but it can create problems; she is no respecter of persons, and may all too obviously decide to have a snack when you are standing at the supermarket checkout counter, or talking to your minister's wife or your father-in-law. Fortunately, people who are not used to breastfed babies sometimes don't realize what she is doing.

Now that your baby can sit up, and perhaps creep and stand, she likes to nurse sitting up, too, straddling your lap and regarding the world as she eats. She is quite dogmatic about this; you may wonder what's wrong as you try to make her lie down on your arm and nurse, and she wriggles and complains, until you discover she has a change in mind. She may also like to hold onto the breast that she is not drinking from, as if it might go away before she gets to it.

MENSTRUATION AND PREGNANCY

Because you are a successful nursing mother, you probably are finding that your menses continue to be suppressed. You probably will not menstruate until the baby is from eight to eighteen months old. Until you have had at least one period, and probably two or three, you are unlikely to conceive again.

Don't count on it, though! People have conceived before that first period; one doctor feels that this can often be traced to a few very busy days, or perhaps an illness of mother or baby that led the mother to nurse less frequently, so that lactation was reduced or suspended "long enough to let an egg slip through." If you do not wish to get pregnant, use a contraceptive. It is not a good idea to take birth control pills—even the mini-pill—as long as you are lactating (see pp. 41–44). Use a barrier contraceptive—such as the sponge, a condom, or a diaphragm—together with spermicidal jelly. If you used a diaphragm in the past, you may find that you need a new size after pregnancy and labor.

When your periods do resume, they will not affect your milk supply. Someone might tell you that you "can't" nurse on the days when you are menstruating, or that the baby will be fussy on those days, or that the milk will diminish. Not so. In some cases, the taste of the milk does change for a day or two; sugar content goes down and sodium up, temporarily. Some babies object but most don't seem to care. Sometimes, however, you yourself are irritable during or before your period, and this will be reflected in your baby's behavior; he may be cranky too, or want to nurse more, for reassurance.

What if you become pregnant while you are still nursing? While it might be a strain on you to nurse all the way through pregnancy, there is no need to come straight home from the obstetrician's office and wean the baby. You can plan on weaning him very gradually over a period of weeks, as described in chapter 14.

Some mothers never wean when they become pregnant again, and thus find themselves, at the end of nine months, with two nursing babies! This event is common enough nowadays to have a name, "tandem nursing" (see chapter 2). Some mothers find that the taste of the milk changes, becoming "weaning milk"—more salty, less sweet—and the baby loses interest; or their milk supply dwindles to nothing during pregnancy, and the baby weans himself. Some find that their breasts become sensitive in early pregnancy, and nursing is uncomfortable. Occasionally, a mother complains of pain in the breast while nursing. These discomforts are presumably an indication from Mother Nature that nursing should stop, and that the present baby should receive his love and attention in ways other than the breast.

Nursing during late pregnancy can cause uterine contractions; in fact, some obstetricians prescribe gentle use of a breast pump to initiate labor when a woman is overdue. If you have any history of miscarriage or premature delivery, you probably should avoid nursing during pregnancy.

CHANGES IN THE LETDOWN REFLEX

After the baby passes the six-month mark and is beginning to get nourishment from sources other than your body, you may find that the letdown reflex no longer operates promptly when he is put to the breast. He may have to suck for fifteen seconds or more before the milk lets down. Gradually, the interval will become longer and longer as your baby grows older and begins to wean himself. This delay in milk flow is reason in itself for some babies to lose interest in the breast, at or around the age of nine months.

CHANGES AT NINE MONTHS

In *A Baby's First Year,* Dr. Benjamin Spock wrote of the bottle-fed baby:

Around nine months of age babies begin to divide into two groups as far as feelings towards the good old bottle are concerned. Of one the mother says: "He's getting bored with it. After a couple of ounces he stops to fool with the nipple and grin at me. He likes milk from the cup." Such a baby seems ready for gradual weaning. Other mothers will say: "She loves her bottle more than ever . . . she usually drains it to the last drop, stroking it and murmuring to it. She's gotten suspicious of the cup lately." Such a baby seems to be saying, "I'm nowhere near ready to give it up."

Exactly the same things are true of the breastfed baby. Some babies will wean themselves rather abruptly, at or around the age of nine months. You start by giving the baby a cup of milk at breakfast, or perhaps at dinner, because you are busy, the baby is too restless to nurse, and it just seems easier. By and by, the baby expects a cup at every meal, and your own milk supply diminishes correspondingly. Without really noticing it, you find he is weaned. He may cling to one favorite feeding, such as early morning, or to a bedtime snack, for a few more weeks—and then, all by himself, he is through with nursing and ready to go on to more grownup things.

Other babies at the age of nine months don't give up the breast at all. They become even fonder of being cuddled and nursed, and while they may nurse only three or four times in twenty-four hours, those feedings are terribly important to them. Others may come to their mother many times during the day for a quick comfort-nursing. With such a baby, you can plan to continue nursing as long as is convenient for you, and as long as you both enjoy being a happy nursing couple.

CHAPTER 13

The Working Mother: How Breastfeeding Can Help

If you're returning to work after your baby is born, you're not alone. Since 1987, 52 percent of mothers have returned to work before their child's first birthday. In one large sampling of working mothers, 76 percent were back at work before their babies were thirteen weeks old.

The reasons for this vast change in American women's lives are varied. It's the unusual couple, these days, that doesn't need two incomes to make ends meet. Most single mothers have no choice but to work. Many women are having their first child after years of education, training, and building a career; they can't be blamed for wishing to continue the work to which they've devoted themselves for so long. Whatever your own reasons, know that returning to work after your baby is born may not be easy, but it is possible.

While work is one of the most common reasons given for weaning, in reality breastfeeding can be one of the working mother's most comforting supports. Some mothers believe, or are told, that you can't breastfeed and work full time outside your home; it's too tiring or it's logistically impossible. In fact, many mothers have returned to work eight weeks after childbirth and have nursed their babies through toddlerhood.

329

Another advantage to breastfeeding if you work is the measure of protection it will give your baby against the illnesses passed around in group day care. Day-care children have an unfortunate tendency to bring home every cold in town. They're simply catching all the bugs in their first three years that children who remain at home usually catch when they begin school. While your baby, breastfed or not, will probably catch his fair share of colds, the protective factors in your milk will help guard him against many serious bacterial infections and secondary complications. (However, do be careful as you select a day-care situation. Group day-care centers that are less than antiseptic in their standards of cleanliness can spread serious illnesses.)

THE SCHEDULE

Many working mothers, breastfeeding or not, adopt a totalitarian daily schedule. From the moment the baby wakes at his customary hour, whether it is 7:00, 6:00, or 5:00 A.M., the mother's day belongs to the schedule. If she has not showered by 6:15, her blouse is not ironed by 6:30, the baby is not fed, dressed, and ready to go to the sitter's by 7:00—if one stage of the morning's preparations is delayed —the entire schedule falls to pieces. Not only will that mother be late to work, but she will be flustered, will perhaps snap at her husband, and will feel once more she has not kept her balance atop the tightrope that stretches between motherhood and the workplace.

Breastfeeding can make a working mother's grueling schedule easier. An early morning nursing is a peaceful start to the day. Mother and baby can say a long hello to each other while the rest of the household sleeps. Once done, the baby, satiated and secure, will be far more willing to entertain himself with a few toys while his mother puts the morning events in motion. And she will do so with the calmness that always follows a satisfying nursing. Some working mothers take the baby to bed with them at night to have as much time together—as much skin-to-skin contact and nursing—as possible. If you would prefer not to have the baby in bed with you all night, take him in when he first wakes at 4:00 or 5:00 A.M. Have a long quiet nursing, lying down while your husband sleeps. You may all doze off again for another hour or two, your milk supply encouraged, and your contact with the baby extended. And you won't have to squeeze a nursing into the harried morning routine.

Nursing can help you prioritize the way you spend your time with your baby. When a working mother returns home, she may see only the dishes still in the sink, the unmade beds, and the laundry to be done. Tired and anxious to keep the house in order, she may feel she can't visit with her baby until the house is neat and dinner started. If she hurries to get the worst of the mess out of the way, precious time with the baby is lost. The baby probably is tired, too, and would like nothing more than a long, quiet cuddle. If his mother forgets the housework for an hour and nurses him, both will be refreshed. The dinner preparations will seem less intimidating, the laundry less urgent. It will suddenly be difficult to remember what happened at the office that day. Some mothers find that a peaceful nursing replaces the glass of wine they used to relax with at the end of the day.

Most working mothers never feel comfortable just sitting. But when you're nursing, the baby gives you a reason to do that. You don't have to get the chores out of the way to earn time with the baby. Breastfeeding will help you remember that what the baby needs most of all is you.

GUILT

Along with her grueling schedule, guilt is the working mother's most difficult hurdle. The stress of meeting the demands of being a mother, wife, employee or employer, housekeeper, and individual can lower many a woman's self-esteem. She may feel at times that she is not fully succeeding in any of her roles. The satisfaction of successfully breastfeeding can restore her confidence and counteract the working-mother blues. The breastfeeding working mother knows that in the things that really matter, she is doing a bang-up job. (And remember that guilt can plague any parent, even mothers who stay at home!)

A particularly tormenting worry among working mothers is that their babies can't tell the difference between them and the sitter. Never mind that every baby knows exactly who his mother is, a working mother may sometimes feel insecure in her place as the center of his world. When nursing mothers have this fear, they can remember that breastfeeding is the one thing they do with their babies that no one else can do. One working mother discovered, "I felt so good about being able to work and nurse that it made me more tolerant, proud of myself, and it was easier to adjust to being back at work since I didn't feel like I was losing my relationship with my baby." Your nursing baby will reassure you after separations that your bond is as special and close as when he first gazed at you. When you see how he wriggles as he hears your voice when you walk in after a day at work, when you feel how his body relaxes against your own, and how he settles down for a long cuddle and satisfying nursing, you'll know that for him, you are unique. When you are apart, you'll still feel reassured. The baby sitter may be very nice, but you are his mama with the warm breast full of milk. It makes all the difference in the world.

GETTING READY TO GO BACK TO WORK: A TIMETABLE

While sixteen weeks of maternity leave would be an ideal minimum, most women find eight to twelve weeks is all their employers will allow. If you must return in eight weeks, or even six weeks, don't despair. You can still nurse your baby if you plan carefully.

IN THE FIRST FOUR WEEKS AFTER BIRTH, your first priority is to establish your milk supply and become a nursing couple with your baby. Nurse whenever the baby wants to nurse. Don't allow yourself to worry, and don't think about work. Enjoy your baby. Frequent, long, and relaxed nursings will give you the bountiful milk supply you need. (See chapter 11, pp. 263–65).

AFTER THE FOURTH WEEK, begin to learn to pump or manually express your milk (see next section, pp. 334–35). Pumping and expressing are learned skills and require practice, and you will need a couple of weeks to get the hang of them.

AT SIX TO EIGHT WEEKS, have your husband or someone else other than yourself give the baby a bottle of expressed breast milk. Before this point, the baby is still learning how to nurse from your breasts. Nursing from a rubber nipple requires a completely different sucking motion and can confuse some newborns so much that they won't switch back easily to a breast. Later, your baby may be set in his ways and may not accept a bottle; he can practice without difficulty in the second month.

AT AROUND TEN TO TWELVE WEEKS (or one to two weeks before you return to work), gradually introduce the sitter and your baby in your own home. Spend some time with the sitter and the baby so that the sitter sees how you care for the baby. Then, when he isn't hungry, leave the baby with the sitter in your home for short periods. Then leave them together for several hours. Build up to the amount of time that you will be away when you are working. Make sure the sitter understands the importance of breastfeeding to you. (One mother took her sitter to La Leche League meetings so she could share the mother's enthusiasm for breastfeeding.) Teach her how to thaw your stored breast milk (see Storing Your Milk, pp. 342–44) and ask her not to feed the baby just before you are due to arrive at home. If your baby will be cared for by a family day-care provider or a day-care center, rather than a sitter in your home, follow the same plan but introduce the baby to the sitter in her home or at the center.

WHEN YOU FIRST RETURN TO WORK, cancel all activities except working and being with your baby. (Consider returning to work on a Friday. Knowing the weekend is ahead may help you ease into the separation.) Forget the housework; let your husband do it, hire a cleaning service, or don't do it at all. Save laundry and grocery shopping for the weekends. Go to bed early. Eat hearty, nutritious meals. Drink plenty of fluids—don't pass a water fountain at work without drinking, keep a bottle of water or juice nearby as you work, and don't sit down to nurse without something to drink beside you. On weekends, you can cook the meals for the coming week. It helps to double-batch every meal you make.

SAVING YOUR MILK: PUMPING AND MANUAL EXPRESSION

What do you do about nursing your baby during the hours that you are at work? If you have to go back to work right away, the most straightforward solution, of course, is to take the baby with you. We've heard of a few organizations—the editorial offices of a woman's magazine, an ad agency, several bookshops, a major charitable foundation—that let the new mother bring her baby to work and keep a crib or playpen in the office, either on an occasional or regular basis, at least until the baby is at the getting-into-mischief age; often the whole staff enjoys the baby's company. Taking the baby to work is of course more manageable if the mother is at the executive level and has an office of her own.

Some working mothers—television and movie performers, for example—bring baby and sitter onto the set with them and nurse during breaks. A few farsighted corporations have their own built-in day-care area, where mothers and fathers can enjoy a lunchtime break with the baby, and where at least a midday nursing can be managed. However, for most working mothers, full lactation is best maintained by pumping or expressing milk while you are away from the baby. The earlier you return to work, the more important it is to learn to express or pump your milk to maintain your supply and continue breastfeeding.

Once mastered, collecting your milk can become a comfortable part of your daily routine. The usual system is to pump your milk during the work day in the ladies' room or in some other private place, store the milk in a refrigerator or on ice, and take it home or to the sitter when you pick up your baby in the evening (see Storing Your Milk in this chapter). That day's milk thus constitutes the next day's feedings for your baby while you are at work again. Many mothers also pump a little extra and keep it in the freezer, as a backup supply.

PUMPING OR EXPRESSING: WHAT'S BEST FOR YOU?

Everybody is different; for some mothers, manual expression (literally, with their own hands) is easy, once learned, and they greatly prefer it over putting a cold plastic object against their skin. Others hate trying to express with their hands, but find a manual cylinder-type pump comfortable and easy to use; however, since each brand of manual pump has a slightly different size and shape of flange, users may have to experiment to find the one that fits them best. Some mothers find the manual pumps uncomfortable ("a primitive device," one mother called it) and the electric pump ideal. Still others don't like even the thought of being connected to a noisy electric motor. You may have to experiment to find out whether hand expression works for you, or whether you will be more comfortable with a pump; and whether a manual pump will suit you, or whether you want to rent or buy an electric one.

Both pumping and manual expression are easier to learn if you first watch someone else do it. Your prenatal childbirth and breastfeeding classes may give some instruction. An experienced friend may be your ideal instructor. Videotapes on all aspects of breastfeeding, including pumping and expressing, can be ordered. Two of the best are *Breastfeeding Techniques That Work!* (Vol. 5, "Successful Working Moth-

In manual expression, the hand gently compresses the breast to move milk down and out *(see text, p. 337)*.

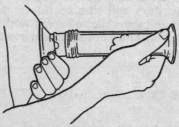

A hand-operated or cylinder breast pump is the choice of many mothers. This hand position is preferable; holding the pump from below protects the wrists and elbows from strain.

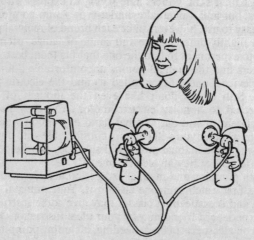

An electric pump is efficient and allows emptying of both breasts simultaneously; electric pumps may be rented as well as purchased.

ers," and Vol. 6, "Hand Expression") by pediatric nurse practitioner Kittie Frantz, and *Breastfeeding and Working Mothers,* produced by the University of Minnesota. (See Appendix, p. 391.)

LEARNING MANUAL EXPRESSION

Expressing your milk by hand is truly an art, and mastering it will save you the cost and inconveniences of a pump. To express your milk manually, begin with a light, tickling massage to stimulate your letdown reflex. Place your thumb on top of your breast and your first two fingers below your breast. Both your thumb and your fingers should be about an inch behind your nipples so that they are positioned over the milk ducts (see chapter 2). Then roll your thumb and fingers outward so that the milk in the ducts flows ahead of them (top illustration, facing page).

Achieving letdown as you express is essential to collecting more than an ounce or two. When the milk lets down, rotate your hand around the breast. Repeat this motion until you have drained the ducts or until your letdown has subsided. A rolling motion, rather than squeezing, pulling, or sliding, will help you avoid bruises or skin burns. Express milk from the second breast and then repeat both breasts. An excellent illustrated summary of this technique can be ordered from La Leche League.

Don't be discouraged if you obtain no more than a few drops the first few times you try manual expression. Practice when the baby naps and your breasts are brimming. Practice when you have a spontaneous letdown (once in the morning —when your letdown reflex is strongest—should be enough in the beginning). Practice early in the morning or during naptime before the baby wakes. Don't worry that you are "using up" your milk before the baby nurses; if you express milk regularly, your milk supply will adjust to the increased need. In addition, your baby is better at stimulating your breasts than the most skilled manual expression or pumping and will be able to draw out milk you have not.

LEARNING TO PUMP: EQUIPMENT

The first step in successful pumping is choosing the right pump for *you*. Samples of manual pumps, instruction in both pumping and manual expression, and electric pump rentals may be available near you from a La Leche League leader, a lactation consultant, or another health-care provider. Several good manual pumps are available in drugstores at reasonable prices. If you plan to use a manual pump, look for the cylinder variety or the piston-style, rather than a bicycle-horn pump. Bicycle-horn pumps, with a rubber bulb you squeeze to create suction, can cause serious nipple damage and are generally ineffective anyway. Cylinder pumps can create a powerful suction as well, but you can control its strength.

If you are not comfortable with manual expression or hand pumps, consider an electric pump. These pumps will draw out your milk with very little effort on your part. Some electric pumps are made to be used on both breasts simultaneously, which offers a major boost to production by taking advantage of your letdown more effectively; this is the system mothers of twins use to develop their increased milk supply.

While an electric pump can cost hundreds of dollars to buy, one may be rented from a pharmacy or a lactation consultant for a small fee (less by far than the cost of synthetic milk! See Appendix, p. 391, for sources). New electric and battery-operated pumps are becoming available that are small enough to fit in your handbag, and they cost less than the older models, too. However, the effectiveness of the small electric and battery-operated pumps is less than that of a manual pump, even in practiced hands.

If you can't afford to rent an electric pump indefinitely, it may be worthwhile to do so while you are building up a supply of milk in your freezer. Call La Leche League, a lactation consultant, or your pharmacist to find one. It is possible that your medical insurance will cover the cost of an electric pump if your doctor prescribes it. With all pumps, read the manufacturer's instructions carefully, and clean the pump properly.

While you are learning to pump, save any milk you do collect. It will come in handy if there are days you can't pump and also during your baby's growth spurts. One mother says, "When my baby started sleeping through the night at four weeks, I would wake up early leaking milk. So I would pump milk at 5:30 or 6:00 A.M. and freeze it, and then feed Ben at 8:00 A.M. when he woke up. By the time I went back to work at nine weeks, I had thirty 5-ounce bags of milk in the freezer. I didn't run out until he was six and a half months old."

HOW TO USE A MANUAL PUMP

The first time you pump, you may not get much milk. Success comes with letting down your milk as you pump, in the same way you let down as your baby nurses. Pumping is best done in a place where you can relax, so that letdown can occur: Practice at home, first. Follow the same suggestions given for learning manual expression (p. 337) in choosing the best times to practice.

To use a manual pump, follow the manufacturer's instructions about assembly and cleaning. Fit the pump over one breast; hold the pump from below so that you pull the plunger out with your palm facing upward; that way your wrist will flex forward. If you hold the pump from above, you will bend your wrist backward on each stroke; the strain may eventually give you tennis elbow (see middle illustration on p. 336).

Begin pumping, pulling the plunger slowly away from you to create suction, then sliding it toward you so the suction ceases. When your letdown action occurs, some instructions tell you to hold the suction of the pump on your breast, rather than continue to pump; however, that is not what your baby does: your baby sucks and swallows, about once a second, releasing suction with every swallow. If you develop the same rhythm of suction and release with the pump, your breasts will respond well and you will protect yourself from soreness.

Because letdown happens simultaneously in both breasts, once you have learned to pump, you may want to collect milk dripping from the other breast while you are pumping. This is easily done by holding a cup or baby bottle over the free nipple. By the time you move to the second breast, your first letdown may have subsided, but the breast will respond to the stimulation again. You may find, with practice, that you can let down your milk repeatedly in a single pumping session.

The first few times you pump, the whole process may seem clumsy and awkward. Be patient—it gets easier. While you are still learning to pump, be careful that you don't pump so frequently or with such strong suction that your nipples become sore. If you practice while you are letting down or when you are brimming with milk, your nipples are less likely to become sore.

The key to successful hand pumping is allowing your letdown reflex to do the work. Experiment with positions and tricks to help you let down as you pump. Strive to have your letdown reflex as conditioned to the pump as it is to your baby. Don't worry, you will not interfere with *that* conditioning; any response can be conditioned to several stimuli, just as we stop the car out of habit when we see a red traffic light, but also when we see a sign that says "Stop." Ideally, you should be able to get your letdown started with a couple of pumping actions. If you then use a pump-and-release rhythm, mimicking your baby's nursing rhythm, the milk will spray freely into the pump almost by itself. Mothers who learn this technique do not find pumping so tiresome.

When you've learned to let down as you pump, you may well be producing more milk than the pump cylinder can hold. Also, if the pump cylinder starts to become full while you are pumping, you may want to empty it into a bottle; when there is less air space in the pump, suction is reduced and efficiency goes down. Put one or two plastic nurser bags, supported within nurser bottles, in front of you. Each time you've filled the pump's cylinder with 2 to 3 ounces of milk, empty it into the bags. That will also reduce the chance that you might accidentally spill the collected milk as you pump. When you have done expressing your milk, simply extract the plastic bags from the bottles, close them with a twist tie, date them, and put them in the refrigerator or freezer. If you plan to drop the milk off at the sitter's the next day, you'll simply need to keep it chilled overnight in the refrigerator; milk that is to be stored more than two days probably should be frozen. So, milk you collect on Friday, destined to be fed to the baby on Monday, should be in a freezer over the weekend.

In time, after three to four weeks, you may find yourself pumping 8 to 10, even 12 ounces a day. One mother found that by the time her baby was five months old, she could easily get 18 ounces! Many mothers, however, never pump more than 3 to 6 ounces. Others find they can manage a great deal one day and very little the next. Regardless of how much milk you can pump, it will benefit your baby and your milk supply. Continuing to stimulate your breasts during separations from your baby, whether you save the milk or not, will maintain production and help you nurse for a longer time. Pumping will also keep you from getting uncomfortably full, which makes you more likely to leak at inopportune times.

LEARNING TO USE AN ELECTRIC PUMP

Electric pumps come with manufacturer's instructions, of course; pay careful attention to the cleaning process, and to the level of suction, which should never be allowed to become uncomfortable. Practice at home; practice during the likeliest times for success at first, as described for manual expression; and teach your letdown reflex to work while you are pumping, as described above in using a manual pump. Electric pumps are generally the ultimate choice of women who are donating to milk banks, or who are maintaining a milk supply for a preterm or ill baby. They are effective, but they are by no means necessary. As a working mother, you are pumping only the two or three feedings you would be giving your baby anyway, if you were together; any method you find comfortable will be fine.

PUMPING AT WORK

Some enlightened organizations provide a pumping station—a private room with chairs, electric breast pump, sink, and refrigerator—for nursing mothers to use while at work. However, an office with the door closed or a women's lounge is a good place to pump. (Don't settle for a bathroom stall unless there's no alternative.) One mother discovered a locked supply closet to which she obtained the key; when she was ready to pump, she locked herself in, taped up a picture of her baby, and pumped undisturbed.

Set up a routine for pumping; it will calm your mind and help condition your letdown reflex. Wash your hands and arrange your pump, a storage bottle, and a picture of your baby in front of you. Think about your baby and about nursing him. (Take along a sleeper the baby has worn. Your baby's scent can be a powerful letdown stimulator.) Breathe deeply. Lightly stroke your breasts with your fingertips. When you are relaxed and ready, fit the pump to a breast and let the milk flow.

Pumping and storing milk at work may raise a few eyebrows, but not nearly so many as you might fear. One mother found that her colleagues reacted with fascination. "They wanted to see the milk, asked if it hurt to pump, and wanted to examine the pump," she said. If someone does react negatively, and lets you know it, brush it off the way you would any intrusion into your private life. You have chosen to do this for your baby and yourself; no one else's opinion matters. It is more than likely that your proud example will enlighten your co-workers and encourage other working mothers to breastfeed, too.

STORING YOUR MILK

Breast milk is a remarkably sturdy fluid. Fresh breast milk contains elements that keep bacteria from growing in it for several hours after it's been expressed. (Synthetic milk, in comparison, is an unstable substance that spoils quickly.) However, because you will be giving your breast milk to your baby, always store and thaw it with care.

Breast milk should be stored in sterile plastic nurser bags, baby bottles, or small plastic containers. (Glass containers can be used for storage but they are bulky and breakable). Refrigerated breast milk must be used within forty-eight hours. If frozen in the freezer compartment of a refrigerator, breast milk can be kept two to four weeks. If kept in a separate freezer at 0°F, it can be kept six months or more. Once thawed, breast milk should not be refrozen.

Freeze milk in small quantities so that if the baby doesn't drink a lot at a feeding, none is wasted. Breast milk is much more fully utilized by the baby than is synthetic milk, so your baby will take fewer ounces of your milk than an artificially fed baby would take from a bottle. Try to estimate how much your baby may take at each feeding; a very young baby may not want more than 2 to 3 ounces at a time, a three- to six-month-old may take 4 to 6 ounces or more. Remember that the milk will expand as it freezes, so leave some room in the containers. Date each container, and use them in the order in which they were frozen. To add milk to already frozen batches, cool it in the refrigerator first, then pour it on top of the frozen milk.

To thaw breast milk, run cool tap water over the plastic bag of frozen milk. Very gradually, raise the temperature of the tap water until it is warm, but not hot. When the milk is thawed, insert the plastic bag in a nurser bottle. If you wish to heat the milk after it has been thawed, put the bottle in a pan of warm water on the stove and heat it very slowly until it is just warm, no hotter than your own body temperature. Thawing milk over direct heat on the stove, however, will heat it too quickly and alter its valuable elements. Never use a microwave oven to heat breast milk; it heats too hot and will eliminate many of the immune factors in the milk, as well as the helpful enzymes and the vitamin C. In addition, milk heated in a microwave will be hotter at its core than at the surface; it can feel just warm to you but be dangerously hot for your baby.

Many companies keep a small refrigerator for the employees' use. Put your bottles of milk in a paper bag and no one will know it's not your lunch. If there is no refrigerator, bring a small ice chest for your milk. If you work far from your home, or if the weather is hot, keep your milk cool or frozen the whole way home—although breast milk, with its living antibacterial cells, can safely go unrefrigerated longer than cow's milk (see chapter 3, pp. 62–63). There are also insulated bags with shoulder straps on the market, made just for transporting breast milk (see Appendix, p. 391.)

THE WORKING MOTHER'S NURSING SCHEDULE

A typical working mother's day begins when the baby wakes. If your baby is an early riser, nurse him in bed before your husband is awake. If your baby sleeps a little later, express a bottle of milk before the first morning feeding, and save it for the baby's lunch. Nurse once more when the baby wakes, just before you leave for work, or at the sitter's house. Then go to work.

At work, if you are free to take a break when you wish, pump your breasts once in the morning and again in midafternoon. Once you are comfortable pumping, you may be able to get 8 or more ounces in twenty minutes. In the afternoon, you may find you get half that much, but at the end of the day you may well have 10 to 12 ounces to give to the sitter for the next day. If you are able to pump only during your lunch hour, pump a little longer; increasing your demand will increase your supply. Or try to arrange to have twenty-minute breaks in the morning and afternoon in exchange for a shorter lunch hour. Try to pump at the same times each day so that your letdown reflex and peak production periods can become conditioned to those time intervals. Store the milk in a refrigerator at work or a thermal container.

Nurse again as soon as you get home or at the sitter's house. If your baby is not being cared for in your home, let the sitter know in advance that you want to nurse him for fifteen to thirty minutes as soon as you are reunited. Pay the sitter for this extra time if necessary. Many working mothers find this particular nursing creates a crucial sense of being reconnected with their baby. Or, if your baby stays at home during the day, lie down in a dark room with the bare baby against bare you and rest and nurse; the skin contact is calming for both of you. Nurse again before the baby goes to bed.

Many mothers nurse several times in the evening and once again at night. Some mothers find a night nursing to be the most peaceful and pleasant of all. If you and the baby are just barely awake and are shortly back asleep, a 2:00 A.M. nursing will not tire you. Keeping the baby in bed with you or in a cradle beside your bed in these early months will make these night nursings even less tiring.

All in all, try to fit in four to five nursing sessions from the end of one working day to the beginning of the next, in addition to your pumping sessions. On weekends, nursing during the day as well as at night will build up your supply for the coming week. This amount of nursing will keep your milk production up for as long as you and the baby wish to keep nursing.

TIME-SHIFTING: HOW BABIES FIT THEMSELVES INTO YOUR SCHEDULE

A frequently seen phenomenon of babies with working mothers is the reversal of their waking and sleeping patterns. In studying working mothers and their babies, Irene Frederick, M.D., and Kathleen Auerbach, Ph.D., have found that a baby will sleep for longer periods during his mother's absence and be wakeful when she is present. This adaptation may protect the breastfeeding relationship, ensuring that mother and baby will nurse when they are together. You may find that your nursing baby stays awake longer in the evenings and takes longer naps during the day than the baby of your friend who stays at home. Surely, this time-shifting is the highest compliment a baby can give his working mother.

In some cases, mother and baby can get on the same

schedule so effectively that by three or four months of age, the baby sleeps while the mother is away: the baby receives no bottles, and the mother doesn't pump her milk either, and yet the baby is fully breastfed and gaining well. Enough nursings are fitted into the hours they have together to maintain lactation.

SUPPLEMENTING WITH SYNTHETIC MILK

If you have to return to work while your baby is under five or six months old, and you really can't bear to pump or you've not found a pump that works well for you, you will probably be able to maintain a milk supply with frequent nursing at night and on the weekends, letting the baby have synthetic milk during the weekdays. Do this cautiously. It can be deleterious to your milk supply, especially in the first months, and it reduces the protective benefits breast milk has for your baby, as well as the beneficial hormonal effects on you.

Some mothers set a goal of pumping until their babies are six months old, and only then allow the sitter to use synthetic milk or introduce solid food. While one study suggests that mothers who pump their breasts to compensate for missed feedings are more likely to nurse for a longer period than those who do not, many mothers find a combination of synthetic milk while separated from the baby and nursing while together to be the best solution for them, especially after the baby is several months old. If you do not plan to save your breast milk and will supplement with synthetic milk for one to two feedings during the day, you will probably still have to express or pump a little milk at work in the first few weeks, to relieve discomfort and minimize leakage. Pump or express just enough to be comfortable. Pumping more than you need to for comfort will cause your breasts to continue to produce extra quantities during your working hours. Let your baby nurse liberally, meanwhile, and your milk-production schedule should gradually coincide with your working schedule.

INTRODUCING A BOTTLE

Wait until your baby is six to eight weeks old to introduce a bottle of expressed breast milk. Start any earlier and you may be tampering with your milk supply and interfering with your baby's suckling skills. Six- to eight-week-old babies, experienced nursers that they are, may be less confused when asked to alternate between two different milk sources—their mother's breast and a glass-and-rubber substitute. Later on, at three and four months, their preferences may be firmly set, and they might refuse any substitution. Lactation consultants consider the eight- to twelve-week period to be the best "window of opportunity" for introducing the bottle. (Some babies will take a bottle in the first five or six months and begin refusing it later; by then, they may be very happy with a cup or spoon to sip from.)

A week or two before you return to work, have your husband or someone else other than yourself give the baby a bottle once or twice every few days. Introduce the bottle somewhere other than the place where you usually nurse. Leave the room; some babies will refuse the bottle as long as they know their mother is near. Experiment with different types of rubber teats. Many babies will gladly accept a bottle but are picky about the kind of nipple used. If one is rejected, try another type.

Babies' reactions to bottles vary. Some babies will take a bottle, even from their mothers, as happily as they'll breastfeed. One mother said, "I was sure he wouldn't take the bottle from me. Ha! He nuzzled into my chest and acted just as he did when he nursed. He caressed his hair and stretched his legs and happily drank." Or, it might take the baby a minute to discover that it's his beloved breast milk in there. Said another mother, "At first, he played with the bottle's nipple and made funny faces at the taste and at the texture of the nipple, but once he tasted the breast milk, he drank almost three ounces."

A few babies will refuse a bottle no matter when or how

you introduce it. One mother found that her baby, upon her return to work, would not take a bottle from anyone. She said, "He took it only a couple of times when hunger won out. We eventually gave up trying, and he soon drank from a cup anyway." Occasionally, a baby will drink only from a cup with a spout, rather than accept any substitute for his mother's breast. Most babies younger than three months, however, will come around with the gentle persuasion of their father, the baby sitter, and their appetite.

LEAKING

This is not the time for silk designer suits. Leaking is a sign of a terrific letdown reflex, but also an inconvenience: One mother's letdown seemed to be triggered by the slight adrenaline surge she felt just before speaking up at business meetings. Cotton pads in your bra will help keep your blouses dry and are available at maternity clothing shops. Putting pressure directly on your nipples with the heel of your hand will stop the flow. To be discreet, cross your arms in front of your chest and press against your nipples with the backs of your hands. Or press against the breast with your upper arm while you touch your hair or an earring. Only another nursing mother will know what you are really doing. As soon as you have a chance, pump to relieve the fullness and to capture the overflow of milk. Spontaneous leaking should disappear as your letdown reflex becomes fully conditioned to responding only to the baby and the pump.

COPING WITH FATIGUE AND STRESS

The fatigue and stress of working full time while your baby is very young can be overwhelming. One mother describes her exhaustion: "I try to get to bed by 10:00 or 10:30 P.M. to counteract fatigue, but sometimes there is so much to do and never any time just for me. Also, there was a period of several months when the baby got up in the night. Those times were very difficult. Sometimes, after I had nursed him back to sleep, I'd lie awake worrying about how tired I'd be the next day. A few times, I was so exhausted I took a long lunch and went home to sleep.

"When my baby was about nine months old, I had a week when my husband was gone most of the time, and the baby was waking up in the night. I was incredibly stressed, crying when anyone asked me how I was, tired and feeling very sorry for myself. I talked about my feelings with anyone and everyone, preferably other working mothers. I wanted to know how they managed. I discovered that everyone gets exhausted and stressed and doubts her ability. I also learned that I needed ongoing support from women in situations similar to mine and that I needed to make time for myself."

Fatigue and stress overwhelm nearly every working mother at some point, and not just those who are breastfeeding. Because working mothers have no time "just to talk," they are astonished at the difficulty of combining motherhood and work, and believe that they alone find it so hard. No working mother has time for what she needs most of all—the support of other mothers whose circumstances are the same.

There may be a La Leche League group of working/ nursing mothers near you that meets in the evenings or on weekends. If not, or if organized groups don't appeal to you, you might find another breastfeeding working mother you can call when you have a question or need encouragement through a rough spot. A lactation consultant is always available by phone. Women at work with whom you've had only a professional relationship in the past may turn into your most valued supports, even if you only have time to chat as you pass each other in the ladies' room. Several good books have been published lately on working mothers— reading even a few pages of a helpful one before you fall asleep each night will fortify you (see Appendix, p. 391).

THE HELPFUL MATE

Your husband can be a deciding factor in your ability to continue working. If your husband truly carries at least

50 percent of the household and child-care duties, you are already a long way toward meeting the challenge of working and mothering. Unfortunately, many husbands don't comprehend what the full load of caring for a house and children entails. They may support your choice to work and say they'll help out, but may not know how or not really comprehend what that means.

Even when your husband intends to help and tries to help, he may not be doing things the way you would. Your husband's idea of an adequate meal or a clean room may differ from yours. The constant inadequacy of the help can be infuriating to women; as a result, many men feel that there is no point in offering to do things, because their wives always get mad and tell them they've done it wrong, anyway.

One way out of this is to learn to accept what he finds adequate, at least for now. So what if he leaves the laundry in the dryer and it all gets wrinkled. So what if he doesn't yet understand that "washing the dishes" includes putting the leftover food away, wiping the counters, and scrubbing the pots and pans. You don't have to learn to tolerate disaster—like the working mother who came home to find her husband and two-year-old son throwing peanut butter at the walls for the dog to lick off—but you can be a bit broadminded. You, after all, may not be perfect at jobs he takes seriously; one couple have been married for ten years and yet she never remembers to save the gas receipts or write down the car mileage, information he keeps meticulously; another wife reflects that she still can't see why her husband was so upset when he found her stirring a can of paint with a screwdriver.

To keep your peace of mind, you can settle for what he does do. You can talk about the most important jobs; and you can also gradually teach him your jobs, with attention and thanks, rather than just expecting him to know them simply because he lives in the same house and must have seen you do them a million times.

Another step toward fair partnership is to make a list of every single chore that absolutely has to be done regularly, from picking up the dry cleaning to scrubbing the bathtub. Remember to list nursing the baby as your most important job. For his part, perhaps cooking dinner can be his most important job. There's no need to be inflexible about who does which job, but refer back to the list from time to time to see how much is actually being taken on by each partner.

Real partnership comes with sharing what Jeanne Stanton, author of *Being All Things,* calls the "psychological burden." She writes, "Someone has to think about what the family will have for dinner, not just who will cook it and who will clean it up." She advises dividing jobs by project rather than task. "Don't say, 'You cook, I'll clean up.' Instead say, 'You take care of dinner Wednesday night.' That means planning the menu, doing the shopping, cooking, clearing the table, and cleaning up. Then, for one day of the week at least, a piece of both the physical and the psychological burden is set aside." She also suggests giving your husband those jobs he is most likely to do well, such as driving to do errands and shopping or "other jobs that require more physical strength than skill, like scrubbing the kitchen floor and cleaning the bathroom."

The third critical element to managing working and motherhood, along with support from other working mothers and from your husband, is time to yourself. It may seem impossible on some days, but just a hot bath or a walk around the block can make you feel renewed. Some mothers find that extra B-complex vitamins in their diets really make a difference. (See pp. 316–17.) Get all the rest you can, any way you can. Lie down on the couch to nurse or to play with your older children, take the commuter train to work and sleep on the way instead of driving, shut your office door and nap during your lunch hour. And view each nursing as a small but intense vacation from the world, a moment when you and your baby exist only for each other and the clamoring demands on you are nothing but a muffled murmur.

IT REALLY DOES GET EASIER

Fatigue and stress can affect your milk supply in the early weeks. However, after two to three months, your milk production is established. As long as you continue to drink plenty of fluids, it may well not be affected by a stressful period. One mother found, "Regardless of how exhausted I would get, I always seemed to have enough milk. It was as if my body knew what my priorities were."

Even so, when most stressed and exhausted, a working mother may feel that she doesn't have any more to give; that she simply cannot answer another need, another demand. And then one day, perhaps around three or four months after returning to work, life seems a little easier. A day this week, then two next week, runs smoothly. She manages to get to the baby sitter's on time and doesn't forget to bring extra diapers; she is prepared for her 10:00 A.M. meeting, and that evening, while her husband does a load of laundry, she and the baby peacefully rock and nurse. *What's happening?* she wonders. *Is it actually getting easier, or am I getting better at this?* Both, say experienced working mothers. Life does get easier as the baby grows and as your husband learns to help out. But your ability to manage the demands of your life calmly and efficiently will increase more than you thought possible. Make time for yourself, enjoy your baby, and be proud—you are an accomplished woman and a loving mother.

CHAPTER 14

Nursing Your Older Baby

CHANGES AT THE END OF THE FIRST YEAR

The older baby really enjoys nursing. You can see that it means more to him than just a way of filling his stomach, and that you mean more to him because of that. He wants to nurse for comfort and reassurance, as much as for food. If you leave him with a sitter, he welcomes you home by scrambling into your lap for a swig of milk. If he hurts himself, or is frightened, nursing consoles him. When he is tired and ready for bed, nursing is his soothing nightcap. Often, he likes to nurse sitting upright, unless he is sleepy, when he goes back to lying in your arms like a little baby. Often, an older baby likes to play by putting a finger in your mouth while he nurses, stroking your face, or patting your hair (see illustration on p. 358).

Many babies do not have a visual association with the breast until they are twelve months old or so. To such a baby, the things that mean "Mother's going to nurse me" are being held in the nursing position, having her undress, and feeling the breast against his cheek. Perhaps because he does not look at the breast as he nurses, the sight of the breast has in itself no meaning for a surprisingly long time. Some babies, of course, do make visual association earlier, and may dance up and down in their cribs, anticipating being nursed, whenever they catch a glimpse of mama dressing or undressing.

353

TALKING

Naturally, as the baby learns to talk, he can tell you when he wants to nurse, in whatever terms your family uses. This can be disconcerting, as when a toddler climbs into your mother-in-law's lap, plucks at her blouse, and asks, politely, "Mi'k?" Some babies even make jokes with their minuscule vocabularies, like the sixteen-month-old who started to nurse, then pulled away from the breast in mock haste and said, "Hot!" and burst into laughter.

The ability to converse can be handy. The baby, who at eight months imperiously insisted upon being nursed right that minute in the middle of the Sears Roebuck housewares department, can at twelve or fourteen months be dissuaded by verbal explanations: "Pretty soon," "When we get to the car," and so on. Some families develop a private term for nursing that both mother and baby can use in public.

HOW LONG WILL YOU BE NURSING?

When you are down to one or two or three feedings in twenty-four hours, your baby is not exactly "breastfed" because she is getting most of her nourishment from one or more other sources. But she is still a nursing baby, and those one or two feedings may be very warm and dear moments for both of you. There's no need in the world to cut off abruptly just because someone says the baby is "too old" to nurse, or no longer "needs" to nurse. Suppose she hangs on to a pre-bed snack, or likes to welcome you home by nursing, until she's two or more? Why shouldn't she? How many children of two—yes, and three and four—have you seen in the supermarket sucking on a bottle for dear life? Cherish these moments of closeness with your older baby; all too soon she will be a baby no longer. There's no need to stop nursing altogether until you or your baby are really ready to quit.

WEANING CUSTOMS

In the United States, the rigid child-care systems of the 1920s and subsequent decades included abrupt weaning. When a doctor decided that it was time, a patient ceased breastfeeding. He may have instructed the mother to give no more access to the breast whatsoever; the mother should take "drying-up" pills, bind her breasts, restrict fluid intake, and cease producing milk as promptly as could be arranged, while the baby was expected to complete the transition to being fully bottle- or cup-fed, with equal speed.

This system is workable only when lactation has been mismanaged to such an extent that milk production is already very inadequate, so the baby gladly abandons the unsatisfying breast for the bottle that fills his stomach. Engorgement and distension are not too much of a problem when feedings are suddenly halted, if the mother has not been secreting much milk anyway.

But such sudden weaning is rough on both parties if it is undertaken when the baby is still nursing happily, and the mother is producing well. The mother has to be a stoic indeed to obey orders to cease nursing completely. However, even during sudden weaning, letting the baby drink off enough milk, once or twice, to ease the mother's discomfort, probably provides an insignificant amount of stimulation. There is hardly a mother in existence who, in this predicament, hasn't resorted to the forbidden relief of allowing the baby to nurse one last time.

Fortunately, most pediatricians today approach the mothers and babies in their care with more sensitivity. The concept of natural weaning, gradually, and with the consent of both parties, is now accepted as a better method. You may find, however, that even if your doctor agrees with the concept of gradual weaning vs. sudden weaning, he pressures you in subtle ways to give up breastfeeding before you or your baby are really ready. He may say, casually, that if a baby is nursing for longer than a year, it is only because the mother is indulging herself. He may imply that you are insecure in some way and are trying to keep your baby dependent on you. He may suggest that nursing is developmentally inappropriate for a baby of your baby's age (whatever that age is); that it's time to find another way to communicate with your baby. If you find your confidence shaken by such comments, remember that this is a decision to be made by you and your baby. No one else's opinion—for that's all this type of comment is—matters. You and your baby understand each other completely and know what is best.

Weaning without intervention often takes place very slowly, as the baby's interest in the breast wanes; some people call this "baby-led" weaning. The baby who abruptly loses interest at nine months provides the exception; he may go from five meals a day to none in the space of three weeks. But the baby who goes on to nurse for many months longer is more apt to lose interest in the breast very gradually. Sometimes you are too busy to feed him; sometimes he is not interested in nursing. Gradually, you forget about one meal and then another, until he is nursing regularly only at one time in the day, his favorite feeding, which is apt to be either the early morning feeding, the bedtime feeding, or upon his mother's return from work.

Of course there are days when he is tired, or teething, and "backslides" to taking two or three feedings again for a while. But the general trend continues. Slowly the favorite meal, too, is abandoned. He sleeps through his early morning feeding or sometimes gives up his evening meal because you are out for the evening, and then begins going without it even when you are at home. A day goes by when you don't nurse him at all; then, a week later, two days go by. Now, your milk is really almost nonexistent. Still, occasionally your baby likes to lie at the breast and recall his infant comfort. Then one day you realize he hasn't nursed in a week. Perhaps he remembers, and tries again, but the empty breast is really not very interesting. He may nurse for a moment, and then give up, perhaps with a comment. One twenty-monther suddenly asked for the breast after three weeks of not nursing; he tried it briefly, and gave up, remarking matter-of-factly to his nearby father, "Nope, Mama's mi'k aw gone."

With this kind of weaning, there is no crying, heartbroken child who cannot understand why the dearest person in the world is denying him the thing he wants most; there are no discomforts, no problems. It is so gradual that often a mother cannot remember just exactly when the nursing stopped. Neither can the baby.

Sometimes a mother can't help wishing that the baby would get things over with and give up the breast, much as she loves to nurse him. Without any definable reason, she may just be ready to move on. At this point, a mother may feel restless whenever she sits down to nurse; she may be impatient and even resentful of the baby's demands. Weaning should begin when either party is ready to stop; in this situation, the mother may need to help the baby give up nursing.

You will probably be able to see how to encourage your baby to wean herself, without making things hard for either of you. Give her lots of other kinds of attention. Anticipate her needs for food and drink. By keeping an eye on how long she has gone since the last meal, you can forestall her hunger pangs with food. Once she asks to nurse, a battle may ensue if you say no. You can avoid that by offering healthy snacks and juice *before* she notices she's hungry and thinks of nursing.

You can sometimes tell a toddler to wait if you are busy, or even promise to nurse her some other time, at bedtime perhaps. Don't begrudge her the breast if she really longs for it, and don't be too sudden. Let her linger on with the favorite meal for a few days or weeks. When she wants to nurse only once a day, it is hardly a great inconvenience for you, and you can satisfy prying relatives who ask, "When are you going to wean that baby?" by saying, "I am weaning her." One meal a day soon dwindles to an occasional meal, and then to none. What a pleasant, peaceful way to bring to a close the pleasant, peaceful experience of nursing your baby.

THE NURSING TODDLER

The nursing toddler is a perfectly normal phenomenon in many cultures. Psychologically and biologically, there is no reason why a two- or three-year-old should not still nurse. Nursing is terribly important to some toddlers; they obviously draw immense reassurance and security—as they begin to explore their world—from being able to return from time to time to the breast.

Mothers are likely to keep the second and subsequent babies on the breast longer than the first. The more familiar one becomes with breastfeeding, the less susceptible one is to fad, fashion, or criticism; so the baby is not weaned according to the customs of others. Also, the very essence of the nursing relationship is to set no rules, to just let it happen; the more a mother becomes attuned to this receptivity, the less likely she is to be arbitrary about weaning; and so breastfeeding, for comfort and affection rather than nutrition, lingers on.

Nursing a toddler: Anything goes, in nursing an older baby. This child likes to nurse sitting astride her mother's hip.

The mother with the nursing toddler must expect some criticism. "What are you going to tell his kindergarten teacher?" is the commonest wisecrack. Interestingly, toddlers can understand this, and learn to nurse clandestinely, in privacy only, never asking to nurse or trying to nurse in front of strangers or disapproving relatives. Often, nursing becomes what one researcher has dubbed "the secret bond" between mother and child. One mother and her nursing toddler spent a month visiting in-laws who would have been appalled to learn that their twenty-month-old grandchild was still being breastfed. Without discussion, the mother simply said, "I think I'll put the baby to bed now" (or "down for a nap") whenever nursing was in order. Mother and baby disappeared upstairs, and nursed as they wanted. The baby kept the secret well, never asking for nursing except when they were alone, and the grandparents never knew.

THE DEMANDING NURSER

Two-year-olds can be both negative and bossy, and one sometimes sees a nursing toddler who has learned to wield his demand for the breast as a weapon over his mother. Perhaps the mother is intellectually convinced that she must not "reject" her baby by refusing the breast. She gives in and nurses even when she doesn't really want to; when it means leaving her company, or interrupting a shopping trip, or when she has just sat down for dinner. She feels secretly resentful, and she is right! The mother of a two-year-old doesn't have to be, and shouldn't be, the omnipresent, all-giving mother that the same baby needed at two months. Nature decrees that both mother and baby should be feeling moments of independence.

Under these circumstances, a dutiful mother sometimes prolongs a nursing relationship that is really a running battle. The mother resents nursing, at least some of the time; the baby feels the resentment and becomes even more demanding and aggressive about nursing, wanting reassurance more than ever, but also using the demand as a weapon. When he feels angry at his mother, he roars, "Titty! Titty!" no matter how unwilling she is or how awkward the moment, until she gives in.

This situation takes some management. One needs to be especially careful to meet the basic needs of hunger and thirst. Toddlers need to eat every three or four hours when they are awake; yet in many households, regular meals are six hours apart or more. In addition to giving him snacks, you may be better off feeding the toddler his own lunch or dinner ahead of the rest of the family, rather than making him wait past his endurance for something to eat.

Sometimes a toddler asks to nurse just for lack of anything better to do. What do mothers do when they're bored or restless? Go to the refrigerator for a snack, right? A baby, too, will sometimes ask to nurse when he would be just as happy with some company or amusement. It's the mother's job to sense these needs, and to adjust as the baby grows; she is not doing the baby any favor if she allows him to get so hungry he can't think straight, or if she substitutes suckling for a romp on the lawn or being read to, at an age when the baby needs to be exploring and experiencing more and more.

Sometimes a mother clings to the comforting nursing relationship when her baby is ready to outgrow it. A woman who has an unhappy marriage might tend to postpone weaning her child. The youngest child in a big family is sometimes encouraged, and not just by the mother, to cling to his infant ways, including nursing. And late weaning, like early weaning, can become fashionable. In nonnursing circles, the announcement that you nursed the baby for two years has a certain, satisfying shock value. But among some groups of nursing mothers, one can get the feeling that long nursing has become competitive, with the mother who nursed thirty-two months enjoying more status than the mother who nursed twenty-two months.

Finally, some mothers use the nursing relationship aggressively. This kind of mother will snatch up her toddler and put him to the breast almost forcibly, because he is making too much noise or straying too far, and she wants to quiet him; paradoxically, she is nursing the baby so she can take her attention off him. Also, it's not just the mother who can use breastfeeding unfairly. In one family, older brothers and sisters habitually carried the toddler to Mom and told him to nurse, just to keep him out of their way and their toys.

When the nursing relationship has deteriorated to the point where either partner uses the nursing to manipulate the other partner unfairly, then it ought to be stopped. That is not a happy nursing couple anymore; relations between mother and child need to be rebuilt on a more grownup basis.

TANDEM NURSING

Suppose a mother is still nursing a toddler agreeably when the new baby comes along? Some mothers nurse through pregnancy and continue to let the older baby nurse, at least occasionally, after the new baby has arrived. "It's so important to him," is the usual feeling. This so-called tandem nursing can be reassuring all around—although there are some physiological drawbacks (see chapter 2, p. 41, and chapter 12, p. 326). The main danger is that the mother begins to feel it is an obligation rather than a pleasure. She needs to listen to her own body and her own heart. If nursing during pregnancy becomes uncomfortable or wearing, she should gently stop. If after the birth she feels resentment, feels that the older baby is taking the newcomer's milk or too much of her attention from the newborn, she should stop. Being resented is much harder on a child than being weaned.

In this case, the resentment is not an emotion over which one should feel guilty; it is a biologically natural phenomenon. Animal mothers dissociate themselves from their young ones as the young ones mature and before the next babies arrive. In wild horse herds, a mare may be followed by her yearling and even her two-year-old, and she will graze with them and keep company with them, but she will kick and nip them if they try to nurse. Viola Lennon, a La Leche League founding mother who had a large family quite close together, was asked how it happened that she never found herself tandem nursing? "Because Mother Vi didn't let it happen," was her sensible response.

Weaning a toddler, when you have had enough of breastfeeding, is common sense, too. How long to nurse is a matter to be decided between you and your baby, and at this point, you both have equal rights. Weaning is part of the baby's growing up, but it is sometimes part of the mother's growing up, too.

TODDLER WEANING PROBLEMS

What if the toddler has been freely indulged in nursing, and now at the age of two or three, is nursing many times a day, often at night, and has a temper tantrum if nursing is denied or postponed even for a few minutes? Weaning such a child by just refusing the breast may be pretty traumatic for the baby, the mother, the rest of the household, and even for the neighbors. Tact and perhaps a little duplicity are called for. In rural Mexico, mothers put a little chili pepper on their breasts. (Angostura bitters, a nonalcoholic flavoring sold in liquor stores, might be gentler and safer.) When the child reacts to the bad taste, the mother feigns surprise, offers sympathy, and agrees that it's too bad the milk has turned so funny-tasting. A few tries over a few days is usually enough to discourage future nursing, and meanwhile the mother can be sure to spend extra time going for walks, playing, and giving the youngster other attention.

In some parts of the Pacific region, women wean late-nursing children by painting their breasts or nipples an odd color with a harmless dye; the changed appearance is sufficiently alarming to discourage the child. Food coloring would be safe to use if a fed-up mother wanted to try this dodge. A practice in Europe in weaning two- or three-year-olds is that the mother takes a four- or five-day trip, visiting relatives, while the father and other members of the household take care of the youngster. The mother who has let herself slip into a longer and more demanding nursing relationship than she enjoys has really earned a little vacation. Usually in her absence, the toddler will grow accustomed to being happy without nursing. Although he may ask to nurse when she first returns, the firm statement that the milk is all gone now, coupled with lots of affection but the refusal to let him try nursing, should soon put an end to the problem, and without the child having had to endure the active rejection by the mother that he might have experienced had she been physically present during the first days of weaning. Leaving town for a few days can also serve just to lessen the toddler's dependence on nursing without stopping nursing altogether. When the mother returns, she may find he is perfectly happy with a bedtime nursing and no longer asks to nurse all day long. La Leche League does not endorse separation and recommends baby-led weaning instead (see p. 356).

AFTER WEANING

If a baby is weaned abruptly, the mother's breasts first fill with milk, and then gradually become empty and slack over a period of several days. Slowly, as the breasts change to the nonproductive state, they return to their former, smaller size; this will take about six months. If a baby abandons breastfeeding very gradually, over a period of many months, the breasts return to normal during that period. By the time the baby is nursing once every few days, the breasts are producing almost no milk, and their appearance is pretty much as it was before pregnancy. Long after the baby has ceased nursing altogether, it remains possible to manually express a few drops of milk from the breasts. Gradually, the drops that are expressed change in appearance to the yellowish look of colostrum. Finally, perhaps a year after weaning, even this milk disappears.

When breastfeeding ceases entirely, it's only natural to feel a little sad, especially if this is the last child you plan to have. Some of this reaction is hormonal (see chapter 2, p. 19, and chapter 6, p. 147), but some of it is a very natural regret. Breastfeeding is soothing and comforting to mothers, too, and it brings a special closeness. Sometimes we feel sad at giving it up.

NURSING AN ADOPTED BABY

The mother who is planning to adopt a baby may well wonder if it wouldn't be possible to give that baby—and herself—the benefits and joys of breastfeeding. Techniques do in fact exist by which a woman who has breastfed in the past can at least partly feed an adopted baby from the breast; this is called relactation. Even a woman who has never given birth, or perhaps never even been pregnant, can develop a little milk production, using proper technique; this is called induced lactation. Both processes are described in detail in chapter 2, pp. 48–51.

Milk production in the adoptive mother is a result of sucking stimulation and is initiated by nursing the new baby as long and as often as possible, before and after bottle-feedings, during the night, and so on. Some babies are cooperative and some are not; in general, the younger the baby, the more willing it is to nurse without much recompense. There are some physical impediments to developing a truly adequate supply of breast milk for an adopted baby. The mother who has never given birth must develop secretory tissue as well. The mother who has previously lactated may produce milk tailored to the needs of an older baby or toddler, not to a newborn (see chapter 2, pp. 40–41). And, in the absence of a subsequent pregnancy, milk production tends to dwindle over time in spite of sucking stimulation.

A full milk supply is not the aim of nursing an adopted baby; the aim is to facilitate the emotional attachment process, and make the baby a member of the family. Progress is considerably more likely if the adopting mother uses a nursing supplementer, a feeding device worn around her neck that trickles synthetic milk into the baby's mouth while he nurses (see illustration on facing page). The new baby is thus fed on synthetic milk, but he obtains it by nursing at the breast, which stimulates milk production.

Many mothers who reestablish or induce lactation feel that nursing an adopted baby, even if they can never forgo supplementation, is worth the trouble. One experienced nursing mother who nursed her adopted baby said, "You have to focus on the relationship, not on the quantity of milk. She nursed like any other baby—to go to sleep, for comfort—and she still nurses like any toddler. That is the real payoff; it's a perfectly wonderful way of mothering." Other experienced nursing mothers feel that nursing an adopted baby produces the nursing experience for the baby, but not for the mother. The supplementer is a nuisance, diminishing the spontaneity, and the hormonal side effects of peace and joy may be reduced as well. One experienced breastfeeding mother who also nursed an adopted baby confessed that she resented the process, but added, "She thinks she's a breastfed baby. I can resolve the resentment in my heart." The adoptive mother who has never nursed a

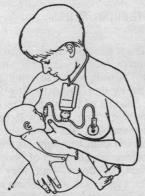

The Supplementary Nutritional System, or SNS, allows this mother to give her baby additional synthetic milk while he is breastfeeding, through a small tube taped to her breast. The SNS stimulates the mother's milk production by encouraging extra suckling, and is used to increase or re-establish a milk supply *(see text)*.

biological child is likelier to consider that nursing her adopted baby is a very rewarding experience. That may be because she is not measuring the nursing against a different kind of experience in her past.

If you are considering nursing an adopted baby, read the section on induced lactation and relactation in chapter 2. You will benefit from the advice of a lactation consultant and the support of other mothers who have relactated. Information on relactation and nursing adopted babies may be obtained from La Leche League International. It is important, in considering nursing an adopted baby, to have the help of an enthusiastic doctor. Many doctors have never heard of such a thing, but may become supportive if presented with some of La Leche League's and other literature on the subject. Tact and discretion are also called for in presenting the idea to social workers and agencies. A foster mother was forbidden to breastfeed her infant charges on the ground that the milk was not pasteurized. One couple were refused as adoptive parents when the agency discovered that the mother planned to try to nurse the baby.

EXTENDING MOTHERING SKILLS

Breastfeeding is not an end in itself, although it may seem so in the weeks and months in which you are learning about it and enjoying it. The goal, of course, is a happy and healthy baby and a fulfilled mother. Breastfeeding does so much to ensure this. The benefits of the nursing relationship linger long beyond weaning. Your baby will be healthier for months, perhaps years. And don't you have the feeling that he is a happier person than he might otherwise have been? Happy nursing babies are all kinds of people—introverts, extroverts, thinkers, or doers—but they tend to share certain basic traits: a generous, affectionate nature, coupled, after weaning, with an almost comic self-sufficiency. Probably your youngster, too, has these qualities, which are typical of the little child who has spent most of his first year of life, or longer, as a happy nursing baby.

And for you, the benefits of being half of a nursing couple

continue, too. Looking back over the months of nursing, you remember the big pleasures, not the little problems. Do you sense how much you have learned? Dr. Richard Applebaum says that breastfeeding teaches "receptivity." Think of the difference between "passive" and "receptive." There is a partnership implicit in being receptive, a partnership that is the very nature of the nursing relationship.

The warmth and receptivity one sometimes first develops as a nursing mother doesn't vanish with the milk. It can extend into the rest of your life, *for* the rest of your life. It can become the heart of your relationship to your husband, to your family, to the rest of the world. Our society values achieving; it does not much value perceiving. The nursing mother, however restricted and unfeeling her own upbringing might have been, learns more and more about perceiving, about awareness of others, about reaching goals by means of receptiveness instead of aggressiveness.

We live long lives now, and many women have small families. Women have more education than in the past and more access to the world outside the family. There are many years ahead, and many opportunities, to put the lessons of the nursing relationship to work in other ways. If there's one thing every part of society could use right now—from the crowded cities to the medical establishment, from the arts to big business—it's the receptive way of achieving together instead of the course of being at odds with nature and against each other. The nursing relationship is a glimpse of how things can be. Some of this enlightenment can carry over into the rest of your life. Perhaps in the return of breastfeeding we are witnessing a small but contagious sample of revolution, a humanizing revolution of our own culture.

References

The references given here are by no means a complete list of the sources used in the preparation of this book. From the research literature we have attempted to select for you: 1. studies or authors directly cited in the text; 2. the best and most reliable studies we have found on most topics covered in the text; and 3. major "review" papers, where they exist, that will lead you to a wider range of studies. In this section, each reference is listed only once, under the chapter to which it most directly pertains.

There are many general books, both scientific and popular, on breastfeeding and related topics. In a separate list, we have selected some we consider interesting and reliable for additional reading. La Leche League International and the *Journal of Human Lactation* are also excellent sources of information on breastfeeding.

References
PART I

Chapter 1: The Nursing Couple

Bevan-Brown, M., 1950. *The Sources of Love and Fear.* Coulls, Somerville, Wilkie, Ltd., Dunedin, New Zealand.

Bowlby, J., 1969. *Attachment and Loss.* Vol. 1. Basic Books, New York.

Bowlby, J., 1953. *Child Care and the Growth of Love.* Penguin Books, Baltimore.

Brody, S., 1956. *Patterns of Mothering.* International Universities Press, New York.

Deutsch, H., 1945. *The Psychology of Women,* Vols. I, II. Grune and Stratton, New York.

Escalona, S., 1952. Interaction of mother and child. In: *Problems of Infancy and Childhood, Transactions of the Sixth Conference.* Josiah Macy Jr. Foundation, New York.

Lindbergh, A. M., 1955. *Gift from the Sea.* Pantheon, New York.

Middlemore, M. P., 1941. *The Nursing Couple.* Cassell & Co., London.

Montagu, A., 1961. Neonatal and infant immaturity in man. *J.A.M.A.,* October.

Montagu, A., 1971. *Touching: The Human Significance of the Skin.* Columbia University Press, New York.

Newton, N., 1951. The relationship between infant feeding experiences and later behavior. *J. Ped.,* 38:28-31.

Smith, H., 1765. *Letters to Married Ladies.* Quoted in: G. F. Still, 1931: *A History of Paediatrics.* Oxford University Press, London.

Thirkell, A., 1959. *Love at All Ages.* Alfred A. Knopf, New York.

Winnecott, D. W., 1957. *Mother and Child.* Basic Books, New York.

Chapter 2: How the Breasts Function

Andran, G. M., F. H. Kemp, and J. Lind, 1958. A cineradiographic study of breastfeeding. *Brit. J. of Radiology* 31:156.

Andrusiak, M.S.W., and M. Larose-Kuzenko, 1987. The effects of an overactive let-down reflex. *Lactation Consultant Series* Unit 13. Avery Publishing Group, Garden City Park, New York.

Asselin, B. L., and R. A. Lawrence, 1987. Maternal disease as a consideration in lactation management. *Clin. Perinatol.* 14(1):71-87.

Auerbach, K. G., and J. L. Avery, 1980. Relactation: a study of 366 cases. *Pediatrics* 65(2):236-42.

Auerbach, K. G., and J. L. Avery, 1981. Induced lactation: a study of adoptive nursing by 240 women. *Am. J. Dis. Child.* 135:240-43.

Belevady, B., S. Pasricha, and K. Shankar, 1959. Studies on lactation and dietary habits of the Nilgiri hill tribes. *Ind. J. Med. Res.* 47:221-34.

Bradshaw, M. K., and S. Pfeiffer, 1988. Feeding mode and anthropometric changes in primiparas. *Human Biology* 60(2): 251-61.

Byers, T., S. Graham, T. Rzepka, et al., 1985. Lactation and breast cancer: evidence for a negative association in post-menopausal women. *Am. J. Epidemiol.* 121:664-74.

de Carvalho, M., S. Robertson, A. Friedman, and M. Klaus, 1983. The effect of frequent breast-feeding on early milk production and infant weight gain. *Pediatrics* 72:307-11.

Casey, C. E., and K. M. Hambidge, 1983. Nutritional aspects of human lactation. In: *Lactation: Physiology, Nutrition and Breast-Feeding,* M.C. Neville and M. R. Neifert, Eds., Plenum Press, New York.

Chao, S., 1987. The effect of lactation on ovulation and fertility. *Clin. Perinatol.* 14(1):39-50.

Chayen, B., T. Nergesh, and V. Uma, 1986. Induction of labor with an electric breast pump. *J. Reprod. Med.* 31(2):116-18.

Cronin, T. J., 1968. Influence of lactation upon ovulation. *Lancet,* 2:22-24.

Dewey, K. G., D. A. Finnley, and B. Lonnerdal, 1984. Breast milk volume and composition during late lactation (7-20 months). *J. Pediatr. Gastroent. Nutr.* 3(5):713-20.

Egli, G. E., N. S. Egli, and M. Newton, 1961. The influence of the number of breast feedings on milk production. *Pediatrics* 27(2):314-17.

Engelking, C., and J. Page-Leiberman, 1986. Maternal diabetes and diabetes in young children: their relationship to breastfeeding. *Lactation Consultant Series* Unit 5. Avery Publishing Group, Garden City Park, New York (Review paper).

Golapan, C., 1958. Effect of protein supplementation and some so-called galactagogues on lactation in poor Indian women. *Ind. J. Med. Res.,* 46:317-22.

Gould, S. F., 1983. Anatomy of the breast. In: *Lactation: Physiology, Nutrition, and Breast-Feeding,* M. C. Neville and M. R. Neifert, Eds., Plenum Press, New York.

Gwinn, M. L. et al., 1990. Pregnancy, breastfeeding, and oral contraceptives and the risk of epithelial ovarian cancer. *J. Chron. Dis.* 43:559-68.

Hartman, P. E., and J. K. Kulski, 1978. Changes in the composition of the mammary secretion of women after abrupt termination of breast feeding. *J. Physiol.* 275:1-11.

Hytten, F. E., 1954. Clinical and chemical studies in human lactation. *Brit. Med. J.* 1:175-249.

Ing, R., J.H.C. Ho, and N. L. Petrakis, 1977. Unilateral breastfeeding and breast cancer. *Lancet* 2:124-27.

Johnston, J. M., and J. Amico, 1986. A prospective longitudinal study of the release of oxytocin and prolactin in response to infant suckling in long term lactation. *J. Clin. Endocrinol. and Metabolism.* 62:5.

Karra, M. V., et al., 1986. Changes in specific nutrients in breast milk during extended lactation. *Am. J. Clin. Nutr.* 434(4):495-503.

Kippley, Sheila, and J. Kippley, 1989. *Breastfeeding and Natural Child Spacing, rev. ed.* Couple to Couple League International, 3621 Glenmore Ave., Cincinnati, OH 45211.

Koetting, C. A., and G. M. Wardlaw, 1988. Wrist, spine, and hip bone density with variable histories of lactation. *Am. J. Clin. Nutr.* 48:1479-81.

Lawrence, R. A., 1989. *Breastfeeding: A Guide for the Medical Profession.* Revised edition. C. V. Mosby, St. Louis.

Lawrence, R. A., 1987. The management of lactation as a physiologic process. *Clin. Perinatol.* 14(1):1-10.

Layde, P. P., et al., 1989. The independent associations of parity, age at first full term pregnancy, and duration of breastfeeding with the risk of breast cancer. *J. Clin Epidemiol.* 42:963-73.

McTiernan, A., and D. B. Thomas, 1986. Evidence for a protective effect of lactation on risk of breast cancer in young women. *Am. J. Epidemiol.* 124:353-58.

Neifert, M. R., S. L. McDonough, and M. C. Neville, 1981. Failure of lactogenesis associated with placental retention. *Am. J. Obstet. Gynecol.* 140:477-78.

Neville, M. C., 1983. Regulation of mammary development and lactation. In: *Lactation: Physiology, Nutrition, and Breast-Feeding*, M. C. Neville and M. R. Neifert, Eds., Plenum Press, New York.

Neville, M. C., J. C. Allen, and C. Watters, 1983. The mechanisms of milk secretion. In: *Lactation: Physiology, Nutrition, and Breast-Feeding*. M. C. Neville and M. R. Neifert, Eds., Plenum Press, New York.

Neville, M. C., R. P. Keller, J. H. Secort, et al., 1988. Studies in human lactation: Milk volumes in lactating women during the onset of lactation and full lactation. *Am. J. Clin. Nutr.* 48:1375-86.

Neville, M. C., and M. R. Neifert, Eds., 1983. *Lactation: Physiology, Nutrition, and Breast-Feeding*. Plenum Press, New York.

Neville, M. C., and M. R. Neifert, 1983. An introduction to lactation and breastfeeding. In: *Lactation: Physiology, Nutrition, and Breast-Feeding*. M. C. Neville and M. R. Neifert, Eds., Plenum Press, New York.

Newton, N., 1978. The role of the oxytocin reflexes in three interpersonal reproductive acts: coitus, birth, and breastfeeding. In: *Proc. Serano Symposium*, L. Caranza, P. Panceri, and L. Zichelli, Eds., Academic Press, London.

Newton, N., and C. Modahl, 1980. New frontiers of oxytocin research. In: *The Free Woman: Women's Health in the 1990s.* van Hall, E. V., and W. Everaerd, Eds., 1989. The Parthenon Publishing Group, Park Ridge, N.J.

Newton, M., and N. Newton, 1948. The let-down reflex in human lactation. *J. Pediatr.* 33(6):698-704.

Newton, N., and M. Newton, 1950. Relation of the let-down reflex to the ability to breast feed. *Pediatrics* 5:726-33.

Newton, N., and M. Theotokatos, 1979. Breast-feeding during pregnancy in 503 women: does a psychobiological weaning mechanism exist in humans? In: *Emotion and Reproduction: Proceedings of the Serano Symposia, Vol. 20B*, L. Carenza and L. Zinchella, Eds., Academic Press, New York.

Olsen, C. G., and R. E. Gordon, Jr., 1990. Breast disorders in nursing mothers. *Ann. Fam. Pract.* 41(50):1509-16.

Paulos, J. A., 1988. *Innumeracy.* Farrar, Straus & Giroux, New York.

Pederson, C. A., and A. J. Frange, Jr., 1979. Induction of maternal behavior in virgin rats after intracerebroventricular administration of oxytocin. *Proc. Nat. Acad. Sci. USA.* 76:6661-65.

Pryor, K., 1963. *Nursing Your Baby.* Harper & Row, New York Revised edition, 1973, Pocket Books, New York.

Riordon, J., and F. H. Nichols, 1990. A descriptive study of lactation mastitis in long-term breastfeeding women. *J. Human Lact.* 6:53-58.

Roepke, J. L., and A. Kirksey, 1979. Vitamin B_6 nutriture during pregnancy and lactation: effects of long term use of oral contraceptives. *Am. J. Clin. Nutr.* 32:2257-64.

Salber, E., et al., 1966. The duration of postpartum amenorrhea. *Am. J. Epidemiology,* 82:347-50.

Salmenpera, A. L., 1984. Vitamin C nutrition during prolonged lactation: optimal in infants while marginal in some mothers. *Am. J. Clin. Nutr.* 40:1050-56.

Sharma, S. D., 1974. Effect of oral contraceptives on quality and quantity of milk secretion in human beings. *Ind. J. Med. Res.* 62:964.

Thomsen, A. C., T. Espersen, and S. Maigaard, 1984. Course and treatment of milk stasis, non-infectious inflammation of the breast and infectious mastitis in nursing women. *Am. J. Ob. Gyn.* 149:492-95.

Tovarud, S. V., and A. Boass, 1979. Hormonal control of calcium metabolism in lactation. In: *Vitamins and Hormones: Advances in Research and Applications,* 37:303-47.

Woolridge, M. W., 1986. Aetiology of sore nipples. *Midwifery* (2):172-76.

Woolridge, M. W., and Chloe Fisher, 1988. Colic, "overfeeding", and symptoms of lactose malabsorption in the breast-fed baby: a possible artifact of feed management? *Lancet,* 8:382-84.

Woolridge, M. W., et al., 1990. Do changes in pattern of breast usage alter the baby's nutrient intake? *Lancet* 336:395-97.

Worthington-Roberts, B., J. Vermeersch, and S. R. Williams, 1985. *Nutrition in Pregnancy and Lactation.* Times Mirror/Mosby, St. Louis.

Chapter 3: Human Milk

Acheson, E., and S. Truelove, 1961. Early weaning in the aetiology of ulcerative colitis. *Brit. Med. J.* 00:929-33.

References

American Academy of Pediatric Committee on Drugs, 1989. Transfer of drugs and other chemicals into human milk. *Pediatrics.* 84:924-36.

Applebaum, R., 1970. Modern management of successful breastfeeding. *Pediatr. Clin. North Am.* 24:203-25.

Asquith, M. T., P. W. Pedrotti, D. K. Stevenson, and P. Sunshine, 1987. Clinical uses, collection, and banking of human milk. *Clin. Perinatol.* 14(1):1273-85.

Auerbach, K. G., and L. M. Gartner, 1987. Breastfeeding and human milk: Their association with jaundice in the neonate. *Clin. Perinatol.* 14(0):89-107.

Barger, J., and P. Bull, 1986. A comparison of the bacterial composition of breast milk stored at room temperature and stored in the refrigerator. *Int. J. Childbirth Educ.* 2:29-30.

Bartmess, J. E., 1988. The risk of polychlorinated dibenzodioxins in human milk. *J. Hum. Lact.* 4(3):105-07.

Belec, L., et al., 1990. Antibodies to human immunodeficiency virus in the breast milk of healthy, seropositive women. *Pediatrics* 85:1022-26.

Berlin, C. M., 1987. The use of drugs during pregnancy and lactation. *Publ. Health Rep.* Suppl:53-54.

Bounous, G., P. A. Konshavn, A. Taveroff, and P. Gold, 1988. Evolutionary traits in human milk proteins. (Review article.) *Med. Hypotheses* 27:133-40.

Britton, J. R., 1986. Discordance of milk protein production between right and left mammary glands. *J. Pediatr. Gastroent. Nutr.* 5(1):127-29.

Carvalho, M. D., M. Hall, and D. Harvey, 1981. Effects of water supplementation on physiological jaundice in breastfed infants. *Arch. Dis. Child.* 56:568-69.

Carvalho, M. D., M. H. Klaus, and R. B. Merkatz, 1982. Frequency of breastfeeding and serum bilirubin concentration. *Am. J. Dis. Child.* 136:737-38.

Chandra, R. K., 1979. Prospective studies of the effect of breast feeding on incidence of infection and allergy. *Acta Paed. Scand.* 68:691-94.

Chaney, N. E., et al., 1988. Cocaine convulsions in a breast-feeding baby. *J. Pediatr.* 112:134-35.

Chen, Y., S. Yu, and W. X. Li, 1988. Artificial feeding and hospitalization in the first 18 months of life. *Pediatrics* 81:58-62.

Cunningham, A. S., 1979. Morbidity in breast-fed and artificially fed infants. *J. Pediatr.* 95:685-89.

Cunningham, A. S., 1988. Breastfeeding, bottle-feeding, and illness: an annotated bibliography, 1986. In: *Programmes to Promote Breastfeeding.* D. B. Jelliffe, and E.F.P. Jelliffe, Eds., Oxford University Press, Oxford.

Cunningham, A. S., D. B. Jelliffe, and E.F.P. Jelliffe, 1991. Breastfeeding and health in the 1980s: A global epidemiologic review. *J. Pediatr.* 118(5): 659–66.

Davis, M. K., D. A. Savitz, and B. I. Graubard, 1988. Infant feeding and childhood cancer, *Lancet,* 8:365-68.

Dolan, S. A., et al., 1986. Antimicrobial activity of human milk against pediatric pathogens. *J. Infec. Dis.* 154:722-25.

Drake, T. G., 1930. Infant feeding in England and in France from 1750-1800. *Am. J. Dis. Child.* 39:1049-51.

Fulton, B., and L. Moore, 1990. Radiopharmaceuticals and lactation. *J. Hum. Lact.* 6:181-84.

Garza, C., R. J. Schanler, N. F. Butte, and K. J. Motil, 1987. Special properties of human milk. *Clin. Perinatol.* 14:11-32.

Goldman, A. S., S. A. Atkinson, and L. A. Hanson, Eds., 1987. *Human Lactation Vol. 3: The Effects of Human Milk on the Recipient Infant.* 400 pp. Plenum Press, New York

Goldman, A. S., and C. Garza, 1987. Future research in human milk. *Pediatr. Res.* 22:493-96.

Goldman, A. S., C. Garza, et al., 1982. Immunologic factors in human milk during the first year of lactation. *J. Pediatr.* 100:563-67.

Goldman, A. S., C. Garza, et al., 1983. Immunologic components in human milk during weaning. *Acta Paed. Scand.* 72:461-62.

Goldman, A. S., C. Garza, et al., 1990. Molecular forms of lactoferrin in stool and urine from infants fed human milk. *Ped. Res.* 27(3):252-55.

Goldman, A. S., R. M. Goldblum, and C. Garza, 1983. Immunologic components in human milk during the second year of lactation. *Acta Paed. Scand..* 72:461-62.

Goldman, A. S., and C. W. Smith, 1973. Host resistance factors in human milk. *J. Pediatr.* 82:1082-90.

Goldman, A. S., L. W. Thorpe, et al., 1986. Anti-inflammatory properties of human milk. *Acta Paed, Scand..* 75:689-95.

Gyorgy, P., 1960. The late effects of early nutrition. *Am. J. Clin. Nutr.* 8:344-45.

Hambidge, M. K., 1977. The role of zinc and other trace metals in pediatric nutrition. *Pediatr. Clin. N. Am.* 24:95-106.

Hamosh, M., and A. S. Goldman, Eds., 1986. *Human Lactation, Vol. 2: Maternal and Environmental Factors.* Plenum Press, New York.

Hanson, L. A., S. Ahlstedt, B. Anderson, et al., 1984. Protective factors in milk and the development of the immune system. *Pediatrics* 75(suppl.):172-76.

Hartman, P. E., S.E.G. Morgan, and P. G. Arthur, 1986. Milk letdown and the concentration of fat in breast milk. In: *Human Lactation, Vol 2: Maternal and Environmental Factors.* M. Hamosh and A.S. Goldman, Eds., Plenum Press, New York.

Heird, W. C., 1986. Potentially harmful effects of human milk upon the recipient infant. In: *Human Lactation, Vol. 3: The Effects of Human Milk on the Recipient Infant.* A. S. Goldman, S. A. Atkinson, and L. A. Hanson, Eds., Plenum Press, New York.

Heymann, S. J., 1990. Modeling the impact of breast-feeding by HIV-infected women on child survival. *Am. J. Pub. Health* 80(11):1305-09.

Hide, D. W., and B. U. Guyer, 1985. Clinical manifestations of allergy related to breast- and cow's milk-feeding. *Pediatrics* 76:973-75.

Host, A., S. Husby, and O. Osterballe, 1986. A prospective study of cow's milk allergy in exclusively breast-fed infants. *Acta Paed. Scand.* 77:663-70.

Hytten, F. E., and A. M. Thomson, 1961. Nutrition of the lactating woman. In: *Milk, the Mammary Gland and Its Secretion,* Vol. II, S. K. Kon and A.T. Cowie, Eds., Academic Press, New York.

Insull, W., Jr., J. Hirsch, A. T. James, and E. H. Ahrens, Jr., 1959. The fatty acids of human milk II: Alterations produced by manipulation of caloric balance and exchange of dietary fats. *J. Clin. Invest. 3:443.*

Jelliffe, D. B., 1955. *Infant Nutrition in the Subtropics and Tropics.* World Health Organization, Geneva.

Jensen, A. A., 1987: PCBs, PCDDs and PCDFs in human milk, blood, and adipose tissue. *Sci.Total Environ.* 64(3):259-93.

Kasdan, Sara, 1956. *Love and Knishes.* Vanguard Press, New York.

Kramer, M. S., 1981. Do breast-feeding and delayed introduction of solid foods protect against subsequent obesity? *J. Pediatr.* 98:883-87.

Labbok, M. H., and G. E. Hendershot, 1987. Does breast-feeding protect against malocclusion? *Am. J. Prev. Med.* 3:227-32.

Lifschitz, C. H., et al., 1988. Anaphylactic shock due to cow's milk protein hypersensitivity in a breastfed infant. *J. Pediatr. Gastroent. Nutr.* 7:141-44.

Macie, I. C., and H. J. Kelly, 1961. Human milk and cows' milk in infant nutrition. In: *Milk, the Mammary Gland and Its Secretion.* Vol. II, S. K. Kon and A. T. Cowie, Eds., Academic Press, New York.

Mata, L., et al., 1988. Promotion of breastfeeding in Costa Rica: the Puriscal study. In: *Programmes to Promote Breastfeeding.* D. B. Jelliffe and E.F.P. Jelliffe, Eds., Oxford University Press, Oxford.

Mayer, E. J., R. F. Hamman, E. C. Gay, et al., 1988. Reduced risk of insulin-dependent diabetes mellitus (IDDM) among breastfed children: The Colorado IDDM Registry. *Diabetes* 37(12):-1625-32.

Mellies, M. J., T. Ishikawa, P. Gartside, K. Burton, J. MacGee, K. Allen, P. Steiner, D. Brady, and C. Glueck, 1978. Effects of varying maternal dietary cholesterol and phytosterol in lactating women and their infants. *Am. J. Clin. Nutr.* 31:1347-54.

Minchin, M., 1989. *Breastfeeding Matters.* Rev. ed. Allen & Unwin. Sydney, Australia.

Morrow-Tlucak, M., H. Haude, and C. B. Ernhart, 1988. Breastfeeding and cognitive development in the first two years of life. *Soc. Sci. Med.* 26:635-39.

Neville, M. C., et al., 1986. Changes in milk composition after six months of lactation: the effects of duration of lactation and gradual weaning. In: *Human Lactation, Vol 2: Maternal and Environmental Factors.* M. Hamosh and A.S. Goldman, Eds., Plenum Press, New York.

Neville, M. C., and J. Oliva-Rasbash, 1987. Is maternal milk production limiting for infant growth during the first year of life in breast-fed infants? In: *Human Lactation, Vol. 3: The Effects of Human Milk on the Recipient Infant.* A. S. Goldman, S. A. Atkinson, and L. A. Hanson, Eds., Plenum Press, New York.

Peterson, R. C., and W. A. Bowes, 1983. Drugs, toxins and environmental agents in breast milk. In: *Lactation: Physiology,*

Nutrition and Breastfeeding, M. C. Neville and M. Neifert, Eds., Plenum Press, New York.

Pierse, P., J. Van Aerde, and M. T. Clandinin, 1988. Nutritional value of human milk. (Review article.) *Prog. Food Ntr. Sc.* 12:421-47.

Rivera-Calimlim, L., 1987. The significance of drugs in breast milk: pharmacokinetic considerations. *Clin. Perinatol.* 14:51-70.

Rogan, W. J., 1986. Epidemiology of environmental chemical contaminants in breast milk. In: *Human Lactation, Vol. 2: Maternal and Environmental Factors.* M. Hamosh and A. S. Goldman, Eds., Plenum Press, New York.

Romney, B. M., et al., 1986. Radiolnuclide administration to nursing mothers: mathematically derived guidelines. *Radiology* 160:549-54.

Schrago, L., 1987. Glucose water supplementation of the breastfed infant during the first three days of life. *J. Hum. Lact.* 3:82-86.

Schwartz, R. H., et al., 1987. Acute urticarial reactions to cow's milk in infants previously fed breast milk or soy milk. *Pediatr. Asthma, Allergy, Immunol.* 1:81-93.

Sheard, N., and W. A. Walker, 1988. The role of breast milk in the development of the gastrointestinal tract. *Nutrition Reviews* 46:1-8.

Slade, H. B., and S. A. Schwartz, 1987. Mucosal immunity: the immunology of breast milk. *J. Allergy Clin. Immunol.* 80:346-56.

Soisa, R., and L. Barness, 1987. Bacterial growth in refrigerated human milk. *Am. J. Dis. Child.* 141:111-12.

Specker, B. L., 1987. Sun and vitamin D: Cyclical serum in breastfed babies. *J. Ped.* 110:744-47.

Specker, B. L., et al., 1987. Effect of vegetarian diets on Vit. D in breastfed babies. *Ob.Gyn.* 70:870-74.

Still, G. F., 1931. *The History of Paediatrics.* Oxford University Press, London.

Taguchi, S., and T. Yakushiji, 1988. Influence of termite treatment in the home on the chlordane concentration in human milk. *Arch. Environ. Contam. Toxicol.* 17:65-71.

Takeda, S., Y. Kuwabara, and M. Mizuno, 1986. Concentrations and origin of oxytocin in breast milk. *Endocrinology Japan.* 33:821-26.

Victora, C. G., et al., 1987. Evidence for protection by breastfeeding against infant deaths from infectious diseases in Brazil. *Lancet* 2(8554):319-21.

Wagner, V., and H. B. von Stockhausen, 1988. The effect of feeding human milk and adapted milk formulae on serum lipid and lipoprotein levels in young infants. *Eur. J. Pediatr.* 147:292-95.

Williams, R. J., 1956. *Biochemical Individuality.* John Wiley and Sons, New York.

Chapter 4: How the Baby Functions: The Body

Auerbach, K., and L. M. Gartner, 1987. Breastfeeding and human milk: their association with jaundice in the neonate. *Clin. Perinatol.* 14:89-107.

Avoa, A., and P. R. Fischer, 1990. The influence of perinatal instruction about breast-feeding on neonatal weight loss. *Pediatrics* 86:313-15.

Brazelton, T. B., 1970. Effect of prenatal drugs on the behavior of the neonate. *Am. J. Psychiatry* 126:95-100.

Brewster, D. P., 1979. *You Can Breastfeed Your Baby . . . even in special situations.* Rodale Press, Emmaus, PA. 596 pp.

Butte, N. F., et al., 1984. Human milk intake and growth in exclusively breastfed infants. *J. Ped.* 104:187-95.

Danner, S. C., and M. C. McBride, 1988. Sucking disorders in neurologically impaired infants. *Breastfeeding Abstracts.* 7(1):13.

Dewey, K. G., and B. Lonnerdal, 1986. Infant self-regulation of breast milk intake. *Acta Paed. Scand.* 75:893-98.

Lennon, I., and B. R. Lewis, 1987. Effect of early complementary feeds on lactation failure. *Breastfeeding Rev.* 11:24-26.

Lindmark, B., 1990. Maternal use of alcohol and breast-fed infants (letter). *N. Engl. J. Med.* 322:338-39.

Little, R. E., et al., 1989. Maternal alcohol use during breast-feeding and infant mental and motor development at one year. *N. Engl. J. Med.* 321:425-30.

McBride, M. C., and S. C. Danner, 1987. Sucking disorders in neurologically impaired infants: Assessment and facilitation of breastfeeding. *Clin. Perinatol.* 14(1):109-30.

Matheny, R., and M. F. Picciano, 1986. Feeding and growth characteristics of human milk-fed infants. *J. Am. Diet. Assoc.* 86:(3):327-31.

Mathew, O. P., and J. Bhatia, 1989. Sucking and breathing patterns during breast- and bottle-feeding in term neonates. *Am.J. Dis. Child.* 143:588-92.

Meier, P. P., 1988. Bottle- and breast-feeding: Effects on transcutaneous oxygen pressure and temperature in preterm infants. *Nurs. Res.* 37:36-41.

Meier, P. P., and G. C. Anderson, 1987. Responses of small pre-term infants to bottle- and breast-feeding. *Am. J. Mat. Ch. Nurs.* 12:97-105.

Meier, P. P., and E. J. Pugh, 1985. Breast feeding behavior in small preterm infants. *Am.J. Mat. Ch. Nurs.* 10:396-401.

Minchin, M. K., 1989. Positioning for breastfeeding. *Birth.* 16:67-80.

Saarinen, U. M., and M. A. Siimes, 1979. Role of prolonged breast feeding in infant growth. *Acta Paed. Scand.* 68:245-50.

Simoes, E. F., and S. M. Pereira, 1986. The growth of exclusively breastfed infants. *Ann. Trop. Paed.* 6:17-21.

Steichen, J. J., et al., 1987. Breastfeeding the low birth weight pre-term infant. *Clin. Perinatol.* 14:131-37.

Weatherly-White, R.C.A., D. P. Kuehn, P. Mirrit, J. I. Gilman, and C. C. Weatherly-White, 1987. Early repair and breast-feeding for infants with cleft lip. *Plastic and Reconstructive Surgery.* 79(6):879-85. See also Fisher, J. C., Discussion. Ibid. 79(6):886-87.

Whitehead, R. G., A. A. Paul, and E. A. Ahmed, 1986. Weaning practices in the United Kingdom and variations in anthropometric development. *Acta Paed. Scand.* (suppl.) 323:14-23.

Woolridge, M., 1986. The "anatomy" of infant sucking. *Midwifery* 2:164-71.

Chapter 5: How the Baby Functions: Behavior

Barr, R. G., and M. F. Elias, 1988. Nursing interval and maternal responsivity: effect on early infant crying. *Pediatrics* 81:529-36.

Bell, R. Q., 1974. Contributions of human infants to caregiving and social interaction. In: *The Effect of the Infant on its Caregiver,* L. M. and L. A. Rosenblum, Eds., John Wiley and Sons, New York.

Berham, J. C., G. R. Pereira, J. B. Watkins, and G. J. Peckham, 1983. Nonnutritive sucking during gavage feeding enhances growth and maturation in premature infants. *Pediatrics* 71:41.

Blauvelt, H., 1956. Neonate-mother relationships in goat and man. In: *Group Processes, Transactions of the Second Conference.* Josiah Macy Jr. Foundation, New York.

Brazelton, T. B., M. Z. School, and J. S. Robey, 1966. Visual responses in the newborn. *Pediatrics* 37:284-90.

Condon, W. S., and L. W. Sander, 1974. Neonate movement is synchronized with adult speech: interactional participation and language acquisition. *Science* 183:99.

DeCasper, A. J., and W. P. Fifer, 1980. Of human bonding: Newborns prefer their mothers' voices. *Science* 208:1174-76.

Ekman, P., and H. Oster, 1979. Facial expressions of emotion. *Ann. Rev. Psychol.* 30:527-54.

Ferguson, D. M., et al., 1987. Breastfeeding and subsequent social adjustment in six- to eight-year-old children. *J. Child Psychol. Psychiatr. and Allied Discip.* 28:378-86.

Field, T. M., R. Woodson, R. Greenberg, and D. Cohen, 1982. Discrimination and imitation of facial expressions by neonates. *Science* 218:179-81.

Goren, C., M. Sarty, and P. Wu, 1975. Visual following and pattern discrimination of facelike stimuli by newborn infants. *Pediatrics* 56:544-49.

Haith, M. M., T. Bergman, and M. J. Moore, 1977. Eye contact and face scanning in early infancy. *Science* 198:853-55.

Herbinet, E., and M. C. Busnel, Eds., 1981. *L'aube des Sens: Ouvrage collectif sur les perceptions sensorielles foetales et neonatales.* Stock, Paris.

Klaus, M. H., and P. H. Klaus, 1988. *The Amazing Newborn.* Addison Wesley, New York.

Lipsitt, L. P., 1977. The study of sensory and learning processes of the newborn. *Clin. Perinatol.* 4:163-86.

Marmet, C., and E. Shell, 1984. Training neonates to suck correctly. *Maternal Child Nurs.,* 9:401-07.

Newman, J., and B. Wilmott, 1990. Breast rejection: a little-appreciated cause of lactation failure. *Can. Fam. Physician.* 36:449-53.

Newton, N., 1971. Psychologic differences between breast and bottle feeding. *Am. J. Clin. Nutr.* 24:993-1004.

Rohde, J. E., 1988. Breastfeeding beyond twelve months (letter). *Lancet,* 2:1016. Also Tangermann, R. H., et al., ibid.

Salk, I., 1960. Effects of normal heartbeat sound on behavior of newborn infant: implications for mental health. *World Mental Health,* 12:4-7.

Chapter 6: Parents and Innate Behavior

Bottorff, J. L., 1990. Persistence in breastfeeding: a phenomenological investigation. *J. Adv. Nurs.* 15:201-09.

Brazelton, T. B., 1983. *Infants and Mothers.* Rev. ed. Delacorte Press, Lawrence, New York.

Cohen, S. P. 1987. High tech—soft touch: breastfeeding issues. *Clin. Perinatol.* 14(1):187-95.

Eibl-Eibesfeldt, I., 1989. *Human Ethology.* Aldine de Gruyter, New York.

Elander, G., and T. Lindberg, 1984. Short mother-infant separation during first week of life influences the duration of breast-feeding. *Acta Paed. Scand.* 73:237-40.

Goodine, L. A., and P. A. Fried, 1984. Infant feeding practices: Pre- and post-natal factors, affective choice of method and the duration of breastfeeding. *Can. J. Pub. Health.* 75:439-44.

Jelliffe, D. B., and E. F. Jelliffe, Eds., 1978. *Human Milk in the Modern World.* Oxford University Press, Oxford.

Jimenez, M., and N. Newton, 1979. Activity and work during pregnancy and the postpartum: a cross-cultural study of two hundred and two societies. *Am. J. Ob.Gyn.* 135:171-76.

Kemper, K., B. Forsyth, and P. McCarthy, 1989. Jaundice, terminating breast-feeding, and the vulnerable child. *Pediatrics* 84:773-78.

Kemper, K., B. Forsyth, and P. McCarthy, 1990. Persistent perceptions of vulnerability following neonatal jaundice. *Am. J. Dis. Child.* 144:238-41.

Kennel, J. H., and M. H. Klaus, 1971. Care of the mother of the high-risk infant. *Clin. Ob. Gyn.* 14:926-54.

Klaus, M. H. and J. H. Kennell, 1982. *Parent-Infant Bonding.* C.V. Mosby, St. Louis.

Klaus, M. H., J. H. Kennell, and N. Plumb, 1980. Human maternal behavior at the first contact with her young. *Pediatrics* 46:187.

Lozoff, B., G. M. Brittenham, M. T. Trause, J. H. Kennell, and M. H. Klaus, 1977. The mother-newborn relationship: limits of adaptability. *J. Ped.* 91:1-9.

Millard, A. V., 1990. The place of the clock in pediatric advice: rationales, cultural themes, and impediments to breastfeeding. *Soc. Sci. Med.* 31:211-21.

Modahl, C., and N. Newton, 1979. Mood state difference between breast and bottle-feeding mothers. In: *Emotion and Reproduction: Proceedings of the Serano Symposia, Vol 20B.* L. Carenza and L. Zinchella, Eds., Academic Press, New York.

Mori, M., et al., 1990. Oxytocin is the major prolactin releasing factor in the posterior pituitary. *Endocrinology 126(2)* 1009-13.

Newton, N., 1955. *Maternal Emotions.* Hoeber, New York.

Newton, N., 1971. Psychological differences between breast and bottle feeding. *Am. J. Clin. Nutr.* 24:993-1004.

Newton, N., 1978. The role of the oxytocin reflexes in three interpersonal reproductive acts: coitus, birth, and breast-feeding. In: *Clinical psychoneuroendocrinology in reproduction: Proceedings of the Serono Symposia,* Carenza, L., P. Panceri, and L. Zichella, Eds., Academic Press, New York.

Newton, N., D. Foshee, and M. Newton, 1966. Experimental inhibition of labor through environmental disturbance. *Ob.Gyn.* 27:371-77.

Newton, N., and C. Modahl, 1989. Oxytocin—psychoactive hormone of love and breast feeding. In: *The Free Woman: Women's Health in the 1990's.* van Hall, E. V., and W. Everaerd, Eds., Parthenon Publishing Group, Park Ridge, New Jersey.

Parke, R. D., 1979. Perspectives on father-infant interactions. In *The Handbook of Infant Development,* J. D. Osofsky, Ed. John Wiley and Sons, New York.

Pruett, K. D., 1987. *The Nurturing Father.* Warner Books, N.Y.

Raphael, D., 1977. *The Tender Gift: Breastfeeding.* Schocken Books, New York.

Rohde, J. E., 1988. Breastfeeding beyond twelve months (letter). *Lancet,* 2:1016. Also Tangermann, R.H., et al., ibid.

Taylor, P. M., et al., 1986. Early suckling and prolonged breastfeeding. *Am. J. Dis. Child.* 40:151-54.

Waletzky, L. R., 1979. Husbands' problems with breast-feeding. *Am. J. Orthophyschiat.* 49:349-52.

Waletzky, L. R., 1979. Breastfeeding and weaning: some psychological considerations. *Primary Care.* 6:341-55.

Waletzky, L. R. 1982. The romance and power of breastfeeding. *Breastfeeding Abstracts.* 2:5.

Weisenfeld, A., et al., 1985. Psychophysiological response of breast and bottle-feeding mothers to their infants' signals. *Psychophysiology* 22:79-86.

Whitehead, R. G. 1985. The human weaning process. *Pediatr.* 75:189-93.

Chapter 7: Helping and Hindering

American Academy of Pediatrics Committee on Nutrition, 1980. Human milk banking. *Pediatrics.* 65:854-00.

American Academy of Pediatrics Committee on Nutrition, 1982. The promotion of breast feeding: policy statement based on task force report. *Pediatrics.* 69:654-61.

Asquith, M. T., P. W. Pedrotti, D. K. Stevenson, and P. Sunshine, 1987. Clinical uses, collection, and banking of human milk. *Clin. Perinatol.* 14(1):173-85.

Baum, J. D., 1979. Raw breast milk for babies on neonatal units. *Lancet* 2:898.

Baum, J. D., 1982. Donor breast milk. *Acta Paed. Scand.* 299 (Suppl) :51-54.

Brewster, D. P., 1979. *You Can Breastfeed Your Baby . . . even in special situations.* Rodale Press, Emmaus, PA.

Canadian Paediatric Society Nutrition Committee, 1985. Statement on human milk banking. *Can. Med. Assoc. J.* 132: 750.

Carballo, M., 1988. The World Health Organization's work in the area of infant and young child feeding and nutrition. In: *Programmes to Promote Breastfeeding.* D. B. Jelliffe and E.F.P. Jelliffe, Eds., Oxford University Press, Oxford.

Edwards, G., 1985. The lactation consultant: a new profession. *Birth* 12:9-11.

Frantz, K., P. Fleiss, and R. Lawrence, 1978. Management of the slow-gaining breastfed baby. *Resources in Human Nurturing, Mongraph* (1):287-308.

Jelliffe, D. B., and E.F.P. Jelliffe, Eds., 1988. *Programmes to Promote Breastfeeding.* Oxford University Press, Oxford.

Jelliffe, E.F.P., 1988. Breastfeeding modules for integration into the curriculum of health professionals. In: *Programmes to Promote Breastfeeding.* D. B. Jelliffe and E.F.P. Jelliffe, Eds., Oxford University Press, Oxford.

Koop, C. E., and M. E. Brannon, 1984. Breast-feeding—the community norm. Report of a workshop. *Public Health Rep.* 9:550-58.

Meara, H., 1976. La Leche League in the United States: A key to successful breastfeeding in a non-supportive culture. *J. Nurs. Midwif.* 21(1):20-26.

Mortimer, P. P., and E. M. Cooke, 1988. HIV infection,

breastfeeding, and human milk banking. (Letters.) *Lancet,* 9:452-453; see also R. S. Tedder, ibid.

Naylor, A. J., and R. A. Wester, 1988. Providing professional lactation management consultation. *Clin. Perinatol.* 14(1): 33-38.

Naylor, A. J., and R. A. Wester, 1988. Health professional education: a key to successful breastfeeding promotion programmes. In: *Programmes to Promote Breastfeeding.* D. B. Jelliffe and E.F.P. Jelliffe, Eds., Oxford University Press, Oxford.

Popkin, B. M., M. E. Fernandez, and J. L. Avila, 1990. Infant formula promotion and the health sector in the Philippines, *Am. J. Public Health* 80:74-75.

Winikoff, B., and E. C. Baer, 1980. The obstetrician's opportunity: translating "breast is best" from theory to practice. (Review paper.) *Am. J. Ob.Gyn.* 138:105-17.

Winikoff, B., V. H. Laukaran, D. Myers, and R. Stone, 1986. Dynamics of infant feeding: mothers, professionals, and the institutional context in a large urban hospital. *Pediatr.* 77:357-65.

Winikoff, B., M. Myers, V. H. Laukaran, and R. Stoinew, 1987. Overcoming obstacles to breast-feeding in a large municipal hospital: applications of lessons learned. *Pediatrics* 80:423-33.

World Health Organization, 1981. *Contemporary Patterns in Breastfeeding: Report on the WHO collaborative study on breast-feeding.* WHO, Geneva.

World Health Organization, 1981. *International Code of Marketing of Breastmilk Substitutes.* WHO. Geneva.

Young, S. A., and M. Kaufman, 1988. Promoting breastfeeding at a migrant health center. *Am. J. Pub. Health.* 78:523-25.

Chapter 8: The Practical Politics of Breastfeeding

Auerbach, K. G., 1990. Breastfeeding fallacies: their relationship to understanding lactation. *Birth,* 17(1):44-49.

Bauchner, H., J. M. Leventhal, and E. D. Shapiro, 1986. Studies of breast-feeding and infections. How good is the evidence? *J.A.M.A.* 256:887-92. ("The Yale Study.")

Bergevin, Y., C. Dougherty, and M. S. Kramer, 1983. Do infant formula samples shorten the duration of breastfeeding? *Lancet* 1:1148.

References

Block, B. S., 1990. Breastfeeding your baby. (Book review.) *N.Engl. J. Med.* 322:1324-25.

Clement, D., 1988. Commerciogenic malnutrition in the 1980s. In: *Programmes to Promote Breastfeeding.* D. B. Jelliffe and E.F.P. Jelliffe, Eds., Oxford University Press, Oxford.

Cunningham, A. S., 1981. Breastfeeding and morbidity in industrialized countries: an update. In: *Advances in International Maternal and Child Health, Vol. I.* D. B. Jelliffe and E.F.P. Jelliffe, eds., Oxford University Press, Oxford.

Cunningham, A. S., 1988. An historical overview of breastfeeding promotion in Western Europe and North America. In: *Programmes to Promote Breastfeeding.* D. B. Jelliffe and E.F.P. Jelliffe, Eds., Oxford University Press, Oxford.

Cunningham, A. S., 1988. Studies of breastfeeding and infections. How good is the evidence? A critique of the answer from Yale. *J. Hum. Lact.* 4:54-56.

Cunningham, A. S., D. B. Jelliffe, and E.F.P. Jelliffe, 1991. Breastfeeding and health in the 1980s: a global epidemiological review. *J. Pediatr.* 118(5):659-66.

Garza, C., and B. L. Nichols, 1984. Studies of human milk relevant to feeding practices. *J. Am. Coll. Nutr.* 3:123-00.

Habicht, J. P., J. DaVanzo, and W. P. Buitz, 1986. Does breastfeeding really save lives, or are apparent benefits due to biases? *Am. J. Epidemiol.* 123:279-90.

Johnstone, H. A., and J. F. Marcinak, 1990. Candidiasis in the breastfeeding mother and infant. *J. Ob. Gyn. Nurs.,* 19:116-21.

Kemper, K., et al., 1989. Jaundice, terminating breastfeeding, and the vulnerable child syndrome. *Pediatrics* 84(5):924-36.

Kramer, M. S., 1988. Infant feeding, infection, and public health. *Pediatrics* 81:164-66.

Lumley, J., 1987: Does it work? Obstacles to breastfeeding research. *Pediatrics.* 79:1040-44.

McKinney, W. P., D. L. Schiedermayer, et al., 1990. Attitudes of internal medicine faculty and residents toward professional interaction with pharmaceutical sales representatives. *J.A.M.A.* 264(13):1693-97.

Minchin, M., 1985. *Breastfeeding Matters: What we Need to Know about Breastfeeding.* 348 pp. Allen and Unwin. Ltd., North Sydney, Australia.

Minchin, M., 1987. Infant formulas: a mass uncontrolled trial in perinatal care. *Birth,* 14:25-35.

Neifert, M., S. DeMarzo, J. Seachat, et al., 1990. The influence of breast surgery, breast appearance, and pregnancy-induced breast changes on lactation sufficiency as measured by infant weight gain. *Birth,* 17(1):31-38.

Palmer, G., 1988. *The Politics of Breastfeeding.* Pandora, London.

Reiff, M. I., and S. M. Essock-Vitale, 1985. Hospital influences on early infant-feeding practices. *Pediatrics* 76:872-79.

Stokamer, C. L., 1990. Breastfeeding promotion efforts: why some do not work. *Int J. Gyn OB* 31(Suppl.1) :61-65.

PART II

Chapter 9: Before the Baby Comes

Brown, M. S., and J. T. Hurlock, 1975. Preparation of the breasts for breastfeeding. *Nurs. Res.* 24:488.

Dick-Read, Grantly, *Childbirth without Fear,* Fourth Ed., 1979. Harper and Row, New York.

Eisenberg, A., H. E. Murkoff, and S. E. Hathaway, 1987. *What to Eat When You Are Expecting,* Workman Publishing, New York.

Korte, Diana, and Roberta Scaer, 1990. *A Good Birth, a Safe Birth,* Rev. ed. Bantam Books, New York.

Noble, Elizabeth, *Essential Exercises for the Childbearing Year.*

Chapter 10: In the Hospital

Ehrenkranz, R. A., and B. A. Ackerman, 1986. Metoclopramide effect on faltering milk production by mothers of premature infants. *Pediatr.* 78:614-20.

Frantz, K., 1980. Techniques of successfully managing nipple problems and the reluctant nurser in the early postpartum period. In: *Human Milk: Its Biological and Social Value*. Excerpta Medica, Amsterdam.

Frantz, K., 1988. Recent knowledge concerning practical management. In: *Programmes to Promote Breastfeeding*. D. B. Jelliffe and E.F.P. Jelliffe, Eds., Oxford University Press, Oxford.

Walker, M., and J. W. Driscoll, 1989. Sore nipples: the new mother's nemesis. *Mat.Ch. Nurs.*, 14:260-65.

Chapter 11: One to Six Weeks: The Learning Period

Eiger, M. S., and S. W. Olds, 1987. *The Complete Book of Breastfeeding*, 2nd rev. ed. Workman Press, New York.

Hautman, M. A., 1979. Folk health and illness beliefs. *Nurse Practioner* 4:26-34.

Kitzinger, Sheila, 1989. *Breastfeeding Your Baby*. Knopf, New York.

La Leche League International, 1987. *The Womanly Art of Breastfeeding*, 4th rev. ed. New American Library, New York.

Morse, J. M., and J. L. Bottorff, 1989. Leaking: a problem of lactation. *J. Nurs.Midwif.* 34:15-20.

Spector, R. E., 1979. *Cultural diversity in health and illness*. Appleton Century Croft, New York.

Chapter 12: The Reward Period Begins

Ladas, A. K., 1972. Information and social support as factors in the outcome of breastfeeding. *J. Appl. Behav. Sci.* 8:110-12.

Stanton, J. D., 1988. *Being All Things: How to Be a Wife, Lover, Boss, and Mother (and Still Be Yourself)* Doubleday, New York.

Chapter 13: The Working Mother: How Breastfeeding Can Help

Auerbach, K. G., and E. Guss, 1984. Maternal employment and breast-feeding: A study of 567 women's experiences. *Am. J. Dis. Child.* 138:958-60.

Broome, M. E., 1981. Breastfeeding and the working mother. *JOGYN Nursing* May-June, 201-202.

Frederick, I. B., and K. G. Auerbach, 1985. Maternal-infant separation and breast-feeding: the return to work or school. *J. Reprod. Med.* 30(7):523-26.

Katcher, A. L., and M. G. Lanese, 1985. Breast-feeding by employed mothers: a reasonable accommodation in the work place. *Pediatrics* 75(4):644-47.

La Leche League International, 1985. *Manual Expression of Breast Milk:* The Marmet Technique. Reprint No. 27. La Leche League International, Franklin Park, IL.

Quiggin, A. B., 1967. Mothers in the labour force: Every day is the hardest. *Med. Serv. J. Can.* 23:609-12.

Reifsnider, E., and S. T. Myuers, 1985. Employed mothers can breast-feed, too! *Am. J. Mat. Ch. Nurs.* 1:256-59.

Shepherd, S. C., and R. E. Yarrow, 1982. Breastfeeding and the working mother. *J.Nurs. Midwif.* 27:16-18.

United States Department of Labor, Bureau of Labor Statistics: NEWS, Washington, D.C., USDL 87-345.

Chapter 14: Nursing Your Older Baby

Family Health International, 1988. Consensus statement: Breast-feeding as a family planning method. *Lancet* Nov.:1204-05.

Gerrard, J. W., 1982. Untoward effects of weaning. *Can. Med. Assoc. J.* 126:1133-34.

Waletzky, L., 1977. Weaning from the breast. *World J. Psychosynthesis* 9(4):10-14.

Waletzky, L., 1979. Breast feeding and weaning. *Primary Care* 6:341-55.

West, C., 1980. Factors influencing the duration of breastfeeding. *J. Biosoc. Sci.* 12:325-28.

Whitehead, R. G., 1985. The human weaning process. *Pediatrics* Suppl: 189-93.

Appendix

SOURCES OF BREASTFEEDING INFORMATION AND SUPPLIES

For fast help with breastfeeding problems

1. Call the maternity ward of your hospital and ask the nurses if someone can help you with breastfeeding advice. Some hospitals maintain a breastfeeding hot line; sometimes a nurse specializing in lactation is available by phone. You may actually get more and better information on the phone than you got when you were in the hospital. If your hospital cannot help, try another.

2. Call La Leche League's main office, (708) 455-7300, or toll-free number, 1-800-LA LECHE. The league offers telephone counseling and also can put you in touch with the La Leche League leader who lives nearest you, usually within twenty-four hours.

3. Locate a lactation consultant. Look in the Yellow Pages under Lactation Consultants or Health Services; ask your hospital; or write the International Lactation Consultants Association (see p. 392).

Mechanical aids to lactation

One chemical aid to lactation in the early days is a nasal spray containing oxytocin, the letdown hormone. Metaclopramide is another drug that can be helpful to mothers who are separated from their babies (because of the baby's hospitalization) and must maintain a milk supply by pumping (see p. 278).

Donating milk to a milk bank is very stimulating to your own milk supply. If there is a milk bank in your area, discuss the idea with your doctor. If you are returning to work within a few weeks, pumping milk and storing it in your refrigerator will both stimulate your supply and build up a stock of milk for the sitter's or day-care center's use. See chapter 13 for more information on pumps and pumping.

A useful pamphlet is *Manual Expression of Breast Milk: The Marmet Technique*, Reprint No. 27, April 1985, La Leche League International, 9616 Minneapolis Avenue, Post Office Box 1209, Franklin Park, IL 60131-8209.

Organizations

International Lactation Consultants Association. An organization of board-certified professional lactation counselors (see pp. 181–83). For information or to locate an L.C. near you, write International Lactation Consultants Association, 201 Brown Avenue, Evanston, IL 60202.

La Leche League International, 9696 Minneapolis Avenue, Franklin Park, IL 60131. Business offices: (708) 455-7730. Breastfeeding help-line: 1-800-LA LECHE. (See pp. 174–83.)

Mothercare: The National Association of Postpartum Care Services Diana McQuiston, 4414 Buxton Court, Indianapolis, IN 46254. Phone: (317)293-7763. This organization provides referrals to consumers for more than sixty individuals or companies that provide mother-to-mother help after the baby is born. Publications are available, including a quarterly newsletter, and there are national conventions for providers of services.

Children in Hospitals, 31 Wilshire Park, Needham, MA 02192. Barbara K. Popper, Founder. Phone: (617) 482-2915.

Breastfeeding Resource Centers. An independent program originating with La Leche League, these resource centers offer breastfeeding information and assistance—usually in the local language—in areas where the League's mother-to-mother approach is not feasible. Breastfeeding Resource Centers are in operation in many developing countries. They are run by medical care givers, missionaries, teachers, and other concerned individuals, who distribute accurate breastfeeding information and materials to mothers and health-care professionals. Instruction pamphlets and other breastfeeding education materials have been translated into many languages for distribution through these centers. For information on locating or starting a Resource Center, write to La Leche League.

Publications
Magazines and journals about breastfeeding
Breastfeeding Abstracts. Quarterly publications for health professionals; abstracts and reviews of current publications in the area of human lactation. La Leche League International.

New Beginnings. La Leche League's bimonthly journal about breastfeeding; personal stories, photos, research updates; free with annual membership.

Mothering magazine: a monthly magazine oriented to the noncommercial, nonsexist, environmentally sound view of motherhood and family life, with emphasis on breastfeeding. P.O. Box 532, Mt. Morris, IL 61054. Subscription service: 1-800-545-9364.

The Journal of Human Lactation. Peer-reviewed scientific articles on breastfeeding, as well as essays and commentary, book reviews, and a monthly overview of recent publications in the medical literature. Subscriptions: *Journal of Human Lactation,* Human Sciences Press, Inc., 233 Spring Street, New York, NY 10013. Editorial Office: 2240 Willow Road, Homewood, IL 60430.

Books about breastfeeding
Sources of books. Even the biggest bookstores can carry only a fraction of the books that are published each year, so you shouldn't be surprised if a book you want is not on the shelves of bookstores in your neighborhood. However, most bookstores will be glad to order any title you ask for, if they can find it in *Books in Print,* a catalog that lists the publisher and price of every current book. Often a shop can obtain the book you want in a few days, by mail or through local wholesalers.

The Birth and Life Bookstore is a mail-order house run by mothers that specializes in books related to pregnancy and early childhood. It publishes a newsletter/catalog with hundreds of titles, including many of those listed below. Write or phone to be put on the mailing list: The Birth and Life Bookstore, P.O. Box 70625, Seattle, WA 98107. Phone: 1-800-736-0631.

La Leche League International operates a mail-order store offering many books about breastfeeding and child care. Write or phone for their catalog: Order Department, La Leche League International, 9616 Minneapolis Avenue, Franklin Park, IL 60131. Phone: (708) 451-1891. La Leche League also publishes a great many pamphlets, journals, and other literature about breastfeeding; for information about special LLLI publications, see p. 399.

Some recommended books
Breastfeeding:
Best Feeding: Getting Breastfeeding Right for You. M. Renfrew, Chloe Fisher, and Suzanne Arms. 1990. Celestial Arts, Berkeley, Calif. A favorite of many lactation consultants.

Breastfeeding Your Baby. Sheila Kitzinger, 1989. Alfred A. Knopf, New York. Wonderful photographs of all colors, ages, and types of nursing mothers, with many varieties of breast shape and size, of baby age and behavior, of family surroundings and situations. The message: you're not alone.

The Complete Book of Breastfeeding. M.S. Eiger and S.W. Olds, 2nd Revised Edition, 1987. Workman Press, New York.

The Nursing Mother's Companion. Kathleen Huggins. Revised Edition, 1990. Harvard Common Press, Boston. Useful problem-solving section.

The Womanly Art of Breastfeeding, La Leche League International, 4th Revised Edition, 1987. New American Library, New York. La Leche League's guide to better mothering through breastfeeding. Photographs. Highlights are available on audiotape from La Leche League (see p. 397).

Technical information (see also Reference sections, especially for chapters 2, 3, and 8):
Clinics in Perinatology: Breastfeeding. R.A. Lawrence, Ed., 1987. W.B. Saunders, Philadelphia. An important selection of research papers about lactation and human milk.

Human Ethology. Irenaus Eibl-Eibesfeldt, 1989. Aldine de Gruyter, New York. The evolution of human behavior and similarities across cultures.

Human Milk in the Modern World: Psychosocial, Nutritional and Economic Significance, 2nd Edition, 1989. D. B. Jelliffe, E.F.P. Jelliffe, and L. Kersey, Eds. Oxford University Press, Oxford.

A Practical Guide to Breastfeeding. J. Riordan and K. Auerbach, 1991. C. V. Mosby, St. Louis. A reference text for nurses and lactation consultants, with many contributors. Illustrated.

Parenting and general topics:
The Amazing Newborn. M.H. Klaus, and P.H. Klaus, 1988. Addison Wesley, New York. Wonderful photographs and information about newborn behavior.

Don't Shoot the Dog! The New Art of Teaching and Training. Karen Pryor, 1985. Bantam Books, New York. A guide to using positive reinforcement with children and adults.

A Good Birth, a Safe Birth. Diana Korte and Roberta Scaer, Revised Edition, 1990. Bantam Books, New York. The best book out on locating and negotiating a good birth environment.

The Joy of Twins. Pamela Novotny, 1988. Crown Publishers, New York. How mothers manage twins and multiples, including breastfeeding. Invaluable for parents of twins; lots of important tips if you have two children very close together, as well.

The Nurturing Father. K. D. Pruett, 1987. Warner Books, New York. A psychologist's studies of the experience of fathers caring for babies and small children, and the benefits of this nurturing to the children.

Working mothers:
The Breastfeeding Guide for the Working Woman. Anne Price and Nancy Bamford, 1983. Simon and Schuster, New York.

The Woman Who Works, The Parent Who Cares. Sirgay Sanger and John Kelly, 1987. Little, Brown, Boston.

Being All Things: How to Be a Wife, Lover, Boss, and Mother (and Still Be Yourself). Jeanne Deschamps Stanton. 1988. Doubleday, New York. Practical and comforting suggestions for the stressed-out working mother.

Videotapes

Breastfeeding Techniques That Work!
  Written and produced by Kittie Frantz, R.N., C.P.N.P.
  Vol. 1: First Attachment, 1986.
  Vol. 2: First Attachment in Bed, 1986.
  Vol. 3: First Attachment after Caesarean, 1986.
  Vol. 4: Burping the Baby, 1986.
  Vol. 5: Successful Working Mothers, 1988.
  Vol. 6: Hand Expression, 1988.

A series of tapes designed for teaching use in hospitals, childbirth classes, and breastfeeding clinics. Also useful for the new nursing mother; Volume 5, showing many working nursing mothers, is especially informative and reassuring. Available for preview rental or purchase; in color ½″ VHS or Beta or ¾″ U-matic. Some tapes are available in Spanish. Write to: "Breastfeeding Techniques that Work," 10546 McVine, Sunland, CA 91040.

Breastfeeding and Working Mothers, 1986. University of Minnesota Media Distribution. Available in color ½″ VHS or ¾″ U-Matic. Write to: Box 734 UMHC, 420 Delaware Street SE, Minneapolis, MN 55455. Or call (612) 624-7906.

Breastfeeding Your Baby: A Mother's Guide. 1990. One hour. Made with the cooperation of La Leche League International. Available from Medela, Inc., P.O. Box 386, Crystal Lake, IL 60014, or through La Leche League.

Audiotapes

The Womanly Art of Breastfeeding. High points of La Leche League's manual on breastfeeding. Two-cassette set, 90 minutes, from Order Department, La Leche League International, 9616 Minneapolis Avenue, Franklin Park, IL 60131. Phone: (708) 451-1891.

La Leche League conferences and physicians' seminars. La Leche League sells tape recordings of a wide variety of breastfeeding-related lectures and panel discussions, from La Leche League's international conferences and medically accredited physicians' seminars. Write to the order department for the current list and prices (see above).

International Lactation Consultants Association Conferences. Leading researchers present the latest in breastfeeding research and management at annual ILCA conferences. For a list of available tapes, write the International Lactation Consultants Association, 201 Brown Avenue, Evanston, IL 60202.

Products

Drugstores, maternity stores and catalogs offer a wide variety of accessories for the nursing mother, ranging from nursing pads to sop up leakage, to special clothing and furniture. Some of these products are useful and some are not; for example, you should avoid using nursing pads with plastic coatings, which may keep the breast wet and encourage soreness.

Two main sources for breastfeeding equipment and supplies are La Leche League International and Medela, Inc. La Leche League publishes a catalog offering books, clothing, equipment, and nursing supplies; the profit from these items supports La Leche League's breastfeeding counseling services around the world. To ask about equipment or to get on the mailing list, write or call Order Department, La Leche League International, 9616 Minneapolis Avenue, Franklin Park, IL 60131. Phone: (708) 451-1891. La Leche League magazines such as *New Beginnings* carry advertising for nursing-related products, including nursing nightgowns, toys, cookbooks, and so on, many of which are made by home-based, mother-run industries.

Medela, Inc., is a manufacturing company that began by making nursing bras and expanded to a complete line of nursing equipment developed with the cooperation of La Leche League and its medical board of advisors. All of the Medela products listed here can be ordered through La Leche League or directly, from Medela, Inc., P.O. Box 386, Crystal Lake, IL 60014.

Nursing equipment: Breast pumps

Ameda/Egnell Lact-b electric breast pumps: over 1,200 rental depots nationwide. Electric and hand pumps for sale. Available from La Leche League International or Ameda/Egnell Corp., 765 Industrial Drive, Cary, Il 60013. Phone: 1-800-323-8750.

Medela electric breast pump. Available from La Leche League or Medela, Inc., P.O. Box 386, Crystal Lake, IL 60014.

Manual pumps. Several brands are available in drugstores and wherever baby supplies are sold. Avoid the rubber bulb or "bicycle horn" type, in which suction results from squeezing a bulb; the suction created is too powerful. The piston-type manual pumps vary in size of collector and other details. Look for a pump in which the milk does not come in contact with rubber gaskets or other areas that are hard to clean (see pp. 338–41 for further discussion).

La Leche League International offers several different styles of manual pumps, with various prices and advantages. Call the League order department for further information.

Nursing Supplementers

The Medela Supplemental Nutrition System or SNS. Carries supplement to the nursing baby from a plastic bottle hanging around the mother's neck. A valve in the bottle cape prevents the milk from flowing until the baby sucks, thus reinforcing active suckling. Available from La Leche League or Medela (see above).

Nursing bras. These bras have a flap that unhooks and lets down so the baby can nurse. Available at maternity shops and department stores.

Nursing pads and breast shells. In cooperation with La Leche League, the Medela corporation has developed a line of breast shells and pads for treating inverted nipples, soreness, leakage, and engorgement. Available through LLLI or Medela.

Nursing footstool. Another product of Medela. Some mothers swear by this handy stool, which props your knee up at just the right height to ease your lower back while you nurse.

Baby body packs. There are many types of backpacks and front packs on the market today; you may have to do a little experimenting to find which ones are comfortable for you. La Leche League offers the *Dr. Sears Baby Sling*, which makes it easy to nurse the baby unobtrusively.

La Leche League Publications

In addition to products, La Leche League International offers a wide variety of publications for nursing mothers and medical care providers. Many are available in quantity at bulk prices. Write or fax for current prices and lists. LLLI, P.O. Box 1209, Franklin Park, IL 60131. Fax: (708)455-0125.

A sampling:

Free: product, book, and parenting resources catalogs. List of publications available in translation (34 languages; pub. #508); Directory of LLLI Representatives (#504).

Breastfeeding information pamphlets. Sample topics: nutrition and breastfeeding, breastfeeding after a Caesarean birth, nursing with breast implants, breastfeeding the baby with Down's syndrome, diabetes and breastfeeding, and many other subjects; available individually or in bulk, at a very low price. Write for list and prices.

Breastfeeding rights packet (#78). Resource material for mothers involved in divorce, custody, employment, or other legal controversies that threaten their continued breastfeeding.

Lactation Consultant Series, Kathleen Auerbach, Ed. Information and study units on a wide variety of topics related to lactation. LLLI also provides study outlines and summaries of past examinations, to prepare for the board-certified lactation consultant exam.

Leaven. Monthly journal for LLLI leaders.

New Beginnings. Monthly journal for LLLI members.

Books: La Leche League self-publishes a sizable list of books by members, leaders, and medical advisors, ranging from cookbooks and cartoons to child-care guides. Write for current catalogue.

Posters of breastfeeding mothers, in several languages, are available as well as T-shirts, mugs, and other items bearing the LLLI logo or mottoes.

Index

Page numbers in italics refer to illustrations.

Index

Index

Facial mimicry, 138–39
Family practice physicians, 213
Feces
  as indicator of milk intake, 266
  meconium, 117
  odor, 67, 123
Feedings
  See also Suckling patterns
  at bedtime, 322–23
  cluster feedings, 134–35, 239
  duration, 111, 239
  duration, in older babies, 144–45, 311, 322
  for first time, 231–33
  four-hour schedule, 263
  frequency, 27, 239, 263–64
  frequency, and menstruation, 42–43
  frequency days, 259, 273, 309
  lack of interest in, 243–44
  of newborn babies, 236–38
  night feedings, 239–40, 263, 272, 292–93
  night feedings, at five months, 312
  night feedings, giving up, 323–24
  oversleeping by baby, 271
  patterns, 239, 263–64
  patterns, changes after six months, 322
  patterns, fluctuations in, 299–300
  rapid, 111
  scheduled, 43, 263
  schedules. *See* Feedings, patterns
  time limits, 240–41, 247
Fetal Alcohol Syndrome, 91
Fathers, 17–18, 324
  bonding by, 154

See also Husbands
  innate behaviors, 154–55
Fatigue (babies)
  See also Sleep (babies)
  from feeding, 111
Fatigue (mothers), 36, 315–16
  See also Sleep (mothers)
  thyroid activity and, 317
  vitamin B-complex and, 316
  vitamins and, 316–17
  in working mothers, 348–49
Fats, in milk, 73–75
Fitness, 228
Fleiss, Paul, 176
Food and Drug Administration (FDA), 88
Foods. *See names of specific foods*; Solid foods
Formula kits, 253
Formulas. *See* Synthetic milks
Frantz, Kittie, 106, 179, 189, 241, 337
Frederick, Irene, 345
Frequency days, 259, 273, 309
Froehlich, Edwina, 175, 177
Fullness, signs of, 243
Fussy babies, 264–65, 286, 287, 288, 315

G

Gartner, Lawrence, 119
Gellius, Aulus, 166
Genital herpes, 97, 216–217, 236
Gerber Products Company, 196
German measles, 97
Goldman, Armond, 69
Golopan, C., 45
A Good Birth, a Safe Birth, 179, 206
Gordon, Jay, 121
Grandmothers, 22, 222, 281

406

408

441